Preface

The rapidly changing expectations of the clients of the construction industry are posing a challenge. The players in the construction industry have been invited 'to **join** with government and major clients **to do it entirely differently**' (*Rethinking Construction* — The Egan Report, DETR, 1998). Many of the major clients of the industry are committed to dramatic change — but without prescribing the way it should be done. They have adopted what can be called a 'success targeted approach'. They have challenged themselves and the complete supply chain to find ways of delivering the change by *Rethinking Construction*.

If we are indeed to do it differently we have to understand **the need.** Without that understanding we will not be willing to invest time in learning, developing and using a new toolkit — that of **thinking differently.** This book is written as a contribution to that new toolkit to help **make the difference**. There are tantalising rewards for those who grasp the opportunities, and risks to those who are not prepared to change.

Many readers will prefer to address the application before investing effort in getting to grips with the tools to do it. We have therefore divided the book into three parts and provided many cross-references to allow you to choose your route.

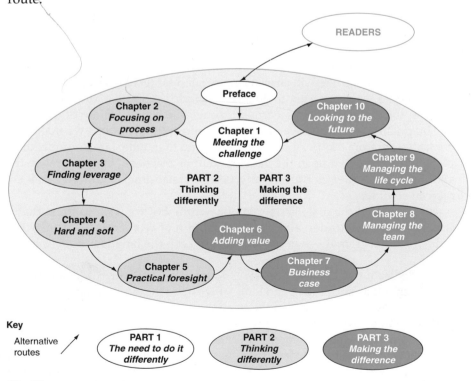

Fig. P1.

In the Preface and Part 1 of the book we set out the need to think differently to meet the Egan challenge. In Part 2 (Chapters 2–5) we explain the toolkit — that of thinking differently — which we believe is required to meet the challenge. In Part 3 (Chapters 6–10) we talk about making the difference in the life cycle of the total construction process.

We have purposely written the text so that after reading Part 1 you may progress to Part 2 or Part 3 according to your taste. Those who feel the need to read about the way in which we can make a difference should progress immediately to Part 3. Those who prefer to understand something of the toolkit should go first to Part 2. Another strategy might be to speed read one section before reading the other in depth. We hope that by making the purpose of each part and, in turn, of each chapter reasonably clear you will be able to choose a strategy which is appropriate for you. There is a risk in this approach which is that we might be accused of repeating ourselves in places — particularly between Parts 1 and 2. We have consciously made some points which are important in more than one context. Depending on how you have chosen to read the book, you may or may not have read the point earlier set in a different context. A good example is the importance of recognising our different points of view in teamwork. We try always to build on an earlier point and bring new learning to a repeated point.

The overall success targets for the book are to enable you as a construction player to:

- deliver new customer focused strategies
- work back from success
- realise values by integrating people and process
- generate simplicity out of complexity by process mind mapping
- inject practical rigour
- create tools for managing uncertainty.

The success targeted process of this book consists of four phases. Firstly, while writing the book we have prototyped the ideas with a range of construction players. Secondly, we ask you to read the book. Thirdly, we ask you to return the feedback form at the end of the book. Fourthly, we will analyse the feedback and publish the results on the internet. We will endeavour to synthesise the feedback to produce agreed success targets and then report on progress to those successful conclusions. We will chart as many successful changes as we can within the resources we can muster to do it. We include in Chapter 10, as a start to this process, the lessons we have learned through the actual writing of this book.

The practical examples we have used to illustrate the points we make in the book all stem from our personal experience and that of the large number of people who have helped us in the development of this book. We have made them anonymous in order to prevent any misunderstandings or not to break commercial confidences.

We have used the male gender in our writing but we wish to stress that this is not because we undervalue the contribution of women to the construction industry — far from it — we use it purely to keep the language as simple as we can.

We dedicate this book to our wives Karen Blockley and Trudi Godfrey who have been totally supportive and long-suffering in the absence of their husbands as we talked for long hours on the telephone, read e-mails of latest drafts, met in the evenings over bought-in pizzas.

We thank Jim Hall for reading a draft of the whole book and for providing several insights. We thank Martin Thomas for discussions from which many illuminating ideas emerged. We thank Tony Allum, Stephen Barr, Adrian Baxter, Hugh Beasley, Liz Daly, Daniel Godfrey, Jim Haile, David Hall, David Hancock,

Doing it differently

systems for rethinking construction

David Blockley and Patrick Godfrey

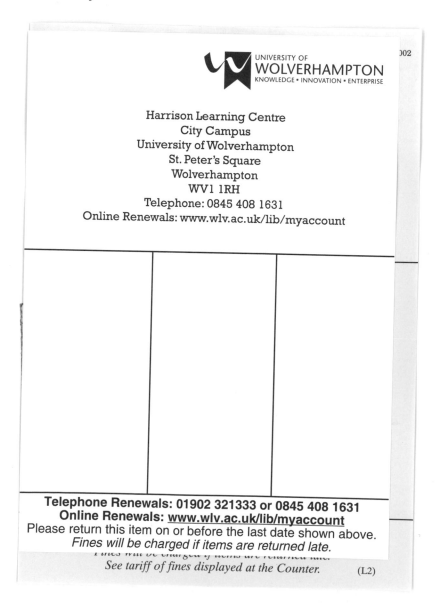

Thomas Telford

Published by Thomas Telford Publishing, Thomas Telford Ltd, 1 Heron Quay, London E14 4JD.
URL: http://www.t-telford.co.uk

Distributors for Thomas Telford books are
USA: ASCE Press, 1801 Alexander Bell Drive, Reston, VA 20191-4400
Japan: Maruzen Co. Ltd, Book Department, 3–10 Nihonbashi 2-chome, Chuo-ku, Tokyo 103
Australia: DA Books and Journals, 648 Whitehorse Road, Mitcham 3132, Victoria

First published 2000

A catalogue record for this book is available from the British Library

ISBN: 0 7277 2748 6

© David Blockley and Patrick Godfrey, and Thomas Telford Limited, 2000

This book is published on the understanding that the authors are solely responsible for the statements made and opinions expressed in it and that its publication does not necessarily imply that such statements and/or opinions are or reflect the views or opinions of the publishers. While every effort has been made to ensure that the statements made and the opinions expressed in this publication provide a safe and accurate guide, no liability or responsibility can be accepted in this respect by the authors or publishers.

Typeset by Gray Publishing, Tunbridge Wells, Kent
Printed and bound in Great Britain by Halstan & Co, Amersham, Bucks.

Norman Haste, Marcus Hayes, Paul Honeywell, Jason Le Masurier, John Lofty, Tony Madden, Keith Marr, John Murphy, Derek Pollock and Roger Wyatt for providing material and for making suggestions, commenting on specific pieces and helping us to improve our original text. We thank Vassos Chrysostomou for a useful discussion on CALIBRE and for permission to include Figs 9.20 and 9.21. We thank Neil Allan, Jitendra Argawal, Alberto Bernardini, Arturo Bignoli, John Davis, Bill Dester, David Elms, David Muir Wood, David Platt and Norman Woodman for many helpful and interesting insights. We thank all other colleagues at Halcrow, and past and present research assistants and postgraduates at the University of Bristol who have helped form and hone many of the ideas which inspired this book.

Last but not least we thank Ann Fitzgerald for her ability to fix up meetings when diaries seemed totally full and to keep Patrick generally well organised.

David Blockley
Patrick Godfrey
Bristol

Acknowledgements

Figures 7.9 and 9.9 are reprinted with permission of The Free Press, a Division of Simon & Schuster Inc., from *Competitive advantage: creating and sustaining superior performance*, copyright 1985 by Michael E. Porter. Figure 8.10 is reprinted with permission from Simon & Schuster, London, from *The seven habits of highly effective people* by S.R. Covey. Figure 8.3 is reprinted with permission of HarperCollins Publishers Ltd, London, from *The one minute manager builds high performance teams* by K. Blanchard, D. Carew and E. Parisi-Carew. Figure 6.10 is reprinted with permission of Nicholas Brealey Publishing Ltd, London, from *Re-engineering the corporation* by M. Hammer and J. Champey. Figure 3.4 is reprinted with permission of Random House, London, from *The fifth discipline* by P. Senge. Quotations are reproduced by permission of Butterworth-Heinemann, Oxford, from *Management teams* by R.M. Belbin and by permission of Random House, London, from *The fifth discipline* by P. Senge.

Doing it Differently: what people are saying

"I hope you find this book *Doing it Differently* an informative and useful text. It is a book that provides numerous tools, techniques and case studies that will help those motivated to change the way things are done within Construction to succeed.

I also hope that it will encourage both clients and Industry to explore the concepts outlined in the Government's Report – *Rethinking Construction* and help them to continue to develop its basic ideas focused on the customer process and people."

Sir John Egan
Chairman of the Construction Task Force

"When *Rethinking Construction* was launched in July 1998 it led to a wide range of responses in construction. Many of these have stemmed from concerns of individuals regarding their own understanding of the whole picture and what they can do to make things better. In *Doing it Differently – Systems for Rethinking Construction*, David Blockley and Patrick Godfrey challenge readers to stand aside from present roles and look at every aspect of Construction, starting with why a particular construction product is required at all. After reading *Doing it Differently* one can see why the key route to construction improvement is through Rethinking and one has the tools to make it happen."

Martin Reynolds
Chairman Construction Round Table 1998/99
Member Movement for Innovation Board 1998

"With the increasing involvement of competition in the water industry and at a time when water companies are required to reduce their charges substantially and yet meet higher quality standards, there is a real need for change. The innovative ideas in this book will certainly help us to reduce construction costs and deliver an even better standard of service to our customers."

John Browning
Managing Director Bristol Water Holdings plc.

"This is a serious and impressive work, which covers a lot of ground. It will help those who are committed to changing the industry to create structures to do so, whether in one area or in totality. It offers a whole range of powerful tools, which will be particularly useful to those with the personal drive to apply themselves to Rethinking Construction. It is packed with examples that help to flesh out a rigorous analysis of how the industry can improve."

David Fison
Executive Vice President, Kvaerner Construction

Contents

Part 1

The need to do it differently

1. Meeting the challenge

1.1   Change is inevitable

Relationships in the construction industry are changing. There is a fog that clouds the 'willingness to pay' of clients and the quality of the service they expect.

On the face of it, there is a surplus of demand for many of our products such as motorways, railways, and airports — that is why many of them are so congested. Yet clients and their customers are dissatisfied. Many of us feel that we can do a great deal better.

Why is it that it takes years of uncertainty and substantial cost to get planning permission to build what is needed — yet clients want us to start work on site within weeks of an instruction to proceed? Why is it that contractors are expected to absorb an order of magnitude greater risk than hitherto on a margin of one percent or two? Why is it that returns on investment are not sufficient for reinvestment in people or the process of delivering satisfactory products?

Change is inevitable. Change carries risks but also creates opportunities for those who see them and grasp them. Current opportunities are exciting. Success will require courage and the faint-hearted will fail. We believe that it will help us greatly to have a rigorous framework of **Systems for Rethinking Construction**.

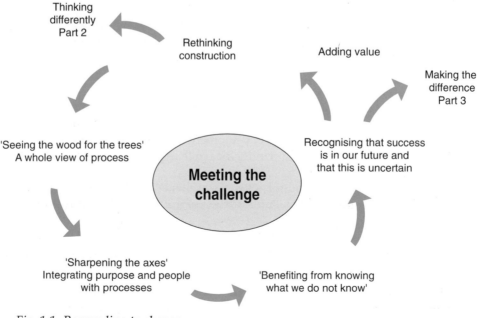

Fig. 1.1. Responding to change

1.2   Targeting success for this chapter

The success targets for this chapter are that, after reading and thinking about it, you will:

- be sufficiently convinced of the need for **change** to read on;
- recognise the relevance of **Rethinking Construction** to the future of our industry;
- agree that current initiatives need to be **understood as a whole**;
- be prepared to put in the effort to get to grips with **thinking differently** and **making a difference**;
- be interested in exploring further the idea that we can get to an essential simplicity in complex systems by **focusing on process**;
- feel that the message is relevant to **your particular needs**.

1.3   Rethinking construction

Are you satisfied with the performance of the construction industry? It seems that many of us, both inside and outside the industry, think we could do a lot better. Perhaps that is why a group of clients have asked that we all rethink construction together. In effect, the construction industry has been challenged through the Egan report (*Rethinking Construction*, 1998, Box 1.1) to improve its performance.

We suspect, however, that most construction players are feeling somewhat tired of the new initiatives and 'bolt on' processes being thrown at them. Latham, Quality Assurance, Quality Management, Total Quality Management, Business Process Re-engineering, CDM, Lean and Agile Construction, Partnering, Supply Chain Management, Value Management, Best Practice, Benchmarking are just some of the recent initiatives. Yet, while some benefits have been delivered, most construction players we meet are profoundly dissatisfied at having inadequate or inappropriate initiatives imposed on them. None are the complete answer — indeed some have downright failed. We, as an industry, seem to have developed 'initiative fatigue'.

Why is it, for example, that:

- customer satisfaction in construction projects is low compared with most industries, yet construction is an essential provider for the continuing improvement of the standard of living, health and safety enjoyed in Western Europe?
- most construction professionals feel under pressure and dissatisfied with their status?
- in spite of the use of fixed price lump sum procurement, the cost and programme of some major projects escalates — in some cases uncontrollably?
- pre-investment in research and development to improve the process is minuscule compared with successful industries such as pharmaceuticals or software development?
- returns on investment and turnover are at unsustainable low levels?
- construction is seen as a polluter of the environment when it is a practical means to reduce pollution?
- the safety record of construction continues to leave a great deal to be desired when other similar activities such as railway maintenance have improved dramatically over the past decade?

We think that, unfortunately, all of us in the construction industry have been part of an adversarial downward spiral as illustrated in Fig. 1.2. The obsession with cost results in all-round dissatisfaction, leading to further pressure to reduce

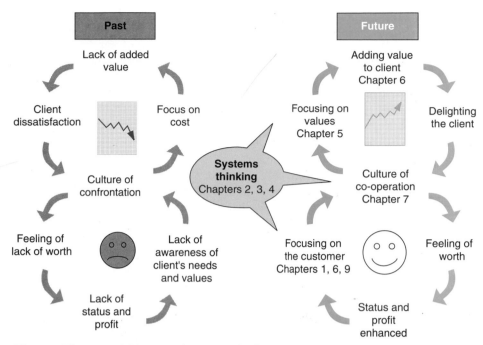

Fig. 1.2. The potential impact of systems thinking

costs. As a consequence of increased competition in a climate focusing strongly on costs, work is being undertaken by constructional providers for inadequate fees.

We believe that, as construction players, we need to focus on delivering value and to *delighting* the client and his customers through a much deeper understanding of their wants and needs from the value chain.

We will illustrate in the book how the introduction of systems thinking into the construction industry, with its emphasis on powerful loops of connected influences and holistically-defined concepts, will help to deliver the success that we all need and want.

What does the Egan Report say?

The industry has performed well — but not well enough. There is large-scale client dissatisfaction with too many projects late and over budget (Box 1.1).

As we have said, there have been many initiatives to change the construction industry — so what is different about *Rethinking Construction*? It is that a group of construction **clients** have said that they want to see an improvement in the construction industry as **a whole**. Importantly, they recognise that they, as clients, are part of the construction process – but, of course, there are still many other clients who do not necessarily see things quite that way. Clients who are publicly accountable need strong reasons not to take the lowest priced tenders.

We think that few would disagree that there is much that can be done to improve the industry, e.g. by cutting waste. However the rewards from those improvements have to benefit all concerned, both clients and the industry itself.

Include the whole team

Latham (*Constructing the team*, 1994) observed that 'there is an acceptance that a greater inter-disciplinary approach is necessary, without losing the expertise of

Box 1.1 *Rethinking Construction — The Egan Report, 1998* **Explanation**

At its best, the UK construction industry is excellent and matches any other in the world. However, it is underachieving with low profitability, and too little investment in capital, in research and development and in training. Too many clients are dissatisfied with its overall performance.

Five key drivers of change are: committed leadership; focus on the customer; integrated processes and teams; a quality driven agenda; commitment to people.

Ambitious targets and effective measurement of performance are essential. Annual reductions of 10% in construction costs and time, a reduction of 20% in defects, together with an increase of 10% in turnover and profits of construction firms are called for (Fig. 1.3). To achieve these targets the industry will need to make radical changes to its processes. These need to be explicit and transparent to the industry and its clients. The four key elements of an integrated project process are: product development; project implementation; partnering the supply chain; production of components. Substantial improvements in the elimination of waste are called for.

The industry must improve working conditions and improve management and supervisory skills. The industry must replace competitive tendering with long-term relationships based on clear measurement of performance and sustained improvements in quality and efficiency.

In summary, the Task Force emphasised that it was not inviting UK construction to look at what it does and to do it better, but that the industry and Government should join with major clients to '**do it entirely differently**'.

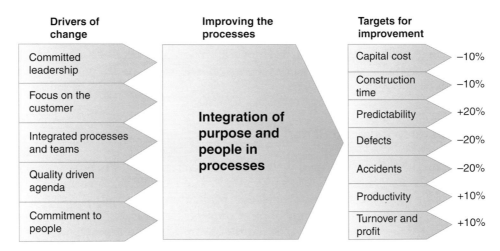

Fig. 1.3. The Egan challenge

individual professions. For example: although there is little doubt that professionals need to understand more clearly the role that each has to play in the building process; it is also important not to lose specialisms that are so important to the industry as it becomes more and more complex.'

Latham recognised that all concerned with construction are interdependent and need to behave as a team. Of course, it is not enough merely to understand each other's roles. Figure 1.4 illustrates some different agendas.

Success may mean quite different things to different people. We need to recognise that we are all interdependent and hence we have to begin by valuing the work of others.

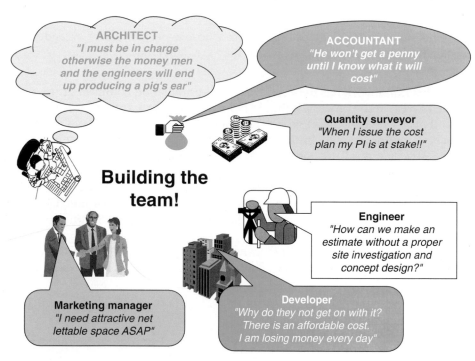

Fig. 1.4. Recognising the worth of others!

We therefore regard the construction players as being the members of the whole team inclusive of clients, design professionals, contractors and subcontractors. We use the term to include everybody who contributes to the supply chain and benefits from the value chain.

1.4   Seeing the wood for the trees

Address the whole process

How much time is used simply to co-ordinate the bits? How much time is spent in rebuilding a new team? How much time is wasted waiting for permission or changing work already done? How much time is spent putting things right? How much of our effort adds value?

While these things can be improved individually, we believe that there is an even greater potential for improvement by addressing the whole of the process from the first vision of a successful outcome to the final decommissioning. We need to address this total process, of which construction is only a part, and to involve all of the construction players. Construction is not just the process of building a new facility, sandwiched between the processes of developing a brief and operating and using the facilities — there is a much wider perspective. Within that perspective we need to focus on what is necessary and sufficient to satisfy the needs of clients and customers with a quality product that fulfils its purpose at affordable cost.

Substantial opportunities could be created through a better total development process. For example, by having better design development processes we could improve construction delivery and the operations of the facilities we build.

To achieve such improvements — i.e. to get such added value — the whole of the need will have to be addressed systematically and co-operatively. We will have to have a coherent framework that relates:

- marketing propositions to delivering success
- customer needs to a delighted client whose expectations are exceeded
- outcomes to the means by which they are delivered
- product to process.

This framework has to be a simple, well-understood common ground for all the players in the process. It should help us all to **get away** from attitudes similar to that of one consultant who is reported (*NCE*, 29 October 1998) as saying, 'I believe partnering can, in theory, bring benefit to all. But at present it is rather like *Animal farm*, all are equal except the pigs — and the pigs are, at present, the clients'.

We know a client who responded on seeing this quote: 'Not bad — since we are the most dissatisfied!' Such positional statements solve nothing. Clients and providers of construction are all in the same boat and have to pull together to be successful.

Therefore, we need to rethink construction so that all of the parties involved have to play a part. We need to find a way to co-operate that can add value to all.

Do less and achieve more

So what is to be done? It seems that the industry has to do less and achieve more. That looks like mission impossible? Certainly, by working harder doing the same things will not be good enough. Tweaking the past will not be sufficient. It is one thing to set targets and to exhort change — it is another to make that change happen. Doing less to achieve more will mean doing things differently.

Box 1.2   Doing less to achieve more   **Example**

An airport on a holiday island was doing so well, it was running out of runway capacity. The first reaction was to decide that extra runway and extensions to terminal and aprons should be built at great cost. Traffic came mainly from the USA with tourists keen to arrive between 3:00 p.m. and 6:00 p.m. so that they could enjoy their cocktails before dinner. A systems approach was suggested and used. The result was that, instead of providing extra capacity for those hours at great cost, a new landing fee structure was worked out. The scheme rewarded those who could land outside of the three-hour period most in demand. The solution redistributed the demand. The result was that the revenues into the airport were doubled at no significant cost.

Box 1.3   Doing better for less   **Example**

A great deal of effort was put into improving the natural lighting in a car park for a shopping complex where competitive advantage was derived from the attractiveness of parking. When eventually customers were asked what they wanted, natural light was a low priority. Instead, they would much prefer to find a space quickly and be close to the shops. The solution was a data management system that directed drivers to available space without hassle; together with relatively higher volumes of parking close to the shops.

Box 1.4   Safeguarding the bits   Example
A group was putting together a specification. Each member of the group had
responsibility for a part. Each member safeguarded his position by adding
in a margin to every estimate he made — just simple prudence. When each
margin was totalled it amounted to 25% of the total cost. There is a need to
be prudent but it has to be considered in the total as well as in the parts.

Box 1.5   The solution is at Luton   Example
A team was working on the need to widen a platform at a railway station
because of heavy passenger congestion. The cost of widening was very great.
The team was joined by an operations manager whose first words, on being
briefed, were, 'The solution is at Luton!' He realised that, if you persuaded
the passengers who wanted to exit by the South exit to sit at the front of the
train, and the passengers who wanted to exit by the North exit to sit at the
rear of the train, there would be no congestion. Not only did this solution
save a considerable amount of money, it also improved the passenger experience because they did not have to walk so far. Now some people in the railway industry use the phrase 'The solution is at Luton' to mean we should
think laterally.

There is a tendency in all management literature to promote a particular
method, the latest technique, as being *the* way to obtain success in all circumstances — this is all that you need to do they say! As we have said, partnering
is one of the latest ideas in a long line. There is a natural tendency to apply successful methods from one industry in one context to the construction industry,
which is likely to be in quite another. This unbolt and bolt-on concept of transfer cannot work.

We subscribe fully to the notion that we can learn from other industries and
other countries. In a sense many of us have been doing that through our own
careers. However, in order to transfer the ideas successfully, we have to understand them and to think them through in the new context. This is why we need
to *Rethink Construction*.

Thus, for example, the development process for a new product in mass production of, say, a car is quite different from that in the construction industry where
products are 'one off'. Companies in the supply chain do have a similar development cycle (e.g. window frames are mass produced) but the end product, the
building, the bridge or the dam is normally a 'one off'. Of course, certain processes are the same no matter what the industry, e.g. business and financial processes. Other processes are similar but within different ways of working. One example
of this is human resources. Still further detailed processes are quite different, such
as product development, technical design and production processes. We shall
see later that by taking a process view of systems we can compare ways of doing
things in different industries and countries much more easily than we can otherwise. We can all then accelerate the turnround for successful rethinking by
becoming experts at doing it.

Take a whole view of quality and value

At a recent conference of project managers the guest speaker asked the audience
to explain how they knew when they were adding value. Apart from 'working

to reduce cost', their answers were less than confident! He then discovered that 95% of them had participated actively in value engineering workshops and there was agreement that value was more than just cost reduction. We believe that, unless we take a whole view of quality and values, we risk major unintended consequences from our decisions and actions. For example, we may reduce the wrong costs in a trade-off decision. We believe that it is risky to stop doing something or to do something differently unless we understand the impact on the customer, operations and business we are supplying.

The words **quality** and **values** are used by many in construction practice to mean only part of what are really much deeper and more powerful ideas. Thus many people write and speak as though quality does not include cost, time and safety, while the ISO 8402 (1994) definition does include them. Likewise value engineering seems to define values in a partial way. It generally restricts its meaning to functionality and misses the richer meaning needed to satisfy customers. That richer meaning is, in the simplest of terms, that:

- we make decisions based on **preferences**
- preferences are based on **values**
- **worth** is a measure of the value we give to something
- **excellence** is the state of having the highest value
- **quality** is degree of excellence
- **fitness for purpose** is quality in construction.

We know that the term 'fitness for purpose' is not used in this way in some construction contracts. We will discuss the legal usage of the term in Chapter 6 with a deeper discussion of the meaning of quality. We believe that these different uses are not adequate reasons for avoiding its proper use as we see it.

Take a whole view of purpose

We define quality as fitness for purpose. What is our purpose? It depends on your view point.

- To a **D**elivery team, purpose may be providing an asset — such as a railway system. If the asset is not of appropriate quality then it could be unreliable.
- To the **O**perations manager, purpose may be running the trains on time — enabled by the asset. If the asset is unreliable then the trains will not be punctual.
- To a **C**ustomer, purpose could be a satisfactory journey by train — using the asset. If the train is not punctual the customer is disappointed and his willingness to pay is reduced or he may complain to the regulator.
- To the **B**usiness manager, purpose might be enhanced shareholder value — from the asset. Customer dissatisfaction ultimately hits revenue and shareholder value.
- To a **R**egulator, purpose may be the need to demonstrate that customer satisfaction is improving at reduced cost to the taxpayer.

This interdependence of purpose is crucial to the ways in which we have to co-operate to add value. Much of custom and practice is based on a historical view of what is needed. This often embraces: (*a*) a lot of unnecessary waste, with safeguards built in at many different levels which, in practice, are seldom used; (*b*) an absence of operational understanding and buildability that could reduce cost and improve value. As has been seen in some of the Private Finance Initiative (PFI) and partnering projects, value adding solutions emerge from dialogue between players pursuing these aspects of purpose. For dialogue to be effective there has to be at least an awareness level of each other's needs and constraints.

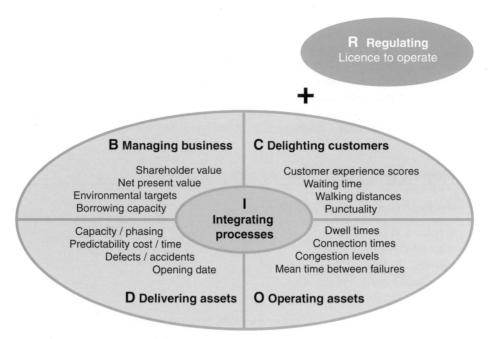

Fig. 1.5. BCIOD+R dimensions of success

What are the dimensions of success?

Much of our rethinking will be built off the six BCIOD+R **dimensions of success** as illustrated in Fig. 1.5. Some success measures, or Key Performance Indicators (KPIs), are shown for each dimension in the figure to illustrate the idea. We will be building our understanding of these dimensions as we progress through the book.

1.5   Sharpening the axes

If we have a set of dimensions for success then we can begin to develop some visibility of what is needed. However, we have to be able to link them up to the actions that will make that success happen.

*We believe that what is needed is not the continual search for the single **method** as **the** way to achieve better practice. We need **new thinking**, underpinned by a strong philosophy, to give us a coherent set of concepts that integrate and add value to the best of the existing ideas. Such an approach will help us clarify what needs to be done and what need not be done. It will allow us to focus on what is necessary and sufficient, and enable us to establish responsibilities and accountabilities. We are proposing the use of **systems thinking** to Rethink Construction.*

Systems thinking provides a set of tried and tested tools. The basic ideas have been used across a far wider spectrum than construction. In this text we will put new emphasis on process and provide new ways of thinking about uncertainty and risk. Through the systems approach we will learn to see wholes as well as parts. We will see interrelationships rather than linear causes and effects and we will see processes of change rather than static objects. We will see connections between physical processes and human and organisational processes, which are necessary to break down the age-old, outdated division between people and their environment. A systems thinker thinks not in straight lines but in causal loops. Senge (1990) provides a first rate introduction to systems thinking for those who wish to read more.

In what follows we will set out and develop this philosophy of approach and demonstrate its relevance to construction. We will not have space to put every aspect of every one of the latest methods that have been suggested for the industry in a systems framework, but we will hopefully set out the means by which it can be done. We will give practical guidance on how the results called for by such as Egan *can* be achieved in the construction industry. We will see how the solution is already within us because it depends upon how we view things. We will come to see that a problem is a solution looking for somewhere to happen!

Integrate purpose and people with processes

The Egan report names five drivers:

- committed leadership
- focus on the customer
- integrated processes and teams
- a quality driven agenda
- and commitment to people.

This in itself is an excellent framework for systems thinking because all five are key attributes of the PROCESS by which success can be delivered. It helps us to recognise the benefits of integrating processes, as it explicitly recognises that the whole is more than the sum of its parts. It rejects the idea that construction success can be achieved by salami slicing the process into separate and discrete activities, each competitively tendered. It emphasises quality for the customer that will help us to see that the complex products of construction are in fact new processes.

In Box 1.6, all of the Egan drivers and the key ingredients are made explicit. Of course this is a superficial way of reminding ourselves of these key factors. In Chapter 2, we will begin to address these issues in a much more fundamental way through systems thinking.

Box 1.6   CLEAR PROCESS   **Explanation**

C   Customer focus
L   Leadership at all levels
E   Ethics and values
A   Awareness of need to improve & learn
R   Responsibilities and duty of care, Risk and uncertainty

P   People, Purpose, Power
R   Roles in teams (the parts that people play), Reward
O   Objectives – should be measurable, Opportunity
C   Culture of quality
E   Environment
S   Success as fitness for Purpose – including business benefit
S   Stakeholders

These key words contain many of the principal ideas used in the techniques such as partnering etc. as mentioned earlier. The basis of those ideas rests in:

- focusing on the clients needs;
- developing a team to deliver those needs on a fair and equitable basis, with opportunities and risks dealt with in an open manner;
- ensuring the rewards for **all** are fair;

- being clear about the values used (measurable business performance and ethical values);
- building a quality culture such that the needs and purposes defining success are clear and agreed;
- ensuring that all are aware of the need to share and learn as appropriate in the circumstances;
- ensuring that the processes (including the supply chain) are clear, so that all of the roles are described and understood and that the skills required are available;
- ensuring that there is no excess 'fat' in the system so all waste is reduced to a minimum.

This simple list of Box 1.6 also includes important ideas often not mentioned, such as considering power in relationships, care for the environment and managing the perceptions of stakeholders.

Process is a peg to which we can attach all other ideas

Our systematic approach to thinking about processes is 'holistic'. This is a jargon word that many people now use to indicate the whole of some system. It has a potentially rich meaning that can be extremely helpful and useful, and which we explore in some depth in Chapter 3. For now, we will content ourselves with the idea that we wish to include the 'totality' of a process as well as the detail — the whole and the part.

The three essential ideas of systems thinking that we will use are:

- parts, wholes and levels
- connectivity
- process.

The example in Box 1.7 illustrates a simple successful application of systems thinking. In Chapter 3, we will focus on the first two bullet points. We will be seeking, through systems thinking, effective leverage to deal with so-called **wicked** problems – these are problems that do not seem to be resolvable by traditional methods and certainly not by linear thinking.

In this part and in Chapter 2, we will focus on the third bullet point, namely process. We will begin to try to remove the fear of complexity by seeking an essential simplicity in complexity through process. To do that we need to conceive the idea of process in a broader way than is usually the case.

Box 1.7 A railway bridge	Example

A design for a large span bridge over a railway track was required. It was found that the structurally economic solution was to have a central supporting column dividing the span into two equal spans. It was realised that the central column was vulnerable to impact from a derailed train. If the column were removed, the entire bridge deck would be brought down. A robust column to resist a derailed train was not practical. The bridge deck was therefore designed to span the entire length under dead load and the central column was used to support live loads only. In that way, in the unlikely event that a derailed train would remove the column, the bridge deck would remain intact unless there happened to be a significant live load on it at the time. The chances of that were considered to be acceptably remote, and therefore an economical, practical, non-vulnerable solution was found.

We think of **process** as the basic tool for describing a system (see Boxes 1.8–1.10). A **system** is simply the highest level process, the top process, that we choose to define for our **purpose**. A **product** is the output of a process. It is normal to keep product and process quite distinct because it is useful in defining what the customer perceives he or she is paying for. However, because products do things and exist through time then they are also processes in a wider system. Process is a generic concept from which other notions spring. It is convenient because it embraces our purposes, our values and what we do.

We will use the idea of process as a peg on which to hang all other ideas such as quality, value, risk, teamwork, etc. As we shall discuss in detail in Chapter 2, all of these ideas can be classified into attributes of who, what, why, when, where and how. They provide a way of unifying all of the current initiatives that basically are trying to help us get from where we are to where we want to be!

Box 1.8   Making a chair   **Example**

A wooden chair can be made in many ways. Think about a hand-built chair made in a woodworking shop by a craftsman. Usually we think about the process that the woodworker will go though to produce the chair and the chair itself as being quite distinct — the process and the product. However, in a more general way we can simply regard the chair as the output of the process. If the chair turns out as the craftsman intended or is even better than he expected, as a work of art, then the process has been successful — as far as he is concerned in that respect (i.e. meeting his objective to produce a work of art as he judges). Of course, if he also designed it in order to sell it and it turns out he can't sell it, then he will not have been successful from that different perspective (i.e. meeting his objective to make some money). The output of a process then has an essential attribute which is to meet the purpose of the process, or in other words to meet the objectives set out at the start of the process. A successful process is one where the output meets that purpose.

Box 1.9   Being a chair   **Example**

Now the wooden chair, the product of Box 1.8 is also a new process — a process of 'being' a chair. That is because it will have a **life cycle** through time from assembly to destruction. The chair will have a value which will change through its life.

However that process of 'being' a chair actually starts as soon as the idea of the chair enters the mind of the craftsman — the product and process are one process. The processes of designing it and making it are an essential part of its being. When it is new (and even before it is actually physically made), it may be worth quite a lot of money (depending on the anticipated or perceived level of craftsmanship). It will also be functional as long as it has been made strong enough and sturdy enough to carry the weight of someone sitting in it. Therefore, as a manufactured object, it has a whole variety of attributes through which we can describe it (price, function, beauty, colour, dimensions, etc.) but the values of these attributes will change through its life (e.g. price will change, functionality may change if it suffers some damage, etc.).

Thus we see that the standard view of product and process is actually, from this description, just one process — the ontological process of being a chair.

We will use that one perspective, as we shall see, to unify our ideas about quality, values, risk, etc.

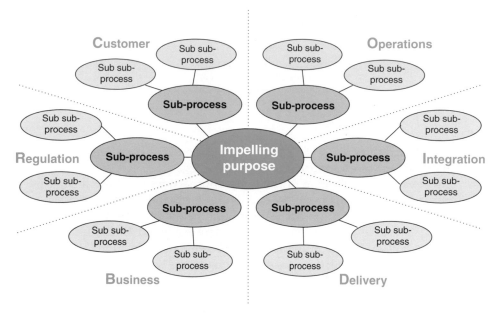

Fig. 1.6. Processes and sub-processes

The top process is a description of the system. It is usually a rather vague high level description, but nonetheless a useful one. All processes have sub-processes. We try to identify all of the sub-processes such that together they are equivalent to the higher process.

Therefore, the second level processes are also a description of the system — but slightly more detailed than the single top process. In turn, each sub-process is made up of sub-sub-processes and so on. Thus we develop a system which can be described at many different levels. Each level is equivalent — in theory — to the top process but at varying levels of detail. Of course, as all modelling is incomplete, the equivalence will never be total, as we shall see in Chapter 4 when we discuss uncertainty.

Box 1.10   The business of making a chair   Example

Now let us think about the process of making the wooden chair of Boxes 1.8 and 1.9 but now as a business proposition where the craftsman will make a number of chairs and sell them. This will be a business with high costs and low sales. The price will be high and the customer will have to be convinced about the quality of the product. At one level we can say that the process is simply described as 'making a chair'. However, it is clear that to go through that process the woodworker must go through a number of sub-processes such as 'making the business case', 'considering the customer', 'designing the chair' and 'building the chair'.

1.6   Benefiting from admitting what we do not know

Traditional predict and provide is suitable when uncertainties are low

The traditional approach to construction is a sequence of processes of brief, design, construct and deliver (Fig. 1.7). This is suitable for a wide range of needs as long as the uncertainties are low. The approach is grounded in need, cost and

Requires low or dependably
predictable uncertainties
at brief / design interface
and clear contractual relations

Fig. 1.7. Predict and provide

subsidy based thinking. Clear contractual relationships based on tried and tested methods are often sufficient to deliver success.

However, the application of the same approach where there is high uncertainty is likely to lead to patchy success, at best, and often to serious disappointments. Examples of such disappointments include the M25, where unpredicted success in attracting customers (users) (Box 1.11) has led to its being seen as a failure. Others examples of prediction failure include Canary Wharf, the Channel Tunnel and, recently, predictions for the Eurostar passenger demand which led to restructuring of the Channel Tunnel Rail Link.

Box 1.11   M25   Example

The planning for the London Orbital M25 motorway was done on a 'predict and provide basis'. The traffic capacity used in the design was therefore on the basis of projections of traffic densities. The whole project was delayed by planning difficulties. The very existence of the road, absence of other planned orbital roads and persistent traffic growth attracted further traffic. The result was that the road became a long parking lot in the rush hour almost immediately it was opened. It has persisted in this state despite the widening of many sectors.

To do it differently and to achieve the Egan targets will require substantial change and consequent uncertainty. Much of it springs from our incomplete knowledge of the future and the unpredictability of people threatened or motivated by change. Of course other industries have achieved and continue to achieve such improvement. They have to. Demand from their customers combined with competitive pressures, provides the environment. In these circumstances predict and provide cannot work.

Thinking driven by need, cost and subsidy has to change to thinking driven by customers and their willingness to pay — all set in the need for a sustainable environment. In a privatised market or a public private partnership, our customer's needs, wants and demands, together with responsible environmental policies, define our purpose. The customer needs are converted to wants by way of their intentions, which in turn are converted to demand if there is willingness to pay. This is the start of the value chain on which our clients and we depend. This is why we believe the change will happen. Those who are not involved in steering that change will be at a serious competitive disadvantage.

However, the change is so radical that we cannot expect to define our future on the basis that it will be similar to our past — with minor improvements. We need to clear the fog, establish what success looks like for the customer and ensure we have a way of **measuring** it. We need to establish, as far as we are able to, what is necessary and what is sufficient to get to success. With a changing environment and changing expectations, we have to be ahead of the game and manage the uncertainties actively and together. It is exciting. It is frightening. It needs courage and a cool head. It can be successful if everyone involved in the value chain and the supply chain can work together. We can have that success, in spite of the unexpected and unintended consequences that arise from even the best laid plans — provided that we work together co-operatively.

1.7 Recognising that success is in our future

Figure 1.8 shows a flexible approach that works towards, and then back from, a clear vision of future success. That success has to be based on values agreed by all concerned. This is a feedback loopy process that integrates design and construction, and that manages out uncertainties and manages in opportunities.

Box 1.12   Creative managing to future success   **Principle**

Our real goals are to:
- harness the creativity of people;
- help them to know their own values;
- understand those of the client and customers;
- have a vision of future success, and to work out how to get it by working back from that future;
- identify and remove the blocks in the progress towards that success.

In order to achieve this success-targeted approach, construction players will have to work together creatively, to know what they value and what they do not value, to think creatively about the risks that they face and the way that they can be overcome.

If the traditional predict and provide approach (Fig. 1.9) is used, when there are significant uncertainties, then you end up where you happen to get to! The process can involve many claims and litigation with no one really knowing just

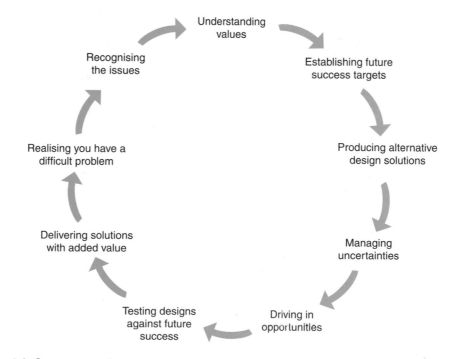

Fig. 1.8. Success targeting

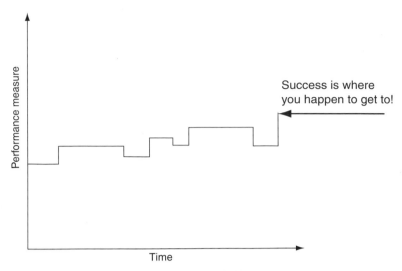

Fig. 1.9. Uncertainties blow 'predict and provide' off course

where it all might end. The added value from the claims process is appallingly low, but if it is the only source of profit it is essential for the success of the provider. The problem is that the uncertainties just blow the whole process off course!

The main reason for this failure is that the real world of practice seems so often to be full of 'messy' complex interacting systems which, despite the spectacular successes of applications of engineering theory, seems at the same time to demonstrate its many inadequacies. We shall call these wicked problems in Chapter 3 — problems that just seem to defy our normal way of doing things these days. All of the issues to do with environmental management, including pollution and global warming, are wicked problems.

Success targeting (Fig. 1.10), on the other hand, recognises that success depends upon a close involvement by all concerned. If everyone is working

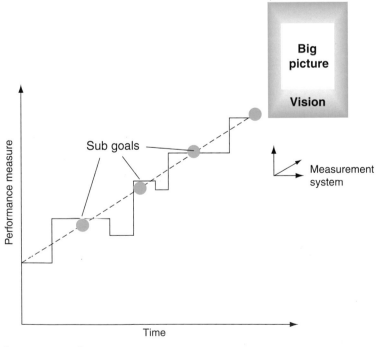

Fig. 1.10. Success targeting

together to deliver an agreed joint success then it is very likely that that success will be reached. It requires a constant and close engagement with events as they unfold. It is practical if it is both co-operative and commercially realistic.

Impelling reasons for systems thinking

We have said that systems thinking will help us to rethink construction. More specifically, we believe that systems thinking will help you to:

- integrate the current initiatives
  see the connection between quality management, value engineering, risk management, etc. more easily;
- see what is common
  understand the relationship between quality and values, functionality and risk, etc;
- reassess the scope of quality and value
  see that these are much deeper and more useful ideas than in common usage;
- recognise the need for radical change
  see the opportunities to add value to your client and to yourself;
- deliver customer focused strategies
  understand the value chain with the customer at the head;
- realise values from processes driven by impelling propositions
  realise the need for a strong creative vision and be able to connect it with practicality;
- integrate people and processes
  see that process is the peg on which to hang all attributes;
- generate simplicity out of complexity
  be able to choose the appropriate level of system description;
- demonstrate practical rigour
  understand how practice can be rigorous and not ad hoc;
- create tools to manage uncertainty
  see uncertainty as fuzziness, incompleteness and randomness and use the Italian flag as a measure (see Box 4.16);
- think in loops and not straight lines
  use diagrams of influence to shed light on complexity.

1.8   A success targeted workshop

Perhaps the following, deliberately fictitious, story of the first few days of a workshop will help us to explore some of these ideas.

Imagine the scene. Bruce, the CEO of United Leisure Industries (ULI), has an idea for a new business opportunity through a chain of public houses and has brought a group together to think through a proposal.

Bruce knows that themed pubs are taking more and more of the market. There are Irish pubs all over the place and doing very well. He wants to invest in Southern England because he feels that this is where they know their customers best. He has to convince his Board that there is something worth investing in — something that will have a competitive edge — they will not be impressed with Welsh rather than Irish pubs! He knows there are significant uncertainties in construction, as only recently a project to provide a theme park with a large helter-skelter ran 50% over budget and acquired an early reputation for breaking down with people in midair! He needs a new idea and knows he has to do it differently for commercial success. He believes it will take something like 3–4 years to get an idea off the ground. The proposal must be something that people will be ready for when the new pubs are launched.

Bruce has asked Sue, the Development Manager of ULI, to lead the team. She will be responsible for the project and accountable directly to him. Together, they have asked the following to form a team:

- Collie, a marketing manager from the Marketing & Sales Department of ULI;
- Stan, a project delivery manager seconded from a contractor;
- Henry from Finance;
- Andrew from a company of engineers and architects;
- Ian, a new recruit fresh from his MBA.

They have two weeks in which to put together a proposal for the Board of ULI. Bruce will be available on day 1 and on the first Sunday (they have all travelled from around the country and have therefore decided to work over the weekend; Bruce has promised them time off in lieu).

Bruce is a bit fed up with the construction industry. He knows it is a difficult industry in which to work. Many of the jobs are underfunded — there are high risks and the future is uncertain. Not only did he have problems with the helterskelter but his previous project suffered because finishes were not ready for the launch; and they were over time by two months and over budget by 20%. He knows that Andrew has been seconded to them to advise them on the Egan Challenge, so he wants to see some results from it. He wants to see the team create a clear vision of success for the scheme. He wants them to work back from that success target to find out how it can be done and what it will cost. Bruce has asked the Finance Director and the Operations Director to give some time to feeding in some ideas to the project and to attend a Directors' briefing at the end.

Sue now has to make this work. She has two weeks in which to do it. She decides that she will need to use Time Boxes because the schedule is so tight. Time Boxes are processes that are very strongly constrained on time. She produced a draft which, after discussion, was agreed by the team (Fig. 1.11).

They decided to split the two weeks into six Time Boxes as shown. Each box is one process involving the whole team. The team would produce Secondary Time Boxes within each Primary Time Box in order to work in smaller groups or individually — but they would come together at the beginning and end of each Time Box process. Ian was made responsible for reporting. Sue agreed with the team that she would remain process owner accountable for overall delivery on time. She is a robust lady who takes the view that 'failure is not an option'.

Sue was pleased that the team readily agreed to her Primary Time Box processes. Andrew had pointed out that if they were to follow the Egan example, they should be very clear about what success looked like in two weeks' time and should begin from there.

'That's not possible,' said Stan, 'how can you define success now — we haven't even started yet?'

'I think we can,' said Andrew. 'We know we have to make a presentation to the Board. We need to understand what the Board wants to see. We have Bruce here to help us with that now — this is not going to change in the next two weeks. We can decide what it will look like right now. We then have to work out how to get to that point.'

Andrew took out his lap top and connected it to the projector which beamed the picture on to the white blank wall. 'Let me get this set up and we can design the story boards. Our presentation will have to contain certain elements. We need to start with an overview, then continue with our vision,' he continued.

'You are right,' said Collie, rapidly picking up the idea, 'and we must include a customer view.'

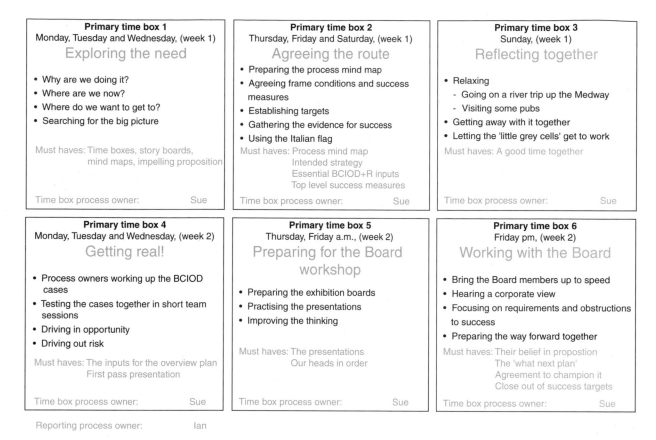

Fig. 1.11. *Primary time box processes*

The team continued to fire in ideas and Andrew captured them on his PC. Eventually they ended up with Fig. 1.12.

'This is the story we have to tell,' said Sue, 'now all we have to do is think up some ideas!'

Fig. 1.12. *Reporting story boards*

'I'm not sure why you want me here,' said Stan, 'I could be doing something a bit more useful. You've brought me in too early — I don't need to get involved yet.'

Sue's reply was quick and sharp. 'Look Stan, believe me, we do need you. Bruce would not have agreed if we didn't think you have a strong role to play. We will need you to prevent us from creating problems later on. Let's have a wager. If we agree that you have not been directly useful at the end of two weeks then I'll buy you dinner one evening — OK?' 'It's a deal,' replied Stan, 'and if I agree that it has been worthwhile the dinner is on me'.

'We need a theme,' said Sue wanting to move the meeting on. 'We have to answer the questions for Time Box 1. These define the success targets for this process. Why are we doing this? What's the big picture here?' They went into a brainstorming session where everybody threw ideas at Andrew who jotted them on flip charts.

Stan felt this was all a bit soft and fluffy so to keep himself looking attentive he took out his cigarettes and proceeded to light up.

'Hold on,' said Collie, 'this is a no smoking area — you can't do that.'

Stan was embarrassed, he had totally forgotten — he was more used to being on site.

'Hold on,' said Collie, 'that's given me an idea. Why don't we have a chain of NO SMOKING pubs?'

'I can't see that working,' said Henry, 'we wouldn't make any money that way. Go into any pub and you come out smelling like a used ashtray — pubs and smoking go together like a horse and cart. We'd lose all our investment within a year!'

'Henry's got a point,' said Sue, 'but he might be wrong. Look how attitudes have changed with respect to smoking over the last 10–15 years. Very few of my friends smoke now — its gone quite out of fashion.'

'That's because there is such a strong health risk,' said Andrew.

'Why not have a chain of healthy pubs?' suggested Ian.

'You know,' said Sue, 'I think you've got something there, it's an interesting suggestion. I think it even has a precedent in that Guinness made a name for itself in the 60s by giving free drinks to people in Irish hospitals.'

'That would help me convince the Finance Director if only it wasn't 30 years ago!' retorted Henry.

Collie was deliberately keeping quiet because she really liked the idea. She wanted the others to have time to think it over and own it. She knew there were problems. For example, some doctors say that red wine in moderation is healthy — but that might change. Her father-in-law is getting on a bit and his doctor has prescribed sherry instead of sleeping pills before he goes to bed! Opinions and judgements change as new evidence emerges in a complex subject such as health. Who knows what will be considered healthy in five years' time.' She decided to keep these thoughts to herself for the moment and bring them in later. After all, they could always develop some contingency plans to cope with unknown future events.

Everyone murmured agreement and heads were beginning to nod.

Ian said, 'Lots of families go out to pubs now — I'm sure a healthy pub would be attractive. People are much more health conscious than they used to be.'

'I think we should follow up on that Ian.' Sue glanced at her watch. 'However, we have covered a lot of ground on this our first day and I think we need a break. Let's wind up for today and get together fresh tomorrow to work up the idea of a chain of healthy pubs.' Collie thought this a good idea. She got on her mobile and asked one of her assistants to prepare some trend graphs of attitudes to health and drinking in this market segment.

The next day was Day 2 — 7% of time had gone — but at least they had a proposition that looked hopeful. Sue was feeling positive. She knew that even if the idea failed to live up to expectations the team was learning fast so the cycle time to develop another idea would be much less. She began by reviewing the previous day. Then she suggested that they should decide to draw a mind map for a healthy pub. Henry was sceptical — 'Why do we need a mind map?' he asked. Sue explained that it provided a framework into which to establish ideas. Then ideas stimulate more ideas — rather like pollinating fruit — some fruit will wither and some will grow big and juicy.

Ian had some special software for drawing mind maps. He began by typing in 'Being a healthy pub', in the middle of the screen. As he did so, they made suggestions. Ian typed them in and they appeared on the mind map screen. Occasionally they deleted items but more often they had to move items as they began to see how ideas related to each other.

'I can see a pattern forming here,' said Sue. She pointed to the image on the wall. 'Over here we have the customer issues and over here we have the delivery issues.'

'That's right,' said Henry, 'and over here we have the business and financial issues.'

They were discovering the dimensions of commercial success with BCIOD+R.

Stan was still not convinced of his need to be there. However, as the days progressed he began to put in objections and to his amazement this generated better ideas. At first, his contributions were small but they grew in importance as his confidence increased. He pointed out that a healthy pub could lose all of its appeal if built on contaminated ground. Andrew wondered if this was true. British Airways had recently completed their new corporate headquarters on cleaned up contaminated land and had won acclaim from all and sundry in spite of its being in the green belt!

Stan began to enjoy himself. He was particularly able to look at the mind map to suggest improvements. He pointed out that heating and ventilation systems are an Achilles heel for the construction industry. This sparked the idea that ULI could work with a manufacturer to develop a really healthy system. It might even have healthy smells, such as new mown hay, injected during the day!

Collie pointed out the need to create a complete experience that was attractive to the target customers. Stan undertook to visit one of the most forward looking suppliers to see if they would consider a partnership on the basis that a new, really healthy, air conditioning system, capable of managing the atmosphere in a pub, could have a much wider market. Perhaps there was opportunity for a supply chain partnership.

Stan was also interested in sustainability — although, like many of us, he was not sure what it meant. He knew about CO_2 omissions and energy usage. He learned that the policy was not just confined to environmental protection and prudent use of resources. It also included provision of high and stable levels of economic growth as well as ensuring social progress that met the needs of everyone. Perhaps a chain of healthy pubs would be seen to be swimming with the 'sustainability tide'. Perhaps if the company adopted such a policy, he would not find himself having to dig people out of holes and coax them down from trees when he started work on a new site.

One issue that Stan did have strong ideas about was standardisation. He believed that it was possible to cut costs significantly by standardising products. However, Collie was opposed. She pointed out the problems of so-called systems building of the sixties — standardisation is without any character — 'it's cheap and nasty,' she said. As they mulled over the issue in the team they realised that Rolls Royce cars are made of standardised components, that the Georgian Terraces in Bath were made from standardised assemblies and that some of the most elegant, modern, fitted kitchen furniture is made using standardised processes. Clearly, many building components are standardised, such as bricks, bolts, steel section etc. The issue was not so much about standardised products but standardised processes! If they could put together the materials in a way that reduces the total man-hour content, particularly on site, they could save money and deliver a much better project. Standardisation makes prototype testing more feasible which, in turn, helps to minimise defects. 'Nice when you can make it work!' thought Stan, but he kept this to himself for the time being.

Andrew had worked in an integrated team before. He had helped to develop and build a sewage treatment plant to recycle sludge that used to be discharged into the sea. He had learned that some of the best ideas for improvement come from people working at the front line — they have to build and use what others have dreamt up — they have to read and interpret the drawings! He felt that Bruce's frustrations with the industry had to be addressed head-on in the presentation. They needed to propose an effective way of getting that front line knowledge back into the design and delivery process. Stan from his site experience and Sue who had been a theme park operations manager rapidly took the point. They decided to include a process of exploring how pubs could be made easier to build and operate, by talking to people who were actually doing it and getting them to help map out the key processes. The process attributes would include not only performance attributes such as cycle times but also a commentary on frustrations and ideas for improvement. They decided to have regular focus group sessions of the most articulate and constructive people to review and challenge the emerging design. They decided to have session facilitators to ensure that assertive designers did not dominate the proceedings.

Henry realised that he had a role to play to help ensure that the business plan was sustainable in spite of the uncertainties they faced. He knew that this would not be achieved by rejecting all risks because low risk opportunities usually have low yield. The trick, he thought to himself, is to be able to recognise the uncertainties and manage them well. He had become particularly aware of this since he had been working the new corporate governance rules that required his director to ensure risks were properly managed. He was aware of the risks of brown field sites. He was very receptive to Collie's suggestion, when it came, that contingency planning for the unknowns was required.

Henry told the team the story of the Housing Association that bought land from a farmer to build some houses. They discovered, after site sampling, that the farm had been near a fireworks factory and there were traces of arsenic in the soil. The cost of carting the topsoil to a landfill site and the tax involved was ten times the cost of the land, even though cattle had grazed there safely for more than 30 years. Andrew suggested they would need a way to identify these issues as the project progressed. It would help if they were ready to answer the question 'what they would they do to minimise these risks?' if asked by the Board.

Perhaps this is a good point to leave our story. Sue and her team followed through the Time Box processes as in Fig. 1.12. They made an excellent presentation to the Board who expressed great interest. We shall have to wait and see if a chain of healthy pubs is ever built! Stan took Sue to dinner after it was all over and thoroughly enjoyed himself. He had been thinking differently and he felt he had made a difference.

(Opposite) Fig. 1.13. Mind map for 'being a healthy pub'

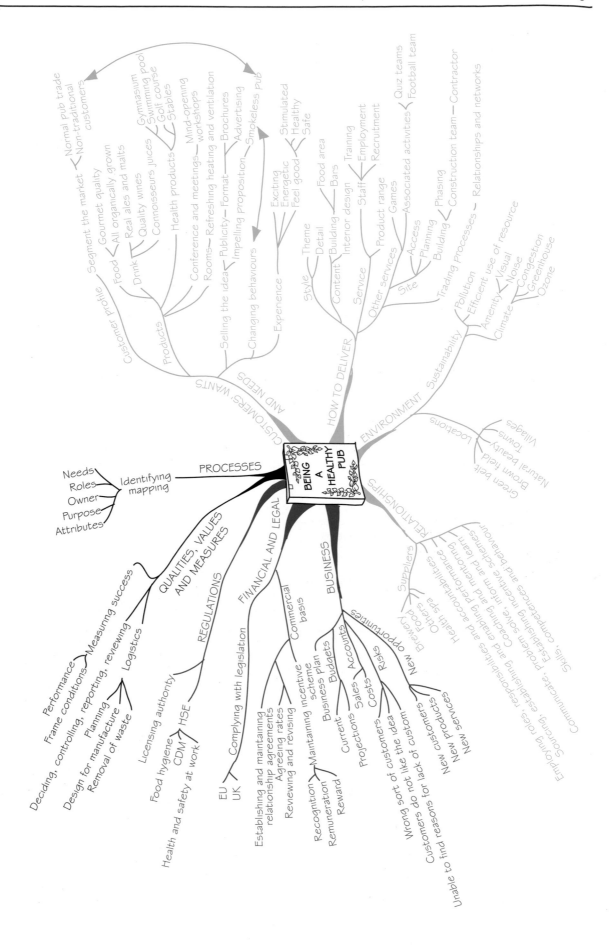

1.9 Checking for success

The success targets for this chapter set out at the beginning were that, after reading and thinking about it, you will:

Success target	Review
• be sufficiently convinced of the need for **change** to read on;	there is a fog that clouds the 'willingness to pay' of clients and the quality of the service they expect. We need to clear that fog. We have been challenged to rethink construction. That provides us with opportunities for both corporate and individual benefit;
• recognise the relevance of *Rethinking Construction* to the future of our industry;	change is inevitable and the pressures for further change are demonstrable. We have to get out of the downward spiral caused by focusing solely on cost;
• agree that current initiatives need to be **understood as a whole**;	there is value in all of the current initiatives — they all have a part to play — but they need tying together into one consistent framework;
• be prepared to put in the effort to get to grips with **thinking differently** and **making a difference**;	in order to change we need to reach out for new ideas. That will take some effort and we have to be convinced that it is worth it;
• be interested in exploring further the idea that we can get to an essential simplicity in complex systems by **focusing on process**;	process is the peg on which we can hang everything else;
• feel that the message is relevant to **your particular needs**.	every problem presents an opportunity — there are many opportunities coming from *Rethinking Construction*.

We hope that we have reached our success targets for this chapter — please use the feedback form at the end of the book.

Part 2

Thinking differently

2. Focusing on process

2.1 Deepening our view of process

If we want to do it differently then quite obviously we cannot continue to do the same things in the same way. It would also not be sensible to do things differently just for the sake of being different. We need to have a clear purpose and we need to be able to map out how we are going to be successful. It will help enormously if the maps we are to use through the journey to success are consistent and able to cover almost everything that we may do. In this chapter, we will develop this new and whole view of process which we will use as a framework for developing our rethinking of construction. In doing so, we hope to take the fear out of complexity by seeing the essential simplicity that focusing on process brings (Fig. 2.1).

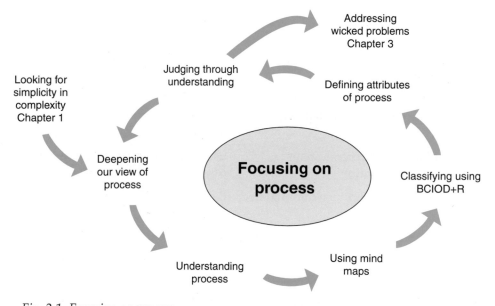

Fig. 2.1. Focusing on process

2.2 Targeting success for this chapter

The success targets for this chapter are that, after reading it, you will be able to:

- describe the central role of process in unifying ideas and techniques;
- write out a full set of attributes for process based on a simple generic principle;
- classify the processes using BCIOD+R;
- demonstrate the importance of creative thinking in modelling process;

- devise an impelling proposition for a product;
- draw a mind map for a product;
- draw a process product mind map to connect vision and practice;
- write down six principles of process;
- explain through values the connection between what we do and what we think about.

2.3 Understanding process

We need a new whole view of process

What does the word process mean to you? Do you think of process as a recipe such as making a cake or a manufacturing process such as the tinning of baked beans? Do you think of inputs being transformed into outputs? We want to widen those views because although those views are very useful as far as they go, we can offer a new and whole view of process that will help us to cut through complexity like a knife. To do that we will need to include factors that are particularly needed when co-operation between people is important. In Box 2.1

Box 2.1 A new view of process	Explanation
Typical current view	**Proposed new whole view**
Process is:	**Process is:**
a task or activity	*a way of getting from where you are to where you want to be*
can only be viewed from one perspective	can be viewed from many perspectives such as function, value, supply, risk
only useful in a restricted way	the central idea on which ideas are 'hung'
only useful when conditions stable and repetitive	useful to help manage risk when conditions are uncertain
inflexible, difficult to accommodate change	flexible — can be used to manage change
only useful when conditions are predictable with low uncertainty	useful to manage high uncertainty
not very dependent on teamwork	totally dependent on teamwork
not seen as being useful across organisational boundaries	essential for work across organisational boundaries
only to be used on a clear problem	useful to clarify 'messy' problems
a lot of work to produce a model	to be used right from the start
limited in the number of attributes used (e.g. time)	used to unify ideas with a rich set of attributes — particularly a clear purpose, definition of success and a process owner.

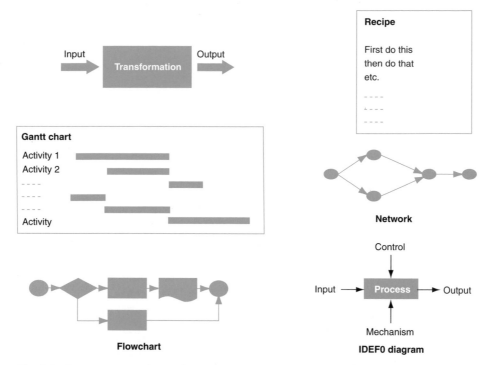

Fig. 2.2. Some current views of process

and Fig. 2.2 we set out some typical current views of process and contrast them with this new whole view we want to use.

All processes must have a purpose

Of course the processes and sub-processes of the chair example of Chapter 1 (Boxes 1.8–1.10) are reasonably straightforward and are included as a first, relatively simple, example. The healthy pub example obviously brings in much more complexity. However, it is clear even from the simple example of the chair that the purpose of the basic process (making a chair) has many facets. Is the purpose artistic, functional or to make money — or all three — indeed have we missed any other purposes? How do we make sure that all aspects of the purpose are covered? If this requires some thought for a straightforward chair, then how much more difficult is it for a chain of pubs or even an airport terminal?

We need to be creative to think about the purpose of a process — including the purpose of a product (as a process).

Encourage creative thinking

We will examine thinking skills, including creative thinking, in some detail in Chapter 5. Creative thinking techniques such as brainstorming require us to extend the scope of our thinking and to look outside of our normal considerations (Box 2.2).

Recognise that there are many points of view

We have already stressed the need to recognise the many perspectives that there

---

Box 2.2   Judgement and creativity   Example

Judgement requires analytical negative thinking. The questions we ask are 'What's wrong with this?', 'What happens when we take this apart?' Judgement is about criticism and confrontation. Edward de Bono pioneered lateral thinking as a way of coming up with new ideas. He argues that thinking is a skill that can be developed just as we develop other skills such as riding a bicycle. He says that thinking is worth practising and he provides lessons and simple tools to help us think more effectively. He provides practical tips to help us develop new ideas — to be more creative. This sort of thinking is positive, synthetic and co-operative.

Here is an example. The problem is that people park for too long in a town centre and block the spaces needed for shoppers. Edward de Bono's thinking group came up with the notion that anyone could park anywhere as long as they left their headlights on — so parking would be self-limiting! That's the creative part — the judgemental part tells us that there would be lots of cars with flat batteries to tow away! Here is another example. In order to give an incentive to a factory not to pollute the river it uses, the Environmental Agency could require it to extract its water downstream of its output!

(Edward de Bono, 1982)

---

are on a system. Thus we must consider the issues from all points of view and not just narrowly from our own. We should recognise that the client, the architect, the civil engineer, the structural engineer, the services engineer, the quantity surveyor, the finance director will all have different needs and priorities.

This is important in team building and to win success (Chapter 8). Likewise we need to consider the various aspects of a system, such as functionality, safety, and business case, and the context in which the process is embedded — particularly environmental issues. We also need to attempt to consider all issues that our process may generate, both intended and unintended. We must explicitly manage the perceptions of all of those who have a stake in the process so that their needs can be managed.

Box 2.3   Treatment of old mines   Example

One of the authors was asked to sit on an advisory committee to the Department of the Environment. The issue was the treatment of some mines. The committee included a vice chancellor, a mining engineer, a geologist, a civil engineer experienced in public utilities, a geotechnical engineer, a property specialist and a specialist in risk management. When any specific case was being discussed it was clear that, in each case, the property specialist framed the problem as being one of property values, the mining engineer as a mining issue, the geotechnical engineer as a ground/surface problem, the geologist in terms of the rock formations, the civil engineer experienced in utilities management in terms of the processes that would have to be thought through and the author spoke of the risk management. Each specialist framed the problem from his own experience and education, and therefore proposed quite radically different solutions in some cases. However, the composition of the group enabled a well-rounded discussion with many points of view being examined. Eventually, the solutions were dominated by technical thinking since that was the dominant background of the group.

> **Box 2.4   Three channel airport**   Example
>
> A major UK airport may have to have three channels for passengers by 2010 under the EU Shengen agreement. The first channel is for those passengers arriving from outside the EU and going on to another destination outside the EU. The second channel is for those travelling from outside the EU into the EU. The third channel is for passengers from inside the EU going to another place in the EU. The various requirements resulted in proposals for physical separation of these channels at great cost. However, since the Shengen agreement does not come into force for several years, virtual separation was mooted. It was found that it might be possible in the future through biometrics. This technology allows individuals to be identified: for example, by video camera pictures of the eye. The technology is not currently available but the risk of its not being developed in time was considered small, as others are already pioneering its use (e.g. in banking). Thus the solution was virtual separation based on biometrics not yet available but using the time available to make it happen. The savings made by not providing physical separation were enormous.

2.4   Using mind maps

Generate ideas about purpose — based on an impelling proposition

We have found that mind maps, as proposed by Buzan (1988), have helped us to generate ideas about purpose. They enable us to think through the issues and enable leaps of intuition. As we saw in Section 1.8, we start by developing an impelling proposition of purpose as typically used in marketing. This impelling proposition is used to express the essence of the product — the most important idea of the product. It can be developed by individuals or through a brainstorming workshop.

Of course, we should not forget that traditionally the impelling purpose of a product is really the province of the client. For the moment, we are assuming here that the design team advising the client (including the construction players working directly for the client to procure the product) are working together as a team. We realise that this is not possible in many cases without a significant change of attitude by those concerned. The client frequently does not want to reveal his competitive edge to construction players (presumably because he feels he cannot trust them). If relationships are such that we do not contribute to the process of determining the purpose of a product then the opportunities we have for adding value are considerably narrowed. However, if we can contribute to the thinking through of the purpose of a process then we can identify many ways of making value visible. We need to help the team to work together to 'add value' and we need to develop the skills to offer to clients.

Figure 2.3 is the mind map of propositions for the chair example of Chapter 1 based on the impelling proposition shown at the centre of the diagram — 'Being a chair hand-crafted for comfort'. Note that we choose the central idea as the process of **being**. This is the idea that encompasses all others. It covers all that can happen — from first vision to final decommissioning.

Thus, as we saw in the healthy pub example, the diagram is built by adding branches as they occur to us. At the simplest level the mind map is simply a technique for taking notes. Here we are using it to structure our thinking about the

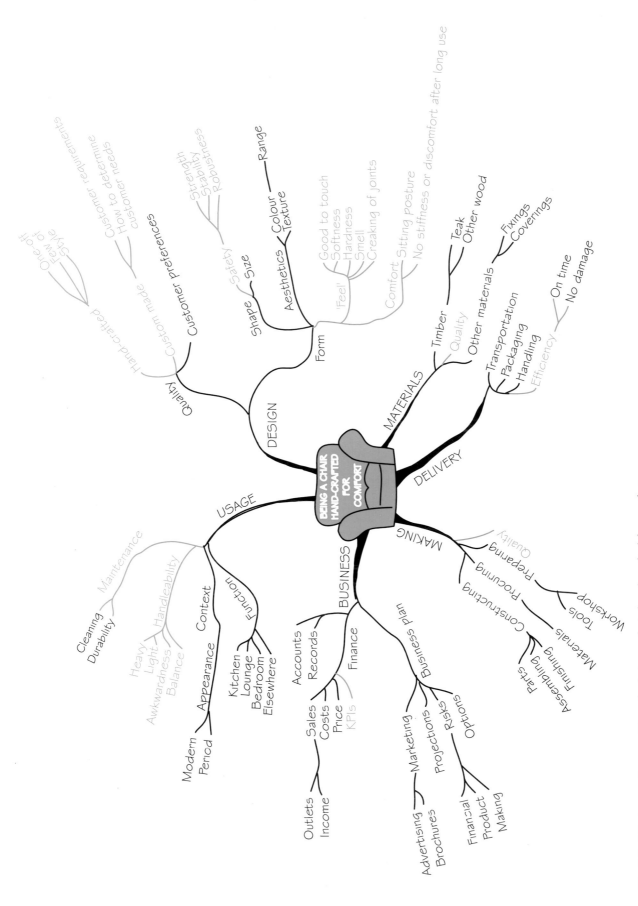

Fig. 2.3. Mind map of propositions for being a chair hand-crafted for comfort

aspects of the basic idea. As you think of ideas and note them, you add branches to the tree. You edit the tree so that the ideas flow in level of generality from the centre outwards. Thus your most detailed ideas will be the leaves of the tree.

Build a process model from the mind map — name the processes

Having generated ideas, we need to convert them into practical action. We do this by creating a process mind map from the ideas mind map. The first requirement is to recognise what the processes are and to **name** them. Perhaps, surprisingly, this is the most difficult requirement to get started on — but when you get the knack it becomes quite easy. The mind map stimulates the thinking through of the system. By turning the ideas expressed as propositions into named processes, we transform this thinking into a practical way forward.

The naming of processes is a practical approach because processes are what people actually do and how things actually behave. In a design process, you have to envisage the processes within the system you are designing and in which the systems will be a part. It is valuable to envisage your product as a system of processes because the success definitions for each process become the criteria against which you can test the anticipated performance of the physical systems — the bricks and mortar. For example, an airport terminal is a means by which passengers and goods transfer from road and rail to air, and vice versa. There are many processes involved with many interactions. The design team can test a proposed solution against the success states by doing a mental 'walk through' of the processes in the proposed design solution — a kind of thought experiment or 'mental simulation'. Of course, it is possible to do a computer-based simulation if the transformations in the process can be modelled (e.g. computer models are used to simulate congestion in a terminal for different rates of arrivals and departures. More commonly, a structural finite element analysis through time of the response of a building to loadings can be used to simulate the effect of a loading scenario).

Thus Fig. 2.3 can be transformed into Fig. 2.6 by building through the levels (Figs 2.4 and 2.5). Each figure is a process model of the product of the chair. Figure 2.7 is the same as Fig. 2.6 but shown as a vertical hierarchy of processes. The top process in both diagrams is the impelling proposition. The second level processes are shown in the next layer. The third level processes are the next layer and so on. Notice that the shaded boxes in Figs 2.6 and 2.7 are special since they reflect the requirements of the impelling proposition. Note also that the other processes are important in delivering a successful chair — but the ones in green are the ones that mark out this particular chair as special. This is where the differential value is added.

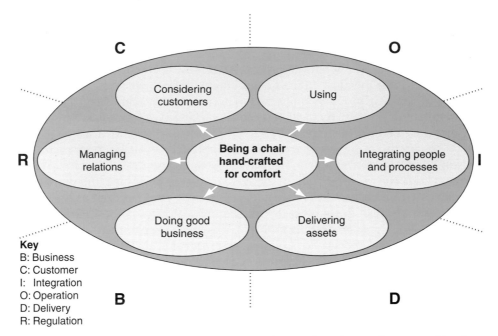

Fig. 2.4. Building a process model for hand-crafting a chair for comfort: top level

Fig. 2.5. Building a process model for hand-crafting a chair for comfort: second level

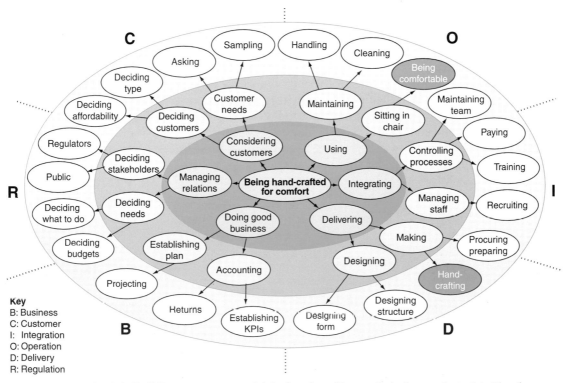

Fig. 2.6. Building a process model for hand-crafting a chair for comfort: third level

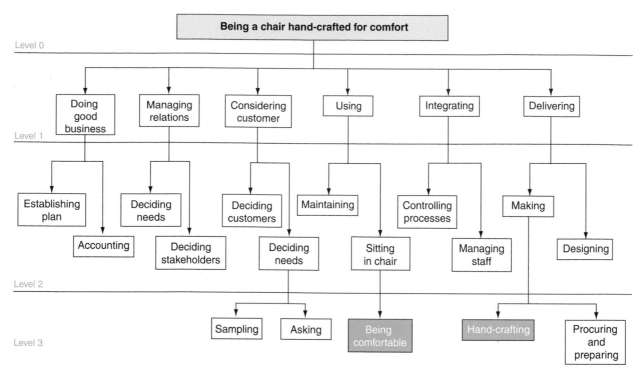

Fig. 2.7. A process hierarchy for hand-crafting a chair for comfort

2.5 Classifying the processes as BCIOD+R

BCIOD+R provide the dimensions of success

We now need to note two things about the subsidiary processes. Firstly, we need to note that the top level description 'Being a chair hand-crafted for comfort' is exactly equivalent to the second level description of six sub-processes as long as we have not missed anything out! This is how we are rigorous. Both descriptions are useful in different ways. The second level process descriptions should be jointly necessary and sufficient for the top one. Secondly, we need to note that the second level processes correspond to six sections labelled BCIOD+R for Business, Customer, Integration, Operations and Delivery and Regulation.

Now, of course, each of these sub-processes can be broken down into further sub-processes. For example, 'delivering' can be made up of 'designing' and 'making'. In turn, 'making' can be made up of 'procuring and preparing' and 'hand crafting'.

Again, these sub-processes are equivalent to the 'parent' process as long as we do not miss anything out! Thus the process of being a chair is actually made up of levels of sub-processes in six dependent areas of BCIOD+R. This categorisation is generic and can be applied at every level from an individual to large organisations and countries (Box 2.5 and Figs 1.5 and 1.6).

Visualise the processes as a snowflake

One way to imagine and think about this 'nesting' of levels of different versions of process is to visualise the snowflake of Fig. 2.8. However much you enlarge a bit of a snowflake, it looks the same. Each of the six subsidiary stars are the BCIOD and R of the process above.

Box 2.5   BCIOD+R are basic processes   **Explanation**

We can examine just how basic by relating them to our personal lives

B   Business processes — looking after our income and expenditure, ability to raise a mortgage, pay for a holiday, etc.

C   Customer processes — relating to our employers, any buyer of our services, any one who we undertake to do something for, etc.

I   Integrating processes — maintaining our diaries and our network of relationships, 'oiling the wheels', etc.

O   Operating — running our day to day activities, daily life; we are born, live and die — this is our life cycle

D   Delivering — providing the deliverables, the products and services for which we are responsible and accountable

R   Regulation processes — observing rules and laws such as driving on the correct side of the road, the law, duty of care as a qualified professional.

Snowflake analogy
No matter how much a component of a snowflake is enlarged, the component is seen to have a similar shape to the original snowflake. Where hard processes are embedded in soft ones the same is true for many of the systems that govern the behaviour of processes for rethinking construction.

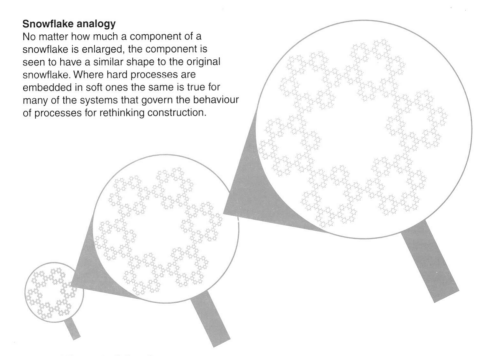

Fig. 2.8. The snowflake of process

The snowflake is similar at every level of definition and the stars fit together in a nested pattern. Clearly, construction processes may not be as symmetrical as a snowflake but the image is a powerful metaphor. For example, the client needs construction as part of his business, so does the contractor, so does his subcontractors. They all have customers, operations, rules and a need to integrate.

Products are processes

It is also important to see that the process of 'being' is not just about the physical product — being starts with the very first idea, the first vision. The gestation period of conception and design is just as much part of the final product as the bricks and mortar eventually are. This is because decisions at this stage make the product what it is and what it becomes. The old distinction between product and process is lost — both are part of the process of being. Product is a particular view of process which is useful because it focuses on what people need, want, demand and buy. However, product and process are not alternatives, they are both part of the process of being.

The processes interact and combine to achieve the whole 'impelling idea'

When we have identified the processes, we have to arrange them into some sort of network of connected relationships. As we have already indicated, this central idea of connectivity will be discussed in detail in Chapter 3. As we shall see there, relationships vary from those expressed in a formal language (e.g. mathematical functions) to those expressed (often necessarily rather vaguely) in natural language as some sort of influence. It is the interaction between the processes at one level that produce the unique properties that may emerge at the higher level. We will formalise that idea in the next chapter when we discuss the idea of a 'holon'.

Processes have friends

Effectively, processes interact by messages being passed between them — just as people interact by word of mouth, letter or e-mail. Each communication is a message. This is the idea at the root of modern IT systems such as the internet and object-oriented programming techniques. It is also the way we are beginning to understand the way the brain works (Carter 1998) in the sense that neurons switch state when a chemical or electrical messenger arrives from another connected neuron. A typical neuron may be connected to ten thousand other neurons.

So just as neurons communicate with connected neurons so, at a very different level, do people communicate with friends and contacts. Thus each process requires inputs from a set of connected 'friend' processes and sends outputs to another set of 'friend' processes.

Therefore, in a complex system, we do not try to write down all of the interactions in a sort of giant matrix equation — rather we simply focus on local interactions with 'friend' processes.

Thus every process has a declared and published set of 'friends' at the same level. The owners of processes which are friends agree to exchange information (inputs and outputs). The number of friends is kept to a minimum. The test to decide which processes should be friends of a process is that information that has been transformed in some way in the process is needed by the friend directly. There are a number of useful rules for this way of thinking about exchanging information which we will explore in Chapter 3.

It works for physical hard systems analysis

In physical hard systems, where we can represent theoretically the transformations from inputs to outputs within a process, we can simulate this message passing directly. This is the basis of the IOPM (Interacting Objects Process Model — Box 2.6) In soft systems where we cannot model the transformations depend-

> **Box 2.6   The Interacting Objects Process Model (IOPM)   Explanation**
>
> A physical object, such as a building structure, can be modelled as a process of action and reaction through time using conventional methods. This process can be simulated on a computer as a response to time varying loads. However, in the IOPM, each beam or column in the structure or each finite element in the analytical scheme is modelled as a process in its own right. In a conventional analysis the physical connections between the physical objects are modelled through the degrees of freedom (dofs) in matrix equations linking action and reaction. In the IOPM, these dofs are effectively channels of communication linking 'friendly' processes. These processes interact by sending messages (down these channels of communication) which are the current values of the state variables such as position, velocity, acceleration, force, etc. Each process (e.g. finite element) transforms an input message from friendly processes into output messages sent back to friendly processes. Each process acts in parallel. The IOPM is so-called because each process is modelled using a set of software objects in an object-oriented computer language such as C++.
>
> The results for standard problems are identical to traditional methods. The technique is versatile, flexible and simple to use. It allows complex transformations (e.g. non-linear 'chaotic' dynamics) to be modelled easily and quickly and can be extended to solve problems beyond the scope of conventional methods.
>
> (Blockley, 1995)

ably, we also cannot simulate them dependably. However, we can monitor the actual message passing in the actual systems, both hard and soft, and we can manage the consequences closely — this is what important aspects of management are about.

A further example of an impelling proposition leading to process mind maps

Figures 2.9–2.11 show a further fictional example for a water company. The interesting idea that emerged from the thinking through of the mind map was the contrast in the 'popular image' of the water industry with that of bottled water. The public, on the face of it, acts irrationally in buying bottled water. They can get at least as good, if not better, quality water from the tap quite freely. So what has driven the significant change to bottled water over the past 10 years or so? We believe the answer is in taste and security. There is a perception that tap water is not of the quality that perhaps it once was — and yet water quality testing shows that not to be the case. There is also possibly a perception that drink sold in a shop is safer than that obtained from the tap. This is compounded by the fact that tap water can often carry a chlorine taste. However, that is soon lost if the water is cooled in a fridge for an hour or so — something you do quite naturally with bottles of water.

The central idea and process for the mind map is still **being** — in this case 'being a Water plc'. However, the impelling proposition that could make a difference is associated with the need for a customer focus — 'supplying fresh clean safe water'. In Fig. 2.10, the processes in which the customer impelling pro-

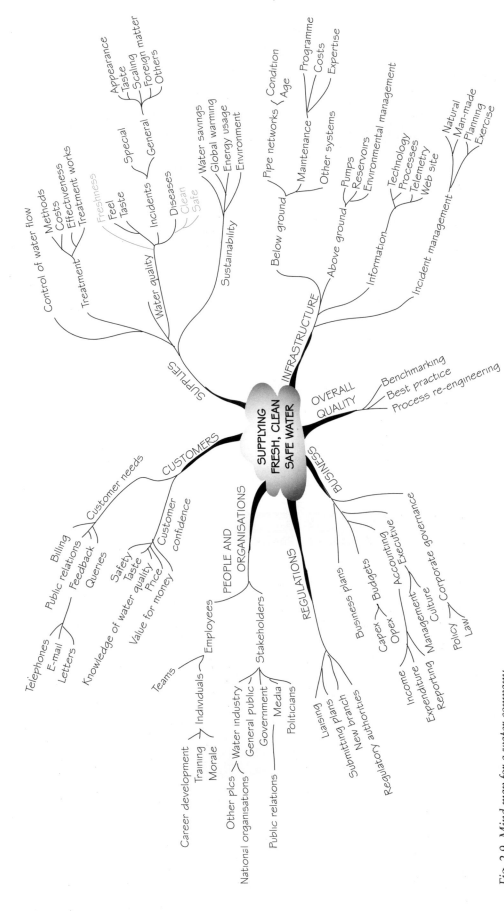

Fig. 2.9. Mind map for a water company

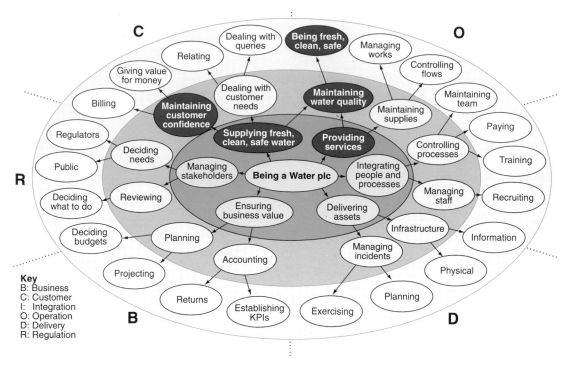

Fig. 2.10. Process model for a water company

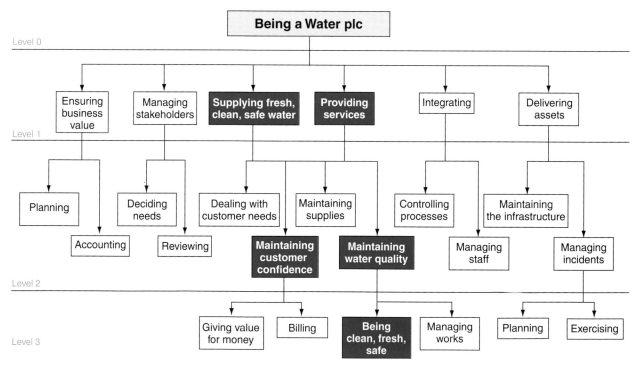

Fig. 2.11. Process hierarchical model for a water company

position appears are highlighted in red. Thus it is easy to see just how each process influences the impelling proposition which drives the marketing of the business.

Note that we have devised fictional impelling propositions with key ideas about marketing the product and then identified the processes required to deliver the proposition. Those key ideas are the first exposure to the values associated with the product and hence of the client. As we have already said, a value is the worth that you give to something and it is that worth you use to make decisions and hence to decide actions.

Process models help build consensus

The mind map quite naturally leads you to other values that may be associated with the product. Since the totality of the process is to deliver the impelling proposition, its success depends upon the success of all of the sub-processes. Thus the maps show how success in each process contributes to the total success. Of course, some of the processes are not held to be as important as others (depending on your role or stake and your point of view). The model therefore presents a way of pulling all of the different views together. In fact, we have found that a major added value in developing these diagrams is that they facilitate team discussion about different views of what is and is not important. They facilitate the building of concensus.

Now we want to focus on a particular process at a particular level and see how we can use the process to integrate many important ideas.

We can hang all sorts of attributes onto the process

Each process has a set of descriptors — just as does anything else. We can describe any object by its name, its size, its weight, its beauty, its cost, etc. These attributes are many and various, hard and soft, precise and vague, low level and high level, informative and uninformative, etc. They represent different aspects, different views, of the object. We choose them for our purpose, as appropriate, to describe, to explain, to persuade, etc.

Likewise, the attributes of a process describe just what the process is and likewise we choose them as we feel appropriate for our purpose. The attributes can be any form of information including text, drawings, measurements — in fact, any file of information. Effectively, each attribute reflects a value — something we feel has enough worth to warrant inclusion and modelling — which contributes to the total value of the impelling proposition. Box 2.7 shows an example of some of the simpler attributes for a chair. In the next section we will begin to give some more general guidelines on how to identify a full set of process attributes.

In this characterisation of process we must be sure not to omit some of the 'softer' issues which cannot be measured quite so easily as the 'harder' ones. For example, how do we measure whether the chair is 'attractive to a discerning buyer' or the level of environmental concern about the use of hardwoods from the rain forest? Clearly, we cannot measure 'softer' factors as dependably as the 'harder' ones but, nevertheless, we can often get a fairly reliable indication on which we can make decisions. We will look at the measurement of soft systems in some detail in Chapters 4 and 6.

Box 2.7 Making a chair — attributes		Example

Process Name   *Being a chair hand-crafted for comfort*

Roles   **Players**
Process Owner   *The craftsman*   *Fred Smith*
Client   *The customer*   *Member of public*
Suppliers   *Timber merchant*   *Bill Jones & Co*
Materials   *Timber etc.*   *Teak*

Purpose   *Dining chair as 'work of art',*
                and saleable

Objectives   *Attractive to discerning buyer*
                Carry 20 stone person

States   *Cost to produce, saleable price (£)*
                Forces in legs from person sitting

Risk   *Cost too high to make profit — quite likely*
                Unable to carry load — very unlikely
                Environmental concern for use of hard woods from rain
                forest — unlikely

Stakeholders   *Family of craftsman — dependants*
                Owner of workshop — rent due

2.6   Defining the attributes of process

Make sure every process has a process owner

Now we can begin to pull together some of the important attributes of a process.

Each process must have a **process owner** — someone who has taken responsibility for the **success** of the process and is accountable for it. Each process is happening for a set of reasons — it has a set of **purposes** that may or may not be clear. Success has to be agreed right from the outset. The success target is a particular set of state variables as we shall see later in Fig. 2.15. The definition of success may change for good reasons during the process — but at any time during the process, the process owner and all of the players in the process must agree about what they are aiming at. When it is not clear or when the various parties in the process have different ideas about the purpose then there may well be problems.

Likewise, all processes involve and rely on **people**. Relationships have an important ingredient called **power**. Power is the capacity to influence another. There are types of power such as positional power, resource power, personal power, expert power and physical power (Handy 1985) and these should be appreciated and understood. We will return to this in Chapter 8. The key person as we have said is the process owner who as well as having a set of **responsibilities** should constantly be seeking and encouraging all of the players in the process to find ways to improve it. The process owner's role is to establish measurable targets and then to provide the **leadership** to identify critical success factors and dependencies such as sub-processes that may be delegated. The process owner as team leader will need to be committed to the **team**. The group of people that plays out the **roles** that make up the process has to be aware of the possibilities and individuals have to know how to be part of a team. The group should develop a **quality culture** to deliver success and that will crucially include a safety culture.

Of course, the most important person of all is the **customer** of the **client** who heads up the supply chain because this is why the process exists at all — to provide the client with what he/she needs to provide the customer with what he/she wants. In general, a person or organisation that receives output from a process, either directly or indirectly, is a customer to that process. Customers, in this general sense, can therefore be internal or external to a company. It is crucial that the process owner understands the needs of the customer and manages his/her perception of the progress towards the agreed goals. It is these goals that define the success that all parties want. In return, the customer rewards the process directly through payment and indirectly through other services such as recommending the suppliers to other people. All of these relationships have to be established and managed and the contractual arrangements then follow. The best form of contract would be one that can be put into the drawer and left there because the relationships are so strong that there is no need to refer to it. In any case, the contract should provide a basis to support the success of the relationship. The contracts are not ends in themselves.

Get to success by managing uncertainty and risk

At the root of managing process is understanding **risk** and managing **uncertainty**. Risk management and its subsidiary processes of hazard identification, risk analysis (whether qualitative and 'soft' or quantitative and 'hard') and risk assessment are essentially bound up in our understanding of uncertainty. Uncertainty is everywhere and we all cope with it in our own way. A process framework provides the coat hook on which we can hang our assessments of value, risk and uncertainty. We will consider these matters in some detail in Chapter 6.

Use six honest serving men to define attributes of process

'I keep six honest serving men,
(They taught me all I knew)
Their names are *What and Why and When,
And How and Where and Who*'

(Rudyard Kipling, *Just So Stories*, 1902)

Our six good men and true provide the means by which systems and therefore processes can be defined so that they can be controlled and improved. The shapes of processes are defined to meet their purpose and are similar at any level of detail in a system even though the procedure by which they are delivered often looks different. In overview we can think of these six good men as providing categories for the various perspectives on process that we must think about. They are shown in diagrammatic form in Figs 2.12 and 2.13 and listed in detail in Box 2.12.

At the highest level the *what* are the customers' needs and wants — shelter, a journey, refreshment, a drink, entertainment or simply to feel good. Then at the next level below the *what* are the facilities that we build to serve those needs. Through these facilities, construction touches the lives of everyone (Box 2.8).

These are the products of construction processes in the sense that a product is a 'thing produced by a natural process or manufacture', as the dictionary tells us. However, each of these 'things' is a complex in itself and, as argued earlier, has a life cycle of its own, which is a process starting at conception and ending at decommissioning.

In general, products from some processes are not the constructed artefacts that result from the core process but are files of information required to support that core process. Products such as reports, specifications — in fact, any documents, even new research theories, computer programmes or software — are products

Fig. 2.12. The six honest serving men

of processes, and each of these has a physical reality (on paper or computer file). This product exists to inform or to instruct and therefore has an existence that is also a process. Thinking of products as processes, in this way, completes our maps of process — the input into one process is the output from another.

Decide what are the 'whats'!

If we think of the whole process of construction as starting from an idea (say for a bridge) and as ending with a reality (the bridge operating and eventually being decommissioned), then in the early stages the 'what' is not the final product (the bridge) but a user need which is a purpose from which an intention to build is derived. The product of these earlier sub-processes is a representation of this intention in the form of shared information. This representation takes many forms, but at the first concept meeting it might be a series of 6B pencil sketches, and immediately prior to the building process on site it consists of the contract documents. Thus the whole process of construction consists of a set of sub-processes each with outputs which are the top level need (e.g. to shorten a journey), an evolving representation of the final product (the bridge) and, the actual product (the actual steel or concrete bridge). At each stage, the players in the processes share a growing commitment to this outcome.

Each of these products/processes or the 'whats' of Box 2.8 have a **form, state, transformation and meta-system**. Let us consider each of these in turn briefly.

Form is about shape, i.e. the physical appearance and size that is familiar — but is also more than just its shape — it is about the 'essence' of its being. This rather abstract idea has practical consequences for the robustness (and, conversely, the vulnerability to progressive damage) of a process. The form of information is the medium in which it is expressed. Thus for a new theory that medium might be the language of mathematics.

State is the set of parameters or variables that describe the process, including Key Performance Indicators (KPIs). These include the 'hard' ones such as length,

```
Box 2.8   WHAT as facilities                              Explanation

Houses, shops, offices, hotels, stadia, airport terminals
Parking places, multi-storey car parks, aircraft stands
Basements, excavations, tunnels, caverns
Culverts, bridges, viaducts, aqueducts, estuary crossings
Rail: depot, mainline, underground, long tunnel,
Roads: rural, urban, trunk, motorway
Coastal protection, harbours, quays, jetties, lighthouses
Warehousing, industrial plant, water treatment works
Dams, reservoirs, power stations, transmission towers
Coal, gas, oil and nuclear power plant, waste disposal works
Etc., etc.

WHAT as milestones and deliverables

Sketches, drawings,
Theoretical models, computer models
Reports
Specifications
Contract documents
```

width, time and weight, and the 'soft' ones such as beauty, culture, team spirit, customer satisfaction, willingness to pay, etc.

Transformation is the change that happens either in the real world 'out there' or in the model of the world that we are using. In a construction project it is the change in the world that happens because of the work done to build some part of the job. At various stages of a construction process the representation of the transformation will be through the various contract documents and theoretical models of what is to be done. In a theoretical process such as the calculation of a stress level in a steel structure there has to be a model of the transformation (e.g. the simulation of stress waves in a finite element analysis) and then the transformation will be through the equations that represent that process (e.g. Newton's Laws, and the elastic behaviour of steel).

The **meta-system** is that which is outside the process that we are concerned with. It is important because through it we decide just what is in our process and what is not. When we identify any process (or indeed anything at all) we have to draw a boundary between what is it and what is it not it! What it is not is in the meta-system, i.e. that which surrounds the system. Again, this may seem unduly esoteric for most practical examples. However, there have been significant occasions when different players in a process have had a different view about that process, which has led to serious difficulties. In fact, this is a common reason for claims litigation (Boxes 2.9 and 2.10). See also Box 9.12, CALIBRE.

```
Box 2.9   Knowing when you are inside a process          Example

A client wanted to refurbish a hotel. He employed a management contrac-
tor and a professional team. They started work on the basis of a cost plan
and a contract. As soon as the contract was signed the client avoided giving
any further instructions to anybody, apparently in the belief that by this
means he would avoid any cost overruns on his account. In practice, the con-
tract made him an essential part of the construction team. The outcome was
bankruptcy for the client and very substantial losses for the other parties.
```

Box 2.10   Designer–contractor interactions   Example

A contractor was appointed after the design work was completed. The assumption was that design can be progressed to an advanced state without addressing specific buildability issues with the contractor. It was implicitly assumed that design is quite separate from construction and that the interface could be managed by the contract. It also eliminated many opportunities to improve the project. It created a substantial risk of claims. It would have been better to establish a process that integrated both the designers and the contractors from the outset.

Box 2.11   Knowing when you are inside a partnering team   Example

Two competitive organisations agreed to co-operate on a project. They employed change management consultants to help the integrated team to work together. They were so successful that they became a third organisation. Back in their parent companies they were viewed with some suspicion. Access to knowledge was frustrated and much of the benefit of co-operation was lost. The key element of trust was lost.

So the *what* define that which we are trying to achieve with a process. We start with an idea and end up with a reality. But *why* are we doing this process in the first place and what resources will we need in terms of people (the *who*), things (which are the *what* from subsidiary processes), time (the *when*), place (the *where*) and money (the values of the resources)? (see Box 2.12).

See that the 'why' question drives the process

The *why* question is the driver of the process — it is the potential that creates the change — it is the pressure that causes the flow. We can draw a direct analogy between potentials (such as differential velocity in mechanics, voltage in electrical systems, pressure head in hydraulic systems, temperature difference in thermodynamic systems) and the *why* that drives social systems. In systems dynamics these are known as across variables that drive the through variables of flow. (In fact, these two variables, the across and through variables, are dual and one can consider either one driving the other, depending on one's starting position.) The through variables of flow are force in mechanics, current in electricity, flow in fluids, heat in thermal systems and change through time in social systems.

Thus the *why* question is fundamental to understanding process. What is the basic need to be satisfied? How does this define the purpose of the process? What problems and issues does this raise that must be solved? How will we know if and when the need is met, the purpose fulfilled and the problem solved? We need measures of success. We will need to articulate what we are trying to achieve in the process in broad terms as a mission and set of aims. Then we will need precisely defined statements of what we are trying to achieve, which will be the objectives of the process. These then define the target we are aiming at, the desired end state of the process. These questions cannot be answered unless we have a clear value system that enables us to order our priorities. We will con-

Box 2.12　Process attributes		Explanation
Who? Roles Functions Players/Actors Owner Client/Customers Stakeholders	**Why?** Purpose Needs Targets Vision/Mission Success/Failure Problem/Issue Creative tension Objectives	**Where?** Place Site Location
What? Form 　Material/Structure 　Connectivity 　Hierarchy 　Robustness 　Language State 　Variables 　Parameters 　KPIs Transformation 　Physical system 　behaviour 　Technology 　Models Meta-system 　Environment 　Context	**When?** Time Start Finish Critical path	**How?** Decision 　Alternative solutions 　Evaluation criteria 　Choice Resource Controls 　Evidence 　Planning 　Prediction 　Imagination 　Scenarios 　Opportunities 　Hazard/Risk 　Proneness to failure

sider these issues in Chapter 6 when we look at what underpins the way we make preferences. One point is clear, however, at this stage, namely that, while money is a good and important measure of our values, it can distort our thinking if it is to be our only measure or if all other measures are to be translated into it.

If we do not make clear our answers to these *why* questions then we will launch into a process not knowing where we are heading. It would be like setting off from Bristol in a car without a destination in mind — a sort of purposeless mystery tour.

The development team and the delivery team must liaise

These issues are important organisationally because usually there is a development team whose job it is to work the relationship between *why* and *what*, and there is a delivery team whose job it is to work the relationship between *what* and *how*. There can be several different *whys* and there is certainly more than one way of delivering but they all have to agree the *what* (what is built, what is done, what is the product) because there has ultimately to be only one *what* — even though that product is a complex set of processes.

So what resources do we need? First we need some people. These are the *who* questions. What **roles** are needed? A role is rather like a part in a play taken by an actor. Another way of thinking about it is as a 'hat' to be worn. It is a set of responsibilities that is taken with a corresponding set of accountabilities. At the highest level in a typical company the roles are the Chairman of the Board, the Chief Executive and the Directors both executive and non-executive. Roles at lower levels in the company include the bricklayers and steelfixers who actually make the construction — without them nothing in the physical world on site would change. The roles are usually generic to the process but the people occupying the roles will change. One person can take on many roles in many processes. Crucial roles are those of the owner of the process, the client and the stakeholders as described earlier. A product has a role which is its functionality, i.e. what it is for — as determined by the designers and users. The piece of wood that is my door has the role of being a door, the bricks that are the building in which I work have the role of keeping out the weather. Neither the wood nor the bricks know they have those roles — the functionality is ascribed by us as users.

All processes will be enacted at some location or locations. The *where* questions are those to do with the place or site. Likewise, the *when* questions are standard items for project management of time and are critically important. Critical path analysis, for example, is a well-known project management tool that helps us to understand the relationships of time. We had an illustration of the use of time boxes in Chapter 1. We will return to time management in Chapters 8 and 9.

The techniques are the 'how'

So the last (but by no means least) set of questions relate to the *how* of process. If the *why* of process drives the change through time of the *who, what* and *where*, then the *how* of process is the means by which this change happens. In symbolic terms the *why* is the driver, the potential that makes change happen. The *who, what, where, when* are the change itself — they are the parameters of the system which will change as the process unfolds. The *how* is the operator which is the method by which the *who, what, where, when* are transformed, are changed through the process from the input state (with nothing at all except a need and a vision) to an output state which is success. This state at the end of construction and start of operations is the *what* (of the constructed facility), the *who* (all of those involved), the *where* (as the location) and the *when* (the time). This is shown in Fig. 2.13 and in symbolic terms is

$$why = how\ (who,\ what,\ where,\ when)$$

Box 2.12 shows some of the decision making terms that determine just *how* the process is to be enacted. Unfortunately engineers tend to jump to the *how* questions rather too quickly. The *how* questions are of course crucial but they need to be driven by the *why* and addressed alongside the *what, where* and *when* questions. TQM and VM encourage users to identify *why* before *how* and to understand the relationship between them. This is simply because success for any construction process is that it fulfils its purpose. If we are clear what the purpose is then we are more likely to fulfil it.

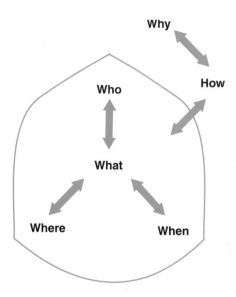

Fig. 2.13. The six men

Assess progress to success

In Box 2.12, one of the *whats* is the set of state descriptors. These are the well-known variables or parameters of a physical model (e.g. sizes, material strengths, loads, etc.) and the other Key Performance Indicators (KPIs) such as % completion, % spend of budget, other financial ratios. They should also include the softer, more difficult to measure, but nonetheless important indicators such as team spirit and safety culture. At company board level the emphasis tends to be on financial ratios as KPIs. We need to be aware that many of the KPIs tend to be historical measures of performance and so using them to steer what we do is rather like driving while looking out of the rear view mirror. We need to be able to use these indicators to project forward to future success and this requires evidence developed through models of future performance.

The idea of a balanced scorecard (Kaplan and Norton, 1996) was introduced in an attempt to provide a more balanced link between financial budgets and strategic goals. This will be discussed further in Chapter 6.

In Fig. 2.14, the performance of a process through time is shown. Progress in the figure is measured by one performance indicator with results in the past and present and projections of possible future scenarios. Failure will occur if the trajectory strays outside of the acceptable region that in this case is above the limit boundary — shown horizontally for simplicity. If the trajectory stays in the green zone then there is no concern for the future of this process; if it is in the white zone then there is concern and perhaps even some partial damage, and action may well be required to put the process back on track. If the trajectory reaches the red zone then there is a serious concern that the process is almost an 'accident waiting to happen' and action must be taken to avoid failure.

Figure 2.15 extends Fig. 2.14 to three dimensions. Those readers familiar with limit state reliability theory will immediately see how this model derives from that theory (Blockley, 1980). The 3-D space in the figure is defined by two performance measures and time. Clearly in an actual problem there are many performance measures (state variables) and the space is multi-dimensional. The 3-D volume shown in the figure then becomes a hyper-volume which, of course, cannot be drawn diagramatically. The figure has been drawn to illustrate conceptually what is happening as one proceeds from an initial state to the final goal state. If the process is successful throughout its life then the trajectory will remain

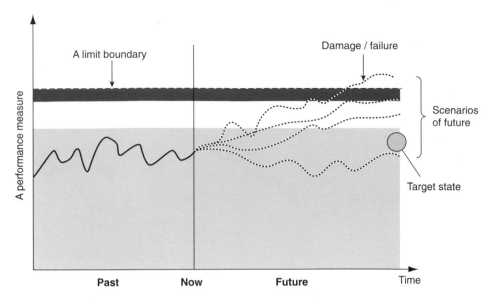

Fig. 2.14. Performance

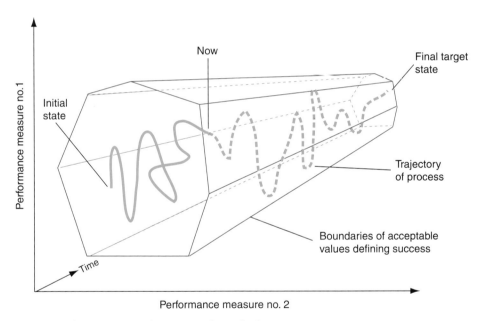

Fig. 2.15. The trajectory of a process through time

inside the region defined as acceptable. In other words to be successful the trajectory of the process must lie in an acceptable region. If there is cause for concern that the trajectory might be approaching the limits of the region then the process owner will need to consider what action is needed to pull the trajectory back safely inside the acceptable region. If it is possible to predict future trajectories through some sort of analysis then the chance of the trajectory straying outside of the acceptable region must be acceptably low. This is, in effect, risk management.

It is important to realise that this diagram applies at one point in time and is the best estimate of past, present and future at that time. As positions change and goal posts move then our ideas about everything contained in the process may have to change — sometimes quite dramatically — and then we will need a new diagram. Therefore, if our vision of success changes and our targets change then we adjust everything in the light of those changes. If evidence about the players in the process emerges such that changes are required then they will be made, and decisions will be made accordingly. The important point is that at any one time we have a clear idea of what constitutes the path to success, as we understand it, at that time. There is no sense in which Figs 2.14 and 2.15 are static with static targets — they are changing dynamically as time progresses.

The business case should contain all of the important 'whys' for BCIOD+R

We have said that the first process to address is that of **managing the business** or ensuring business value. The business case (Chapter 7) sets out and becomes the major *why* driver — it drives the whole project. It is fundamental to identifying the reasons why a particular project is being promoted and why it makes business sense to all of those involved. It addresses all of the issues covered by BCIOD+R — it is prior to project management and sets the context for it.

2.7 Judging through understanding

Be clear about the principles of process management

So let us return to some simple principles of process management. We have said that everything that we do is conceived as a process made up of many interacting sub-processes. Every process has a purpose and success is the achievement of that purpose. Success is always achieved through people either directly or indirectly.

As we have seen, the attributes of a process can incorporate people and purpose. We have six basic principles that we should remember. We will develop them through this book, and they should be borne in mind whenever we are setting about understanding and managing a system of processes. They are summarised in Box 2.13 as **CREATE**.

We will be content merely to note these principles at this stage. We will refer to each of them in later chapters and return to them all in the final chapter.

Construction is based on professional judgement

The thinking on which that judgement is based has to be informed and responsible with a proper duty of care. We have to understand what we are doing and be able to justify it. Our thinking has to be reflective and creative and it has to show practical foresight. As individuals and as teams we have to obtain as much dependable knowledge and information that it is reasonable to assimilate to inform our thinking. It is difficult, if not impossible, to develop and change that thinking without reaching out for new ideas. We are challenged to rethink construction for some quite fundamental reasons that are impelling. We therefore have a duty of care to examine seriously the case for a systems approach to construction.

What we do, as individuals and in groups, depends on what we decide. In turn, this depends on what we understand — the quality of our own mental models. It also depends on what we value and how creative we are in thinking of alternatives and how good we are at judging the worth of alternatives. Decision making is a process as shown in Fig. 2.16 — in fact, it is a generic process.

Box 2.13	CREATE — The six principles	Principle
C	**Customers/Clients**	Focus on them, get to know the totality of their needs because these define the **purpose** of the process.
R	**Role/Responsibilities**	Define and document who is responsible and accountable for what — be sure everyone knows and agrees what **success** is.
E	**Environment**	Name the processes, define the systems and then manage the differences of understanding between people of just what is in the system and what is not. Proactively manage the perceptions of the stakeholders. Watch the outside pressures; financial, political, etc.
A	**Appropriateness**	Make sure the scope and level of definition of the system is appropriate for the purpose. Remember prediction is useful but limited, uncertainty has to be identified and managed.
T	**Testability**	The best and most dependable information is testable. Look for evidence, document it, assemble it, measure it.
E	**Ethics**	Try to be as clear as possible about individual and team values. Encourage a quality culture. Build trust between players.

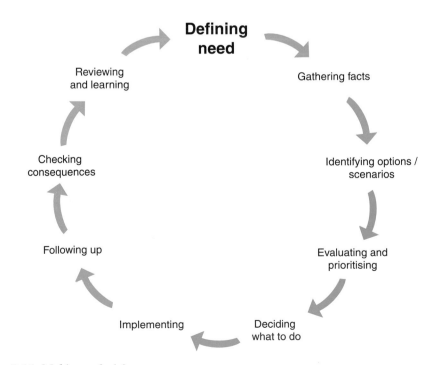

Fig. 2.16. Making a decision

Any such process, as we have said, is inevitably made up of sub-processes. This is because, for example, in many complex and messy problems the major problem is to understand what the problem is — as we shall discuss in the next chapter. Ultimately, at the most abstract level, a process is the transforming of inputs into outputs, i.e. we perceive the world, reflect on it and then act. We are using the word 'reflective' to describe the process within our brains which is partly cognitive and at a conscious level and partly sub-conscious at levels deep within our brains such as those limbic regions which decide our emotional behaviour. The reflective part of the process is that which transforms our perceptions (inputs) into actions (outputs).

Box 2.14   We do what we value   **Principle**

Thus we do what we decide — we decide what we value — we value what we understand (although that understanding may sometimes not be great) — we understand what we think about. Thus what we do depends on our ability to think creatively and to judge what we create against well-balanced criteria.

2.8   Checking for success

The success targets for this chapter set out at the beginning were that at this stage you will be able to:

Success target	Review
• describe the central role of process in unifying ideas and techniques;	process is the core concept on which all other ideas are hung as attributes to represent what the process is. We use process to integrate ideas and to give us a way of seeing an essential simplicity in complexity;
• write out a full set of attributes for process based on a simple generic principle;	the generic attributes can be thought through from who, what, why, where, when and how. Some of the important ones are role, purpose, state, success, place, time and transformation;
• classify the processes using BCIOD+R;	construction processes can be classified in terms of Business, Customer, Integration, Operations, Delivery and Regulation (BCIOD+R). The classification works at all levels;
• demonstrate the importance of creative thinking in modelling process;	it is important to keep open creative thinking and closed judgemental thinking styles apart;
• devise an impelling proposition for a product;	creative thinking is required to express the essence of the product;

• draw a mind map for a product;	the process is helped by drawing a mind map of an impelling proposition for a product;
• draw a process product mind map to connect vision and practice;	the mind map can be used to produce a process product model which connects vision and practice. Successes in each process are the values that contribute to the success of the whole project;
• write down six principles of process; explain through values the connection between what we do and what we think about.	the six principles of process are captured by Customer, Role, Environment, Appropriateness, Testability and Ethic.

We hope that we have reached our success targets. Please use the feedback form at the end of the book.

3. Finding the leverage

3.1 Wicked and messy problems

Conklin and Weil (1999) call them wicked problems; Schon (1983) calls them messy sets of problem issues. We all have them — problems and situations that do not seem to yield to easy solutions. You get the feeling they are rather like sorting out a bowl of tangled spaghetti that seems to get more tangled the more you try to sort it out. Conklin and Weil describe a subtle but pervasive pain in organisations. You recognise it, they say, by complaints such as 'I can't get anything done — I've got to go to another meeting', or 'Why does everything take so long these days?' The pain comes from the clash between what we hope, expect and plan to happen and what actually happens — the reality. It comes from not recognising that some of the problem solving techniques we have been taught are not adequate for wicked and messy problems.

'Some problems are so complex that you have to be highly intelligent and well-informed just to be undecided about them' Laurence J. Peter

3.2 Targeting success for this chapter

The success targets for this chapter are that, after reading it, you will:

- be able to recognise a wicked problem;
- want to look for leverage to tackle such a problem (Fig. 3.1);

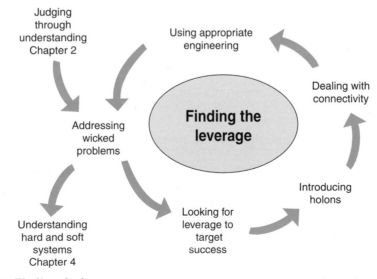

Fig. 3.1. Finding the leverage

- be able to identify that leverage through targeting success within process holons;
- begin to see how to deal with complexity through process holons defined at different levels of definition and you will focus on the local connectivities;
- be able to identify the appropriate level to model your systems.

3.3 Addressing wicked and messy problems

In this chapter we will begin to set out the essentials of the systems approach to tackling wicked and messy issues and problems. They seem to be characterised by the following statements. How familiar do they feel to you?

- You do not seem to understand the problem until you have developed a solution. There does not seem to be a definitive statement of what the problem is and so there really is not a definitive end. There seem to be so many interlocking issues and constraints. There are many unintended consequences of the decisions that are taken.
- There are so many people involved that the whole thing is a social process which comes to an end when there is some sort of agreement or everybody gets tired.
- The constraints on the solution change over time, sometimes quite suddenly and rapidly. It is not so much that the goal posts shift — it seems as if you are being required to play a different game!

The construction industry is full of wicked and messy problems — see Box 3.1.

Box 3.1 Wicked problems	Example
- What is the best route for this new road? - Where should we site this factory? - Design this new airport terminal? - What features should this new building product have? - What should be the requirements for Chartered Engineer status? - Design a new degree programme for engineers of the new century.	

For each of these problems there are so many interacting features that the total effect of a change in one feature cannot really be fully appreciated until the solution is developed and tested in practice — see Box 3.2.

The interactions within Box 3.2 are ones that we can foresee even if we find the outcomes difficult to predict. There are however other classes of interactions that are even more difficult — those that we do not know we do not know about! We will address such incompleteness in Chapter 4.

Wicked problems usually involve people

Clearly, in each of these cases there are many people involved. Wicked problems are usually wicked because so many people are involved — including the clients, their customers, the designers, the contractors, government agencies, the regulators and the general public. Each of these groups and the individuals in these groups have their own needs, aims and objectives — their own agendas. When all of these come together in harmony the results can be astonishing; when they do not — when they clash — then stalemate results and hardly anything gets done.

> **Box 3.2 Interactions within wicked problems .** Example
>
> - If the route for a road is changed to avoid splitting a community then perhaps a natural environmental feature is threatened or the costs of tunnelling becomes prohibitive when running sands are discovered on the route.
> - An improvement in the security of the baggage handling at the airport could affect the mishandled bag rate and the time passengers have to wait for their luggage.
> - Dropping the study of thermodynamics in a new degree programme might produce a generation of civil engineers who find difficulty in understanding the needs of services engineers thereby leading to functional problems and higher costs.
> - The use of brittle steel led to the Sea Gem disaster, which motivated the use of tough steels. This, in turn, mitigated the consequence of unanticipated fatigue problems in the North Sea.

> **Box 3.3 For them to operate together effectively, each of the   Principle
> members of the team needs to be aware of the
> knowledge and skills of each of the other members
> of the team, i.e. to co-operate**
>
> Where there is significant uncertainty and creative thinking is needed to bring about change, then the outcome is not easily predictable at the start. Some of the interfaces between parts of the construction process, e.g. Developer, Architect, Engineer and Cost Planner, cannot easily be prescribed. Each player should have sufficient understanding of the roles of the others so that each can legitimately challenge and contribute to the others' success. The effectiveness of multi-disciplinary development teams depends on this.

In many projects, a great deal of time is spent in *getting the people right*. Many managers would argue that if you can get the people right you are half way there. A good team can usually work with a bad system to success, though inefficiently and with high cost, but rarely does a bad team succeed even with a good system.

Wicked problems are always changing

Change is inevitable and the pace of it seems to increase year by year. You may start a process thinking you are aiming at one set of goals and then, because of changing conditions, you are forced to change direction. It is rather like starting a game of soccer where the aim is to score a goal by kicking the ball under the posts and then being told you are now playing rugby and you should kick the ball over the posts. In fact, it is often so bad now that you are effectively told that you are now playing chess!

The real problem is that we are taught throughout our school and higher education that the power of rational thinking is all that we need — that we can solve these wicked problems by linear, logical processes stepping through the stages of the problem in a clear sequence. Of course, this process works for many problems, e.g. the analysis and design of structures and other engineering science

---

> **Box 3.4   Cycle times**   **Example**
>
> Cycle times, from start of investment to payback, for construction develop-
> ment may be of the order of 5 to 15 years. These times are often incompati-
> ble with market factors which have cycle times of, say, 1 to 4 years. Examples
> of such factors are the price of oil, the market in electronic chips, strategies
> for alliances between airlines, office rentals at Canary Wharf, etc. Unfortu-
> nately, these market factors are becoming more unpredictable (some would
> say chaotic) and solutions influence the outcomes of projects in entirely unex-
> pected ways. Thus a strategy of 'predict and provide' (Fig. 1.7) is no longer
> an adequate strategy for success.

calculations. Although they probably did not seem simple when we were students struggling to understand, they are simple in the sense that they follow a
logical step-by-step sequence to a 'correct' answer. Conklin and Weil (1999) call
these 'tame' problems because they yield to traditional methods in a reasonable
time period. However, if we try to use tame methods on wicked problems, we
run into difficulties.

It is important, however, before we go any further, to emphasise that we must
not 'throw the baby out with the bath water' here! We must not underestimate
the importance of linear, logical problem solving processes. They are *necessary*
to develop the mind, they are necessary for a good education and they have
enabled us to achieve many magnificent things. If you cannot solve tame simple problems, you will probably not be able to tackle wicked and messy ones. It
is just unfortunate that tame simple methods are *not sufficient* for wicked and
messy problems. They lead to the organisational pain described at the beginning
of this chapter.

3.4   Looking for leverage to target success

Solving wicked problems is a social process

The challenge to rethink construction is certainly a wicked and messy problem!
If we use tame simple methods **only** in our attempts to meet this challenge, then
the chances are we will not succeed. Clearly, there are an enormous number of
interlocking issues and constraints to be addressed. Many people are involved
and, although clear targets have been set out, there seems to be no definitive solution to the problem. We probably will not have any deep understanding of the
problem until after we have developed a solution. Certainly the constraints on
the solution will change and are changing, and the decisions that we take will
have many unintended consequences — some for the better and some for the
worse (Box 3.5)!

> **Box 3.5**   **Explanation**
>
> As the old Wiltshire saying goes 'They be always improving things — some-
> times they improves for the better and sometimes they improves for the
> worse!'

Here we can set out only the approach we think is necessary — it is a social process that is needed but one set in a challenging technical environment. As we discussed in Chapter 1, it is no use doing more of the same — there has to be change to do more with less. As Senge (1990) has written:

'Small changes can produce big results — but the areas of high leverage are often the least obvious'.

In our experience, there are many people around who are expert in making straightforward problems complicated. The reverse, that of making complicated problems straightforward, is not so easy!

Box 3.6   Steering a ship   Example

Senge (1990) quotes Buckminster Fuller's illustration of the principle of leverage through a trim tab. A trim tab is a small 'rudder on the rudder' of a ship (Fig. 3.2). It is very small and its role is to make it easier to turn the rudder which, in turn, makes it easier to turn the ship. The larger the ship the more important is the trim tab.

The interesting point here is not just the effectiveness of the trim tab — but that it is not an obvious solution.

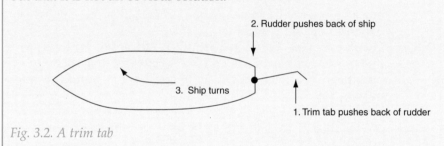

Fig. 3.2. A trim tab

Senge also sets out 11 laws of systems thinking which illustrate the difficulties of getting to grips with wicked problems (Boxes 3.7 and 3.8). These laws are based on at least two important ideas. Firstly, there is usually a delay, often considerable, between cause and effect (Law 7) — most of us tend to think of cause and effect being close in space and time. Secondly, systems tend to have compensating feedback. The harder you work at improving matters, the more effort sometimes seems to be required!

Box 3.7   Senge's Laws of Systems   Principle

1   Today's problems come from yesterday's solutions
2   The harder you push, the harder the system pushes back
3   Behaviour grows better before it grows worse
4   The easy way out usually leads back in
5   The cure can be worse than the disease
6   Faster is slower
7   Causes and effects are not closely related in time and space
8   Small changes can produce big results
9   You can have your cake and eat it — but not at once
10 Dividing an elephant in half does not produce two small elephants
11 There is no one to blame

Box 3.8   Examples of Senge's Laws   Example

No. 1   There are many examples of this law. Mining subsidence has happened in many parts of the UK because the pillars (in pillar and stall
mining) were robbed and hence the remaining ones were overstressed and eventually collapsed (e.g. limestone mines in the Black
Country). Maintenance expenses on many constructed facilities are
high because initial spending was cut. Nuclear waste storage will
leave problems for future generations.

No. 2   All of us feel this one at some time. We seem to be peddling harder
to stay in the same place.

No. 3   Senge quotes a wonderful cartoon from the *New Yorker* where a man
sitting in an armchair pushes over a giant domino encroaching in on
him from the left. He is obviously saying to himself that at last he
can relax. He does not see that the domino is toppling another domino and so on in a chain reaction until the last one comes up to hit
him from the right!

No. 4   This is the 'What we need is a bigger hammer' syndrome. Sometimes
we have to recognise that we need to do it differently.

No. 5   Often we just shift the burden somewhere else. The protective parent who intervenes in a situation on behalf of the child creates a
dependency on the parent.

No. 6   The tortoise is slower but wins the race. Edward de Bono has written
that the slower thinker often produces better solutions because a very
bright person often jumps to an 'obvious' solution and gets trapped
by it.

No. 7   When we are young we feel immortal so the long-term consequences
do not seem real — nevertheless, they are real, as we realise as we
grow older!

No. 8   The trim tab is an example, see Box 3.6. We believe systems thinking
is the trim tab for construction.

No. 9   Cost and safety are often portrayed as opposite sides of weighing
scales as though increasing one means reducing the other to keep
the balance. This need not be so. By best practice you can improve
both, as both are underpinned by a quality culture — but you cannot have them both instantly.

No. 10   Organisations are often designed to keep the interactions opaque.
Rigid departmental boundaries that people cannot cross are all too
commonplace examples.

No. 11   You and your problems are part of the same system — there is no
one to blame. Do not fall into the trap of blaming 'the system'. If you
want to change things then you have to change the way you behave.

Box 3.9   Example

Try smiling as you answer the telephone. It promotes an initial warm reaction the influence of which on the subsequent conversation can be as beneficial as growling could be detrimental to the outcome of the conversation.

> **Box 3.10**   Example
>
> The move to PFI and other similar alliancing agreements can change the perception of the team. The change is from one of constantly seeking out how to make a claim to one of constantly seeking out how to add value. The success of a PFI road building project derived from a recognition that early delivery meant early improved cash flow for the contractor and a shorter period of disruption for the road users.

The lever is systems thinking about process

We believe that the change that will provide the leverage to rethink construction is for all of us in the construction industry to adopt a values driven, success targeted, systems thinking approach.

To do this will require us to take on some further systems ideas which we will introduce in this chapter. Box 3.11 illustrates the first four important ideas that we will need to solve wicked and messy problems.

> **Box 3.11**   **Solving MESSY Problems — TRUE**   Principle
>
> **T**   **Teamwork** is essential, developing good leadership, mutual respect, motivation, strong ethic, all pulling together, agreed roles, common vision towards agreed objectives in identified processes, personal excellence.
>
> **R**   **Resources** have to be at an appropriate level for the process, including individual competencies and teamwork skills, as well as budgets etc.
>
> **U**   **Understanding** has to be promoted; good models of phenomena (physical and social), workshops and 'awareness gap' testing where understanding is poor or risks high; identifying and addressing issues; and sand traps preventing agreements.
>
> **E**   **Evidence** should be used to make decisions, to manage the process and the uncertainty, with a firm grasp on reality. Dependable ways of obtaining, assembling and interpreting evidence are needed to examine processes from different angles and points of view — to walk outside and look in.

Teamwork is essential

Co-operation, through teamwork, is at the root of our systems thinking approach. As we said earlier if we get the people right then we are most of the way there. We need all of the people pulling together with agreed and well-understood roles and responsibilities and clear accountabilities, all moving towards agreed objectives. This requires leadership and good management and a motivational framework. As Senge (1990) so eloquently describes, two of the main requirements are shared vision and team learning (Box 3.12). He sets out the basics for the art and practice of the learning organisation. Although he does not use the language of wicked and messy problems he is addressing the same issues. He urges a new role for managers and leaders which he calls

'... the role of the manager as researcher and designer. What does he or she research? Understanding the organisation as a system and understanding the external and internal forces driving change. What does he or she design? The learning process whereby managers throughout the organisation come to understand these trends and forces'.

This does not mean that managers no longer make decisions — of course they will be involved in many decision processes but they will be consulting and holding dialogues with corporate and local managers. A new view of leadership is required

'... where leaders are designers, stewards and teachers. They are responsible for building organisations where people continually expand their capabilities to understand complexity, clarify vision and improve shared mental models — that is they are responsible for learning.'

We prefer to think of leaders as coaches but the basic idea is the same — that of moving away from the old idea of leaders as the people who tell other people what to do to a new idea of the leader as someone who facilitates. This new leader empowers and enables people as owners of their processes to co-operate with others to add more value than they would if they worked independently.

Box 3.12	SENGE'S FIVE DISCIPLINES for a LEARNING ORGANISATION	Principle
Personal Mastery	A commitment continually to clarify and develop our personal vision, to focus energies, to develop patience and to see reality. It is a cornerstone of the learning organisation (see Chapter 8).	
Mental Models	The deeply ingrained assumptions and generalisations that influence how we understand the world and how we take action (see Chapter 4).	
Shared Vision	This is not about a vision statement that only the Chief Executive and close colleagues own, rather it is a genuinely shared 'picture' of what future the group is aiming at. It can be generated through a process of developing a vision statement. Every process team needs a shared vision (see Chapter 8).	
Team Learning	How can a group of talented people so often perform collectively at a level below the individual talents of any one of them? If you have been part of a great team you recognise the opposite — the heights that can be reached when teams gel. Achieving this is about genuine dialogue, thinking together and getting the chemistry right (see Chapter 8).	
Systems Thinking	A conceptual framework, a body of knowledge and tools — it is still a relatively new set of ideas for seeing processes (wholes and parts), and connections.	

Realistic resources have to be provided

The issue here is not that money, people, time, knowledge, etc., must be available in unlimited quantities but rather that the availability of the resource is managed appropriately. In other words, at the extreme, it is ridiculous to expect more from a resource than is possible. The emphasis is on working together with the client and all of the players in the process to make sure that there is agreement about the level of resource to be used and how it will be managed as the wickedness of the problem is tamed. We must try to avoid the problem that there is not enough resource to do it properly the first time but always enough to 'fix' it when it goes wrong. This is particularly important for systems that are safety critical, but, of course, is also important in rethinking construction, of doing more and better for less.

Understanding has to be promoted

If a process is to be accomplished successfully then all of the players must have a good understanding of all that is necessary to be successful in their particular roles and responsibilities. If you do not understand then you are flying blind. For technical phenomena, if good scientific and engineering models are available then confidence can be high. Of course, while many phenomena are well understood, sometimes we can be rather arrogantly overconfident. For example, the idea of storing nuclear waste underground for centuries without monitoring what is happening would be very dangerous. No one can predict what will happen over such long periods. However, if such storage is monitored closely and suitable training programmes are put in place, then future generations will be able to understand what is happening and take any necessary actions to manage an evolving situation. In that way the uncertainties of the future will be managed. We will not be relying on uncertain and rather technically arrogant and overconfident predictions.

Box 3.13   Example

An environmental risk analyst with a nuclear background was asked at interview what would be the ideal material for a containment vessel for burying corrosive nuclear waste. His answer was a casket made of gold. One of the lessons from ancient Egypt is that gold is one of the least suitable materials — because people are likely to want to steal the casket!

Of course, the essence of understanding of human behaviour both individually and socially is not well developed. We have referred (Box 3.12) to Personal Mastery and Mental Models as key ideas in the learning organisation. It is the job of process owners as leaders to motivate and coach individuals and teams to commit to working through problems and issues. Thus when events do not work out as predicted, the individuals, the teams and the organisations are nevertheless able to manage the process to a successful conclusion.

In summary, while many physical phenomena can be predicted there can be considerable uncertainty which has to be dealt with through conservative decision making (safety factors, etc.) or through techniques such as the Observational Method (Peck 1969), as we shall see in Chapter 9. By direct contrast, human individual and social behaviour is unpredictable since it seems to be infinitely variable — although there are some regularities. This has to be dealt with through good management and relationships defined through contracts. The message from *Rethinking Construction* is that the old emphasis on 'predict and provide' is not good enough. This process of understanding the problem, of solving it completely through predicting what will happen in the future and then providing that solution has worked for tame problems. However, it is increasingly showing the strain for the modern situation with wicked and messy problems.

Effectively, the need to rethink construction derives from the increasing realisation that even so-called straightforward construction projects are wicked problems (although few people presently use that term). The design and construct process has to be more integrated so that there can be a constant review of progress towards eventual success. Prediction will have an important role in that process but the emphasis has to change from predict and provide to one of managing the process to clear success targets. A key requirement is a payment system that motivates and encourages an investment in success.

Evidence must be dependable

Most of us are good at keeping our feet well and truly planted on the ground and do not get attracted into 'flights of fancy'. Nevertheless, imagination is required to manage for the future and to make creative progress but this must always be kept in check by keeping a firm grasp on reality and not being fooled into something that is not feasible. The more appropriate our view of future success the better will be our decisions to get to it. Senge talks of the 'creative tension' between where we are now and where we want to be — this is the potential, the *why*, that drives our new view of process. The trick of personal mastery (Box 3.12) is to keep that tension balanced against your competencies. The balance does depend on having good dependable information. When we are making decisions we really need relevant **evidence** and we must be able to judge how dependable that evidence is. We take information from the past, information from the present, and information we have obtained from predictions about the future, and put it all together. We need dependable measures. Such evidence, coming at you from many quarters, is similar to the detective or the trial judge and jury. They have to put together information which is as different as apples are from oranges to make a judgement or a decision. In effect, we have to add up these apples and oranges to know how much fruit we have.

As we have said earlier we need to de-emphasise the role of prediction. We hasten to add we are NOT saying we should not try to predict, we are NOT advocating the rejection of traditional engineering scientific techniques. The evidence from prediction is crucial. However, the emphasis on prediction in our engineering science education comes from a tame philosophy of problems that yield to prediction. In construction as in other parts of life, prediction is often difficult and highly uncertain. Predicted results have therefore to be taken in the context of that uncertainty and as part of the management of the design and construction process.

Wicked problems have to be managed

Thus it is important to manage the growing issues as a wicked problem evolves. We interact with the physical world. It is not just a matter of understanding what we want to achieve, designing it, predicting what will happen and then getting on and doing it according to the predictions. Rather it is more about immersing ourselves in the issues and working with events as they unfold, using all our knowledge and skills. It is important to recognise that unlike an undergraduate tutorial example there is no perfect solution, no correct answer and no distinctive truth. The solution is rather about getting agreement about **what is best in the context** — it is a social process.

In this concept of management process there is nothing wrong with jumping backwards and forwards in the stages of decision making. However, we recognise that there are times when commitments are made — the decision points (or rather points of choice because decision making is a process), and then we recognise those choices, respect them, prepare for them and live with them. Of course, it is naive to think that we all actually do think in straight lines. Research shows that problem solvers jump about all over the place when they are thinking something through. Nevertheless, when we have to externalise our rationality, the best way to do it is through logic, mathematics and science. But we all recognise that the world is not a cold, rational and logical world — it is one full of emotions and needs, where people behave only partly in a rational way.

An example of a simple tame methodology applied to wicked and messy problems is operations research. This has had an impact in certain specific pseudo tame problems but generally has not had the impact expected of it. Why is this? Because it does not recognise in its basic philosophy that solving problems of this type has to be a social process (Box 3.14).

Box 3.14 Operations Research (OR)   **Explanation**

Operations Research (OR) is the application of the scientific approach to the management of large systems of men, machines, materials and money in industry, business and government. Proponents aim to produce measurements and models. Most of the effort in OR seems to have been concentrated on refining and developing quantitative tools for specific problem situations. For example, linear programming finds the optimal values of a linear function subject to linear constraints. Other examples concern queuing theory, bidding problems and search problems. The intentions are good, the solutions are clever and useful in specific situations but the impact overall is small. There is a gap between OR and practising managers because the theory does not deal with the complexity that managers face. Processes involving people are non-linear and 'chaotic' (in the new scientific sense) with many points of bifurcation in decision making. The scientific method needs to evolve into a systems method. There are signs that through biology this is beginning to happen.

3.5 Introducing holons

Systems thinking is a way of tackling a problem

Systems engineering is a widely used term which means different things to different people. This is quite understandable given that it is still early in its development. The usage in this book concerns *Systems Thinking*. It is not a branch of engineering such as civil or mechanical, it is not a topic such as thermodynamics — it is a way of going about tackling a problem.

We need it to provide the leverage required to rethink construction which is a wicked and messy problem.

There are three essential features of systems thinking. They are:

- holons
- connectivity
- a new whole view of process.

We have already discussed, in Chapter 2, the new whole view of process to enable us to produce complete and consistent maps of what is to be done. Now we will focus on two more notions of systems thinking that are needed to do this properly — holons and connectivity (Boxes 3.15–3.25).

The full meaning of holistic comes from the holon

Earlier we have used the term 'holistic' and we said that we want to develop a holistic approach. The idea originates in biology and is now widely used to indicate an idea of the whole. Frequently, however, the depth of its meaning and usefulness is not appreciated. The concept of a holon is fundamental (Box 3.15) to systems theory (Koestler 1967). We define a holon as a process which is both a whole and a part. As an example you can think of yourself as a holon (Box 3.15). Other examples are given in Boxes 3.16–3.18.

A system is then defined as a set of interacting holons. Thus a system naturally divides into layers of holons — a system is a multi-levelled hierarchy. Note that the use of the word hierarchy here is not implying rigidity or a power structure (as in a strongly hierarchical organisation such as the military), it is merely being used to describe differing levels of description. In any layer the holons are

---

Box 3.15 What are holons?   Example

We can illustrate the idea of a holon by you thinking of yourself as one. In one sense you are a whole and in another you are a part.

You are a whole in the sense that you are a person with your own particular identity. You have sub-systems (holons) which make you what you are. Examples are your skeleton (your structural holon), your nervous system (your information holon), your blood circulation system (your internal energy distribution holon), your digestive system (your energy capture and waste holon). Each of these holons is itself made up of sub-systems (holons). Thus looking downwards further inside of you and continuing on, you eventually get to genes, cells, molecules, atoms, sub-atomic particles and so on, probably *ad infinitum*.

As a whole person you have properties which are unique to you and your level of description. For example, you can walk and talk — none of your sub-systems holons can do that on its own. Thus your ability to walk and talk, your personality, your particular skills and competencies **emerge** from the co-operation of the parts — they are emergent properties which apply at the level of description of you — as a whole.

However, you are also a part. As the poet John Donne said, 'No man is an Island' (*Devotions upon Emergent Occasions*, 1624, Meditation XVII). You cannot live without interaction with your fellow human beings. First of all you are part of your family holon, whether as son, daughter, brother, sister, father, mother or any relation. The family has emergent properties. Perhaps you are part of a 'happy' family or an 'intelligent' family or a 'wealthy' family. You are also a part of many other holons. You are part of the company for whom you work. You are part of a group or team within that work. Of particular interest in construction is that you may be part of a project team with people from other companies. All of these groups have emergent properties such as 'team spirit', 'successful', 'dynamic' or 'team in trouble', these properties emerge from the interactions (the chemistry) between the people in the group. Of course, at even higher levels we are all part of the city we live in and that city is part of the country we live in and we are all part of the human race.

It is a useful exercise to think of emergent properties at each of these levels. Examples are that we speak of a 'beautiful' city, of a 'peaceful' country and of the 'aggressive nature' of the human race. We can encourage useful emergent properties such as good team spirit by helping processes to be co-operative.

Box 3.16   A hard holon   Example

A steel beam in a building is a process holon. It is a whole in that its engineering properties emerge from the material from which it was made and the shape into which it was formed. Thus a steel Universal Beam comprises atoms, molecules, crystals which have the hardness, yield strength and modulus of elasticity, etc. that we associate with steel. The beam also has properties that result from the shape of the beam such as first and second moment of area which depend on flange and web sizes. The behaviour of the beam under load can be modelled, for example, through elastic theory. This attribute of the process holon is the transformation of input (loads) to output (response as movement such as static deflection or dynamic position, velocity and acceleration).

The beam is also a part of the structure in which it is contained. It interacts with that structure and receives loads through its connections as well as from direct loads. The behaviour of the beam as part of the total structure is dealt with by structural analysis — usually through a computer finite element analysis. These are familiar ideas. What is not so familiar is to realise that the beam is also a part of a soft system which conceives, designs, builds, operates, uses and eventually decommissions the structure. The beam is part of the business case for the building.

---

at a similar level of precision of definition. In the layer, above the holons are more general, have greater scope and are less precisely defined. In the layer below, the holons are less general, have less scope and are more precisely and specifically defined.

Holons have extremely important characteristics called **emergent properties**. These are properties that 'emerge' from the interaction of the sub-holons and may make sense only at that level of description. For example, emergent properties of human beings are the ability to walk and talk (Box 3.15). It is in this important sense that the whole may be greater than the sum of the parts (Boxes 3.19–3.25) and we can refer to this as holistic gain.

A hard system is an inanimate one that can be described in terms of an action and a reaction. The engineering science systems of physical things are hard systems. Examples are beams, columns, bridges, dams, reservoirs, etc. The actions are the forces and other demands upon the systems, and the reactions are the response of the systems to those actions usually obtained theoretically through the well-known response analyses of engineering science.

Soft systems involve people, and consist of action, reaction and intention. The extra ingredient of intention makes the understanding and the modelling of soft systems extremely difficult because the behaviour of people is not easy to predict dependably. In fact, there are many points of possible bifurcation (sharply different alternative paths) in the process (Box 3.17).

Box 3.17   Example

A round ball is to be projected through the air. This is a hard system and it is predictable. We can use mechanics to map the trajectory. A soft systems version would be a ball which had a mind of its own and could decide (at as many arbitrary points through the process as it wished) to change course arbitrarily. The hard components of the trajectory are predictable (it is still a ball) but the intentionality changes are not.

Box 3.18   An aeroplane as a holon   Example

A passenger aeroplane is a part of a system which provides a service to customers, flying them between destinations. As a whole, an aeroplane is an
assembly of soft and hard systems involving people such as the flight crew,
the flight attendants, the structure (the airframe), the power (the engines),
the informations systems (the computers and control systems), the fuel and
waste management systems (the fuel to power the engines and the food and
drink for the people on board), etc. That it can fly to a destination safely is
an emergent property of the way the components 'co-operate'.

Box 3.19   The emergent property of gas pressure   Example

Many of the common engineering properties emerge from sub-systems. Perhaps the easiest to understand is that of gas pressure. This results from the
cumulative effect of millions of molecules buzzing around in a random fashion colliding with the side of the container in which the gas is held, and the
total effect of all of these collisions is the pressure.

Box 3.20   Why holons?   Explanation

Holons:

• help us to describe complex problems simply;
• can be used for both 'hard' physical systems and 'soft' systems involving
  people (see Chapter 4), and to combine them;
• enable us to clarify relationships and accountability;
• can be used to map the path of change from where we are now to where
  we want to get to;
• are a means of identifying added value as an emergent property;
• are particularly useful in managing co-operative systems.

Box 3.21   What are holons?   Explanation

Holons:

• are processes — they do things;
• are parts (of other holons);
• are wholes (made up of sub-process holons);
• all have action and reaction (hard) and some also have intentionality (soft);
• change through time, and a description at a point in time is a 'snapshot'
  of the state of the process.

Box 3.22   Principle

Emergent properties are the reason why the whole
is more than the sum of its parts.

Box 3.23   What is a system?   **Explanation**

- A system is a hierarchy of process holons (Fig. 3.3).
- At the top there is only one process holon.
- Each process holon consists of sub-process holons and sub-sub-process holons according to the level of precision of definition.
- A layer of holons is at a similar level of precision and definition. The holons interact at the same level to form a description of the whole system at that level. The transformations in each process holon produce the change. A process model of these transformations, available usually only for hard systems, can be used to simulate change. The success of the holons at any level should as far as possible be a necessary and sufficient condition for the success of the holons above.
- The layers above are more general, have greater scope and are less precisely defined.
- The layers below are more specific, have less scope and are more precisely defined.

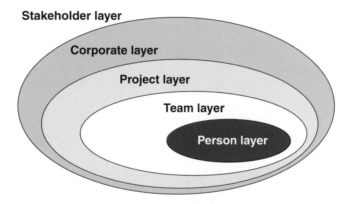

Fig. 3.3. Hierarchy of layers for a project

Box 3.24   We define a holon by its attributes   **Explanation**

- Process holons have attributes of *what, why, when, where, who* and *how* (Fig. 2.12, Box 2.12).
- The product of a process holon is an output which is part of the *what* — and it is a new *process*.
- The emergent properties of a process holon are part of the state of the *what* — they 'emerge' from the interactions between the sub-holons. The sub-holons do not exhibit these properties.
- A process holon is connected to 'friend' holons at the same level to which it sends and receives messages.
- A process holon is connected to a higher level holon in which it has a role (i.e. a set of delegated responsibilities) and to which it is accountable in a specifically recognisable way, e.g. through precise objectives or measurable performance parameters.
- A process holon is connected to sub-holons to which it has delegated a role and from which it requires accountability.

Box 3.25   Chains of holons   Example

Value chains are the connected holons that interact to generate value.
Supply chains are the chains of supplier process holons that interact to generate a product for the customer at the top of the chain.

These are not chains in the sense of linearly connected links — rather they are processes which **interact to a common purpose**. Thus the value chain and the supply chain are part of the system of process holons. Every process holon should deliver value (that should be the meaning of success). Only some process holons are suppliers in the usual sense of the word and so the supply chain is a sub-set of the systems hierarchy. By improving the interactions, emergent properties of value are improved.

In a wider sense all processes send output to other processes and, in that sense, are suppliers.

A high level description of the value chain of processes for a contractor may be: detecting the customer; tendering; preparing a contract; planning; executing a contract; finishing the contract; evaluating the contract; supporting the contract.

Box 3.26   Changes   Example

Intentions change in even the best-planned projects. During construction of an offshore tower a major oil spill occurred elsewhere. All available tugs were requisitioned for a month. Float-out was delayed by four months until a suitable weather window occurred.

Scale is important

If we focus on a particular holon we are focusing on a particular level of definition of what we understand of the world. As humans we naturally focus on the human scale. As we move away from that level, it becomes increasingly difficult for us to understand what we find. We need tools (including theoretical tools) to help us. Looking inward to the deepest understanding we have of sub-atomic particles, which are not really particles but events, and to string theory and super string theory, we find it increasingly difficult to probe those areas, and only a few of us can understand it. There seems to be a law of diminishing returns in as much as the further we go, the more energy is required to investigate it experimentally. Presumably there has to be a limit — but who can guess where that is. So at the bottom of this hierarchy are the unknown and probably unknowable infinitesimally small holons. Likewise, if we look upwards we have the same difficulty. We are citizens of the world (the theory of *Gaia*, Lovelock J, 1992, is perhaps a description of an emergent property of the whole world). The world is part of the solar system which is part of the Universe. What is at the top of this hierarchy is again unknown but it is the large infinity and maybe it is what some mean by 'God'.

There are no fundamental holons only appropriate ones

So we now have a way of looking at any system. We see it as a process holon and as part of a hierarchy. It has properties that apply to it and to its sub-holons.

It has some properties that have 'emerged' from the co-operation of its sub-holons.

Immediately there is a new question — what is a fundamental holon? Usually in western thought fundamental is somewhere deep down in the hierarchy of our understanding. Thus we tend to think that an understanding of atomic physics is more fundamental than an understanding of engineering mechanics. In systems theory this is not the case because all levels are equally valid — the issue is not whether the holon is fundamental but whether it is **appropriate** — but appropriate for what? The answer must be 'for helping us to do what we want to meet our **purpose**'. If we want to understand the behaviour of sub-atomic particles then we use holons at that level, or if we want to build a bridge we use engineering mechanics — both are appropriate for different problems or answering different needs.

So this is a major tool in our systems tool kit — the concept of a process holon. Straightaway we have a way of getting at complexity. We now know that by finding the appropriate level we can begin to represent our system in a way that we can actually handle because it is **appropriate to our need**. This is a reflection of how in practice it is done. A board of directors is not interested in detail unless it has a specific impact at their scale or level of interest. Conversely, the process owner for designing fixing bolts needs only to know enough about the 'big picture' to know where his process fits into the scheme of things.

Find appropriate process holons

So how do we seek to find appropriate process holons? We start at quite a high level — one which may not be as precise as we might wish — and work down. It is important to realise that as we look upwards from any given holon to a higher level of holon then we reduce the complexity at the expense of some precision of definition. However, these higher level holons are important because of their scope. For example, if we are running a large organisation with many employees and are executing many complex projects then we think at the level of the organisation itself and what it is about. This is exactly what the Chairman and Board of Directors have to do. They cannot think about the mass of detailed concerns, i.e. all of the individual projects going on within that organisation — no human could — but they look for the emerging properties of that large organisation and manage them — these are the high level performance measures. Of course, as we shall see later, in order to manage them they may have to drill down occasionally into the lower layers of the organisation in order to deal with a specific issue. For example, a site foreman has perhaps been the subject of a particular case of discrimination and the Board have to make sure that the policy is changed to accommodate the lesson.

However, if and when we find the appropriate level in the hierarchy for us to address our wicked problem, then it is quite likely that on its own it is not sufficient. We then have to identify the sub-process holons in order to get to process holons that will do the things that need to be done. This is especially likely at the start when we are trying to get to grips with the issues within our wicked and messy problem. For example, if we are concerned with the risks of a particular project to the organisation as a whole (a high level holon) we will probably have to look in more detail, at lower levels than the Boardroom.

Look for necessity and sufficiency

In order to move from a higher level to a lower level, we need to identify what lies below each holon. We need to think through all of the process holons that make up the higher level process holon. We can do that, for an existing set of processes, by asking how responsibilities are delegated downwards and what accountabilities are reported back. We can look for the sub-processes that are **necessary** for the success of the high level process and also for those that might be **sufficient**. We also look for those that are neither necessary nor sufficient. In the initial stages of dealing with complexity we need just to name the processes at each level until we get to the level which is appropriate for our needs.

This is part of the process of identifying the system as we discussed in Chapter 2. If we are dealing with an existing situation we are describing (and later possibly re-engineering) the processes that are actually being done. If we are designing a new process for producing a new product then we are thinking through what needs to be done. If we are designing the new product itself then we are thinking of the processes which make up that product. It is important in defining what we want to be part of our system and what we can take as outside the system. Of course, there will be an interaction between the system and its environment (or meta-system) but we will not be concerned with representing or modelling that meta-system. Thus if we are designing a very large long span bridge, we might well be concerned with the impact of the project on the financial health of the company as part of the business plan. In order to assess that, we may need to examine the control procedures within the company to assess that the risk is acceptable (see Chapter 6). In doing this assessment, we may need to look upwards to examine the process holons of which the bridge is a part (i.e. the company's portfolio of projects and the state of the borrowings of the company, etc.).

Therefore, while complexity is still a difficult idea, the concept of a holon and hierarchy gives us a tool for crystallising the essential processes that need to be understood and controlled in order to achieve what we want.

3.6 Dealing with connectivity

Look for relationships

One of the characteristics of wicked, messy problems, that we stressed earlier, is that there are so many interlocking controls and constraints that it is difficult to 'see the wood for the trees'. In tame simple problems we are able to express the relationships between the parameters of the problem in quite simple terms. For example, we know that the influences that are important in the amount by which a beam will deflect under load are the load itself (size, nature and distribution), the geometry of the beam (span, second moment of area) and the material of which the beam is made. Our knowledge is so well established for very simple problems that we can actually write down a functional relationship between these terms for say a simply supported beam with a central point load, and be confident that under the simple precise conditions (knife edge supports, knife edge load, uniform geometry and material) we can predict the deflection to a high degree of accuracy. Problems then arise when we use these ideas in practice — for example, when we apply the formula to beams in actual buildings which are not quite as precisely defined as in the laboratory because of the way in which they are connected to columns and to floors. The more we move away from those simple laboratory conditions the greater the uncertainty. We will examine this in more detail in the next chapter when we look at uncertainty and how we establish dependable evidence.

A central issue here is that although the functional expressions of influence are critically important in our understanding of phenomena — they are necessary but they are not sufficient. They are not sufficient because wicked and messy problems do not yield easily to such models.

There may be subtle influences

The systems approach recognises that the relationships between cause and effect in wicked and messy problems may be very subtle and the effects over time of interventions are not obvious. Sometimes the obvious actions do not produce the obvious, desired outcome. There are many **unintended** outcomes and consequences. Some are unwanted (e.g. a failure). Where this is so we have to manage risk knowing we cannot predict all outcomes.

Focus on local connections

We can, reasonably easily, examine a holon and identify its connections locally with its immediate friends or neighbours — we can do that by observing the interactions. For example, consider yourself as a holon again. You know with whom you interact through your relations, friends and colleagues. Thus for a particular wicked problem (e.g. dealing with a relationship that is in difficulties) you can identify the other holons in the system with which you interact. The difficulty is that, while you influence a friend directly, you may also influence that friend indirectly because he receives a message from another of your friends! These interactions are the stuff of soap operas. In abstract terms a holon influences a neighbour directly but can influence almost any other holon in the system indirectly. In chaos theory this is known as the 'butterfly effect', where theoretically the flapping wings of a butterfly in one country could indirectly cause a windstorm in another country. The reason is that instabilities in the system may be such that a small perturbation causes a large change in behaviour.

Thus we can see that there may be a 'web' of interconnectivity between holons which we must at least try to control if we are successfully to reach the conclusions we desire.

Filling a glass of water revisited

Figure 3.4 is taken from Senge (1990). We prefer to represent the feedback loop as in Fig. 3.5. Senge's diagram represents stages in the process. We think of the feedback loop as a process with sub-processes.

The generic sub-processes are perceiving, reflecting and acting (see Chapter 5) on the world outside of us which has an objective existence (see Chapter 4). In this example, the world outside of us is the physical glass and the *flowing water*. The *tap position* used by Senge is a state variable in the process of *acting by turning the tap*. Senge's *current water level* is a state variable in *perceiving the water level*. Senge used a *perceived gap* in his diagram. Instead, we use *thinking about the gap* (which together with the target desired water level is the process of reflecting).

See the loops of influence

Figure 3.6 shows the essence of a systems diagram of this sort. The key is to see loops of influence rather than straight lines — it is not a linear chain.

The feedback loop is a an idea familiar to most of us but few of us use it. We need to appreciate the depth of its implications. Linear thinking implies a one

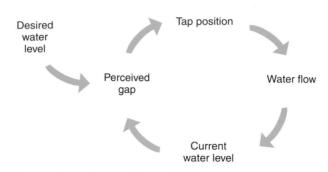

Fig. 3.4. Filling a glass of water (Senge 1990)

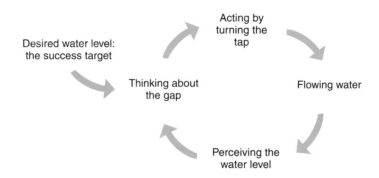

Fig. 3.5. Filling a glass of water

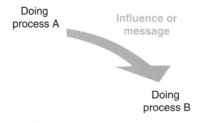

Fig. 3.6. A systems influence diagram

Box 3.27   Vulnerability of water supply   Example

The Engineering Director of a water company identified that the water supply to a large part of the area served was vulnerable to damage to a canal from which the water was extracted. Small damage to the canal could produce disproportionate consequences. This was exacerbated by the fact that the canal was not owned by the company and so the maintenance programmes that the company would like to see were not in place. The top level process holon is *maintaining a constant supply of water to all customers*. The success target for the process is absolutely clear, water has normally to be available without disruption to the customers, but if a major incident were to happen then supply had to reconnected within 48 hours. It was clear that major damage to the canal would not be repairable in 48 hours. An analysis of the processes revealed that contingency processes were required to increase the flexibility of the systems and to reduce the vulnerability to events that were difficult to control.

Box 3.28   Airline safety through soft systems action   Example

The Chief Executive of an airline recognised that safety was paramount. In order to motivate the maintenance crews to keep safety at the top of their minds he gave them free flights to holiday destinations on the aeroplanes they themselves were maintaining. The process holon here was *ensuring flight safety*. The sub-process holon of maintaining the aeroplane had a number of success targets — but an important one was making sure that no maintenance worker compromised the safety of the aircraft.

---

way cause. Linear simple thinking sees the process of filling the glass with water as 'I am turning the tap to cause the glass to fill to the required level'. Actually, we could say that 'the level of the water in the glass is causing my hand to turn the tap'. (Of course we do not do that because we know the intention is within the owner of the process whose hand it is!). However both statements are incomplete. We need to see this process holon as one with clear objectives which the process owner aims at through the interacting sub-processes. These co-operate such that as the state of the process reaches the desired state, the state variable (the tap position) is controlled to a successful conclusion (the glass filled to the desired level).

The connectivity between processes is clearly potentially complicated since, at first glance, every process seems to influence every other. However, if the process owner focuses on interactions through direct connections only, he can leave the influences of indirect connections to **emerge** as the process develops. The trick here, if you are a process owner, is not to waste time trying to anticipate indirect influences because they are almost entirely unpredictable. The point is that these indirect messages actually come via a direct connection anyway. You therefore manage the influence of indirect messages as they emerge as the process unfolds by directly managing your progress to your success target. You manage progress by: (a) focusing on each particular process; (b) thinking about the inputs you need and get; (c) obtaining dependable evidence; (d) reflecting and making decisions; (e) acting by sending outputs to those processes to which you are directly connected. Thus although your KPIs are direct measures of evidence they provide the means for also controlling indirect influences.

Thus inputs to our process are received from friends and the outputs are sent to friends and that is all that you need to understand and represent. This is directly analogous to the way people interact. We communicate with those people we know. If you know someone then you can speak to them directly. If you want to influence someone you do not know then you have to speak to them through a third party — your capacity to influence them becomes indirect. We all receive inputs from friend process holons whether personal friends, the media or the physical environment. If we want to send outputs out to other than these friend process holons then we must do it through them. Marketing is a good example of how one sets about influencing people indirectly.

Of course, if a direct connection is needed and does not exist then it can be made in a way analogous to introductions between people. It is also analogous to the connections between neurons in the brain. There is evidence that certain neurons are connected through early life experiences (Carter 1998). Children who do not have these experiences have mental deficiencies in certain areas of activity. The neurons are process holons which cluster to form higher level process holons such as language processing in the cognitive brain or emotional reactions in the limbic region.

Clearly, if two process holons are directly connected then the information passed between them, the inputs and the outputs, needs to be defined.

Therefore, we have a way of handling the complexity of connectivity where everything seems to influence everything else. We think about each process holon individually and locally and make sure we know to which process holons it is directly connected. In a physical process this is hard wired. For example, as in Box 2.6, every finite element is a holon which is connected by its degrees of freedom to other elements. The total connectivity is expressed by the global matrix equation for the system. Correspondingly every process owner in a soft process will have a good idea of what information he needs to succeed and what connections he needs or has to develop as his process unfolds.

Of course, we have also to think about the content of messages that are sent to the neighbouring holons and that depends upon our understanding of the system. We recognise that all of these holons are acting in parallel.

Robustness derives from connectivity

There is another benefit to this way of thinking about connectivity and that is that it provides us with a way to look at the robustness of a system. As yet this is a very underdeveloped aspect of systems theory. We have to be concerned that a system does not fail when subjected to a small amount of damage. Our system must not be vulnerable to damage which results in disproportionate consequences. The failure of the block of flats at Ronan Point in 1968 is a classic example where the blowing out of one panel in a high rise panelled construction caused a consequential collapse of the whole of one side of the building. Robustness and its converse, vulnerability, are attributes of the *form* of a system. If the interconnections between the holons are damaged then the messages are not what they should be and the system degrades. A new theory for examining how this occurs has been developed by the first author (Lu Z., Yu Y., Woodman N.J., Blockley D.I., 1999). This is a specific example illustrating how a systems way of thinking can lead to new ideas and techniques (i.e. a new theory of vulnerability).

> **Box 3.29** Example
>
> Two teams were working on different aspects of the same project. One team had a great team spirit: the leader and process owner was highly respected and encouraged everyone. The other team had poor team spirit because the team leader tended to set people against each other. This was unintentional — he was just a very poor communicator — and this led to major misunderstandings within the group. Nevertheless, the project was going well. Then a small but significant setback occurred owing to a change of mind by the client. Considerable pressure was put on both teams. The first team responded to the challenge and thrived on it and went on to success. The second team collapsed and had to be replaced. A small change by the client had produced big consequences for the project team. The process owner who had delegated processes to these two teams should have recognised that lack of robustness in the second team and managed it away (if necessary, by replacing the leader) before the event.

3.7 Using appropriate engineering

The purpose of this chapter has been to present the basic ideas of the systems approach. The first trick of dealing with complexity is to find the:

- level of description, i.e. the appropriate process holon that you need to meet your purpose and satisfy your needs;
- sub-process holons that you must design in and then execute in order to obtain the success you want;
- process holons that are friends.

You then focus on each process holon in turn. You remember that each one may happen in parallel. You then work through the process attributes of who, what, where, why, when and how as described in Chapter 2. This is what we like to call appropriate engineering. It enables the bringing together of the physical science and engineering processes (the physical phenomena) with the human and organisational process into one common language. It enables us to describe and model a system (with physical and human phenomena) so that we may manage it to the result we desire. It is a language for managing a system — no matter how complex. Of course, it does not substitute for poor thinking or incompetent people and is not therefore a panacea. However, it is, as we have said before, a tool with the leverage we need and want.

Looking from the inside and the outside

Since a process holon is both a whole and a part it is quite natural to view it from the outside looking in (as a whole) and from the inside looking out (as a part). This becomes important in considering the business case — for example: when considering your client and his needs. In Chapter 7, we will point out that the project team could consider themselves from various angles. Too often, groups appear to be inside looking in and totally concerned with themselves, totally self-absorbed. It is helpful to look out to attempt to see what others are seeing. The most difficult of all is to get outside of the group and to look in as others do. Then you begin to see how others see you, and you begin to see that the world owes you no favours and that in order to change the world you have to change the way you interact with that world. If you use the idea of a holon as a part and a whole, then that type of thinking is so much easier.

A consultancy practice was formed by one man with one secretary. The practice thrived because his skills were creative and businesslike. He delivered what the clients wanted. He took on new staff and the practice grew to about 40 people. At first this was fine but problems began to creep in — they were losing efficiency and people felt under pressure. The boss asked people to work harder and longer hours but things did not seem to improve. The clients were not as happy as they had been and everyone was overstressed. The founder felt under pressure since his business seemed to be slipping away from him. He began a review of what was wrong. Instead of taking the process gently, he started to blame some of his staff before they had chance to explain what was wrong. The staff became unhappy and there was a lot of internal disagreement. In the meantime, the clients were increasingly unhappy and pressure grew on the company (Fig. 3.7).

The founder consulted a friend who was able to help him look at the practice from the outside looking in. He realised he had to let go and to be a leader rather than the autocratic boss he had become. Although he had nurtured the practice from its beginning he had now to see things more clearly from the point of view of others. As he did this, the practice began to thrive again as people realised their potential.

Fig. 3.7. Overwork and stress

3.8   Checking for success

The success targets for this chapter set out at the beginning were that, at this stage, you will:

Success target	Review
• be able to recognise a wicked problem;	a wicked messy problem is one that does not yield easily to traditional linear thinking. It has many interlocking issues and constraints. There are many unintended consequences of previous decisions. There are many people involved so it is really a social process of finding agreement. The goalposts seem to be constantly on the move;
• want to look for leverage to tackle such a problem;	leverage comes from applying systems thinking with three essential ingredients; holons, connectivity and process, through which you target success;
• be able to identify that leverage through targeting success within process holons;	process holons are wholes and parts. Each one has a whole range of attributes through which it is described and represented. There is a process through which success is agreed between the players and stakeholders. Responsibilities may be delegated to a sub-process owner and the sub-process owner is accountable for the success of that sub-process;
• begin to see how to deal with complexity through hierarchical process holons and you will focus on the local connectivities;	process holons receive inputs and send outputs to friends and that defines the connectivity. We deal with the complex interaction between processes by focusing on local connections only;
• be able to identify the appropriate level to model your systems.	the appropriate level for your systems model is the one which delivers your needs and meets your purpose. It is at that level you target success. Of course, you also enable the process owners of the sub-process to target success at their appropriate level.

We hope that we have reached our success targets for this chapter — please use the feedback form at the end of the book.

4. Hardness and softness

4.1 People are crucial to success

Any thinking about how to reach success must involve thinking about people. There is not much that happens in the world that is not influenced by people one way or another. We must therefore think about processes and systems that involve people. In this chapter we will see that all hard systems are embedded in soft ones.

4.2 Targeting success for this chapter

The success targets for this chapter are that, after reading it, you will be able to:

- distinguish between a hard system and a soft system (Fig. 4.1) and describe how hard systems are embedded in soft systems;
- describe the subjective, the inter-subjective and the objective;
- relate the common perception of the term 'objective' to the process of measurement;
- describe the relationship between the truth and the dependability of information;
- state the four sufficient conditions for dependable information;
- describe uncertainty in terms of FIR — Fuzziness, Incompleteness and Randomness;

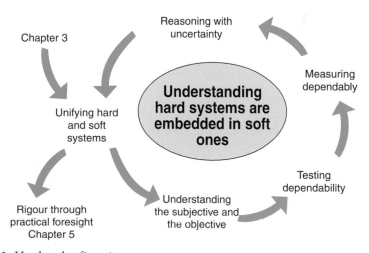

Fig. 4.1. Hard and soft systems

- think about the dependability of evidence;
- understand why there is a need to integrate hard and soft systems into one theory of process.

4.3   Unifying hard systems and soft systems

Hard systems are physical, soft systems involve people

In Chapter 3, we said that the leverage to solve wicked and messy problems will come from systems thinking. The foundations of the approach were laid in the ideas of process, holons and connectivity. In this and the next two chapters, we need to build some superstructure on those foundations before we can begin to deliver added value into the business case (Chapter 7), the people (Chapter 8) and the project life cycle (Chapter 9). In this chapter, we want to distinguish between hard and soft systems and develop our understanding to the stage where we can see how the two can be combined into one system of thought in Chapter 5. We want to do this because we will show that the distinction between hard and soft systems has outlived its usefulness. This is because we will show that all hard systems are embedded in soft systems and because we humans are intimately part of the physical world we live in.

Hard systems are physical systems that are commonly said to be 'objective' — they do not depend on who is interacting with the system. Hard systems are independent of the observer and hence the same for all of us. Our collective understanding has developed through the physical sciences particularly those that underpin engineering such as mechanics. Our ability to model and hence predict bounds on the behaviour of hard systems is good although there are many outstanding issues still to be addressed. Hard systems comprise an action and a reaction — for example in structures a load (such as wind or imposed load) and a response (a deflection or strain). Fundamental limits on predictability have emerged from quantum mechanics and deterministic chaos theory (Argawal J., Woodman N.J., Blockley D.I., 1998).

By contrast soft systems are human and social systems — they involve people. Our collective understanding has developed through the social sciences. Our ability to model and hence predict bounds on the behaviour of soft systems is poor. Soft systems comprise action, reaction and intention — for example, a request (from the boss), an action (doing something) and a purpose (the reason for the request and the action). The role of prediction in soft systems is very limited. The emphasis is on management and control.

Hard systems are easier to manage than soft ones

The parameters of hard systems are measurable, the methodology is clear and the results are normally dependable. Relationships between them are expressible as functions that are dependable and usually deterministic. They are hard in the sense that they are clear, quite precise, predictive and testable. Although few of us thought of these subjects as easy when we were/are struggling to understand them for the first time, we can recognise that through the theory that has been developed over the last few hundred years we can and do use that science reasonably easily. This is especially so in recent years as the manipulative difficulties have largely been removed with the use of larger and faster computers. Thus in the sense that these calculations do not present undue difficulties much of the time — they are relatively easy to solve and, in this sense, hard systems

Box 4.1   Models of systems   Explanation

A hard system:	A soft system:
1. comprises action and reaction	comprises action, reaction and **intention**
2. has a purpose which is a function that derives from the soft system in which it is embedded.	has a set of purposes which derive from the **needs** and consequent intentions of the players in a process
3. has an objective existence in Popper's World 3 (see Section 4.3)	has an objective existence in World 3 but also has a significant subjective (World 2) content
4. dependable measurements are central	dependable measurements are difficult
5. has relationships which can be modelled in formal language	has relationships which can normally only be expressed in natural language or by statistics
6. has models which are deterministic or stochastic	needs systems thinking models
7. is usually associated with physical sciences	is usually associated with social sciences, management and marketing
8. is successful on tame problems	needed to solve wicked and messy problems
9. is clear and reasonably predictable	can be vague and difficult to predict, needs grounded judgement
10. has measurable data	has little measurable data

are easy! Of course, this should not imply that there are not still some outstanding difficulties in hard systems. Metal fatigue and soil behaviour are two obvious ones as well as the evolving issues in chaos theory and limits on the predictability of non-linear deterministic systems.

Conversely, we use the term soft systems for those associated with the social sciences because they are rather difficult to pin down, not very precise, and dif-

Box 4.2   Hard and soft systems   Example

Hard systems	Soft systems
Performance of a beam	Performance of a team
Snow loads on a roof	Customer needs
Water flow in a channel or pipe	Information flow in a company
Traffic engineering predictions	Strategy to create customer satisfaction
Extreme wind load assumptions	Dealing with environmental protesters
Pressures on a retaining wall	Work pressures on people
A cost plan	A business case

ficult to test. Measurement is difficult, evidence is hard to find, methodology is crucial and often subject to debate and models tend to be almost always expressed in natural language. Thus few soft system theories, if any, have the dependable predictive capability of the physical sciences. Although statistical inference is widely used, it is often difficult to interpret. Consequently soft systems are difficult, interpretation is often very subjective, and it is easy to 'waffle' around the subject but difficult to write something that penetrates to the heart of the problem. Therefore, in soft systems there are no easy answers and, in this sense, soft systems are hard!

Following on from our discussion in the previous chapter about wicked problems and the systems approach, it is clear that, up to present times, hard systems have largely yielded to the so-called tame approach with the clear technological successes of modern times. However, our successes in the social sciences are much more difficult to identify. For example, one of the most influential social theories of the last century, Marxism, has virtually collapsed.

In this chapter we will work with this distinction between hard and soft systems. Then in Chapter 5, we will purposely integrate them because we want to produce a systems methodology that is usable for any system hard or soft. Practical construction systems always involve both since, as we shall see, hard systems are always embedded in soft ones.

Box 4.3   Soft system are systems in practice   Principle

In the actual practice of construction, we cannot afford to leave anything important out just because it is inconvenient or just too tricky to deal with. We cannot define systems in a way which makes it easier for ourselves — we have to define them as they are in total.

This means that we need systems thinking for both hard and soft systems for overall success.

Most of the challenges in rethinking construction arise from aspects of human behaviour. Engineering has a well-developed engineering physical science but a totally under-developed social science. Approaches that ignore the human and social dimensions to engineering usually disappoint all concerned.

Interestingly , the recent developments in non-linear dynamics are also beginning to blur this distinction between soft and hard systems. This is happening in the sense that even in a hard deterministic non-linear process there may be conditions under which it becomes unpredictable, and softer emergent properties may be found using computer simulations.

Hard systems are embedded in soft systems

All designed hard systems have a function which is a role in a process. For example, a beam in a structure has the function of carrying the loads from the floor slab. A dam has the function of holding back the reservoir water. The steel and concrete of which the beam and the dam are made does not 'know' it has that function — it has no intentionality. The function is ascribed to a hard system by us, the people who conceive it, design it, build it and who use it. We are also the ones who decide when the hard system has failed and we decide the criteria of failure. Clearly, some functions are obvious as in these examples. Others are less clear and the uses to which a system is put may be unintended. For example, a bridge designed to carry road traffic was almost certainly not designed to be used as a shelter by homeless people. In one case, the cost of repair to concrete damaged by the fires lit by homeless people to keep warm under a bridge was substantial.

Natural systems such as lakes, mountain ranges, etc. do not have a designed function but nevertheless they may have several roles in soft systems. For example, lakes and mountains are frequently a crucial part of the tourist industry. They have the role of attracting tourists by the very fact of their existence. They may also have an infrastructure role in that the lake is a reservoir to supply water. Similarly, these natural systems play a part in the environmental processes of climate etc. Some of these we understand reasonably well (e.g. short-term weather forecasting) and some we do not understand at all well (e.g. global warming).

For our purpose as construction players, every hard physical system has a role to play which is ascribed by a soft system. That role will be identified through our understanding of the process in which it is a part. If we do not understand that role we may well not value it sufficiently. For example, the role of the tiger in conserving the environment of India is intuitively appreciated by many but that does not seem to prevent other people from shooting them in such numbers that their extinction has become a real possibility. The role of animals and other creatures in the natural world is complex and only partly understood. The role of designed systems built by the construction industry is usually clear though sometimes the consequences of building a large facility are not fully appreciated (e.g. large reservoirs have produced earthquakes under the weight of water).

The important idea here is that all hard systems are understood and managed through soft systems. It is helpful to conceive all hard systems as being embedded in soft ones.

Box 4.4   Every hard system is set within a soft system   **Principle**

In the past we have failed to recognise this because we have failed to realise that humans are intimately connected to their environment.

Box 4.5   Soft and hard systems are integral   **Principle**

The distinction between the human and physical worlds has outlived its usefulness. The idea that humans are apart and quite separate from their physical environment is no longer tenable. They are integral.

A large proportion of success or failure of construction projects depends on the co-operation (working as a single system) of soft and hard systems. By including holons that integrate the systems we can manage the emergent property of integration and so achieve substantial added value.

Box 4.6   Integrating safety   **Example**

The success of a shopping mall development over a railway depot depended on integrating the customers' perceptions of safety, the behaviour of the emergency response teams, the behaviour of the construction teams and the safety systems provided. Had they not been integrated, when it is clear that in an emergency they have to work together, the business case could have been seriously damaged and the development delayed. The integration also enabled the wasteful, no added value, processes to be removed.

4.4   Understanding the subjective and the objective

Effective measurement is critical to success. It is crucial to establish dependable information in any system, hard or soft. However we need to make it absolutely clear what we mean when we speak of objective and subjective information. These important ideas are often used in a way which confuses them with measurement as understood in hard systems. People's judgements, decisions and behaviour are based on their perceptions. Since judgement is so central to construction, an understanding of measurement is of profound practical importance to achieving the improvements we are looking for.

We perceive the physical world 'out there'

Outside of any one of us is a physical world that we can reach out to only through our five senses, namely sound, sight, smell, touch and taste. We hear noises from a machine, we can see it and we can touch it and even smell it — but what is it really like 'out there' outside of us? If our eyes were sensitive to X-rays rather than the frequencies we know as visible light, then our mental images would be quite different. The physical world would seem quite a different place. The objects and people that we call beautiful might be quite different from those we currently value that way. Our mental pictures of the world would be so different that our understanding would be different and so our actions would be different. Our mental models of the world derive from our perceptions which we reflect upon and then act upon in a continuous sequence of second to second, minute to minute and hour to hour daily events. We will examine this reflective practice loop further in Chapter 5. Popper (Magee, 1973) called this **physical world** 'out there' which we can reach only through our senses his **World 1** (Fig. 4.2).

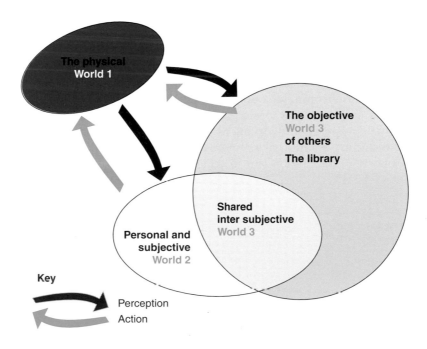

Fig. 4.2 The three worlds of Karl Popper

We perceive our own personal world

We all have our own personal and private thoughts and reflections. Some of these cannot be shared with others — for example, I cannot share with you the actual pain I feel in my stomach. Of course, I can attempt to describe it to you, as I may do to the doctor, but this is not easy because we just cannot share the actual pain, the actual perception. Popper (Magee, 1973) called this world of private thoughts and reflections a **World 2** — a **personal subjective** world entirely of our own.

We share perceptions

Of course, while some of our perceptions and thoughts are private to us and remain stuck in our personal subjective World 2, many others can be and are shared — that is what language is all about. We all see the same moon and two people in a room see the same furniture. We share those sorts of perceptions and thoughts, and through that sharing over a very long period of time has evolved language and knowledge. But when two people see the same furniture do they actually see the same thing? These perceptions are inter-subjective, i.e. shared. However, each of us perceives things slightly (and sometimes dramatically) differently, and then the processing we perform on our perceptions inside our brains is personal and therefore likely to be different. We learn to identify things such as colours, shapes, smells, etc., and these become part of our language — we do not even stop to consider that when I say that chair fabric is green and you agree, whether we are both actually experiencing exactly the same perceptions. Colour blind people certainly do not. **The point is that we agree that the fabric is green** and rarely, for all practical purposes, do we disagree even though our personal subjective World 2 perceptions will probably be different. We learn to call green what we call green and usually there is no problem for most of us.

How can we characterise the world of knowledge?

In like manner, through language, we construct relationships between these concepts. Some of these are true and some are not. By that we mean, in common-sense terms, that some correspond to the facts, to the way things actually are, and some do not. For example, fictional stories are real in that they exist quite outside of any one individual — but they are not true. However, the fact that I exist at the time of writing these words is factually true. Popper called this information as being in the **objective World 3**. One way to think about World 3 is to imagine it as all of the books in all of the libraries in the world or on the internet. Knowledge in World 3 has an objective existence in the sense that it exists **outside the mind of any one individual,** even though it was created by many individuals. **World 3 has an objective existence although it derives from our subjective minds.**

Objective information is different from being objective

Thus objective information may be true or false. We have to be wary of the common usage by most people that objective information is somehow dependable and reliable — it is not — there is a confusion here with measurement which we will come to. As we shall see, dependability is a very important characteristic which we need to understand but it is quite **different from being objective.**

We recognise patterns

We can only access the **physical** World 1 and the **objective** World 3 through our own **personal** World 2. We can think of information as sets of patterns. Our minds organise our personal perceptions into patterns. We need not concern ourselves here about the nature of those patterns whether they are electrical impulses (as in a digital system) or chemical or even numerical or symbolic. We have some patterns in our brains. When a pattern is formed the mind no longer has to analyse or sort information — all that is required is enough to **trigger** the pattern and the mind then follows it. Unless there are competing patterns, anything remotely like the established pattern will be treated just as if it were that pattern.

We all have a point of view

The patterns that we have are formed as a combination of our genetic inheritance and of the experiences we have gone through since we were born. These form our 'world view' or our **point of view**. Each of us has a unique point of view but, of course, we share similarities as we explore groups of holons. Thus engineers tend to think along similar lines as do accountants or sociologists. There are gender differences and there are differences between cultures. We have to think carefully about our points of view when we consider the need to think differently. Mind set is a pattern of thinking which we return to subconsciously, when we are under pressure for example. If we wish to change that mind set, we have to practice hard to establish the new patterns.

When we approach a wicked problem, when we define the roles and responsibilities and choose players to take them on, we have to be acutely aware of the influence of the points of view being expressed.

Box 4.7 **Insiders and outsiders**   Example

One important example that we discussed in Section 3.27 was that of having the point of view of an insider looking in, an insider looking out or an outsider looking in. Think about a project team of which you are part. Which point of view do they take?

There is active and passive information

The text of this book consists of patterns of marks on a piece of paper which all who understand English will be able to read and use. This is **passive** information because it changes only very slowly as the book deteriorates and the print become difficult to read perhaps. There may also be updates and reprints. The information that we use professionally, codes of practice, regulations, the theories of engineering science are all written down, like this book, using natural language or a formal language (such as mathematics) as passive information. This information may change over time but only very slowly. Likewise, in the history of computing, information on computer discs as digital patterns has so far been passive information since it changes only slowly.

The information in our brains is not like this — it is **active** information because it is constantly changing; it is dynamic and it may be self organising. We get a glimpse of this sort of information when we use neural nets or other high speed modelling of artificial intelligence. Likewise and interestingly, most of the files on computers on the internet are passive. However, because web pages are changed regularly and the system is so massive, then the whole system is actually dynamic and has some emerging active characteristics.

Passive	Active
Changes slowly	Changing dynamically
Examples:	**Examples:**
Text of this book,	Information in our brain
Codes of practice	Social values
Data on computer discs	Information on the internet

We link between patterns of information

These patterns, active or passive, are intended to represent things in World 1. The patterns of the sound 'cat', the patterns of the visual image of a cat, the patterns of the smell of a cat, the patterns of the letters of the word are all representations, are models, of a cat that are linked in your mind. When you perceive a cat the perceptions you receive are matched with those you already have and you recognise a cat. This is the basis of language and it is a process — a process of linkages to form language and understanding. For further examples of how the brain operates on patterns see Carter, 1998.

We also form these patterns to create **relationships**, e.g. 'I like cats' is a relational pattern in my brain, as is 'that cat is bigger than the other cat'. These patterns are the basis of language, of choice and hence of decision making. They are the basis of all communication and co-operation and hence of mathematics and scientific knowledge. Thus through language we have a way of representing things in physical World 1 and objective World 3, which enables us to get what we need to satisfy our various needs.

So how do we know which patterns are true and which are not? In one sense, in the every day sense, this is a trivial question and is not problematic — a statement is true if it corresponds to the facts. However, in order to measure soft systems and to address wicked problems using a systems approach, we need to think a little more deeply about an issue that philosophers have been discussing for thousands of years!

4.5 Testing dependability

If we have a statement expressed in any language (i.e. expressed according to some **agreed** rules about what a pattern of symbols means), then how do we establish whether or not it is true? That is, how do we ascertain if the statement corresponds to the facts? (We should note in passing that there are other definitions of truth that philosophers use — we are using the commonsense idea of truth here.)

We establish whether or not we think a statement is true by testing it — or if that is not possible then we test the source from which the statement comes. To test a statement we look for inconsistencies within it or with other previous statements or agreed statements. According to Popper (Magee, 1973) this is the root of the growth of scientific knowledge.

However, in order to test the truth of a statement we need a meta-language in which to express that truth. The meta-language is part of a meta-system that encompasses the system we are concerned with. Everything in the meta system has to be agreed and uncontroversial — otherwise we would need to bring it into the system. The problem is that this leads to an infinite regress, in the sense that if we wish to test the truth of statements in a meta-language, then we need a meta-meta-language and so on ad infinitum!

In the systems approach we are comfortable with the notion of a meta-system with its meta-language because it is the next level up in the process holon hierarchy. We are less concerned with the truth of some evidence, only that it is sufficiently dependable and **useful for our purpose**.

There are testable and non-testable statements

The first criteria we use to establish the truth of a statement is to ask — is it testable? Let us examine the difference between testable and non-testable statements. You and I are sitting together in a room and we both observe a small statuette on a desk. I make two observations: the statuette is heavy and the statuette is beautiful. You disagree — you say the statuette is not heavy and it is ugly. How do we resolve this disagreement?

The first one is easy — we can weigh the statuette. Let us assume that we find it has a mass of five kilograms. You may find it easy to lift five kilograms — I may find it difficult. Nevertheless, we can agree on its mass and, if that information is useful (for example to lift it on a sling), we can agree on using it. The reason we agree is because we agree that the process of weighing is dependable and we accept the result. In fact, the measurement is an experiment in which the statuette is put into one-to-one correspondence with a standard mass. As long as it is done properly the result is more or less dependably independent of the person doing the weighing and he/she will get the same result each time.

So that is one half of the disagreement sorted out — what about the other? How do we establish the truth about the beauty of the statuette? Unfortunately, there is no easy test or measurement. However, we are not totally at a loss because we can ask others. We can ask many other people, friends, artists, experts — anyone! The problem is that we will get lots of different answers. So we value the opinions differently — just like the judges at an ice skating competition or beauty competition. In fact, the voting procedure is a measurement although we may not normally think of it as such! Thus although commonsense tells us that the true mass of the statuette is five kilograms, it does not tell us whether the statuette is beautiful. We have a dilemma, which is entirely because it is difficult to measure beauty dependably. What is more, can we be confident that measurement of beauty leads to truth?

Dependable information is more useful

In fact, of course the concept of truth is slippery — philosophers have been pursuing it and arguing about it for a very long time! The commonsense idea is satisfactory for everyday usage and that is how we normally deal with it in construction practice. However, this is letting us down when we consider difficult matters of uncertainty and risk, as we shall see in Chapter 6.

In order to avoid these difficulties with truth, we should instead focus on the idea of **dependability** — which is the commonsense idea of truth anyway! Dependability is a measure of the extent to which we decide we can use a statement, or more generally a hypothesis or scientific theory, in making a decision. We straightaway accept that dependability will depend on the context of the decision. It will also depend on the appropriateness of the models we are using to represent what we are deciding about. We cannot think about truth that way since it is absolute. For example, if the statue is a present for a friend and we know that she perceives it to be beautiful; then we can accept the statement 'the statue is beautiful' is a dependable measure of the suitability of the present.

Box 4.8   Judgement, truth and dependability   **Principle**

Judgement, truth and dependability are different things. In order to manage the behaviour of a system involving people and complex physical processes we have to make judgements. We should try to ensure that our judgements are dependable for a decision in a particular context rather than true in all contexts.

Box 4.9   Brent Spar   Example

The public were persuaded that Brent Spar contained many tons of oil that would pollute the ocean if Shell were to proceed with their original plans to dispose of it deep in the northern Atlantic. It was not true that Brent Spar was a 'toxic time bomb' but nevertheless disposal in mid-Atlantic was prevented.

Base decisions on dependability not truth

Construction players (and indeed all practitioners) need information to make decisions. They need to be able to justify those decisions and, to do that, they need to know that they can rely on the information — they need to know that it is dependable. For example, if the results of a linear elastic analysis of the response of a concrete structure under an idealised wind load is useful in deciding what steel reinforcement to use and helps to produce a structure which will be safe, then **for that purpose in that context** the results of that analysis are dependable. The results are not true in the sense that the strains in the structure will be exactly as predicted. Indeed they may be very different, as anyone who has tried to measure them will tell you. This can be for a variety of reasons such as creep and shrinkage or because the material has strains outside of the elastic region. Nevertheless, the purpose of the elastic analysis was not to predict those strains but rather to produce a safe design — the two are very different. The reason why such an analysis might produce a safe design lies in the safe theorem of plastic theory and in the practices of structural design that have been used before and are being used again (Blockley, 1980). Of course, if the analysis were actually to be true then the designers could have total confidence in the dependability of the analytical results because truth is sufficient for dependability — but it is not necessary.

Box 4.10   **Principle**

Truth is sufficient for dependability — but it is not necessary

---

Of course, this begs the question of how we decide when a statement is dependable for a defined purpose. In systems thinking we look for **evidence**.

There are four sufficient conditions for dependable evidence

We want to be able to test if some information we have is dependable. The tests, which if successful are conditions for the dependability, were first set out in Blockley (1980) and are shown in Fig. 4.3.

Notice that together they are sufficient conditions and not necessary. That means that you can have dependable information that has not passed these tests (but it will be difficult to establish that), but if the tests have been passed then you know you have dependable information. Thus there will be many dependable statements about which it is very difficult to get dependable evidence.

The first step is to set up an experiment to test the statement as a hypothesis. As we have said, we will interpret the idea of an experiment very generally. It is the taking of action upon the external world and recording the consequences. In hard systems it is common for an experiment to be repeated many times over under precisely controlled conditions. At the other end of the spectrum it may be possible to perform an experiment only once because it is self-destructive. The results may be highly interactive with the observer as in many soft systems experiments. In some disciplines it may not be possible to perform an experiment directly, e.g. history or archaeology. However, historians can look for evidence and may perform indirect tests. A famous example was the Kon Tiki expedition that successfully tested the hypothesis that the early inhabitants of South America could have sailed across the Pacific. Of course, it did not prove that they actually did.

Clearly, the more repeatable the experiment the more sure we can be of the data we obtain from it and the more highly tested the hypothesis.

Given the first step, that the test is repeatable, the second step is to check that the state of the system is the same in each repeated experiment. A simple example of where it may not be the same is a Euler strut. There is a point of bifurcation in the elastic response of a long slender strut to an applied load — the strut may buckle one way in one test and another way in another test. In general, in non-linear systems there are points of bifurcation or instabilities which are such that the behaviour in one simulation may be quite different in two separate and seemingly similar tests (under very small changes in initial conditions). More

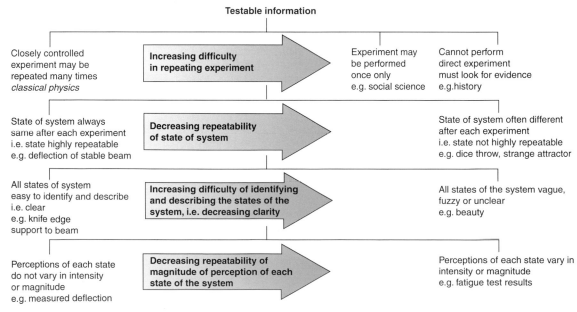

Fig. 4.3 Conditions on the dependability of information

commonplace examples are the faces of a dice, since every throw of the dice may produce a different face (which is the state of the system) selected from one of the six by the random roll of the dice. Human behaviour is another everyday example — but one that is much more complex as, unlike the six faces of the dice, the number of states is infinite! Sudden changes of behaviour form points of bifurcation which make human behaviour fiercely non-linear. As we shall see later, we can use statistical reasoning to deal with the variations in the repeatability of the state of the system as long as we can obtain sufficient data over large enough populations.

Given the first two steps of this testing process to establish dependability then the third step is to test the clarity of the descriptions of the state of the system. In classical physics the experimentalist purposely chooses clear states in order to eliminate this problem. This is, for example, why concrete beams are tested on knife edge supports in the laboratory under controlled conditions. In soft systems it may well be necessary to use rather vague terms (such as team spirit). In engineering practice, it is common and justifiable to use vague terms if they are appropriate, as we saw in Chapter 2. Thus in a preliminary discussion with the architect, a structural engineer might refer to 'high' stresses when discussing conceptual changes to a design. Of course, if asked he would be able to put a range of actual values which are 'high' stresses in that context — but the point is that in a certain context such a vague description can be useful.

The fourth and final step, given the first three, is to check that the magnitudes of the actual measurements are repeatable. This is the familiar checking of the scatter in experimental results. For example, if you plot a graph of the applied load against the deflection of a simply supported beam in a laboratory, you should get a nice straight line. However, in a fatigue test the number of cycles to failure will vary a lot between tests and you may get a large scatter.

Figure 4.3 illustrates the different disciplines under various combinations of these conditions. The hard sciences fulfil the conditions on the left-hand side of the figure and the dependability degrades at each level as you move to the right. Thus soft systems tend to be on the right-hand side of the figure.

Note again that these four conditions are sufficient and not necessary. As history is at the top right-hand corner the conditions cannot be used to test historical hypotheses. For example, they cannot be used to test the date of your birthday because that was a one-off event. That does not mean that if you tell me the date of your birthday I cannot treat it as a dependable piece of information. In order to do so I need appropriately dependable evidence obtained in some other way because the date is not testable directly by experiment. However, there may be evidence — e.g. a birth certificate. I might worry that it is a forgery so then I would have to go to the registry and check the certificate. Clearly, it is also possible that your entry in the registry is wrong — perhaps someone slipped up all of those years ago! In this sort of situation, at some stage, we have to be willing to accept the evidence and make a decision based on that judgement. The amount of detective work and resource we are prepared to expend must depend on the context of the problem we are trying to solve.

4.6 Measuring dependably

Hard systems are understood through system models with parameters

We are familiar with hard systems analysis — it is the engineering science of structures, hydraulics, etc. These systems of structures and water pipes, etc. are described in terms of parameters such as span length, geometry, loading conditions, material properties, etc., which are precisely defined and measurable. Mathematical relationships are developed between these parameters to describe system behaviour and to enable prediction. Thus, for a simply supported beam with span l, central point load W, elastic modulus E, second moment of area I we can predict the deflection d confidently as

deflection $d = Wl^3/48EI$

In general, this is $y = g(x_1, x_2, x_3, ..., x_n)$, where y, x_i are the parameters and $g(\cdot)$ is a model of the system behaviour — in this case a simple beam on knife edge supports, the sort of experiment that all first-year civil engineering undergraduates will perform.

Now as we move away from the defined conditions under which this prediction has been tested, we may become increasingly concerned about the uncertainty in the relationship between the formula (which is accurate in a laboratory test) and the actual beam in an actual structure. There are two types of uncertainty in this new situation, namely parameter uncertainty and system uncertainty.

The parameters may be uncertain

Parameter uncertainty is the uncertainty about the values of the parameters that we may use to calculate the deflection. For example, is the load exactly 2 kN? Is the span exactly 5 m? Is the elastic modulus exactly 200 N/mm^2? The designer must ensure the beam is safe so, in order to be sure, safety factors or load factors or partial limit state factors are included in the calculations. The values are chosen (usually in structural design by Code of Practice committees) so that we can be sure that our predictions are safely cautious. A more advanced approach, as we shall discuss later in this chapter, is to treat these parameters as random variables and hence to calculate a probability that the deflection will be between a certain range of values **given the system model is dependable.** This is the topic of probabilistic reliability theory.

The system models will be uncertain

If we have uncertainty in the systems model then we are uncertain of the relationship between the equation $y = g(\cdot)$ and the actual system. This is a much more difficult problem and is one not yet satisfactorily solved in probabilistic reliability theory. If the equation is badly wrong then no safety factors can prevent failure. Engineers have to judge whether or not a model is appropriate, and they do that by effectively testing when it has been used before and under what circumstances: i.e. they look for evidence that the model (in this case the formula) is dependable.

The basic structure of a hard system is that of action and reaction. This occurs in various forms whether as Newton's Third Law or as load versus strength or as demand versus capacity. There is effectively a struggle between the demands upon the system and the capacity of the system to cope with that demand. The designers, the builders and the users are all trying to ensure that the demand will never exceed the capacity, i.e. the system will function through all of its life cycle.

Thus the issue, familiar to practising engineers, concerning the use of hard systems analysis, is really the extent to which the models of the actual system are being used appropriately (i.e. to provide fitness for purpose). This depends on the context which, as we have said, is a soft system. In the past we have failed to recognise this because we have failed to realise that humans are intimately connected to their environment. Of course, this is an issue of systems identification because one can always draw a border around any system (hard or soft) and focus entirely on that which is within it. In scientific research this is quite permissible in order to discover new relationships — however, in practice the construction process is a social process which always has at least one hard system embedded within it.

We therefore have, in practice, to treat the results of hard systems analysis as evidence in the soft systems decisions that have to be made. Of course, the soft systems should be made as hard as is appropriate so that all of the results are used to the best effect.

Measuring is an experiment

The notion of measurement in hard systems is familiar and so we will discuss it only briefly here. Measurements are experiments in which the object to be measured is put into one-to-one correspondence with a standard unit. For example, the length of a building is put into one-to-one correspondence with a standard metre tape. The process of measurement is independent of the observer and is therefore objective. However, it is worth distinguishing between the common usage of the terms subjective and objective when applied to hard measures.

Construction players speak of objective measurement. For example, if we measure the length of a line then we are at the left-hand side of Fig. 4.3 — all of the criteria are satisfied. The measurement is repeatable, the state of the system is clear and repeatable (as long as you have a good tape measure) and within tolerance you will get the same length each time you perform the measurement and whoever does it. Therefore, the test is in Popper's World 3 (shared information), it interacts with Popper's World 1 (the physical and social world 'out there') and it is dependable. When the engineer says the measurement is objective he/she really means that it is objective and dependable. This distinction is important when we consider measurement of soft systems because these measurements can be objective and dependable to a degree which we can judge using the criteria of Fig. 4.3.

Now imagine that we do not have the equipment to measure the line. We have to estimate it either by pacing it out or just by looking at it. Clearly, now the dependability of the answer drops. There is objectivity here in the understanding of the measurement criteria (i.e. what we mean by a metre length) but not in the estimate of the magnitude (i.e. how many metres there are) — this is subjective. The estimate is effectively a thought experiment where we **imagine** putting a tape into one-to-one correspondence with a line. It is repeatable but the state of the system is less clear (e.g. if we pace out the line, how long is our pace and are all of our paces the same?). This is quite distinct from a judgement about a soft measurement, as we shall see later.

The point here is that we will always prefer a dependable measurement to a subjective estimate. Unfortunately, sometimes the information is not available nor are the resources required to find it. Data is often sparse and relationships expressed on a graph seem to resemble 'plum puddings'.

Soft systems are not easy to represent

A soft system, as we have said the name implies, is one where it is often not easy to identify what it is. The edges are uncertain and unclear, it is not easy to describe what is going on within it — the relationships within it are unclear and it is difficult to predict what will happen. Models of soft systems do not enable easy or dependable predictions even under quite tightly defined conditions. These are issues of system identification, system representation and modelling.

Box 4.11   **Principle**

**The construction process is a social process and is
therefore a soft system**

People have intentionality

The root of the reasons for these difficulties is, as we have said earlier, that soft systems always include human beings, and human beings have intentions — they decide what they want and when they want it. The motivation behind their decisions is rarely obvious and usually very difficult to identify.

Just as in a hard system there is action and reaction, demand and capacity, but there is this extra element — the intentionality of the human being. This is the ingredient that makes it difficult to model and hence to predict a soft system. In Chapter 3, we said that a soft system is rather like throwing a stone through the air (a hard system) — but the stone has a mind of its own (intentionality) and decides to change its trajectory part way through (Box 3.15). It will do this many times over. This means that the relationships are non-linear, with bifurcations and instabilities at regular intervals. It means that there are inherent limits to our predictive capability of soft systems.

The emphasis in soft systems therefore is not on prediction but rather it is on control, it is on the management of the process. We will see in Chapters 6 to 8 how hard and soft systems can be pulled together in a process holon for the management of all systems whether hard, soft or any degree of hardness/softness in between.

Soft systems are difficult to measure

Measurement in soft systems is not easy but it can be done. There are both hard and soft parameters in soft systems and the models of the relationships between the parameters are soft. Repeated measurements of hard system variables such as height and weight of people can be used to relate to, say, the number of heart attacks — but the relationships will be inexact and usually have to be interpreted statistically. The predictive capability of such relations will be problematic if the basic causal mechanisms are not understood. Of course, that begs the question of what constitutes causality and that is a basic issue in the social sciences. Here we will argue that if a model is dependable in that the four criteria as described in Fig. 4.3 are satisfied (the left side) then the model is causal.

What of the basic measurement process for soft concepts such as beauty? How do we measure soft systems?

As we said earlier there is a way of measuring beauty and that is to take a vote among a group of people chosen for a reason. Clearly, if we test a voting process against the criteria of Fig. 4.3 there can be a lot of uncertainty about a result. It is a well-known problem for opinion polling where the choice of representative samples etc. is critical. However, opinion polling has the luxury normally of being able to take large samples with clear questions. In soft systems we are often concerned with sparse evidence about imprecise ideas. It is important, therefore, that these measurements are judged against some understanding of the types of uncertainty that we shall examine in Section 4.6.

We can identify four types of problem

In Chapter 2, we referred to wicked and messy problems as distinct from tame problems. Now we can examine types of problem as dealt with by existing theoretical techniques. We will characterise a problem as a doubtful or difficult question to which there may be a number of possible answers, which have to be considered and evaluated in the decision making process. Four types of problem are shown in Box 4.12.

Box 4.12 Types of problem		Explanation
Type	**Consequence of adopting proposed solution:**	**Examples**
1. Deterministic	Are known for certain	The behaviour of a floor slab according to a theoretical model
2. Probabilistic	Are precisely identified but only probability of occurrence is known	The depth of water over a spillway
3. Fuzzy	Are approximately identified so that only possibilities or fuzzy consequences are known	Human error in a design calculation
4. Open world	Some (precise or fuzzy) have been identified	Environmental impact of traffic congestion

Type 1 problems are the well-known deterministic ones. The power of this simplest of assumptions is clear for physical systems such as those dealt with by Newtonian mechanics. These are tame problems. Most of the past successes of applications of engineering science have relied on the fact that for certain regular and repeatable situations this model is appropriate. Note that the consequences of adopting a proposed solution are known for certain only within the model (Popper's World 3). The actual consequences in the world 'out there' (Popper's World 1) are uncertain and depend entirely on how good the model actually is in representing that physical world. The ability to solve Type 1 problems is necessary but not sufficient for good construction practice.

Type 2 problems are an extension to Type 1 in that a probability measure is attached to a set of possible outcomes and consequences. In the literature this is often referred to as decision making under risk. It is the basis of probabilistic risk and reliability theory. The ability to solve Type 2 problems is neither necessary nor sufficient for good construction practice. However, solutions can be helpful if the basis of the calculations is properly appreciated — otherwise they can be seriously misleading.

Type 3 problems are a further extension of Type 2 with explicit recognition that there may be lack of precision in defining some of the terms.

In all of these three types there is an in-built 'closed world' assumption. This means that all of the outcomes and consequences are, it is assumed, known. There is no room for unforeseen and unintended outcomes and consequences in the formulation of the model. Thus when a probabilistic analysis is carried out, it is implicit that the chance of some outcome is measured **relative to the set of all other identified outcomes**.

Type 4 problems are 'open world' problems which are more like the wicked problems discussed in Chapter 3. Here only some of the possible outcomes and consequences are identified and known — there is a recognised possibility of unforeseen and unintended outcomes and consequences of a particular decision — this is much more like real world problem solving.

4.7   Reasoning with uncertainty

In all systems, uncertainty is a key issue. In any process we are attempting to move towards a success target. To do this we need to make decisions within each process. Decisions depend upon information derived from the past, present and future. We examine past experiences and case histories from which we have hopefully learned. We look at the past performance of the process and the key players within it. We examine the present state of affairs within the process through an audit or other observations. We consider future scenarios through scientific prediction or through mental simulations or thought experiments about what might happen. We try to anticipate unintended consequences of the options we are considering and we make contingency plans to cover some eventualities.

Our effectiveness in putting all of this information together depends on how uncertain it all is. Managing uncertainty is a key to success targeting.

Uncertainty is FIR

We divide uncertainty into three types, namely fuzziness, incompleteness and randomness. In our systems hierarchy, as described in Chapter 3, we have levels of definition which correspond to the notion of fuzziness. The attributes of each process holon are described by patterns which are clustered at these various levels.

Box 4.13	Uuncertainty is	FIR	Principle
F	Fuzziness	Imprecision of definition	
I	Incompleteness	How can we know what we do not know?	
R	Randomness	The lack of a specific pattern	

Fuzziness can be a benefit

What do we mean when we speak of a *large* strain in a concrete structure. Obviously what we do mean depends upon the context. A large strain in an uncracked section where cracking is not to be allowed is not the same as a large strain in a cracked section — perhaps forming a concrete hinge.

The intellectual tradition of the western world is based on precision. The value of fuzzy or imprecise words has perhaps not been appreciated. Edward de Bono (1971) calls such words *porridge* words. He argues that *porridge* words allow high level questions to be asked when there is not enough information to ask precise ones. They allow overview explanations when we do not need or cannot provide detailed ones. They enable us to leapfrog over areas of difficulty, imprecision or ignorance to allow us to carry on to a point where we can make a useful assessment. They can prevent too early a commitment to a specific idea which closes off potentially beneficial options.

Of course, many construction players are familiar with the idea that detail is required only to the level which enables you to solve the problem. This is contained in the idea of fitness for purpose. The more detailed an explanation, the more likely it is to be wrong. We use 'black boxes' (the 'primitive' holons below which we just cannot go because we do not have any understanding of what the sub-holons of a black box are) — no matter how much detail we go to we end up with a 'black box' in the end. In systems theory, however, we can consciously choose those holons that we are going to consider as black boxes within our system because we do not need to explore beyond that level of detail.

Zadeh in the 1960s suggested a theory of fuzzy sets which has developed into a variety of theories of vague and approximate reasoning. This work is leading to new and important insights into the mathematical analysis of uncertainty which is beyond the scope of this book but which is the basis of the Italian Flag which we will use later (Cui W.C., Blockley D.I., 1990, and Hall J.W., Davis J.P., Blockley D.I., 1998).

Here we will deal with fuzziness and imprecision of definition simply by attempting to ensure that we use the appropriate level of modelling in the holistic hierarchy. However, it is important to recognise and be as explicit as possible about the differing levels of fuzziness in our models and to recognise that in many problems a rather high level and vague statement may be appropriate.

Box 4.14	Principle

**We need to recognise that fuzzy statements
are appropriate for some processes**

Incompleteness is often missed

Incompleteness is perhaps the most important aspect of uncertainty since it is the one least appreciated by most of us.

Incompleteness concerns that which we do not know. Let us distinguish straight away between 'that which we do not know we do not know' and 'that which we decide we do not want to include in our system' probably because we judge it is not relevant. For example, when studying the stresses in a steel structure we do not need to include parameters concerning environmental impact. Theories of small deflections of beams leave out the strain energy due to shear because it is small. Engineering theory is full of such sensible simplifications. Thus if we know that we have not included something in a model of the system then we have done that knowingly, and if subsequently those matters we have left out become important then we can include them. Of course, in areas of difficulty the effects of these omissions must be monitored carefully.

However, what of those phenomena that we do not know we do not know? This is the essential worry about incompleteness. For the vast majority of situations perhaps the concern is not real and can be forgotten — however, in the case of high risk projects where chances of a catastrophic event are small but the consequences are enormous, we must be concerned.

Clearly, the lesson for us in this is what phenomena are happening today that we do not know about in our decision making process? The answer to that is that all we can do is have the **humility to recognise the limits to what we know** and to manage our processes carefully, so that if and when such phenomena arise

> **Box 4.15   We cannot know what we do not know**   Example
>
> An outstanding example of this is the Dee Railway Bridge which collapsed
> in the UK in 1848. At the Commission of Inquiry all sorts of explanations were
> given for the accident — but they did not mention what we now know to
> have been the real cause, namely lateral torsional buckling of the cast iron
> beams. The reason they did not mention it is simple — at that time they had
> no understanding of it. The beams had been designed using a formula
> derived by Fairburn in 1812 for spans of about 12 feet. Over the years between
> those tests and the building of the Dee Bridge the formula had been used
> quite successfully on longer and longer spans. It was not until the Dee Bridge
> that the mode of behaviour of a beam over that span changed from simple
> deflection in Fairburn's tests to lateral torsional buckling (a good example of
> a change in the second criteria of Fig. 4.3). How could they know what they
> did not know?
>
> (Sibly and Walker, 1977)

we can recognise them and deal with them before lives are lost. This again
emphasises the need to focus on the management of process. It is particularly
important for viciously wicked problems such as BSE, global warming, nuclear
waste disposal and genetic engineering. It is also relevant, for example, to the
financial health of a developer during a recession or the possibility that our
product will be made obsolete by a new invention.

Randomness is the only uncertainty in probability theory and statistics

The definition of what is meant by the term random is actually problematic and
controversial. Following Popper we will define randomness as the lack of a specific pattern. The pattern can be anything — a sequence of numbers, a picture,
a digital signal, a graph, a sound, a chemical, etc. Imagine a sequence of numbers. If there is an obvious pattern, for example 2, 4, 6, 8, etc., then we have no
difficulty in seeing it is non-random. If there is not an obvious sequence, however, then we are not sure — it seems random but is it? So we choose as many
tests as we can think of and as soon as we find a sequence then we can declare
it non-random. However, if we try many different tests and we do not find a
sequence then we can declare it random — but are we sure? How can we be sure
that some rather more clever statistician will not come along and say to us 'have
you tried the X test?' and when we do then we find a sequence? Clearly, this is
a matter of testability just as we discussed for truth and dependability. As the
pattern fails more and more tests, and the tests are more and more ingenious,
then we can grow ever more confident in our belief that the sequence is random
— but we can never be totally sure! Thus again it is a matter for deciding on a
level of appropriateness, a level of evidence, a matter of using an appropriate
number of tests, so that when we use the result in a decision process we get a
dependable decision.

Whether a pattern is random also depends on the process by which it is formed
and its place in a pattern of patterns. For example, a set of numbers drawn in
the National Lottery as 2, 4, 6, 8, 10, 12 could be randomly drawn since the chance
of this sequence is exactly as any other.

There are patterns over populations of data — random variables

The above discussion applies to complete randomness with no patterns at all — a uniform histogram or probability density function. However, there is a stage in between total randomness on the one hand and a completely deterministic pattern (effectively a fixed sequence) on the other. This is the realm of statistics where there are patterns between parameters but they are identifiable only over populations of data. We cannot rely on the patterns to occur between specific individual samples of the data. For example, although there is a strong relationship between smoking and lung cancer it is a statistical one — we all know of the 90 year old who has smoked 20 cigarettes a day since he was 15 and of the young man who died of lung cancer having never smoked in his life. It is the relationship over a population of many people that demonstrates the connection.

Statistics and probability theory are about the treatment of parameters as random variables. These random variables have an associated probability measure which is distributed over a range of values of the magnitude of the parameter to indicate what values are likely to occur. An example is the famous bell-shaped normal distribution — there are many others. It is beyond the scope of this book to discuss probability theory and randomness, but it is important to realise that randomness in parameter values is only one aspect of uncertainty — parameter uncertainty (Blockley, 1980). For a good introduction to probability and statistics for civil engineers, see Benjamin and Cornell (1970).

When two or more random variables are statistically related then one can derive joint probability density functions which indicate the likelihood of two or more values occurring together. Of course, to measure such data is difficult and so it is rarely available. The deterministic relationships of hard engineering science are therefore used to model the system, and simplified emergent measures of the probability density function are used such as the mean, variance and covariance and other higher order statistics to perform the necessary calculations. The choice of these measures and their values requires some difficult judgements.

Subjective judgements can be made using probability

Another interpretation of the random variables of probability theory is that of the Bayesian Theory (Benjamin and Cornell, 1970). Here the probability measure is not of chance but of **belief**. It is therefore a theory for manipulating subjective judgement and, as such, would be very powerful were it not for the severe limitations of the axioms of the theory. The main one is that the theory requires a complete set of judgements since **no incompleteness is allowed** (the probabilities must sum to one) and rare is the person who knows all of the possible futures within any serious problem. Another large practical limitation is the difficulty of expressing dependencies between related random variables as conditional statements. The idea of incompleteness is completely missing from probabilistic risk analysis and reliability theory. However, interval probability theory (Cui, Blockley, 1990) was developed to avoid this restriction. Research continues into an important area of the manipulation of subjective judgements which will be applicable to soft systems analysis (Hall, Davis, Blockley, 1998).

Measure evidence using the Italian flag

In process modelling we are concerned to find evidence that the process is moving towards success and that there is no build up of difficulties that might bring about failure — we will call that the **hazard** content (or the banana skins!) of the process in Chapter 6. The evidence will come from many sources of various types and there is a need to collect it, digest it, interpret it, learn from it and make decisions using it. Some evidence will be favourable and some will be unfavourable (Box 4.16). The judgements about it will be inter-subjective and hence objective in the sense of Popper's World 3. However, the dependability of the judgements will have to be assessed.

Uncertainty can be dealt with in a soft way simply by people judging it subjectively and sharing those judgements with others before decisions are taken. The other way is a harder way of using mathematical logical reasoning based on Interval Probability Theory. Our view is that a combination of these two approaches should be used for the most difficult and important projects. The mathematical manipulations will help to avoid logical errors but the mathematics is not rich enough yet to represent all of the aspects that need to be considered. Ultimately, judgements are about agreement concerning the models used as being

---

Box 4.16 **The Italian flag of evidence from Interval Probability Theory (IPT)**	**Explanation**

In order to have a measure of evidence that can be used on Type 4 problems in Box 4.12 we need to assess quite separately the evidence in favour of and the evidence against the proposition that a process is heading for success. We do this by measuring (by voting or by individual judgement) on a scale [0,1] evidence in favour and colouring it green as shown in Fig. 4.4. Evidence against is assessed on a scale [0,1] and is coloured in red starting from 1 and working back to zero. The difference in the middle is white and makes an Italian flag.

There are three interesting special cases.
Evidence = [1,1] which is all green and means that there is complete evidence for and no evidence against (no red).
Evidence = [0,0] which is all red and means that there is complete evidence against and no evidence for (no green).
Evidence = [0,1] which is all white and means there is no green evidence for and no red evidence against and so we really 'do not know'.

If the evidence is for example [0.4, 0.9] then there is 40% green and 10% red and 50% white.

Figure 4.4 shows a simple model of a process with two sub-process holons which are both necessary for the success of the top process. The players who own each process associate an Italian flag with that process. The flag represents their view, based on evidence, that the process will be successful. Clearly, there is something wrong in Fig. 4.4 since the flags are inconsistent in a rather blatant way for the purpose of an example. This means that the process owners when they realise this inconsistency can discuss the reasons for it and decide on adjustments or on what needs to be done to ensure success. This type of social process can enable the team members to admit what they do not know and hence take action to manage it.

It is important that soft social processes are grounded in logic and so we provide some brief outline mathematical details. Figure 4.5 illustrates Italian Flags for a set defined on a variable X. Figures 4.5(a) and 4.5(b) are the probability density functions for the classical case with no 'do not know' white area. Figures 4.5(c) and 4.5(d) show the equivalent distributions with the corresponding Italian Flags.

---

appropriate to solve the problems with which we are faced. In the final analysis, if we have to justify ourselves against our peers in a court of law under tort, we can perform only to the level of the group to which we claim we belong with our level of expertise. In other words, we must judge uncertainty with a level of responsibility and accountability that is in accordance with the expertise we claim to have.

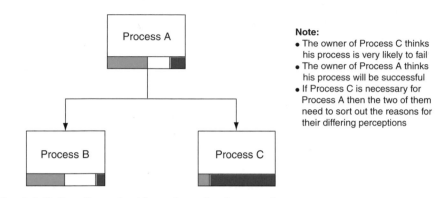

Note:
- The owner of Process C thinks his process is very likely to fail
- The owner of Process A thinks his process will be successful
- If Process C is necessary for Process A then the two of them need to sort out the reasons for their differing perceptions

Fig. 4.4. Italian flags of evidence for a simple example

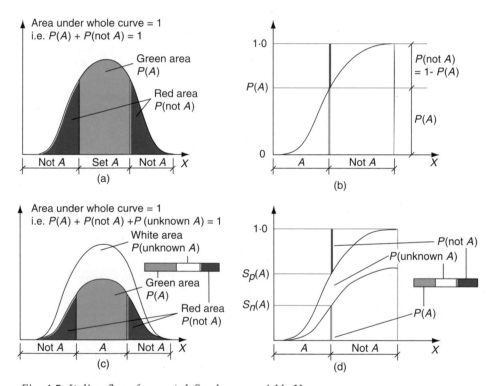

Fig. 4.5. Italian flags for a set defined on a variable X

4.8 The Italian flag story

Jo, the Managing Director of West Enton Water plc, had a problem. Her Chairman had expressed concern about the supply to the people in Zone D of her patch. He pointed out there was only one source and the supply was vulnerable.

She had spoken to Fred, the Engineering Director, with no real meeting of minds. She decided to call a meeting of the main players to share the issue and look for a solution she could take to the Board.

'What's this all about?' Fred, the Engineering Director had arrived early at the meeting. 'I've got this problem sorted, why do we need a meeting about it?' Edith too was early — she was the Customer Services Manager. 'Surely there is an issue here Fred — we have to make sure the customers have a continuous supply, don't we?' 'I've just got better things to do today,' thought Fred to himself.

Just then in came Jo, quickly followed by Tony, the Water Quality Director.

'As I see it,' said Jo getting down to business straightaway, 'we have a problem with the supply to Zone D. The purpose of this meeting is for us to look at it and to decide what to recommend to the Board on Thursday. We have an unacceptable vulnerability. If we get a major incident we could be in big trouble. I want to get some clear direction today.'

'But the chance of anything happening is very small,' said Fred. 'I've assessed it and I think we are OK.'

'I agree the chance is small,' said Jo. 'It's the vulnerability I'm worried about. If there is an incident the consequences could be enormous. Just think of all that disruption, and the compensation payments would be horrific.'

'It's what we call a low chance high consequence risk,' said Fred. 'But I agree there is a vulnerability there. I've not felt the risk was high enough to put forward any scheme though — there are so many other priorities for our budgets.'

'OK,' said Jo, 'I understand where you are coming from Fred and I think you are probably right. However, I think we've got to put our minds around what we might do about this. If we conclude that we leave it as it is, then that's what we should recommend to the Board. So what are the options Fred? Can we put in place a contingency plan?'

'As I see it,' said Fred thinking quickly, 'there are five options.' He wrote them up as bullet points on the flip chart.

1. Do nothing.
2. Buy in water from Eastham Water plc.
3. Build a new pipeline so that we can by-pass any incident and extract water upstream of the incident.
4. Develop a new source from a canal or borehole.
5. Pump water from one of the other zones.

Jo responded immediately. 'Well, leaving option 1 aside for the moment — if we can do option 5 then the problem is solved!'

'Hold on,' said Fred, 'we can't cover all our customers in Zone D that way — that's why it's not in our normal operations plan.'

'I can't support that then,' said Edith, 'the customers must come first.'

'I agree,' said Jo.

'There's also a doubt about water quality,' said Tony. 'We may have a mixing problem from two different chlorination processes. The treatment works in Zone D are different. I don't think the water from Zones A, B and C is suitable — I need to check.'

'Well that seems to rule out option 5 then,' said Jo. 'Option 2 isn't on since we really have enough water already,' she continued, 'the Board won't contemplate buying more in. We would have to go into a long-term agreement for a daily or weekly supply that we would need only in an emergency.'

'Option 3 looks very expensive,' said Jo. 'Is that so Fred?'

Fred was beginning to warm up at the prospect of a nice juicy piece of contract work. He had been thinking. He began a long account of how option 3 could work. They all listened attentively. After he had finished Tony said, 'That option seems OK to me.'

Edith said, 'Yes, it seems OK but looks too expensive.'

Jo said, 'I think option 3 is OK technically but we've got to do better on cost.

What about option 4?'

'I could go along with option 4 as long as the risk to quality was acceptable,' said Edith.

Tony had been sitting quietly thinking. 'There are risks in option 4 — but they could probably be handled OK,' he said. Fred added that there was a new potential source nearby — might be expensive to drill but it could probably do the job.

'Well,' said Jo. 'We have five options and some disagreement because option 5 seems the best from a financial and business point of view but is technically not on. The water mixing issue might be OK — we don't know yet — but the fact is we can't reach some of our customers. So shall we all agree on option 4 then and I'll put the processes in place to work up a solution for the Board? I think they may end up deciding not to do anything in view of the cost — but heaven help us if we do get an incident!'

Jo got up to leave.

'Just a moment,' said Tony, 'I've heard about this new technique where you use an Italian Flag to express your uncertainty in your judgements.' He went on to describe the idea briefly.

'The problem seems to be with option 5,' he said. We would like it to be the one we choose — but we have heard arguments against it — mainly from Fred and me! As I said, I am actually a bit uncertain about it — I do need to do some checks.'

'OK,' said Jo sitting down again, 'let's try it. Can we all draw our Italian Flags for option 5 in the first instance?

The result was:

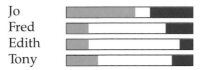

Jo
Fred
Edith
Tony

'That's interesting,' said Jo, ' I'm firmly in favour from my overall perspective but with major problems that really rule it out. There is too much red in my flag for a yes. But you are all unsure — you have put in a lot of white! Explain.'

'Yes, I felt I had to say no,' said Fred, 'because you were pressing me for a judgement. Actually I needed to express my need to don't know. Let's just bullet point the green and the red. What are the reasons for the low green folks?'

They wrote down

- may do the job
- its cheap
- its simple.

What are the reasons for the red?

- may not do the job
- may be a water quality issue.

'Interesting,' said Jo, 'it directs to the two obvious questions about option 5 but which we didn't allow ourselves to ask because of the time pressure I put on you. Will it actually do the job and is there a water quality issue?

Can you give me a week to work on it? I think I may be able to find a way round it,' said Fred.

Much to Fred's relief, Tony said, 'I agree that's a good idea.'

'Right,' said Jo, 'I do need some clear answers fast and I'll not pretend otherwise — I wanted to get some clear steer today to the way we progress this. However, we'll meet early next week and defer the decision until then. I'll have to defer the item at the Board as well which could be a bit embarrassing. If we've got to spend money on a feasibility or design study I want to get on with it.'

One week later they met again. Tony and Fred revealed that the problems could be overcome and that option 5 was indeed practicable. They had identified a small pipeline which at very small cost could connect the vulnerable customers and then they could pump water into the Zone D. They had not identified a need for that pipeline before because in normal circumstances it was not required. However, it would greatly increase the connectivity and hence the robustness of the pipe network. There was not a water quality problem with the mixing of water.

'Well,' said Jo, 'we were about to embark on an expensive exercise in evaluating these options with option 4 at the top but now we have a clear recommendation for option 5. Let's sum up what we've learned.

1. **Vulnerability and risk are different**. We are vulnerable in the sense that some small damage to our source could cause disproportionate consequences to our customers. So even though the chances are small there is a strong case for increasing the robustness of our network.
2. **Italian flags enabled us to express what we did not really know**. We had some evidence for and some evidence against with a lot of uncertainty in the middle. The flags helped us to pick out the essential questions and to take a difficult decision to make more time.
3. Team dialogue enabled us to **see the problem from a different point of view** (in our case vulnerability rather than risk) and through it we found a new opportunity.
4. **Slower thinking can produce better solutions**. We allowed ourselves not to be pressurised into a quick decision. If we develop a different point of view we can look for new solutions.

Well done everybody and thank you!'

4.9 Checking for success

The success targets for this chapter set out at the beginning were that, after reading it, you will be able to:

Success target	Review
• distinguish between a hard system and a soft system and describe how hard systems are embedded in soft systems;	hard systems are physical ones comprising action and reaction — we understand them largely through the physical sciences. A soft system involves people with intentionality and is difficult to predict. All hard systems are embedded in soft systems because it is people who ascribe functionality;
• describe the subjective, the inter-subjective and the objective;	subjective information is Popper's World 2 of the self. Perceptions which are shared are inter-subjective. Information built on these shared perceptions is in Popper's World 3 and is contained in all of the books in all of the libraries in the world and on the internet. It is objective in the sense that it exists outside any one individual but it may be true or false;

• relate the common perception of the term 'objective' to the process of measurement;	measurement is a process. The measurements of classical physics satisfy the four jointly sufficient conditions of repeatability and clarity. As these conditions are relaxed so the dependability of the measurement process diminishes. Common perception is to confuse 'objective' with highly dependable;
• describe the relationship between the truth and the dependability of information;	truth is obtained when information corresponds to the facts. It may only be demonstrated in a system through a defined meta-system. Truth is a sufficient condition for dependable information but is not necessary;
• state the four sufficient conditions for dependable information;	1. The repeatability of an experiment set up to test a proposition. 2. The repeatability of the state of the experiment. 3. The clarity of the state. 4. The repeatability of the magnitude;
• describe uncertainty in terms of FIR — Fuzziness, Incompleteness and Randomness;	uncertainty is fuzziness (imprecision of definition), incompleteness (how can we know what we do not know?) and randomness (lack of a specific pattern);
• think about the dependability of evidence;	realise that decision making requires the gathering of evidence from the past, present and future together with an assessment of its dependability;
• understand why there is a need to integrate hard and soft systems into one theory of process.	the distinction between the human and physical worlds has outlived its usefulness. The idea that humans are apart and quite separate from their physical environment is no longer tenable. They are integral. We are embedded in environmental processes. We need to deal with hard and soft systems as one.

We hope that we have reached our success targets for this chapter — please use the feedback form at the end of the book.

5. Rigour through practical foresight

5.1 The need for rigour

A framework for rethinking construction cannot be complete without addressing how we think about the future. We cannot any longer assume that the future looks similar to the past. We cannot assume that trends that we have come to recognise will continue. The rates of change and the demands on people to cope with the change are key elements in our systems. The intentions of people are both the primary force for success and at the roots of the future. Our route map based on the connectivity of people driven processes has provided a basis for mapping what we are doing and where we want to get to. We now need to develop some of the ways in which people can think their way to construction success rigorously through **practical foresight**.

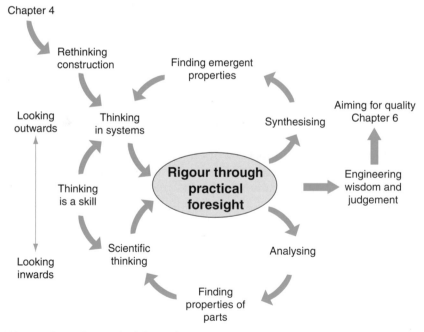

Fig. 5.1. Rigour through practical foresight

5.2 Targeting success for this chapter

The success targets for this chapter are that after reading it you will be able to:

- state how logical and scientific rigour is part of practical rigour (Fig. 5.1);
- describe the difference between scientific thinking and systems thinking;

- state how reflective practice is a theory of practical competence;
- contribute to a workshop to address a wicked set of problems;
- describe the relationship between creative and judgemental thinking and between analysis and synthesis.

We also hope that you will think that thinking is a skill that is worth practising whether you are a junior engineer, a company director, a student or a professor, old or young.

5.3 Rethinking construction

We have said that rethinking construction requires systems thinking. In the earlier chapters we focused on the central *systems* ideas of layers of interacting process holons. Now we ask you to think about *thinking* and how we may be able to process our ideas more effectively. We will set out the relationship between systems thinking, creative thinking, judgemental thinking and scientific thinking.

We agree with Edward de Bono (1971, 1976) who believes that thinking is a skill that can be developed whatever your academic prowess and whatever your age provided that you are willing to learn. In our observation there are clever people who are not effective thinkers and there are people who may not have passed academic examinations but who are very effective thinkers. We think that whatever your innate mental ability to process information it is always possible to improve your thinking skills.

There are many ways to contribute to the rethinking of construction and we all should try to appreciate and encourage a rich variety of them.

We have talked of wicked and messy problems and contrasted them with tame problems. We believe that wicked problems can be tackled only with some understanding of the tension between the long-standing academic notion of engineering as applied science and the way in which engineering is practised. Practitioners have always had to address the soft issues even though they have tended to do it implicitly and not explicitly. The improvements we have seen in our understanding of hard systems, through science, has left them dominated in practice by soft system issues.

Our behaviour is influenced by our culture and heritage. In order to think differently we need to examine just how the tradition of scientific enquiry is still strongly part of that culture and heritage. We need to explain how we see scientific enquiry as part of a wider discipline which Donald Schon (1983) called Reflective Practice. We need to point out that the traditional route of logical rational thinking (as exemplified through mathematics and science) is necessary but not sufficient for wicked problems. We need to examine just how this difference has inhibited the development of engineering into a fully fledged intellectual and rigorous practical discipline. We need to be able to recognise and reinforce the rigour of good practice.

Engineering is about doing and doing is a process

In the simplest of terms, scientific thinking is about knowing something but engineering is about creating something. Engineering is about planning, designing, constructing and operating complex systems — it is in the final analysis about *doing and doing is a process*. Of course, all of us recognise that in order to do anything we must know something — it is the classic chicken and egg problem (see Box 5.1). Of course, science is really also about the process of knowing, of establishing true and precise knowledge. Thus in science and in engineering both knowing and doing are inextricably bound together — in fact, so much so that the question 'Which comes first — knowing or doing?' becomes meaningless.

Box 5.1   **Principle**

To know you must do and to do you must know

So why is it that society — all of us — tends to value knowing more than doing? Simply it is because without knowledge the things we can do are limited. This is why we want our children to have a 'good education'. We believe that knowledge is the key to a happy and successful life. However, this has been, in western intellectual thought, taken to extreme — to the extent that knowing is considered to be so superior to doing that doing is relegated to an inferior status. Knowing is clever and done with clean hands. Doing is for the not so clever who get their hands dirty. Rational scientific knowing is logical and rigorous. Practice is non-rigorous and ad hoc.

We reject these views as mistaken. Rethinking construction requires us to challenge them. For example, the reason why practice is seen to be non-rigorous is that with any significant action there is normally significant uncertainty. This means that there is always a lack of fit between what we know and the consequences of what we can do. Construction problems are usually open world problems. The route to success requires us to manage the uncertainties, and the methods we use for managing them are often dismissed as ad hoc. Uncertainty, you will recall, consists of imprecise concepts (Fuzziness), much that we do not know and we do not know that we do not know (Incompleteness) and much that seems to have patterns only in populations of data (Randomness). The knowledge on which the action is based is often not as clear as it might be. In these cases, we have to exercise judgement. When people are found to have made mistakes their judgement is called into question. This is at the root of the general loss of confidence in 'the expert'. If we were instead to be able to celebrate the recognition of what we do not know about the future, it would allow us to manage it more effectively.

Practice can be as rigorous as theory — but in a different way — through systems thinking

A key idea in this chapter is that the rigour of practice is different from the rigour of science and the pursuit of truth. Rigour is the strict enforcement of rules to an end. Logical rigour in mathematics and science requires an exactness and adherence to logical rules that derives from the pursuit of strict truth. (For a detailed discussion in an engineering context see Blockley, 1980.) These same rules are important in practice too because, as we saw in Chapter 4, strict truth and precision are sufficient but not necessary for practice. As practitioners we are interested in dependable evidence which is actually the common sense interpretation of truth. **It is fortunate that strict truth and precision are not necessary for practice — for if it were, nothing would ever get done!**

There is a larger purpose in practice that is complex and uncertain, i.e. to deliver a system that is valued in a rich variety of ways. Practice requires a type of rational judgement that transcends the application of strict logical rules. It requires creative and judgemental thinking which is rational and logical but can, at the same time, create practical solutions despite the limitations of our understanding. It requires the choice of appropriate models of understanding that can *create* a vision of what is needed and then successfully *create* a practical solution that meets the need. Practical rigour requires **creative foresight** and **analysis of hindsight**.

The possible **unintended consequences** of human decision and action are legion and the rigour of practice is about anticipating and managing them. The values associated with success in science are clear cut — truth and precision — whereas the values associated with success in construction are many and various, hard and soft and often difficult to measure.

Practical rigour is required to meet the unceasing and unyielding demands of the actual physical and human world to satisfy the purpose. Gravity, wind, snow, rain and other natural forces are hard task masters. Likewise, in an increasingly competitive world so are customers, clients and employers. To meet them requires creative diligence and **duty of care** to shoulder responsibility so that no stone is unturned and only the practicable minimum is left to chance. Since no system is totally predictable and we do not know everything about everything, judgements have to be made and carried through. Practical rigour requires wise foresight to anticipate what can go wrong and put it right before the consequences are serious. Sloppy and slipshod thinking has no part in practical rigour, but since there is inevitably a lack of fit between theory and practice, sensible approximations have to be made and appropriate models chosen. Every practical possibility has to be considered and every reasonable precaution has to be taken. Measured risks have to be taken. Practical rigour has to be creative in making the vision and in thinking of what can go wrong with the potential solutions.

Practical rigour is a rigour of the open world where uncertainty is profound. Practical rigour is therefore much richer in concept than scientific and logical rigour. In fact, the latter is a subset because it is about completeness of rigour in a closed world. Scientific rigour requires selective inattention to the difficulties that it cannot yet address. Practical rigour does not have that luxury — it must include everything that is relevant. Practical rigour requires the management of incompleteness. Strict logical rigour is usually only possible if incompleteness is left out of the model.

5.4 Thinking as a skill

We need to have open-minded thinking about open world problems

At the end of Chapter 3, we showed that it is quite natural, when thinking in terms of process holons, to look outwards to systems in which your process is a part and to look inwards to sub-systems in which your process is a whole.

We can do this, therefore, for the construction industry as a whole. We will also do this in Chapter 7 when we discuss customer/client focus. Looking outwards we can see that the experiences and lessons learned by other industries ought to be understood and assimilated as they impact on the construction industry. Of course, that does not imply that these experiences are simply and directly transferable any more than the experiences and lessons learned by a personal friend are transferable to another at an individual level. However, they can often be adapted and interpreted to our benefit.

What is required is an open-minded willingness to look for new ideas and lessons — it is central to sustainable development both at a personal level and collectively as an industry.

This, however, does require time and effort that may seem, at least in the particular and in the short term, not to have a real payback and therefore to be not worth doing. However, in the totality, looking at the whole and in the longer term, the investment may well be essential for success in a privatised industry.

Such investment requires a budget which, for the industry as a whole, is the collective research and development budget. In the UK, but not in Japan, this investment is very small and too small for long-term sustainability.

Thus the first requirement for thinking about thinking is to have an open mind which is receptive to new ideas — not uncritically receptive — but one that is willing to put effort, time and resource into examining the most promising ones. It is a matter of mind set.

Everything depends upon our point of view

As we have said earlier, everything we think and do depends upon our point of view, it depends upon the way in which we look at the world. Philosophers often call this our 'Weltanschauung' or our world view. We attribute meaning to something by interpreting it in the light of our experience and education. However, as social anthropologists would point out, our world view is also formed through the culture of the society in which we live. Thus the same issue will tend to be formulated as an economic problem by an economist, as a technical problem by an engineer, as a costing problem by a quantity surveyor, as a creative problem by an architect and as a social problem by a sociologist. Each world view may be quite valid in that it may be internally consistent and that propositions may be deduced from it that correspond with the facts. Box 5.2 and Fig. 1.4.

Road construction is an example of the way different groups can perceive the same issue. As construction professionals, we need to get ourselves recognised as the means by which environmental sustainability is achieved — rather than as the enemy to be fought at the sites of the by-pass at Newbury or the runway at Manchester.

We are changing the way we think about engineering practice

In the minds of many, engineering is an applied science. Others would argue that it is about designing artefacts. Many practitioners would argue that engineering is about managing projects to successful conclusions. Systems thinkers would say that engineering is about managing systems and business people would argue that it is about sustainable business. These are all views about the same thing — engineering (Fig. 5.2).

However, from all points of view logical rational thinking has to be one of the most important ways of thinking.

- Engineering as **Applied Science**
- Engineering as **Designing an artefact**
- Engineering as **Managing a project**
- Engineering as **Managing a system**
- Engineering as **Sustainable business**
  — in **harmony** with the environment
  — **integrating people** and **things**

Fig. 5.2 Some views of engineering

Box 5.2   Views about an integrated transport proposal   Example

An Environmental Terrorist: 'My mission is to be seen to be benefiting the environment, I don't care whether transport is integrated or not as long as I can get publicity for my cause by disrupting its construction.'

A Pensioner: 'I can't drive a car and find getting up and down stairs very difficult. If the buses met the trains then I would not have to wait in the cold. I could take a few presents when I go to see my grandchildren.'

A Politician: 'I have got to be seen to do something about the jams on the M25. Perhaps we could build a very large park and ride scheme. Provided everything links up we could be less than an hour from the city and attracting investment in jobs for my voters.'

A Civil Servant: 'How can we avoid being made to look silly when:
- we do not have the public transport system to start to touch the problem
- it is politically difficult to invest or mortgage public money to build it
- if it is a PPP (Public Private Partnership) project and contractors make a decent profit a select committee will slate us
- to do nothing will cause bigger and bigger environmentally damaging traffic jams'

A Customer: 'It is no good integrating the tubes and the buses when I want to take the laundry to Edna. I would not be seen dead carrying her smalls through the central station in the rush hour. In any case the roads are so jammed and the trains so late that it takes all day to get there and back. I think I will stick to my car — at least I can talk to Edna, on the car phone, when I am in a jam.'

A Transport Operator: 'Yes, integrating transport modes could be a good idea if they would cut out the red tape. How can I invest in a bus station here when it will take longer than the length of my railway franchise to get through the planning process and buy Woolworths next door, let alone get a pay back on my investment.'

A Construction Programme Manager: 'If only somebody would tell me what they want designed and built; I could get on and get it done on programme and to budget. Instead I get it in the neck because they keep changing their minds so costs keep escalating and programme keeps slipping. How can I keep my designers to a lump sum if the variation orders are more than the original contract. No wonder it is a shambles.'

Designer: ' It is sad really, we had to bid this lump sum at below cost knowing that the last thing we could afford to do was come up with a bright idea that delivered integrated transport. Our profitability depends on maximising the variations. We had a good idea. It involved building a passenger transport interchange as a bridge over the railway. We could have had minimal environmental impact and extra revenue from shops. We could have had better customer experience because we could have integrated the information system in the shops with the signalling to make waiting time useful. However, it will cost more to design and so to propose it would be like a turkey voting for Christmas!'

Do you know how the stakeholders see your proposal? Have you asked them?

Logical rational thinking makes sense

We value logical rational thinking because it makes sense. It can be shared and through it we can obtain agreement. It provides the clarity that we seek. It is unsurprising therefore that it is the basis of science and hard systems. It is the basis of much that we do. There is no sense in which it should be rejected — but it has to be seen as necessary but not sufficient to deal with wicked and messy problems. The rational decision making process (Box 5.3) and problem solving process (Box 5.4) are well known. However, these models have one fundamental flaw — they encourage linear thinking.

Box 5.3   Making a decision   **Explanation**

1.   Define the problem
2.   Gather the facts
3.   Get various possible solutions/alternatives/scenarios
4.   Evaluate them
5.   Select a solution/Make a choice
6.   Implement the chosen solution
7.   Follow up
8.   Check the consequences
9.   Review
10. Redefine the problem — go to 1.

They give the impression that thinking your way through a problem step by step is a linear process and, of course, is only the best way if you know the sort of answer you expect before you start! Figures 2.16 and 5.3 are the 'rich pictures' which, as we have seen, give more of the flavour of the loopy nature of decision making.

Fig. 5.3. Problem solving

Box 5.4	Problem solving	Explanation
1.	Define the problem	needs judgement
2.	Set up theoretical model	needs judgement
3.	Deduce the results	needs logical deduction
4.	Interpret the meaning	needs judgement
5.	Make a choice	suspend criticism for a moment
6.	Take action	needs judgement
7.	Evaluate feedback	needs judgement
8.	Redefine problem	go to 1

We cannot always get it right first time

Of course, if we have a tame problem where we know what we want and we have planned our route to success, then we should aim to complete every process 'right first time'. This is the famous maxim of the quality movement. However, when faced with a wicked and messy problem the maxim has to be seen in a different context. We have to see that it applies to each process. However, part of each high level process is deciding what the lower level processes are. We cannot therefore get those right until we have sorted out what we are aiming at in that higher process. So first we have to get the strategy right — the big picture. Then we have to manage that high level process and as we address the issues we design the lower level processes. These processes will include workshops and public meetings and new issues will emerge as the process unfolds. We also need to manage the connectivity between the various processes so that information is exchanged between the process owners in the most effective manner. In other words, we evolve a process model and enact it as the high level process is carried out. Thus we should not think of the process model as static and unchanging — it is dynamic and constantly changing as the higher level processes delegate and accept the outputs from the lower processes.

Think effectively

Edward de Bono has written about the educational trinity of knowledge, intelligence and thinking (Box 5.5). As we have said earlier, his basic thesis is that thinking is much more than 'intelligence in action' — it is a skill that can be developed (Box 5.6).

Thinking is the deliberate exploration of experience for a purpose. Thinking is about finding the patterns in our brains that we talked about in the last chapter.

Box 5.5	Educational trinity (de Bono)	Explanation
Knowledge		the basic material of thinking
Intelligence		an innate quality of speed and extent of processing in the brain
Thinking		the operating skill through which intelligence acts
(de Bono, 1976)		

> **Box 5.6**   **Principle**
>
> ### Thinking is a skill that can be developed

If we lock into the wrong patterns we make mistakes. We need a large repertoire of patterns in order that we can think widely. We perceive, we reflect and we act. Excellence of logic does not make up for bad perception. It is clear that bad logic leads to bad thinking but it is not the case that good logic necessarily leads to good thinking. A line of argument without logical error is not necessarily right, it is just consistent with the starting point. Edward de Bono also identified an 'Intelligence trap' (Box 5.7).

Box 5.7   **The intelligence trap**   **Explanation**

Intelligent people may construct a rational well argued case — and then become trapped by it.

Verbal fluency should not be confused with good thinking.

Ego, self-image, is often based on intelligence and the need to be right.

The critical use of intelligence tends to be more immediately satisfying than the constructive use — negative.

Intelligent people often prefer reactive thinking — real life demands pro-active thinking.

A quick mind jumps to a solution from only a few signals, a slower mind may produce better solutions.

Intelligent people sometimes prefer cleverness to wisdom.

(de Bono, 1976)

Box 5.8   **Effective thinking**   **Explanation**

An effective thinker has a sense of purpose. He is:

- confident but humble — not that he will always be right but that he can turn it on to anything he wants;
- in control — not just drifting along ;
- clear about what he wants to do — clear focus, clear overview;
- prefers wisdom over cleverness;
- is robust and practical when required — does not wallow in nit picking or indecision;
- can appreciate achievement, if any, and is thinking of what is next;
- thinks about thinking — thinks thinking is worth practising — sees arrogance as a major sin.

(de Bono, 1976)

Box 5.9 Some thinking aids	Explanation
Ask who, what, why, how, where and when	
PMI	Plus, Minus, Interesting points
APC	Alternatives, Possibilities, Choices
CAF	Consider All Factors
N&S	Is it Necessary and is it Sufficient for our purpose?
C & S	Consequence and Sequel
FI–FO	Information In–Information Out
EBS	Examine Both Sides
ADI	Agreement, Disagreement, Irrelevance
OPV	Other People's Views
HV, LV	High Values, Low Values
TEC	Target, Expand/Explore, Contract/Conclude
(de Bono, 1976)	

Think creatively

Some people think that creative thought is the province of only a few gifted people. We believe that this view is mistaken. We believe it does not recognise the creativity that we all have to use in our daily lives. If we practice we can become more creative than we would otherwise be. Of course, there are some people who are naturally more creative than others — but that is not to deny that we can all improve. Again, in this section we want to bring out two basic ideas and to point the interested reader into the literature. Creative thinking skills help us to develop practical foresight.

There is some disagreement about whether creativity declines as one gets older (Box 5.10). We certainly know some over 70 year olds who are more creative than some 20 year olds. We suspect that creative thinking results from an attitude of mind irrespective of age.

Data are sets of patterns. We have said that we can think of our thought processes as the matching of sets of patterns. Thus the more a person treats data which look to have nothing to do with each other as though they are related,

Box 5.10 Creativity	Explanation
'Imagination is more important than knowledge'	*Einstein*
'Man's body is faulty, his mind untrustworthy, but his imagination has made him remarkable'	*John Masefield*
'Imagination grows by exercise and contrary to common belief is more powerful in the mature than in the young'	*Somerset Maugham*
'Experience takes away more than it adds. Young people are nearer ideas than old people'	*Plato*

the more likely he is to make data combinations which are unusual (i.e. to think creatively). The kind of person who codes in this way is called a wide categoriser while the opposite kind of person is a narrow categoriser (Box 5.11).

Box 5.11   Width of categorisation   Theory

People who make fine distinctions between bits of input and who require high levels of similarity before they can see relationships (narrow categorisers) are inclined to store information as though it consists of a large number of relatively unrelated bits. Thus, they are less likely to make the kind of cognitive leap involved in creative thinking. On the other hand, a willingness to treat two pieces of data where connections are not immediately apparent, as roughly equivalent, is favourable to the appearance of creativity. Thus creative thinking can be related to the width of categorising. Unfortunately it seems that engineering has attracted students who naturally tend to be narrow categorisers. This is unfortunate because the best engineers and indeed all professionals clearly need to have creative skills. We therefore have to help those who are narrow categorisers to work on the skill of widening their categorising skills when needed, i.e. to nurture their creative skills. The sterile antagonism that can exist between architects, quantity surveyors and engineers often arises because each will not recognise the value that is added by the combination of broad and narrow categorising skills.

Box 5.12   Engineering creativity   **Principle**

Engineering is an art as well as a science.

To maintain competitive advantage we must value and nurture both skill sets in the whole engineer because much of the value he can add comes from integrating the skills.

Thinking together — practical design of workshops

There is one golden rule in developing creative thinking: **keep creative and judgemental thinking apart** (Boxes 2.2 and 5.13). All of the techniques for developing creative thought (for example brainstorming) depend upon this rule.

We have learned that systematic risk management is much more effective if it is undertaken as an opportunity risk management workshop in at least two sessions. The gap should be between the forming, storming (creative identification) processes and the norming, performing (judgemental assessment) processes. The reflection that takes place after storming is often very productive — it is therefore a good idea to allow sufficient time for this to happen.

Adding value through effective thinking

The value that can be added through effective thinking is clear. Wicked problems cannot be solved without open-minded creativity to generate new ideas. However, new ideas have to be critically examined because they must be practicable and they must deliver the purpose. Keeping creative thinking and judgemental thinking apart is critical to success. Construction players need both skills — or at least the teams that support processes need them in appropriate degrees.

Box 5.13   **Keep creative and judgmental thinking apart   Principles**

- Creativity requires positive thinking.
- Creative thinking requires blame free reporting, all ideas are wanted and will be captured.
- Anybody can have a good idea.
- The reception of an idea, however unlikely or seemingly impracticable, may promote the generation of another one.
- Negative reactions suppress creative thinking.
- Almost any idea can be shown to be wrong and sometimes the proof is so convincing that all further thought is discarded.
- Judgement requires analytical thinking which is negative. 'What's wrong with this?'
- Analytical thinking is very important to establish dependable and useful conclusions. However, it stifles creative thought.
- Keep the creative thought processes and the judgemental thought processes quite separate.

Box 5.14   **Notes on the design of creative   Explanation
              thinking workshops**

1. Creative workshops should be limited to about eight people; workshops to obtain consensus may have to be larger.
2. The purpose is to generate a wide range of ideas to meet an objective and to generate consensus on the merits of the ideas and actions needed.
3. You need a facilitator to act as chairperson, recorder and catalyst. Often the facilitator needs an assistant who acts as a scribe writing down all of the ideas on a flip chart or similar.
4. The role of the facilitator is to design the workshop process, to introduce or identify the objectives, promote discussion and, where relevant, to attempt by the end to obtain consensus.
5. The facilitator should try to ensure that nobody feels threatened because they challenge a position.
6. Keep a focus on principle and try to avoid people taking positions.
7. It is often useful to demonstrate the 'shape' of the expected output, e.g. a risk register or a fault tree.
8. It is often useful to break the session into four stages:

   Forming: asking leading questions, getting the issues into the open;
   Storming: asking opening questions, promoting new ideas, brainstorming;
   Norming: summarising, promoting mutual understanding, moving to a basis for solution;
   Performing: finding solutions, fulfilling objectives.

9. It is important to get people to understand that consensus is only possible if difficulties are brought out into the open and faced up to — though this can sometimes itself be extremely difficult the effort is usually worthwhile even if all that is achieved is improved mutual understanding.

   Some tips
   Approach: Recognise many people have preconceived ideas, try to bring them out, air them and accept them if possible. The facilitator should have a struc-
   continued

Box 5.14 continued

tured approach in mind as a basis for moving forward — but needs to be flexible and responsive.

Make ideas explicit: Show acceptance of suggestions by writing them down. Structure flip charts into categories. Use open questions.

When stuck: Humour is a good way to break the ice. Use your eyes to invite contributions from quieter members of the group — still waters often run deep! If the topic is too complicated break it down into sub-holons.

Make progress: If you fall behind then increase pressure for answers. Do not break into sub-groups just for the sake of progress — they are likely to become unbalanced.

Sub-groups and plenary sessions: These are useful where workshops are large. Over about 6–8 people, output is usually reduced in proportion to the number of people in the group.

Handling conflict: Differences of opinion must not be taken personally. These should be seen as helpful to generate new ideas. Keep positive and confident. Always respond quickly to criticism. Avoid voting — you want consensus. Be hard on the problem and soft on the people.

**Box 5.15   It is more productive to address success   Principle
            before failure.**

Address success first because:

- we all want to be successful and we want to be part of it;
- the realisation of what constitutes success motivates creative thinking;
- it usually causes a workshop or team to start thinking together, understanding each other;
- it creates a realisation of interdependence in mutual benefit, which promotes co-operation;
- it creates commitment and promotes consensus;
- it provides us with a stake in the purpose.

Then address what could prevent success, i.e. risks, threats, obstructions, because:

- people are now committed to success so need to know what prevents it;
- identifying risk is seen as a necessary and creative process;
- it promotes lateral thinking and recognition of uncertainty (see FIR Chapter 4).

Note:

The principle is supported by other less formalised processes such as **SWOT** Analysis: **S**trengths before **W**eaknesses, **O**pportunities before **T**hreats. Similarly, in an analysis of needs the requirements for success are addressed before the obstructions to success. Since the lack of a requirement is an obstruction, it is interesting to note that in workshops we usually get twice as many requirements as obstructions. People normally try to be positive in workshops.

Box 5.16   Brainstorming risks to a major railway project.   Example

A large railway company had a major project at the feasibility stage. The views of the legal, the business, the operations and the marketing departments were seriously out of step. The Programme Manager needed consensus before a critical Board Meeting. A workshop was required to identify and assess the risks to the project to meet corporate procedures. The Project Manager decided that a risk workshop involving all the disparate factions would solve his problem. He invited 27 people!

A questionnaire was used to get some advanced understanding of the perception of the issues. The workshop started in a bad mood caused by a major signal failure on the railway delaying eight participants. Twenty eventually turned up of whom seven were deputies. The first session to identify risks was like pulling teeth! Experience suggested that it would be difficult to fulfil the purpose of the workshop!

One of the pre-questions sought to identify what actions would eliminate the risks. One person had responded: 'Don't do the project!'. The facilitator suggested that this was in fact the only **correct** answer! He said that we could add value by accepting this answer as complete and going home! Suddenly everybody was arguing about why the project was needed. After a short break the workshop was reorganised as a success-targeting workshop.

- How will we know we are successful?
- What are the key performance indicators and targets?
- What are the requirements for success?
- What are the obstructions to success?
- What actions are needed to ensure success?

The Programme Manager got his consensus, a list of the strategic risks, a set of key performance indicators and targets and a strategic implementation plan. His recommendation to proceed was accepted by the Board.

The participants in the workshop were delighted because they had enjoyed themselves. It had exceeded their expectations. They had been successful.

5.5   Looking outwards — synthesising the overview

Systems thinking enables us to do many things

Systems thinking helps us to get the big picture — to get the overview — and then relate it to the detail. By looking outwards from your systems and thinking in terms of process holons we can describe our systems *at any level of definition* and we can do it in practical terms by describing what actually is being done or is required to be done. We ask the basic questions of what, why, who, when, where and how and we can fit them together into one coherent picture — the whole — while at the same time having a handle on the parts. We can keep a sense of overall balance.

Then by building our process holons at different levels of description we can cut through the complexity like a knife. We focus on each process holon and its interactions with other process holons and we do it at a level which makes sense and is appropriate.

This big picture helps to motivate people through a shared vision. It helps to create foresight. It helps people to focus on the purpose and then to be constantly thinking back from that future to decide what needs to be done today. Systems thinking can connect the big picture to the practical detail.

We can recognise wicked problems, we can name and then describe the process holons within them. We look for those sub-processes that will respond to tame solutions. We are able to see that all hard systems are embedded in soft ones and we can handle it.

Synthesise holistic gain through creative thinking

We can also recognise the unique nature of synthesis. We are able to recognise that some properties emerge from the co-operation of sub-systems and so the relationships between various points of view and various representations of the systems are compatible and make sense. Synthesis that produces the emergent properties that surpass our expectations is the essence of creativity (Box 5.17). This we call holistic gain (as it comes from an understanding of emergent properties) to provide a win–win solution.

Box 5.17   Providing client delight — holistic gain   Example

A client wanted a new building. He did not really know what he wanted. The design team came up with a rather pedestrian solution which the client rather reluctantly accepted since he was persuaded it was all that was possible. One of the design team then came up with an impelling proposition which pleased the client greatly. The idea was simply that the building should be refreshing. The team analysed the concept as a hierarchy of process holons with success targets. They tested their solution against the success targets for each one by mental simulation and found that their proposal was not at all refreshing. They set to work to evolve the design such that the success criteria were reasonably well satisfied in almost all of the processes. The new design, with no budget increase, delighted the client and his customers whose expectations were exceeded.

We recognise the importance of dependable measurement — even in soft systems. We exercise a duty of care based on a strong sense of ethics (Chapter 6) to make judgements with practical rigour where the uncertainty is significant.

We see, by focusing on process, how many different aspects of complex systems (quality, values, risk, etc.) relate directly to what we actually do. We keep the social interactions working since we depend upon teamwork to reach success targets. We appreciate the importance of vision, clear objectives and success targets.

We see the context in which we wish to use science. This gives us the capacity to use it wisely as we shall discuss later. So it is the analytical approach of the scientific method to which we now turn.

5.6   Looking inwards — analysing the parts

Scientific thinking is necessary but not sufficient

Schon (1983) defined technical rationality (TR) as instrumental problem solving (i.e. based on technique) made rigorous by the application of scientific theory and technique. It is the underpinning idea behind what most of us were taught in our undergraduate technical education — as engineers or architects or other construction players. Technical rationality is a hard systems approach as discussed in Chapter 4.

Engineering science has been very successful but the wicked problems are showing

The knowledge of a professional is based on theory (almost entirely TR hard systems) but honed through years of experience of dealing with these hard systems embedded in soft systems. Engineering education has for many years been based on a reductionist TR approach where the behaviour of the whole is explained from the behaviour of the parts separately. Thus, for example, we consider a civil engineering structure to be made up of simple elements, beams and columns, etc., that we then proceed to analyse quite separately from those to which it is connected. However, we know that a particular beam or column is connected to others so there has to be a way of recognising that in the calculations. Thus we are taught to think of the load paths in the structure. Loads sit on floor slabs that sit on beams that react on columns that react on foundations that react on the ground. Sometimes those elements are designed quite separately from each other, especially if they require different skills such as when the foundations are designed by a geotechnical engineer separately from the superstructure designed by a structural engineer.

More modern analytical techniques, using the power of digital computing, enabled us to begin to see the connectivity in a structure. Finite elements connected together through large matrix equations allow us to model the systematic effects. Nevertheless, the basic approach is reductionist. In that respect it is perhaps analogous to the Iron Bridge at Coalbrookdale. Here a new material (cast iron) was used in an old form (an arch bridge). As we explored the new material, new forms of bridge evolved. There are many similar historical examples. In order to see the systematic emergent properties from a finite element analysis we will need to use the systems approach — we will need to conceive the finite element from within a systems approach. That is exactly how the idea behind the Interacting Objects Process Model (Box 2.6) is evolving.

Technical rationality has been enormously successful in advancing scientific knowledge over the past three hundred years. The whole of our modern technology is based on it. However, there are problems with it — the wicked and messy ones that do not succumb! As we pointed out in Chapter 1, a specific example is simply the number of failures that do occur (Box 5.18).

Clearly, individual failure cases merit individual enquiry to establish what went wrong and the lessons to be learned. However, it is clear that human error, whether at an individual level or at an organisational level, is a major factor; in the sense, of course, that in any engineering project all error is human error, because it is people who plan, design, produce and use the product. As we have said, all engineering technical processes are embedded in soft systems processes. Engineers and technologists in their quest to discover ways of organising nature, and flushed with their successes in the physical sciences, have perhaps rather neglected the extent to which they rely on human infallibility.

Applied science is necessary but not sufficient for practice

What is taught reflects, on the whole, our collective understanding of 'things as they are'. The notion of engineering as 'applied science' is a strong one and with

> **Box 5.18   Failures result from wicked problems   Principle**
>
> Are the underlying reasons for failures just 'Acts of God', technical errors of some kind, or human mistakes?
>
> When is 'failure' actually an outcome of a reasonable risk taken to gain a benefit?
>
> Failures often are the outcome of not coming to terms with a wicked and messy problem.

that notion comes reductionism. It is necessary but not sufficient for successful practice.

The reductionist scientific approach of TR seeks to be practitioner independent or objective — but what we really want is to be sure we have the condition for making our knowledge testable and hence dependable (see Chapter 4). The concepts and relations in TR are written in an abstract generalised form to make it independent of context. Quantification through measurement is crucially important.

Engineering science does not recognise incompleteness

The scientific methodology of TR is one of 'selective inattention'. Thus the approach is the well-known one that, given a difficult issue (e.g. the behaviour of a welded beam):

- we look to see what aspects of it are important;
- we idealise out the difficult bits until we get something that we can isolate;
- we test it in order to get a functional relationship.

This is what is meant by selective inattention. Thus the difficulties of weld quality, and the factors affecting that, would be selected out of the first attempts to understand the behaviour of the beam. Then as we build an understanding of these simpler bits we bring in the complicating factors (such as weld quality) and we rapidly find it almost impossible to derive a functional relationship. We get instead a 'plum pudding' graph or a many to many mapping. Nevertheless, by deriving some complex formulae we attempt to express relationships involving the major factors. However, we are rarely able to include the really important softer issues in such functional expressions.

Thus selective inattention and TR are becoming increasingly inadequate in today's increasingly complex world. In many cases the factors that just cannot be cast into any theoretical formulation (such as sociological, psychological, political and cultural considerations) may be the ones that most influence a solution — especially for engineering infrastructure projects. There is therefore a need for an approach that integrates the outputs of systems and scientific processes of thinking — one that emerges from the practice of engineering itself.

5.7   Reflective practice

This term was first introduced by Schon (1983) in a discussion concerning the role of professionals and the need to define practical competence. Reflective practice is practical rigour — it is the way in which professionals do their work. They perceive the world, they reflect upon it and they act. They do it with rigour, wisdom and foresight.

Schon was concerned with such questions as 'What is the prevailing culture of the professions? To what extent is there rigour in engineering practice? Why is it that professionals often seem to know more than they can articulate (i.e. have tacit knowledge)? Is there a crisis of confidence in the professions?'

Construction professionals are educated as scientists but work as reflective practitioners

There is a tension between the scientific training that most construction professionals get and the way they have to practice. We are taught that truth and precision are the ultimate values but we find in practice that they are rarely available. Consequently, we feel a basic inadequacy which manifests itself in phrases such as 'I'm only a practitioner' or 'I'm only a mere engineer'. The values that we use in practice are rarely those of truth and precision (after all even Newtonian mechanics is no longer thought to be true in the strict scientific sense). The values we use are much richer and more varied as we shall examine in Chapter 6.

Box 5.19   The role of universities   Theory

Nowadays the culture of most professionals is formed through the education and training they receive at university. Schon pointed out that universities are, for the most part, committed to technical rationality (TR). He maintained that the professions paid a heavy intellectual price for being successfully incorporated, over the last century, into the universities. He quotes Thorston Veblen as saying in 1918, 'The universities have a higher mission to fit men for a life of science and scholarship and they are accordingly concerned with such discipline only as will give efficiency in the pursuit of knowledge, whereas the lower schools are concerned with instilling such knowledge and habits as will make their pupils fit citizens of the world in whatever position in the fabric of workday life they may fall.'

Technical rationality is embedded in our institutional context, it governs our understanding of the relationship between research and practice, it forms the norms of the curriculum of professional education. By this culture, researchers are supposed to supply the basic and applied science from which the techniques for practical problem solving are derived. The researcher's role is therefore considered to be superior because it is perceived as being more rigorous. The rule is that rigorous basic and applied science comes first followed by the less rigorous skills required to apply that knowledge to real world practice. Notice that not only are these latter skills secondary, they are often not considered knowledge at all.

(Schon, 1990)

There is a growing crisis of confidence in the professions

So what is the problem with our present culture? There seems to be a growing crisis of confidence in the professions. Consider three examples where the trust of lay people in experts has been damaged. Firstly, there have been financial scandals where people in the City have used their specialist knowledge and positions for personal gain; that is a question of ethics. Secondly, there have been some major technological failures such as Chernobyl and the Challenger which illustrate that even technical experts can get things wrong; that is a question of technical competence. Thirdly, experts disagree in public about some difficult phenomena such as BSE, genetically modified food, the causes of heart disease or environmental pollution; these are questions concerning the limits to what we know. In a culture where science is supposed to provide all of the answers, the lay person can be forgiven for losing confidence in the professionals.

A consequence of this is that there is a growing questioning of the rights and freedoms of the professions. Their licence to determine who shall be allowed to practise is rooted in deeper questions of their professional claims to have 'extraordinary knowledge', and this depends upon our understanding of the nature of knowledge and its relationship with practical competence.

Science is usually portrayed as objective and value free. In Chapter 4, we examined the idea of objectivity and saw that the key to this is actually testability and measurement. We will examine value systems, i.e. the 'worth' we give to something and how we measure it in Chapter 6. Practitioners are frequently embroiled in conflicts of values, goals, purposes and interests. For example, a central difficulty in engineering design is the balance between safety and cost. However, by thinking about that balance more strategically it is often possible to get both because safety is good business. As Senge (1990) puts it, 'You can have your cake and eat it too — but not at once' (Boxes 3.7, 3.8). The reason we fall into this trap is because we tend to look at issues using a 'snapshot' rather than process thinking. Safety, quality and hence cost reductions actually go hand in hand, and far from being alternatives they can in the overall process bring significant savings.

Schon wrote that in solving wicked problems and messes the professional uses 'reflection in action' a kind of knowing inherent in intelligent action. Skilful action depends upon more that the practitioner can articulate. The question is whether these skills are in any sense inferior to the rigour of TR, the scientific approach.

Knowledge alone does not impart capability

Elms (1989) has argued that engineering education tends, for the most part, to concentrate on the giving of knowledge (rather, as one of our colleagues once said, like pouring water into a jug!). Knowledge alone does not impart capability. An engineer must necessarily be technically competent and knowledge is clearly part of that.

However, there are people with a great deal of knowledge but who are not good engineers.

Capability is something more stable, more endurable than knowledge, but tends to be acquired almost incidentally as a by-product of obtaining knowledge. Senge (1990) talks in terms of personal mastery (Box 3.12 and Chapter 8). However, people have argued that these skills cannot (should not) be taught in a university since they rely on personal skills and require the incentive of real responsibility. One of the most fundamental reasons why engineering capability is not taught is that the very nature of engineering is poorly understood. It is fundamentally different from science, since science is truth-oriented and engineering is goal-oriented. Science uses words such as true/false while engineers are concerned with the quality of a solution and use words such as good/bad or better/worse. Engineering researchers are more likely to be looking at 'how' to do something rather than whether something is true/false. At a very fundamental level the very discipline of philosophy is concerned with knowledge and its methodology is aligned with mathematics and science and that is why it is perhaps inappropriate for engineering. The basic flaw in the scientific method is that it deals with what is true/false only and appears not to care about the use of knowledge for good or ill. Such a lack has obvious ethical implications and may indeed be a major cause of some of the major ills of the world. Scientific knowledge is being neither produced responsibly nor used responsibly if it is regarded as being independent of any values. Wisdom is a combination of knowledge and values.

Wisdom engineering is the way we look at things

Where is the life we have lost in living?
Where is the wisdom we have lost in knowledge?
Where is the knowledge we have lost in information?

The Rock by T.S. Eliot (1934)

Elms (1989) argued that wisdom is more than a matter of action and good decision making. Rather it is a quality of the way of looking at things; it is the ability to see the world clearly in a coherent picture. The clarity is simple but not simplistic and depends upon strong underlying conceptual models.

Box 5.20   Wisdom engineering   **Explanation**

'A wise person has to have knowledge, ethicalness and appropriate skills to a high degree. There also has to be an appropriate attitude; an ability to cut through complexity and to see the goals and aims, the fundamental essentials in a problem situation and to have the will and purpose to keep these clearly in focus. It is to do with finding simplicity in complexity. More fundamentally it is to do with world views and the way in which the person constructs the world in which they operate; which is to say, in engineering, that wisdom is to do with having appropriate conceptual models to fit the situation.'

David Elms (1989)

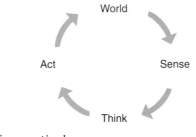

Fig. 5.4. The reflective practice loop

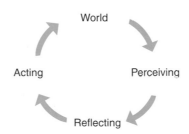

Fig. 5.5. The processes of the reflective practice loop

Box 5.21	Practical intelligence based on Reflective Practice (RP)	Theory

Practice is often held in low academic esteem because it lacks a theoretical basis to provide the rigour. Practice is often seen as merely a collection of particular activities. We will not attempt to produce a full formalism for reflective practice here because that is not the purpose of this book. However, we will present the basic flavour which is the systems approach. We include it here, not because the ideas themselves are important to the practice of engineering, but because we want to develop our understanding of practical competence. Through a deeper understanding of the relationship between knowing and doing, we need it to set the deeper context for rethinking construction and tackling difficult concepts such as engineering judgement and establishing the rigour of professional practice.

The objective of a Reflective Practitioner is to produce 'something' with specific qualities. The 'something' will have an objective existence (in Popper's World 3), e.g. a physical artefact such as a bridge, systems such as an organisation or the expression of a theory in a natural or formal language. The meaning of that objective existence will depend on each person's world view expressed in terms of qualities. The 'something' that the RP produces is a product of a process and indeed the product is itself a new process. If we are successful then the product will fulfil the purpose of the process.

Reflective Practice is by definition dependent on both **practitioner** and **context**. Problem solving is seen as a process. The grounding of the process (the basic concept on which the process is based) is dependability, as we discussed in Chapter 4. Correspondence between the model and the reality may only be approximate (as appropriate) but it must dependably have the required qualities, dictated by its purpose, such as functionality, economy, safety and serviceability. The emphasis is not on having models which are true, accurate and precise, but on a continuous comparison of the model with the reality to lead to a greater understanding of the reality, and proper control of the process to steer a course to success.

The idea of **responsibility** is central to Reflective Practice. The Reflective Practitioner is aware of the limitations of his knowledge and skills and is also very aware of his duties owed both to clients and to other stakeholders such as the general public. Thus the Reflective Practitioner is not concerned principally with the truth of a theory or model, rather he is concerned with his responsibility to act on the basis of the theory or model. The taking of responsibility implies not that one has earned the right to be right or even sufficiently right but that one has taken precautions that one can reasonably be expected to take against being wrong. The RP has a **duty of care** to fulfil a role.

Practical intelligence emerges from the reflective practice loop

As we saw in Chapter 2 we represent human activities as a hierarchy of problem solving processes. In overview the problem solving loop is simply this: we perceive the state of the world (the senses) as sets of patterns in the brain (these patterns may be chemical, electrical, biological, etc., it matters not for this purpose), we interpret our perceptions (think/reflect), we act upon the world (behave) and finally we perceive a new state of the world.

continued

Box 5.21 continued
The RP loop is Fig. 5.4:

$$world \rightarrow sense \rightarrow think \rightarrow act \rightarrow world$$

or in other words a set of processes Fig. 5.5

$$being\ in\ the\ world \rightarrow perceiving \rightarrow reflecting \rightarrow acting \rightarrow being\ in\ the\ world.$$

Our human needs are also patterns which may be in-built or learned. Problems are the result of mismatching patterns. The world (outside of us, i.e. Popper's Worlds 1 and 3 — Fig. 4.2) changes through our actions and we therefore have a new set of perceptions and the loop is repeated. Our attention is the focus of our perceptions and is controlled by the very processes of the hierarchically structured set of processes occurring at different levels of definition and hence understanding. These processes are all occurring in parallel.

Figure 5.6 shows other ways of expressing the RP loop. Figures 5.7 and 5.8 are developments of Fig. 5.5 and show some of the sub-processes within the process of reflecting. They are the issue forming loop, the clarifying loop, the updating loop and the solving loop. These loops operate on the needs, purposes and objectives, the current state of mind, memory, the creative tension that is the difference between where we are now and where we want to be.

In mathematical terms the mind is a many to many mapping or relation between perception and action. We could imagine the relation as a set of rules (as exemplified in expert systems) or a function (as in hard systems) or at the other extreme a poem.

Practical intelligence is an emergent property of this hierarchy of interacting reflective practice loops.

Subconscious patterns influence conscious behaviour

In our subconscious mind this mapping from sensory perception to action is determined but not necessarily determinate. Some of the mappings define skills which may be innate (e.g. playing the piano or driving a dumper truck). The mind receives signals from sense organs and sends signals to various parts of our body. For example, our body temperature control mechanism is of this type. Language is the result of linkages between patterns of sounds (phonemes) and visible marks or symbols (numbers, letters). These linkages are themselves patterns. Understanding body language helps us to win bids. Understanding signals of customer satisfaction helps us to improve profitability.

Learning is the development of new patterns and new linkages between patterns. It is an evolutionary problem solving process central to the building of the mind. We can postulate that clusters of patterns can be linked to word patterns to form higher level, more general words or concepts. We can imagine these concepts are linked in the hierarchy. These linkages occur at all levels so that linkages between high-level concepts may also be clustered to form relationships. These relationships form our understanding and our mental models.

Mental models are patterns representing concepts and relations

To the extent that we are what we think then we are our mental models. They form our world views, they form our opinions, they form our understand-

continued

Box 5.21 continued

ing of the physical world, they form the vision that we want to use to motivate a team to be successful. They may be wrong, they may be misconceptions that lead us to reject an attractive offer, they may be about a pattern of behaviour that helps us to recognise an untrustworthy person. They define willingness to pay and so they define the demand for our services. They are the basis of our judgements that are so crucial to the process by which we decide.

Language is learned from the base of the subconscious mind by a learning process. Our conscious mind is the result of the formation of mental models expressed in terms of language. Through language we can express ideas about ourselves (identity) and about our own knowledge (high level reflection). Through language we reflect and act on the world in a conscious evolutionary problem solving process, which contributes to the building of Popper's World 3 objective knowledge.

Memories are patterns in the mind, and through those which are stored in the conscious mind we have concepts of time and identity. Imagination and creative thinking are the result of forming links between memory patterns which were not previously linked. Scenarios are temporally ordered sequences of events. Through imagination we can build scenarios which have not actually happened both about the present and the future. Note, however, that these links are made between existing patterns in the mind. The richness of these new links must therefore depend upon the richness of the world view. Our potential to create new ideas and better ways of doing things is governed by our ability to form new links and new patterns.

Knowledge is a set of mental models. Some mental models cannot be expressed in natural or formal language and these are part of, but do not define, the subconscious mind (e.g. the rules controlling the heartbeat). Mental models that can be expressed in natural or formal language are part of, but do not define, the conscious mind. Some models can be subconscious some of the time and conscious at other times (e.g. learned skills such as driving a car) and some are almost entirely conscious (e.g. speech). Conscious problem solving is an evolutionary process where actions are taken on the basis of an evaluation of alternative scenarios, which is reflection. Evolution derives from learning which is a loopy process.

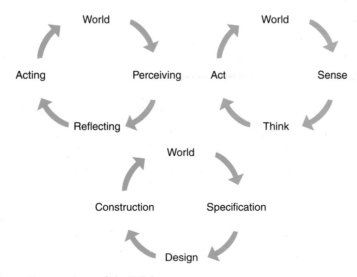

Fig. 5.6. Alternative versions of the RP loop

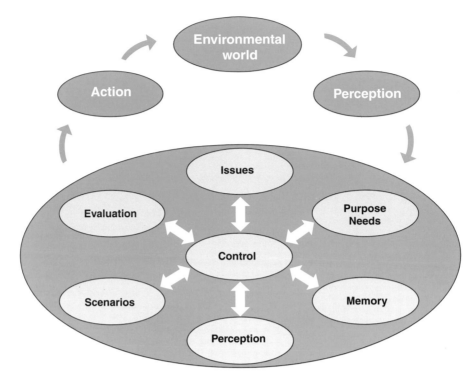

Fig. 5.7. The reflective practice loop (developed)

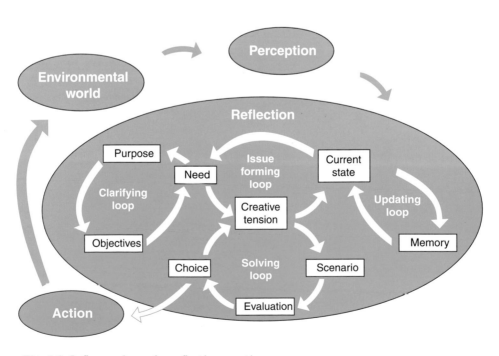

Fig. 5.8. Influence loops for reflective practice

Practical intelligence involves planning scenarios

Consciousness is attributed to an organism when it shows intelligence. We define intelligence as an ability to construct, evaluate and act on alternative scenarios of the future. The richer the ability to construct scenarios the more intelligent we suppose the organisms to be. *Notice that, by this definition, intelligence also includes action and hence is part of reflective practice.*

Box 5.22   Scenarios planning by the conscious ape!   Explanation

Penrose quotes Konrad Lorentz describing a chimpanzee in a room that contains a banana suspended from the ceiling just out of reach and a box elsewhere in the room. 'The matter gave him no peace and he returned to it again. Then suddenly — and there is no other way to describe it — his previously gloomy face lit up. His eyes now moved from the banana to the empty space beneath it on the ground, from this to the box, then back to the space, and from there to the banana. The next moment he gave a cry of joy and somersaulted over to the box in sheer high spirits. Completely assured of success he pushed the box below the banana. No man watching him could doubt the existence of a genuine 'aha' experience in anthropoid apes.'

(Penrose, 1989)

The conscious mind has the ability to build scenarios, hence to make choices to best satisfy needs in a set of reflective practice loops. Thus, by interpretation, the chimpanzee is indeed in possession of a conscious mind. However, the mind is primitive and is unable to form the patterns necessary for written or spoken language although some animals can use simple language and all display some form of body language.

Thus a central characteristic of intelligence, it is argued, is the ability to construct scenarios of what might happen, and this includes the use of tools to manipulate objects in the external world (Popper's Worlds 1 and 3). It involves the ability to construct scenarios in which artefacts already in the world are manipulated to enable the organism to achieve its needs (such as food in the case of the chimpanzee).

Practical intelligence involves using tools

The next level of intelligent behaviour is the ability to make a tool or artefact. This is accomplished by perceiving the world, imagining alternative scenarios, evaluating them and choosing one of them (i.e. design) and then taking action to change the world (i.e. manufacture/construction) so that the chosen scenario is realised. At this level, the chimpanzee would in some way have to see that the position of the box has to be altered to enable him to use it for standing on in order to reach the banana. Further, at a higher level still, the chimpanzee would have to be able to conceive the nature of a box and be able to manufacture it from some available timber.

Tools are artefacts which extend the capabilities of human beings. The need to understand and explain our world is also a high-level human need. In the history of our development, as our understanding has increased, so have we been able to develop more sophisticated tools. Thus the evolution of science has been bound up with practical action. Accordingly, these tools now vary from the simple ruler for measuring length to the complex tools such as cars, bridges and aeroplanes for travel, to buildings and power stations to supply the basic needs of modern life.

Modern nuclear physics is dependent on the engineering of vast particle accelerators. Even though engineers apply science, they are not applied scientists any more that scientists who use engineering are, in some sense, 'pure engineers'!

It is clear therefore that design and manufacture/construction are central to human activity. Design is the construction of scenarios where imagined artefacts (processes) operate to achieve defined needs for some defined people. It is limited only by the imagination of the designers and of the other people involved.

5.8   Engineering wisdom and judgement

Creativity is synthesis

The process of design is both creative and judgemental. The creative process is one of 'opening out' thinking to identify options and alternatives, as we have discussed earlier. The judgemental part is about making sense of all of the creative suggestions and choosing the best ideas and making them work.

Creative thinking is required to spot opportunities for adding value during the design phase of any process. Construction professionals tend, as a whole, to restrict their contributions to their distinctive technical roles. Of course, that is wholly correct in the sense that we should always be aware of our duty of care to act responsibly within our declared competence. However, it is in the creative phase of any process that good ideas and opportunities, no matter from where they come, win on their merits. The ability to make new connections between ideas and to develop the impelling propositions that we talked about in Chapter 2 should be open to all in the team. Construction professionals are good designers and since designing is naturally creative, the same set of thinking skills can be used to identify opportunities to add value to clients and to other members of the team.

During creative synthesis it is important to separate the 'opening out' thinking from the judgmental thinking (Box 5.13). The first reaction to any suggestion should be 'yes' rather than 'no' because even if that particular suggestion turns out to be impracticable, it may nevertheless act as an idea which the team can leapfrog over to a totally new and practical innovation. This suspension of criticism is difficult but crucial if the team is to be genuinely creative together.

Judging is analysing

Of course, the usefulness of the process model has to be judged. This is a closing down thinking process of testing each idea against strict criteria. The process is analytical because it requires us to split the model into each part (in this case each process) and to examine that part on its own. If the part passes the tests and meets the criteria then it is acceptable. If it fails the tests then we must go back into creative synthesis mode in order to find a new idea which will pass the tests.

Thus designing, like any decision making process (see Fig. 2.16), is one of creating possible solutions and then judging their acceptability — keep these two thinking phases apart.

Wise decisions depend on the evidence

Let us now review and summarise some of the ideas of hard and soft systems to help identify what we mean by engineering judgement and its relationship with hard science. We do this because we want to construct a systems process model, which is conceptually the same for both hard and soft systems. Wise decision making must be based on evidence which is as dependable as we can obtain within the constraints of resource in which we have to operate.

Hard systems provide measurable dependable evidence — but there are risks

We have said that all hard systems are embedded in a soft system. That soft system will be an individual, group or organisational process with a specific set of attributes.

Let us reconsider a hard system theory such as Newtonian physics or, at a more precise level, the theory of elasticity as we discussed in Section 4.5. Such a system is expressed using theories such as the formula for the deflection of a simple beam or a finite element model of a dam. Let us look at the relationship between the evidence from the model and the risks we face. We now call these hard system models process holons. The models are patterns of relationships between the qualities of the physical objects such as length, mass and time. The patterns are represented in a formal language, such as algebra, where the terms in the algebra represent measures on these qualities. Thus for Newtonian physics the terms F, M, and a in the equation $F = Ma$ (which is a one to one mapping) represent force, mass and acceleration of a point mass. Weight and acceleration can be measured using agreed procedures that are dependable in that the four conditions of dependability identified in Chapter 4 (Fig. 4.3) can be well satisfied. Likewise the expression $d = Wl^3/48EI$ is a one to one mapping of the relation between the qualities of the beam system relevant to its deflection behaviour. If we understand the relationship between the demands upon the system (the loads on the beam) and the capacity of the system (the strength of the beam), we can get a dependable idea of the risk of failure, i.e. the chance that the loads will overcome the strength.

Dependability deteriorates as we move from theory to practice and the risk becomes more uncertain

As we discussed earlier, these relatively simple relationships soon become problematic for more complex systems, e.g. when one introduces the quality of workmanship into the welding of the beam. Now we can only draw 'plum pudding' graphs because we really do not know how to express the idea of quality of workmanship and how we can measure it. However, we do know how to recognise it and we can see patterns of relationships — it is simply that the four conditions for dependability are relaxed. There is fuzziness and imprecision of definition of what we mean by workmanship and we do not have a repeatable measurement we can use — nevertheless, we can say useful things such as 'when the quality of workmanship is low then the safety of the beam is endangered'. These more general relationships may be expressed in a formal language as an empirical formula or, more likely, in natural language. The knowledge is used in the manufacturing process to make sure the beam is manufactured to specification.

The risks can be calculated as before. However, because the relationships are less dependable then so is the estimate of risk. We need to understand this and to maintain a strategy to ensure we fulfil our purpose.

The dependability of soft systems requires wise judgements and team co-operation

Clearly, when even higher level relationships are considered, such as the impact of a change in the level of inflation on the possible number of applicants for a new post you have advertised, then there is no underlying model you can dependably use. It is not possible to use a formal language to describe the relationships. It is not possible, therefore, to calculate a level of risk dependably.

However, it is possible to make some statements about patterns of relations that represent your understanding of the systems and these are used to make a judgement. Thus as we lose the dependability criteria of Fig. 4.3, we also lose the confidence that dependability brings and we move steadily from a hard system to a soft system. In this case it is imperative that we use all means to test our judgements including team dialogue and discussion to bring out the important aspects to be considered.

Establish the dependability of evidence by subjecting it to as many tests as possible

We are arguing that judgement has to be made on the basis of information that will vary in its testability and its dependability. The only clear way to judge the dependability of evidence is to subject it to as many tests as seems appropriate in a given context.

Therefore, if we are told by someone we respect that the 'moon is made of green cheese' we would perhaps find it interesting! However, if we had to make an important decision based on that particular statement then we would not take much notice of it. The reason is that it does not accord with our commonsense view of the likely nature of the moon and it is not directly testable (except if we had enough resource to ask NASA to launch a lunar mission on our behalf!). Also, the historical evidence that previous lunar missions have brought does not support the statement!

A statement such as 'the majority of customers of the water plc want to see their bills reduced rather than to see more money spent on environmental protection' is more problematic. You would want to assess the dependability of this evidence by examining the process by which it was obtained. If there had been a survey done by a reputable polling company you might be prepared to give it some dependability — but the degree would depend upon the problem you were addressing, i.e. the context.

It is clear, therefore, that our use of both hard and soft systems models depends upon the context in which we are using them.

There is another crucial factor in wise decision making that we must now consider in Chapter 6 and that is the need to be clear about our values.

5.9   Checking for success

The success targets for this chapter set out at the beginning were that, after reading it, you will be able to:

Success target	Review
• state how logical and scientific rigour is part of practical rigour;	practical rigour requires creative and judgemental thinking which is rational and logical but can, at the same time, create practical solutions despite the limitations of our theoretical understanding;
• describe the difference between scientific thinking and systems thinking;	scientific thinking is reductionist which means that the parts can be studied separately to form a view of the whole. Systems thinking is holistic so that it is recognised that there are emergent properties which provide holistic gain;
• state how reflective practice is a theory of practical competence;	the reflective practice loop is the basic loop of perception, reflection and action which appears at all levels from the workings of the low level subconscious mind to high level cognitive decision making;
• participate in a workshop to address a wicked set of problems;	a workshop can be divided into forming, storming, norming and performing sessions. During the storming creative brainstorming sessions no critical negative comments should be allowed. During the norming stage the group is analytical and judgemental;
• describe the relationship between creative and judgemental thinking and between analysis and synthesis.	the key idea in running creative thinking workshops is to keep creative thinking and judgmental thinking sessions strictly apart. Synthesis is positive, creative and opening out. Analysis is negative, judgemental and closing down.

We also stated that you will think that thinking is a skill that is worth practising whether you are a junior engineer, a company director, a student or a professor.

We hope that you now believe that you can, even now, improve your thinking skills.

We hope that we have reached our success targets for this chapter — please use the feedback form at the end of the book.

Part 3

Making the difference

6. Adding value

6.1 A new question

What do people want? What are the rewards? What will it cost? What are the risks? These are major questions on the minds of all of the parties involved in a construction. There is nothing new in these questions — it has always been like this.

So what has to change? Perhaps there is a more fundamental question. How can we know when we are adding value (Fig. 6.1)? We certainly will not know it if we do not have a clear idea about what values are. This applies not only to ourselves but to the whole supply chain of our clients with the customer at the head. Our aim is to help clear some of the fog around the issue of how added value relates to the willingness to pay of clients. We need to recognise our interdependence. We need to know where we are going, who is going with us and why. This is the reason why this chapter is at the start of Part 3 'Making the difference', even though it is a central part of 'Thinking differently'.

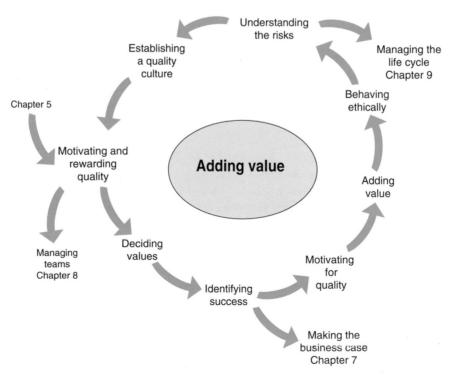

Fig. 6.1. Adding value

6.2 Targeting success for this chapter

The success targets for this chapter are that, after reading it, you will be able to:

- describe how quality depends upon values;
- write down many different values;
- realise the importance of measuring worth;
- set out how companies and individuals can add value;
- describe a hierarchy of needs;
- describe how ethics underpins our values;
- be clear that you need to be clear about your own values;
- see hazards as both hard and soft system 'banana skins' and that risk is in the future;
- describe hazard as a set of incubating preconditions to failure;
- describe how to collect evidence from the past, present and future about the success of a process;
- describe robustness and vulnerability as a property of the form of a system;
- set out the essential ingredients of a quality and safety culture.

6.3 Motivating and rewarding quality

Understanding quality

At the root of each of the new questions we have posed is just one word *quality*. Understanding quality is at the root of understanding value as reflected in the driver for *Rethinking Construction* of a 'quality driven' agenda. It is as defined in ISO 8402 (1994), 'The totality of characteristics of an entity that bear on its ability to satisfy stated and implied needs'.

Unfortunately, the word quality has come to be used in a rather specialised way in quality assurance and quality management schemes and has therefore lost some of its original power. It is too often used only to refer to the functionality of a system, not including safety, economy, sustainability and many other aspects of what we want and need from a process. We have to use the word in the much more general sense of Box 6.1 because our customers, employees and everyone else value our success in wider terms than functionality. We have to do this to create the visibility of the value that we add.

Box 6.1   **Principle**

Quality is a measure of how good the totality is of what we are getting relative to what we want from any process.
Quality is not just about the level of functionality.

cf. Box 6.10

We see products and organisations as processes and so we are concerned with where we are at any time during a process relative to where we want to be at that time and at the end, i.e. the goal, the end state that defines *success*. Quality should be a measure of all of the aspects of a process — all bundled together. The fourth driver for change in *Rethinking Construction* is 'a quality driven agenda' in this total sense.

So how do we identify what success is and how do we know how near to it we might be at any one time? In order to get to grips with these questions we will need to understand clearly how we judge the *relative worth* of things to us — that is our set of *values*.

Before we do that, however, we should just note that the word quality is also used in some contexts to refer to an attribute, characteristic or trait of something. So for a hard system such as a simple beam the qualities or attributes might be *load W, span L, elastic modulus E, second moment of area I*, etc. In this text we will use the word attribute (and the particular process attribute of state variable or parameter — see Box 2.12) for that interpretation of the word quality.

6.4 Deciding values

Understanding our values is central to delivering quality

We make decisions based on our preferences. We have to decide that we prefer one option to another. In order to do that we ascribe a 'worth' to something. A value is quite simply that worth (Box 6.2).

Box 6.2   What is worth?   **Principle**

Worth is the attribute that you use to make a choice.

**Our behaviour depends upon our decisions
which depend upon our choices
hence our behaviour depends upon worth.**

Some of these values are hard and some are soft. Therefore, the worth is sometimes easily measured and sometimes difficult to measure. The danger is that we ignore those values where the worth is not easily measured (Box 6.3). Money is one measure of worth but worth is not necessarily expressible in terms of money.

Box 6.3   Worth of soft values   **Principle**

**The worth of some of the softer values is partly personal, partly shared
and difficult to measure dependably.**

**If we fail to address how to improve those values then we may fail to
add value in soft areas such as customer satisfaction.**

Of course any reasonably complex system will have a large number of ways in which it can be valued. For example, we might prefer one scheme over another because it is safer or because it is cheaper as long as all other things are equal. The challenge is to find the right balance for success. In wicked and messy problems there are many facets to value — Box 6.4.

In Chapter 2, we saw that part of the description of a process holon is made using a set of state variables. Some are hard (such as a set of size parameters for a beam: span, depth, width, etc., and a set of material parameters: elastic modulus, etc.) and some are soft (appearance, workmanship, etc.). For more high-

Box 6.4 Examples of values	Explanation
Customer satisfaction	exceeding expectations, providing what is wanted and needed, fulfilling a desire;
Shareholder value (non-financial)	reputation, good will, customer loyalty, desire to own;
Money	profit, share price, financial measures (such as return on capital, dividend cover, etc.), initial costs, life cycle costs, opportunities, expectations about future value;
Utility	usefulness, utility as in utility theory;
Health and safety	harm, human life, injury, quality of life;
Performance	functionality, reliability, damage, simplicity/complexity;
Buildability	constructability, level of standardisation, waste;
Operations	availability, efficiency, ease, convenience/difficulty;
Environmental Impact	aesthetic, biological, loss of diversity, elegance; pollution, waste, efficiency;
Sustainability	natural resources, energy consumption;
Ethics	individuals, groups, professional standards, future generations.

level business processes these measures are KPIs such as % spend of budget, % completion, return on capital employed or dividend cover. Each of these state variables or performance measures and has a range of acceptable sizes. These sizes will relate to different aspects such as functionality, cost, safety, etc. Thus if a bridge is to span a gap of 20 metres then obviously the span must be greater than or equal to 20 metres for the bridge to be functional. This requirement is conceptually straightforward for hard systems but more difficult for soft systems because the requirements are less precise and difficult to measure dependably.

Measure worth

Our decisions and those of our clients and their customers are based on assessments of soft values as well as hard. The worth of soft issues is often the difference between success and failure.

We define success by allocating particular 'degrees of worth' to particular values. In order to make decisions in which we choose between options, we need to be able to measure worth. It is important, therefore, that we measure the worth of soft values as well as of hard values and that we do it as dependably as we can.

The measurement of soft issues is not easy and the answers we obtain are not always as dependable as we would wish. There is considerable uncertainty in the method as well as the answer. We need to recognise that our purpose in measurement is to provide evidence that is as dependable as we can achieve. We are doing it so that we can agree about the situation and make good decisions together — we are not trying to discover absolute truth. We know that the act of measurement can itself influence the outcome — so the way we measure is very important and can be helpful or harmful. For example, feedback forms used at the end of a seminar may not only help the organisers to improve future seminars but may also help the participant, through the act of completing the form, to reflect on what happened while his feelings are fresh. This helps to reinforce his understanding. If feedback forms are an imposition, they can generate negative feelings and block learning. If they are introduced as part of the process the outcome can be very positive.

Another problem, particularly in construction, is that of timing. Decisions are required yet attitudes and needs may change and so therefore must the measurements that we take. We need to develop risk management strategies to respond to the uncertainty — which we can do as long as we admit it exists. For example, an investment in the corporate headquarters of British Airways was protected by ensuring that the design allowed blocks of space to be let separately to other organisations.

The process of measurement is important

So if the questions we ask often condition the answers we get, then it is essential that we first understand and communicate our purpose in asking the questions and the wider purpose they serve. We need to design them to fulfil that purpose and to continue to test and guide the process to success. This is a similar approach to that used in a product design cycle of design, prototype testing and monitoring to improve the future.

In all of our attempts to understand and assess worth — it really is the **listening and observing, and the collective understanding that follows, that creates the added value**. It is essential to record that understanding so that in time we can begin to notice patterns of behaviour that will help us to improve the way we manage issues in the future.

There is as yet **no agreement about how we should measure soft issues** — other than in specific circumstances such as political elections, or competitions such as ice skating championships. Nevertheless, these measures are essential as long as the process and results are judged appropriate and sufficiently dependable, i.e. fit for purpose. Political elections are an example where we realise that they are imperfect, we know that there are different ways of carrying them out (e.g. first past the post or proportional representation — and there are different ways of doing that), but the results are the basis of our whole democracy.

Measurement is an experiment

As we saw in Chapter 4, measurement is an experiment where we put two phenomena into correspondence (e.g. a line and a metre tape). Because soft processes are essentially social processes, their measurement rests on collective agreement through a process in Popper's World 3 of shared perceptions. That agreement includes the way in which the physical and social worlds outside of us (Popper's World 1) respond to what we do. It therefore includes our collective understanding of hard systems as well. This is because we are constantly testing out our ideas on the physical world, seeing how it responds, modifying our own ideas and then sharing and discussing those ideas with others to obtain agreement.

Box 6.5   Measuring soft issues   Examples

Example 1   Team understanding

How much evidence is there that issues are understood adequately by this team?

| None | Very little | A little | Some | Quite a lot | Considerable | Complete | Don't know |

Where are issues well understood?

....

Where are issues badly understood?

....

What practical action could be taken to substantially improve the understanding of issues?

....

Example 2   Confidence in judgement

What is your level of confidence in your judgement? Please tick the most appropriate box and answer the question below.

| Complete | High | Moderate | Low | Very low | None |

What practical steps could be taken to substantially improve your confidence in your judgement?

....

Example 3   Customer satisfaction

Please indicate how well the process team has met your expectation.

Well below expectation		Satisfies expectation		Well above expectation
1	2	3	4	5

Please indicate, in bullet point form, key issues that have led to the judgement you have made

....
....

The dependability of our measurements of hard systems is generally very good and **agreement about method** is usually not an issue. Therefore, we generally do not argue about the meaning of a metre length or the calibration of a tape measure although we take great care to use appropriate processes of measurement — e.g. to include temperature corrections if significant. The uncertainty in hard systems measurement is usually that either we just do not have the data or the magnitudes of the measurements are highly variable. This is why we may use statistics to try to summarise and make sense of the numbers.

We have criteria (from Chapter 4) through which we can think about the dependability of a soft measure. We need a measuring experiment based on four sufficient conditions. These are the degree of:

(*a*) the repeatability of the experiment
(*b*) the repeatability of the states of the experiment
(*c*) the clarity of the states
(*d*) the repeatability of the magnitudes of the states.

Worth is expressed through choice

To measure worth we need to observe it. Worth is expressed as preferential choice. Thus the measurement of worth can be carried out through any experiment (such as voting, betting or simple comparisons) in which people are asked to make choice and their behaviour can be observed and recorded. Through the experiment we put that choice into correspondence with a scale such as (0,1) or a percentage depending on the nature of the experiment.

The essential variability in the results is because worth depends upon intentionality. The four sufficient conditions for the dependability of the experiment are all difficult. Often the experiments cannot be repeated. The states of the system are often not stable (since people have intentionality they are liable to change their minds in a sudden way — forming many points of bifurcation in the process). The clarity of the state description is often necessarily vague (just what do we mean by good team spirit — although we recognise it when we see it). Lastly, the magnitude of the states (e.g. the number of votes) is highly variable in each experiment.

Assessments can be carried out at various levels. For example, at a high overall level, we can assess customer satisfaction by observing the behaviour of customers and looking for repeatable and discernible patterns in the way people express preference. Alternatively, we can simply ask customers by means of standard questionnaires or focus groups. We could even ask them to draw an Italian Flag (Chapter 4 — although we accept that as this is a new idea some training in its use would be required first). Likewise, if we are attempting to assess team co-operation we can observe team behaviour or, again, simply ask the members of the team.

Voting, betting and pairwise comparison are ways of measuring worth

One way of thinking about a preferential choice is as **a vote**. We can imagine that the system (hard or soft) has under the specific conditions of the experiment voted for a particular result. Thus every point on a graph represents the way the system has voted for a relationship between the two or more variables concerned. The proportional vote for a particular choice is then our measure on the scale (0, 1).

Perhaps the first formal technique for trying to measure soft systems was through so-called Bayesian probability theory where people are asked to make alternative bets in order to find subjective individual measures of belief. The measure here is again a bet on the scale (0, 1).

Another method is to ask people to make a sequence of choices between pairs of measured variables. This is called pair-wise comparison and can be used by individuals or in a workshop to prioritise issues.

Note that in all of these methods the answers should always be applied with caution. As we have stressed, in our experience, the greatest benefit arises not from the calculated weightings but from the understanding generated by the process and the reasons for the choices made. Each of the methods to which we have referred is founded on mathematics which can help to provide consistency and clarity. However, the mathematics is not yet rich enough to model the full range of human judgement. It is beyond the scope of this book to delve into the mathematics behind these techniques. However, it is important that the methods we use are grounded in logic because this helps create dependability. For those readers interested in more theoretical detail the ideas are developed further in Box 6.6.

Box 6.6   Measuring soft issues　　　　　　　　　　**Explanation and theory**

We may use a questionnaire, an interview or a workshop to collect a set of opinions in the form of ticks in boxes, as in Box 6.5. In each case we need to examine carefully the four conditions for our measuring experiment to determine the dependability of the process we have used to obtain our measurements. First, is the experiment repeatable? Second, what is the state of the experiment? It may well be unknown since people can change their minds abruptly between different measurements. Are we aware that this might have happened in our experiment? Third, the clarity of the states are fuzzy (what do 'best practice' or 'some' really mean?). We assess whether the definitions that we are using are appropriate and sufficiently understood by all. Fourth, the magnitude of the results will vary a great deal. We will have direct evidence of this through the actual choices made through the ticks in the boxes.

Providing we think that the definitions of the states are satisfactory for our purpose, we can ask many people for their opinions to try to average out the variations — using classical statistical methods. Alternatively, if we have only a few people involved we can use the measuring process to generate a dialogue and to generate understanding and, where appropriate, to try to attain some sort of consensus. If consensus is not possible then the reason for the differences may be recorded.

The results do, of course, **depend on the context** from which they were derived. They are in no sense context free. Even hard systems measurements are embedded in a set of soft systems values. **Measurement is always done in the context of a purpose.** It is therefore very important that results in one context are only transferred to another context with great care.

Of course, these measurements are made in order to inform decision-making. In the ultimate the responsibility for decision lies with the **process owner** in accordance with his accountability to a higher process owner. However, it is the duty of the process owner to ensure that the decisions of the team are **fit for purpose** as he sees it. Whether personally, or through some social process such as a workshop, the process owner may wish to include judgement in the results.

Voting

Whether formally in the boardroom or electorate, or informally through some consultation process, **voting** is one of the most commonly used methods of measuring a soft issue. This idea can be extended as a way of using the results from questionnaires in a soft measurement system.

Think of each opinion, each tick in a box, as a vote. You can also think of relationships expressed on a graph in this way. Each point on a graph is effectively a vote for a connection between two states (Fig. 6.2) which we will call

continued

Box 6.6 continued

a formal relation *R*. These points can then be used to form measures on the relation.

Think of an individual set of votes from 10 people YNNYYNYYYN as an Italian Flag with no incompleteness (no white). With six votes of Yes and four votes of No we have 60% green and 40% red.

This allows the voters only two choices, Yes or No — which is OK, i.e. fit for purpose, if all we want is a clear-cut decision according to some clear-cut voting rules. However, it does not allow our voters to admit that they do not know. Yet we know that the reasons for the uncertainty may be really valuable information. We can therefore include the white part of the Italian Flag. Now, Yes votes are green, No are red and Unknown are white. If the voting pattern changes to YUUYYNUUYU, then we have 40% green, 50% white and 10% red.

By admitting that we do not know, we are able to plan how to manage it. Through dialogue, or answers to supplementary questions, we can decide on an improved course of action. If the facilitators of the voting respond appropriately to the results, they can get increased buy-in from the participants.

The voting process is repeatable, the states are unknown, the clarity of each state depends on the problem, and the number of votes cast (the magnitudes) will be variable each time we repeat the experiment. The figures can be used mathematically based upon Interval Probability Theory (IPT) and a computer programme — but this is beyond the scope of this book (Cui and Blockley, 1990; Hall, Blockley and Davies, 1998).

Betting

Preferred choice can also be measured through a series of bets. Decision theory was developed in this way using probability as a measure of subjective belief. This theory is called Bayesian probability after a theorem of probability attributed to Thomas Bayes who was an English Presbyterian minister in the 18th century. Respondents are given a series of bets and from them a probability magnitude is derived. Likewise, it is possible to derive a measure of subjective utility (Blockley, 1980). These figures are then used in Bayes Theorem to calculate updated degrees of belief in the light of new evidence (Benjamin and Cornell, 1970). Unfortunately, probability theory suffers from one critical characteristic which is that it is a closed world theory. It assumes that the problem is tame. The mathematical details are beyond the scope of this book but the implication is that results can be seriously misleading if an important possible outcome has not been included. The theory does not allow us to admit what we do not know since all possible alternatives have to be identified in advance and all probabilities must sum to one. This complete identification of all possible futures is often not possible in soft systems.

Making pair-wise comparisons

It is possible to take two sets of variables that may form a graph (or more generally a relation as in Fig. 6.2) and make comparisons between all pairs of

continued

Box 6.6 continued

points — this is known as pair-wise comparison. For example, the points in Fig. 6.2 may be formed by asking for each x_i and y_j — is there evidence of a relation? The answer for each point could be an answer of Yes, No or Uncertain as shown in Fig. 6.2.

Saaty (1981) has developed a technique for pair-wise comparisons. He sets up the problem as a group of people wanting to judge the relative importance of a set of activities in a quantifiable way. He then asks individuals to judge a matrix of relative weights by asking the question — 'of the two alternatives i and j, which is more important with respect to some property and by how much?' A mathematical method involving the calculation of Eigenvalues is then used to provide an overall set of weighted values that can be applied to a set of options in order to compare them.

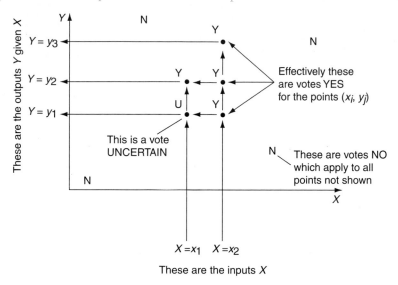

Fig. 6.2. A relation between two variables X, Y as a set of votes

Graphs and relations

Where we are concerned with complex and confusing issues, it is particularly important that the methods we use have a sound underlying logic even if the information may be essentially qualitative. The purpose of the following is to explain how soft relations, including the Italian Flag, relate to simple graphs.

Functions

Figures 6.3(a) and 6.3(b) show familiar mathematical graphs or functions of the form $y = f(x)$. The relationship between one variable and another is called a mapping. In Fig. 6.3(a), the mapping is from one value of X to one value of Y **only** and is therefore called a 1–1 mapping. In Fig. 6.3(b), the mapping is many to 1 since there are three values of X in the figure that result in the same Y. Note that the variable name is X and a particular value or magnitude of X is x.

Plum puddings

In Fig. 6.3(c), we have a so-called 'plum pudding' graph where many values

Box 6.6 continued

of X map to many values of Y. This is a many to many mapping. While it is possible to make sense of most hard systems and some soft systems with 1–1 and many–1 mappings most soft systems are complex 'plum puddings'. Results from experiments in metal fatigue are one example of many to many mappings in hard systems. The impact of a stakeholder on a project is a many to many mapping in a soft system.

Relations

The variables in soft systems are not easily defined and are therefore rarely just single point values as in Fig. 6.3(a). They are rather sets such as B (a set on X) and A (a set on Y) as in Fig. 6.3(c). The example we use later is that in stakeholder management, B is the set *low interest* which is a subset of X, and X is the scale $(0,1)$. Likewise A is the set *low influence* which is a subset of Y and Y is also the scale $(0,1)$.

We may have some knowledge of an input B expressed as a measure on X, say $p(B)$, and we want to know something about an output A expressed as a measure on Y, say $p(A)$. To calculate $p(A)$ we need a relation R between X and Y. The points in Fig. 6.3(c) represent that relation. The total space of all points (x, y) is known as the Cartesian Product $(X \times Y)$. The relation R is a subset of $X \times Y$ and a many to many mapping. We imagine each point as a vote for the relationship existing in a particular region of the space.

In Fig. 6.4(d), we divide R into nine subsets each defined with respect to A and B as shown. In effect we have stepped up a level in the way we describe R. We are now representing R in terms of A and B together with *not A* and *not B*. Instead of R being made up of lots of points, as in Fig. 6.3(c), it is now made up of four subsets of $X \times Y$ as (*A and B*), (*A and not B*), (*not A and B*), (*not A and not B*) which are the nine regions of Fig. 6.3(d). We collect them up into the four regions in Fig. 6.4(a). We thus have a way of representing a high-level relationship R simply in terms of A, B, *not A* and *not B*.

We can think of the number of points in *A and B* as shown in Fig. 6.3(c) as the number of votes for *A and B*. So the strength of an association in a relation can be measured as the proportional number of votes for A and B which can be interpreted as a probability or $p(A \text{ and } B)$. We then repeat that idea for the other regions in the relation as shown in Figs, 6.3 and 6.4. Effectively we now have a high level joint probability distribution over a space of the four subsets of $X \times Y$ which we can use to calculate $p(Y)$ from $p(X)$ and R using the total probability theorem that $p(A) = p(A \text{ and } B) + p(A \text{ and not } B)$.

In Fig. 6.5(a), we show the proportional number of votes as $m_{11} = p(A \text{ and } B)$; $m_{21} = p(A \text{ and not } B)$, etc. The Italian flag shown in Fig. 6.5(b) is for (*A and B*).

Rules as relations

We can express such a high-level relation R as a set of rules in natural language such as:

IF *A and B* **THEN** *C1*
IF *not A and B* **THEN** *C2*
IF *A and* *not B* **THEN** *C3*
IF *not A and not B* **THEN** *C4*

continued

Box 6.6 continued

For example:

IF a stakeholder has *low interest* and *low influence* **THEN** he has *low importance*
IF a stakeholder has *high interest* and *low influence* **THEN** he has *some importance*
IF a stakeholder has *low interest* and *high influence* **THEN** he has *high importance*
IF a stakeholder has *high interest* and *high influence* **THEN** he has *extremely high importance*

If A is the set *low interest* and B is the set *low influence* in the first rule then the left-hand side of the rule expresses one set (A and B) of R in Figs. 6.4(a) and 6.4(b). The right-hand side of the rule is the property $C1$ that emerges from the left-hand side.

Figure 6.4(b) is a repeat of Fig. 6.12 that we shall discuss later when considering how we deal with stakeholders. The label in each box in Fig. 6.4(b) is the decision and hence the action we could take if we assess the status of a particular stakeholder as being in that box. Thus if the status is assessed as *low importance,* as in the first rule, then we decide that minimum effort is all that is needed.

The other three rules express the other subsets of Fig. 6.4(b). Thus the fourth rule says that a stakeholder in this box is of *extremely high importance* and therefore effectively a key player.

Thus together the four rules represent the relation R expressed in natural language. We can see, therefore, how they relate through R to a graph in a formal mathematical language and even to a function $y = f(x)$. We can see that $y = f(x)$ is just a special and very precise form of a general relation.

In our example, R has the emergent property of representing importance. The stakeholder management actions then follow through a further mapping from importance to action. The process of influencing a change in the status of a stakeholder that results from the decision (from Fig. 7.10) can be envisaged as a trajectory through R in time as Fig. 6.4(c). This figure can be compared directly with Fig. 2.15.

Italian Flag

The Italian Flag expresses a measure of the dependability of a set or a relation such as R. In classical probability theory we attempt to produce a probability density function on R, but very often we just do not have the data. If we are able to get measures for the various boxes in Fig. 6.4(b) (for example by taking a vote from members of the team) then we could imagine them to be proportionally distributed as in Fig. 6.5(a) where they all sum to one. The Italian Flag for A and B as shown in Fig. 6.5(b) contains no white, i.e. no unknown votes. In Fig. 6.5(c) we use Interval Probability Theory which allows for unknown votes so that both A and B can have unknown values. Thus m_{13}, m_{23} and m_{33} are unknown for A, and m_{31}, m_{32} and m_{33} are unknown for B. The white region in Fig. 6.5(c) is unknown for A *and* B and provides the white region in the Italian Flag of Fig. 6.5(d). For further details see Hall, Blockley and Davis, (1998).

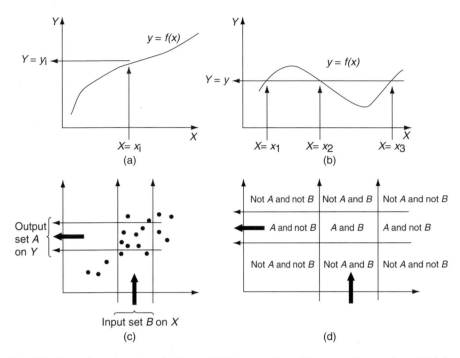

Fig. 6.3. From functions to relations: (a) 1–1 mapping; (b) many-1 mapping; (c) 'plum pudding' relation R; (d) sets on the relation R

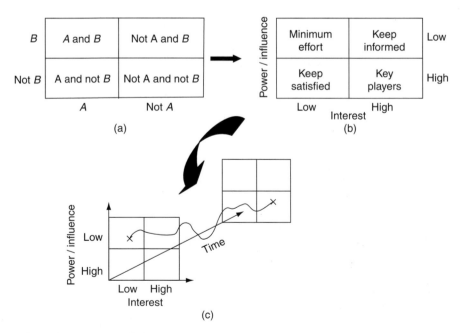

Fig. 6.4. Changing stakeholder's positions: (a) the sets of R; (b) stakeholder diagram; (c) the change process

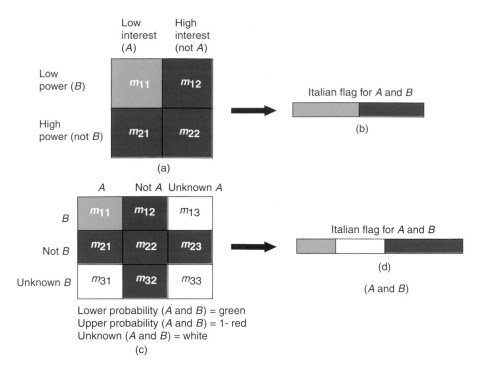

Fig. 6.5. Italian Flags on a relation

Measure future worth

Construction players often have to make choices to trade off differing require-ments that balance the interests of different BCIOD+R process owners. These interests often depend on soft issues such as the value of customer experience in the facility.

Minor defects in a house you have just bought will disappoint you more than if those same defects occur 20 years later — you are entitled to expect something new to be defect free. This illustrates simply the interaction between soft (cus-tomer satisfaction) and hard (number of defects) measures of worth.

In practice, it is the quality of our trade-off decision processes that will be a key element in our ability to meet the Egan challenge. These trade-offs have to include a strong element of foresight with carefully thought-through timings. Too late they can increase costs substantially — too early and the lack of depend-ability may increase. The way in which we manage future worth has to allow for these difficulties.

A measurement system is therefore important. Such a system can enable the setting up of a trading zone where players with different BCOD interests can agree what should or should not be done together with how they will manage the risks. The measurement system will be much more effective if, as for all processes, we are clear about its purpose. It will be more robust if it helps us to admit what we do not know and often cannot know about the future. Admit-ting what we do not know helps us to do something about it or at least to under-stand better the risks we face.

We have all been assessing worth throughout our lives — but we normally make the necessary judgements intuitively. As hard information becomes more readily available and processed, it can tend to dominate the outcomes and sup-press our appreciation of soft issues. Twenty years ago one of the key attributes of a key player in the city was that his 'word was his bond'. Electronic reporting of measurements has to a degree suppressed the cultural recognition of this value, yet if anything soft issues are more, not less, important now and integrity in their assessment is essential. The adoption of soft systems thinking provides a framework for us to improve the process of soft measurement so as to maintain a balance, which is essential to managing the future successfully.

Because measuring worth is so uncertain the process has to be one of continuous learning and development. We normally do it subconsciously. In order to know the worth of measuring worth we need all to start doing it **systematically** now! Obviously it helps to take advice from experts as appropriate (some companies are already appointing knowledge managers and communications managers). However, provided that you do it systematically with caution and much humility you can start today!

6.5   Identifying success

The decision maker (usually the process owner) in every process has to prioritise. See Box 6.7 for the MoSCoW rule to which we have added some extra categories (Note — ignore the 'o's in MoSCoW). This is the first step in making clear what success means. Once that is clear, the decision maker should be looking for opportunities to get that success and perhaps even exceeding it.

Box 6.7   **Principle**

Categorise the success targets using the enhanced MoSCoW rule

The end states for success are:

necessary	these we **MUST** reach — they are essential
highly desirable	these we **SHOULD** reach — we would like to reach
desirable	these we **COULD** reach — we would like but do not expect to reach
a bonus	these we **WANT** to reach — if we can

together with:

new opportunities	these we did not know about when we started but we identified them during the process
to be avoided	these are failure states which must be avoided (ultimate limit states)
might be tolerated	these are partial damage states which we can tolerate in certain circumstances (serviceability limit states)

The requirements specification is one version of success

Success for the hard system is set out in the requirements specification. This is the specific product specification and function, e.g. that a bridge is to carry certain loads across a certain span in a certain location etc. These specifications are well-known and will not be discussed further here.

The soft specification is much harder to be clear about. At the beginning of a large project, this is perhaps the most important aspect to deal with and the one that is rarely addressed systematically. In Chapters 2 and 5, we saw how products such as a chair, a public house and a water plc can be specified creatively by a process model mind map which links creative thinking with the delivery processes. Box 6.8 sets out a further, even more challenging example.

Box 6.8   Delivering a vision   Example

The vision for a new city centre interchange was to provide 'the world's most hassle-free interchange'. The equivalent process is therefore 'being the world's most hassle-free interchange'.

The sub-processes were 'having high financial value', 'having high customer satisfaction', 'integrating people and processes', 'having the world's best connectivity', 'being sustainable' and 'managing stakeholders'. These six processes correspond to the six aspects of a company of BCIOD+R. Each of these sub-process holons was broken down into sub-sub-process holons. For example, necessary sub-processes for 'having the world's best connectivity' are 'having the world's best connectivity from trains to taxi', '... from bus to train', etc.

Specific design solutions for the interchange were then tested against these processes. For example, a typical passenger journey from travelling on a train to boarding a bus was traced by performing a mental simulation or 'thought experiment' of that journey within that design solution. As a result, an assessment of the evidence for success of that design solution against the success target of that process holon was made using the Italian flag as described in Box 4.16. This was repeated for the four top processes giving four Italian flags as measures of the likely success of that design solution in delivering the success targets. This was repeated for all proposed design solutions and the one with the best set of Italian Flags was chosen as the preferred design.

Usually, in a construction project one is putting together new teams to deliver specific versions of success — so how is that shared? It is here that attention is needed in order to deliver *Rethinking Construction*. This is a principal lever for change. How do you create teams with a shared vision and shared mission? We will return to this in some detail in Chapter 8.

The specification that sets out what is required is, in essence, a statement of the success criteria. It could be written as the desired end states for every process at every level in the system. These are the success targets.

Excellence is fitness for purpose

Quality is the totality of what we want from a process. It has two interpretations, namely 'degree of excellence' and 'fitness for purpose' which, as we shall see, are actually the same when the values being used are clearly understood.

Our goal in construction is to produce systems and artefacts that are fit for their intended purpose: in other words, they add value in the manner required. It follows that our measurement of excellence should be based upon our measurement of fitness for purpose. It is for this reason that we are placing so much emphasis on ensuring the purpose of every process is clearly defined. To

---

Box 6.9   The success trajectory   Theory

Let us look at Fig. 2.15 again — and this time let us look for the specification. The acceptable sizes of the state variables are those inside the hyper-volume which is a generalised limit state boundary. Thus, for example, if the performance measures concern structural reliability only (load, strength) then the figure shows the limit state boundaries as used in structural design and reliability theory. If the figure refers to functionality then the hyper-volume refers to the acceptable functional sizes of the state variables. If the figure referred to environmental criteria then the hyper-volume would refer to the acceptable sizes of the environmental state variables. In general, the hyper-volume refers to all requirements — to the specification. The simplest definition of success is that the trajectory of the state variable remains in the acceptable region for the life of the system.

Of course, some acceptable sizes are more acceptable than others. Therefore, each point on the multi-dimensional trajectory has a multiple set of 'degrees of worth' with respect to a given descriptor, and the totality of those degrees of worth is the quality of that point in the process. Our target is to reach a particular level of total quality at the end of the process as set out in the requirements specification. It is effectively a region in the hyper-volume at the end of the process which has a particular set of degrees of worth attached to it. By this interpretation the probability of failure as calculated by classical reliability theory is a measure of the degree of lack of worth with respect to function defined as failure in one or more of the limit states. We clearly prefer a solution with a lower probability of failure at any moment in time and we have acceptable sizes of this probability over which we will not go. However, we also realise that it is only one aspect (a necessary one) of the totality of the worth (quality) of the system.

---

integrate processes within processes it is essential that their purpose definitions are integrated to the purpose of the higher holons. See the section on *Why* in Chapter 1.

As we discussed in Chapter 4, the values for science are truth and precision because the purpose of science is to produce true, precise knowledge. The values for engineering are the fitness for the multifaceted intended purposes of the system.

Box 6.10   **Principle**

Quality is the degree of excellence, which is the state of having pre-eminence or having the highest value.
In construction this is achieved by delivering outcomes that are fit for purpose. Clear purpose is a necessary prerequisite for quality.

cf. Box 6.1

We said that the definitions of quality as excellence and as fitness for purpose are the same. The common confusion that they are different is illustrated by the question 'Which is of higher quality — the Rolls Royce car or the Mini car?' Let us assume we have a Mini which meets the specification for a Mini perfectly — it is of high quality because it is fit for the purpose of being a Mini. Likewise, a

Rolls Royce which meets the specification of being a Rolls Royce is a high quality Rolls Royce. Thus in the sense of quality as fitness for purpose they are equivalent. In fact a particularly good Mini could be of higher quality than a rather poorly put together Rolls Royce. However, if we include in our value system a **preference about the degree of excellence** of the specification then we would all probably agree that the specification of a Rolls Royce is higher than that for a Mini. The confusion between quality as excellence and quality as fitness for purpose is often caused by not being specific enough about the values used in the original specifications. There has to be a clear statement that a Rolls Royce is valued higher than a Mini **if that is what is intended.**

Duty of care to deliver fitness for purpose — the legal test

Quality as fitness for purpose is the success target for all involved. However, it must not be a legal requirement regardless of all circumstances. A legal requirement works against the interests of all involved — **especially the client** (Box 6.11). The reason is that in all projects there are significant uncertainties including, for some, major items of incompleteness where the best solutions will actually emerge as the project develops. If these uncertainties are to be managed in co-operative and interdependent teams, then a legal requirement to deliver absolute fitness for purpose, no matter what the circumstances, will act as a major brake. It will encourage the team to smother the uncertainty with extra safeguards. It will result in an aversion to risk that will reduce the capacity for innovative thinking, and opportunities to add value will not be grasped. It will frustrate delivering the integration of processes and teams.

**Box 6.11   Fitness for purpose clauses in   Explanation
                   design and build contracts**

What is it?

A fitness for purpose clause is one:

- with an absolute obligation to produce something that meets specified requirements
- where the specified outcome is guaranteed
- where it is no defence to say that the reason for failure to meet the required outcome could not be foreseen.

Illustrative examples

1. A contractor signed a fitness for purpose clause for an access road to a business park. The road was specified to have a 20 year design life. The use of the business park changed from offices to include heavy industrial buildings. The road failed after six years. The contractor was liable for the cost of reconstruction. He was unable to claim from his designers because they had used due skill and care in the design. His client had benefited from the change of land use without paying for the necessary upgrade.
2. A tannery wastewater treatment works was designed and built on a fitness for purpose basis to meet environmental effluent standards. The environmental standards were changed. The plant had to be upgraded at the contractor's expense.

continued

Box 6.11 continued

3. A fitness for purpose guarantee was provided for a warehouse floor. The owner changed his warehousing method to use heavier and faster fork-lifts. As a result the floor cracked and degraded rapidly. The purpose had not changed but the loading had increased substantially. It was not reasonable to foresee the change, yet the contractor had to pay for it.

Interests of the customer

It is not generally in the business interest of the customer for the designer to design the infrastructure to meet unforeseen intentions, particularly where the life is measured in decades. It encourages over-design to the cost of the intended customer. The use of the clause demonstrates an adversarial relationship between client and designer and this does not encourage co-operation to add value.

Insurance

In the UK, professional indemnity (PI) insurance does not cover fitness for purpose risk. If a designer chooses to put his balance sheet at risk by accepting a fitness for purpose clause, his PI insurance is likely **to be increased**. Insurers recognise that in the event of a failure, the designer has a conflict of interest. Instead of them working with him to defend the PI insurance, the designer is encouraged to demonstrate that there had been negligence so as to protect his balance sheet with the PI insurance.

Risk from client's intentions

We have shown that engineering success is derived from providing solutions that fulfil their purpose. Specifications can often prescribe solutions and eliminate successful innovation. The designer or contractor can have proprietary knowledge that enables him to offer increased value and to manage technical performance and risk. The payment and reward should be linked to this. However, purpose can also depend upon the future intentions of the owner or operator. In which case the risk can be outside the control of the designer. The problem arises from the absolute nature of the obligation in a fitness for purpose clause when used in place of the normal duty of care.

A way ahead

In practice, the various organisations in the supply chain have a high level of interdependence in achieving success together. The development of 'relationship based' contracts such as partnering, designed to motivate joint success on an open book, risk and reward basis, has enabled substantial performance and cost improvements to be achieved, particularly in offshore oil and gas industry.

There is a case for development of suitable insurance products to provide practical product liability for construction. It would support competent partnering relationships and share the risk of product development, thereby adding value. Innovation would be encouraged to the general benefit of construction users. It could motivate observational risk control and be a useful tool to meet *Rethinking Construction*.

The legal test should be a **duty of care** to deliver fitness for purpose where success depends upon first building relationships and then writing the contracts to serve those relationships. Figures 6.6 and 6.7 show these effects. The construction team cannot be expected to have some magic power for divining the intentions of other parties, especially those of the client and his customers. That does not exclude the client, however, from wishing, quite rightly, to change his requirements part way through a project. However, if he does so, then the consequences have to be understood by all concerned, including the client, and then handled in a co-operative way. An adversarial clause in the contract together with unreasonable changes in the requirements lead inevitably to dissatisfaction all round. A legal fitness for purpose clause will merely make it worse.

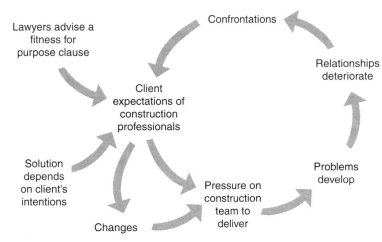

Fig. 6.6. Legal fitness for purpose

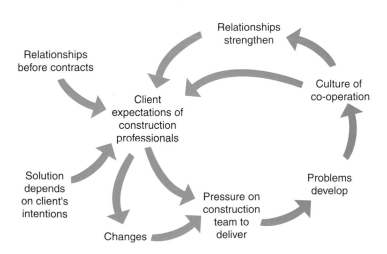

Fig. 6.7. Duty of care to provide fitness for purpose

6.6 Motivating for quality

So why change? What is in it for us? What is the motivation here?

Drive in the capacity to identify and take new opportunities

Figure 6.8 demonstrates the costs of late changes in a project life cycle and hence the possible opportunities for savings if the consequences of these changes are thought through from the start of the project. Likewise, Figs. 6.9 and 6.10 illustrate the opportunities created by co-operative relationships.

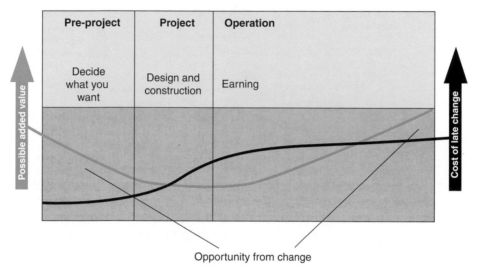

Fig. 6.8. Opportunity to add value

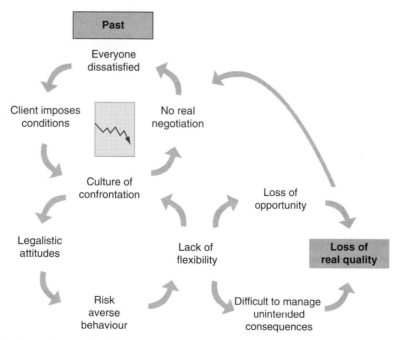

Fig. 6.9. Loss of opportunities

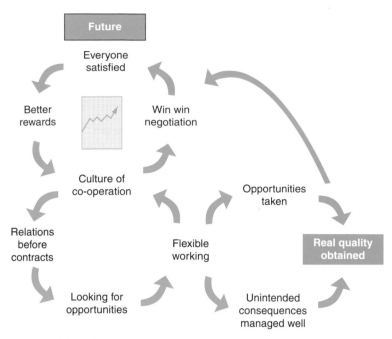

Fig. 6.10. Opportunities taken

We have stressed the idea that failure is often the result of the unintended consequences of our decisions and action. Of course, not all unintended consequences are necessarily unwanted, some are opportunities for unforeseen benefit. This is when a process team can really begin to add value to the client and hence to the team (Box 6.12).

Box 6.12   **Principle**

Opportunities often derive from the unintended consequences of decisions and actions.

A co-operative team culture will enable those opportunities to be taken, the rewards shared and value added for all concerned.

Box 6.13   Opportunity from an unintended consequence   Example

A consultant was asked by the client of a project to advise on the management of risk by the other players. It became clear that the problematic issues were not about risk but rather about being clear about the connection between the vision of the project and its implementation. The decision by the client to ask someone to look at risk management resulted in a significant improvement in a totally different aspect of the project.

The drivers of change are illustrated in Fig. 6.11. The motivation is simple to say but not simple to do — we want to add value to everyone involved and **share the rewards fairly** to sustain long-term relationships. How do we get people to set and attain more efficient and less costly processes? How do we improve

To improve added value

Fig. 6.11. Why change?

quality culture and strategic direction? How do we persuade clients to recognise the added value that the construction players bring? These are all crucial issues for rethinking construction.

We have to do it at the many different levels at which we operate. We will simplify them to the following four levels: society as a whole; organisations; teams; individuals.

Construction is often seen as a cause of problems not as a solution to them

We all want to see social benefits to our quality of life, including the developing world. Construction has a clear role in providing the means for this. It provides for many of the most basic requirements for a civilised society such as shelter, communication networks (e.g. road and railway), water supply and waste treatment.

The relationship between the industry and societal benefit, as a whole, is beyond the scope of this book but essentially the message is the same. If the industry adds to those values which society considers important then society will, in return, recognise that value. Unfortunately, the industry, as a whole, does not usually identify the full range of value adding that it provides because we focus so much on function and cost. If we measure ourselves only on these narrow criteria — and others are expecting other sets of values — then they will be dissatisfied.

The public may reject some new facilities as poor value for money, as a threat to public safety or as an eyesore. From another viewpoint the same facilities may provide a much needed sewage treatment works or a new power station or may even win an architectural prize. These latter values may not be appreciated until there is a breakdown. If that happens then those who rejected the facility will complain about its absence.

Of course, these are complex questions since many of the values held by society are often only recognised when they fail (e.g. major disasters such as Chernobyl, Ramsgate Ferry, BSE). Controversies such as those concerning genetically modified foods strike at basic assumptions about the values that technology can deliver. Construction is often seen as a polluter of the environment rather than the means by which pollution can be controlled. It is therefore essential that the added value of construction to society is identified and disseminated. These questions concern the relationship of the industry to our political systems and the way in which we organise ourselves as a society. They are big issues that deserve a separate volume devoted to them alone and will not be discussed further here.

Successful companies add distinctive value

Success may be defined, for a company, as the reward received for *excelling* at a set of *distinctive capabilities* that have a *special value* to a particular part of the *market place*.

There seem to be two questions at the heart of any decision. 'How does this contribute to our purpose?' 'How does this embody our values?'

Box 6.14   **Principle**

For a company, success is the reward received for *excelling* at a set of *distinctive capabilities* that have a *special value* to a particular part of the *market place*.

If we are collectively to improve the performance of the construction industry we need to harness the commitment of all who are involved. This is where the real systems leverage will come from.

Box 6.15   **Principle**

A vision is a mental picture of a desirable future

A mission is an impelling purpose

Likewise, shared purpose provides a focus for driving strategy. The much scoffed at mission and vision statements are important here. These statements are not as important in themselves as in the **process by which they were achieved** — something that is usually overlooked. Vision and mission statements dreamt up by senior managers and announced to the workforce are indeed a waste of the paper on which they are written since no-one below those senior managers will 'own' them. The key to getting that ownership is the process of deciding on the statements with the people involved.

Successful people add distinctive value

Just as companies succeed by finding a niche in which they can add value, so can individuals. Personal mastery is the phrase introduced in Chapter 3 (Box 3.12 and Chapter 8) for the discipline of personal growth and learning that we hope all of us can attain, which goes beyond competence and skills, although it is grounded in them.

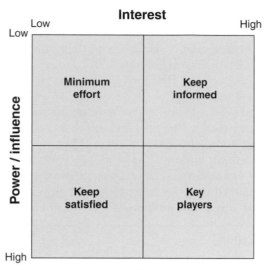

Fig. 6.12. Assessing the stance of stakeholders

Stakeholder needs should be managed

The players and stakeholders in a construction process — the customers, contractors, designers, stockholders, employees, various communities, suppliers and the general public — all have needs and wants associated with construction. Some of these interests will be perceived as positive and some as negative. The new railway might improve the value of property in the area where I live, while the noise from construction will reduce my enjoyment of my garden. There needs to be something in it, some reward, for each of the players and stakeholders.

The first step is to identify who the stakeholders are. Remember stakeholders are the people and organisations that have an interest in the project but are not players. Their stance to the project can be assessed on a scale from total opposition, through indifference to total support. The power of each stakeholder to influence the outcome can be assessed, for example, as high, medium or low. Typical actions required are illustrated in Fig. 6.12 (Johnson, Scholes, 1999).

We look at the different forms of power or capacity to influence in Chapter 8.

We have a hierarchy of needs

The needs of players or stakeholders can be assessed, for any given process, through a hierarchy of needs (Box 6.16) first suggested by Maslow (Connolly, 1980). The most basic needs are food and shelter and if an individual does not have them — they dominate his or her life.

Box 6.16 A hierarchy of needs	Explanation
Self-fulfilment/actualisation	Personal mastery, freedom to choose
Ego and self respect	Recognition, sense of worth, clear values
Social	Friendship, love, belonging, acceptance
Safety and security	Resources, money
Physiological	Food, water, sex, shelter

This distinction is important when dealing with projects across the world between developed and developing countries. If these basics are indeed provided, so an individual feels reasonably secure about them, then the next set of needs relates to a sense of freedom and belonging to a group. This is because 'no man is an island' — we are holons who need freedom to be a whole and belonging to be a part.

The top two needs in the hierarchy, namely self-respect and self-fulfilment or self-actualisation are possibly the most difficult to deliver. Clearly, these highest needs may be fulfilled only by a few at present but we should always keep in mind the target of attempting to provide them for all. These are complex psychological and sociological issues that are the basics of good management practice. The ideas of shared purpose and vision of a group and personal mastery through which individuals find fulfilment are crucial ideas.

Box 6.17 Motivation			Explanation
Motivates people	**Groups**	**Demotivates people**	**Groups**
Success	Success	Failure	Failure
Recognition	Co-ordination	Criticism	Lack of:
Genuine praise	Leadership	Blame	– co-ordination
Resource	Trust	Lack of reward	– leadership
– money	Clear values	Bureaucracy	– vision
– power		Lack of:	– clarity of 'rules'
Freedom		– safety	
Confidence		– security	
Safety			
Security			
Religious beliefs			

The main point here is that in any process all of the parties should identify key players and stakeholders and think through what they need and want, what their various values are and how the needs can be met.

Negotiate needs

Where needs can only be satisfied through interdependence and co-operation then there has to be a negotiation in the team. In *Getting to yes*, Fisher and Ury (1997) point out that many people negotiate from a position or stance that they have taken on an issue. A better approach is to use **principled negotiation** with four basic points (Box 6.18). These principles can be used to negotiate how value can be added for each of the players in a team. This brings us to the important idea of how we add value.

Box 6.18 Principled negotiation	Explanation
People:	Separate the people from the problem.
Interests:	Focus on interests not positions.
Options:	Generate a variety of possibilities before deciding what to do.
Criteria:	Insist that the result be based on some dependable standard.

After: *Getting to yes* by Fisher R. and Ury W. (1997)

6.7 Adding value

Connect vision to action

In every business there is a core set of processes and there are those that support the core business. Every company should identify the distinctive capabilities that have a special value to a customer. Likewise, an enlightened employee will identify what special skills or capabilities he or she has for the company.

Hammer and Champey (1993) show the interrelationship between business processes, jobs, structures, values and beliefs, and management and measurement systems in a Business Systems Diamond (Fig. 6.13).

The diamond is intended to show that each of these four aspects depends on each other intimately. If we think of any organisation (or groups of people from the same or different organisations co-operating in a project) as a set of processes, then the four points on the business system diamond need to be considered. Most organisations and projects are organised around function and not process. We will look in more detail at the business process in Chapter 7. However, it is important at this stage to recognise that if one takes a process viewpoint then the determination of process also influences strongly four other aspects:

- the jobs that people do
- the structures in which they do them
- the management systems and measurements
- the culture of the group.

The balanced scorecard approach

Kaplan R.S. and Norton D.P. (1996) proposed that all businesses could be described in terms of four perspectives:

- business processes: selling, making and delivering, etc.
- financial: commercial management
- customer/client: source of income in return for services/products
- skills and knowledge: basic resources

Kaplan noted that few organisations seem to be able to get these perspectives in balance. As one perspective gets attention the others seem to suffer. One difficulty is that the quality and number of non-financial performance indicators are poor and few and the financial indicators seem to reflect the past. They noted that the principal functions of business, namely operations, marketing, human

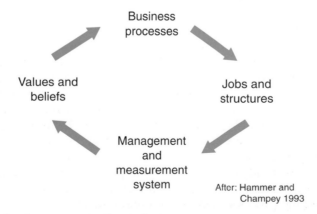

Fig. 6.13. The business systems diamond

resources, tend to operate separately. The idea of a balanced scorecard is to provide a means to ensure each is addressed and not swamped by another through the power of a process owner or other narrow consideration.

It follows that the balanced scorecard is the set of success targets for the processes within the organisation. A typical balanced scorecard is shown in Box 6.19.

Box 6.19 A balanced scorecard		Explanation and Example
AIM: TO GROW SHAREHOLDER VALUE		
Perspective	**Productivity**	**Purpose**
Financial	Better return on resources used Improve high profile projects	Improve return on capital Demonstrate project mix
Customer	Recognised as best provider Satisfied customers	Improve market share Build relations
Business processes	Improved financial measures Improve business relations	Understand competitors better
Skill and knowledge	Satisfied workforce Improved motivation	Improved training Investors in people

The perspectives in the balance scorecard can be readily turned into the high-level processes of the organisation, and the aims and objectives are the success targets for those processes. The balanced scorecard is a natural outcome of a process holon. Such an outcome can be of immense value to top management in attempting to balance the company and to link the overall vision, aims and objectives to the tasks that people actually do.

The approach described by Kaplan and Norton is very similar to that of BCIOD + R as suggested in Chapter 2. These six processes correspond to the four of Kaplan and Norton and, we suggest, are a richer set for the construction industry. Also, by focusing on process, we can link roles, functions, values, quality, risk, and we understand the supply chain, the value chain and any other chain we may care to define. The integrating processes will produce further added value.

Removing waste is removing processes that do not add value

One of the big issues in construction site processes is the reduction of waste. The generic issue here is the identification and removal of non-value adding processes as in Lean Construction. Clearly, this waste reduction by removal of processes must not be interpreted too narrowly because processes that support the core business do not add value directly to the core business (such as paying the wages), however, without that essential service the core business would break down. Therefore, it is essential to recognise that value can be indirect as well as direct to the core business. Many of the difficulties arise at the interface between processes, especially between technical and business processes. One major advantage of thinking holistically at various levels of process is that it becomes natural to think about the interfaces as well as the processes themselves. In many cases, cross-functional processes tend to be poorly owned and so these provide rich opportunities for improvement (Godfrey 1993).

Generate more value through value engineering

Value engineering is the discipline that grew up around the notion that there is a need to identify explicitly the value of every function of every part in an engineering product. The methodology is about creating a climate of work where every part is assessed for the value it brings and every part is examined to see how it might be improved. Of course, if a part is found to be unnecessary then it can be removed. If a part can be redesigned to fulfil its function more efficiently then savings are made. This requires the creative thinking that we discussed in Chapter 5.

Value in value engineering, however, has a much more specific interpretation than we have used in this chapter so far — it is fair price, monetary return or value for money. It is often defined as the ratio function/cost. We should compare that idea with the values in Box 6.4.

We can measure value for money in terms of willingness to pay or in terms of other financial parameters. In order to do that we need to consider the whole business case and we will do that in Chapter 7.

A typical set of values that would be part of a value tree in a value engineering exercise are shown in Fig. 6.14. In a process holon, each of the values set out in the tree is simply a success target. Each success target can be reached through a sub-process holon as shown in Fig. 6.15. In terms of the multi-dimensional space of Fig. 2.15 the values are points in the state space (Box 6.20).

Box 6.20   Values as state variables   Theory

In Fig. 2.15, a process is a trajectory through a multi-dimensional space of variables describing the state of the process. These variables are effectively the criteria for deciding the success of the process and the final required values are the success targets. The weights and the scores given to each value define the location of the success point or region in the state space.

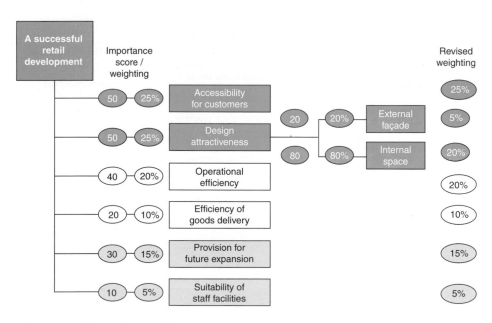

after: Connaughton and Green (1996)

Fig. 6.14. Building a value tree

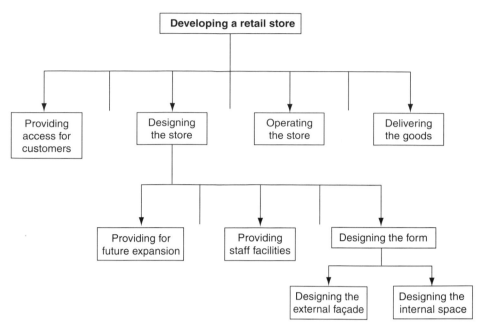

Fig. 6.15. Process model for the value tree of Fig. 6.14

Functional analysis is an analysis of the roles in the system

Another important aspect of a value engineering exercise is to identify the various functions for a system. For example, a function tree for a library is shown in Fig. 6.16. Each part of the library plays a role (which you recall is a function for an artefact) in the process of being a library. Figure 6.17 shows the process model for a library and provides a test against which any particular proposal can be evaluated. Thus a value tree and a function tree are particular aspects or views

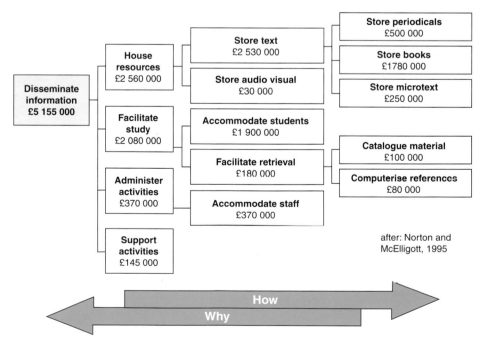

Fig. 6.16. Function tree for a library

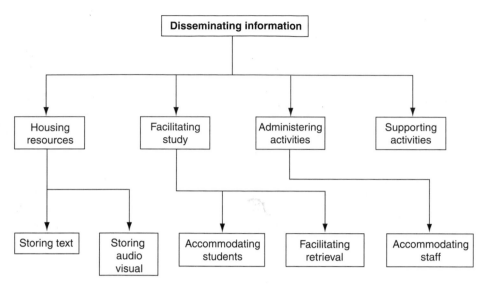

Fig. 6.17. Process model for the function tree of Fig. 6.16

of a process model. The power of the process model is that we use the process to attach values (as success targets) and functions (as roles) to them. One could simply describe the functions as the reaching of success targets.

Through the sub-processes the design team can apply creative thinking to improve the design schemes. Figure 6.18 shows how the cost savings made during this exercise can show payback.

The important point is to find waste — work that neither adds value nor enables value — and to eliminate it. One obvious example is the effort that goes into making, arguing and settling claims which from a holistic viewpoint provides poor added value for everybody — except the lawyers!

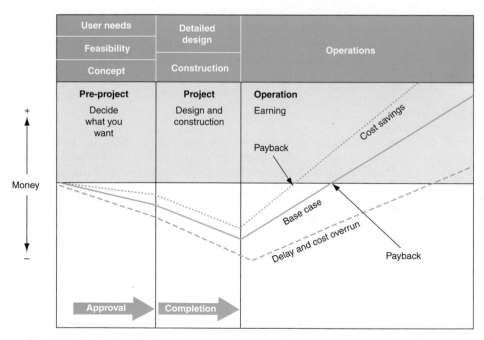

Fig. 6.18. Project cash flow

6.8 Behaving ethically

Our whole enterprise depends upon our values. Underpinning our values are moral or ethical beliefs. Different points of view may derive from different ethical stances. Differences between government and protesters over road building programmes demonstrate the point well. Media debates about the willingness of 'big business' to pay for safety improvements are other examples. By using systems thinking we intend, at least, to improve understanding of these ethical issues to attempt a more rational use of effort and resource than sometimes happens. For example, the escalating complexity and cost of the planning process for the public enquiry into Terminal 5 at Heathrow has been reported at £80 million (*Financial Times*, March 17th 1999) which must represent little added value to anybody. Put another way, it should be possible to reach an acceptable decision by less costly means and so release money saved for other purposes.

Take a duty of care

Professionals clearly have a legal and moral duty of care to deliver quality. The duty of care is a responsibility to act reasonably with respect to a number of constituencies or stakeholders — oneself, family, client, society at large and the physical environment. The taking of responsibility implies not that one has earned the right to be right or even nearly right, but that one has taken what precautions one can reasonably be expected to take against being wrong. Construction is a responsible decision-making activity based on specific values — one of which is to act responsibly by obtaining dependable information (Box 6.21).

Box 6.21   **Principle**

**Morals are concerned with right and wrong
— with what ought to be rather than what is.
They are about defining what is *good*.**

**Ethics is the discipline of moral conduct.
It is a set of standards by which a particular group
or community decides to regulate its behaviour
to distinguish what is acceptable in pursuit of its aims and what is not.**

In ordinary discourse the words morals and ethics may be used interchangeably; for example, we may speak of moral conduct or of ethical conduct and we may speak of moral philosophy as ethics. We may speak of medical ethics or engineering ethics. Of course, there are standards of morality that are related not to specific roles but to all of us — for example, being honest.

Engineering ethics involves normative enquiries aimed at identifying and justifying the morally desirable norms and standards that ought to guide us. Normative questions ask 'What ought to be?' and 'What is good?' Questions are those such as 'When should an engineer blow the whistle on dubious practice?' or 'Whose values should be primary on a large contract in a developing country?' or 'What is a good risk, given that all risk cannot be eliminated?'

Some of the interpretations of that which is known as the 'golden rule', which is the cornerstone of our understanding of how we should behave, are shown in Box 6.22.

Box 6.22	Principle
Do unto others as you would have them do unto you	*Christianity*
Do unto all men as you would wish to have done unto you, and reject for others what you would reject for yourselves	*Islam*
Hurt not others that which pains yourself	*Buddhism*
This is the sum of all true righteousness Treat others, as thou wouldst thyself be treated. Do nothing to thy neighbour, which hereafter Thou wouldst not have thy neighbour do to thee	*Hinduism*

There is no 'golden rule' for construction or for engineering but there is a duty on players to apply their professional knowledge and skills responsibly. One suggestion for a golden rule might be 'the construction player shall at all times apply his/her specialist knowledge and skill in the public interest, with honesty, integrity and honour.' Every professional society has its own rules expressed in a code of behaviour and while they will have much in common, there are many variations.

Box 6.23	Principle
Ethics is about managing differences and making choices about individual, family, work and societal issues.	

Are ethics relative or absolute? Philosophers have tried to find some general and absolute principles and they have failed (Warnock, 1998). So does this mean that anything goes? There is a 'hard core' of principles with which almost everyone would agree. The problem is that it seems always possible to find counter-arguments for any general rule, which places one rule over another. For example, while being honest is a very important principle, there are circumstances where it can be argued that it is best to tell a 'white lie'. This is why judgement is necessary in any system for measuring worth. Some of the important values for construction players are shown in Box 6.24.

Box 6.24 Some important values	Explanation

- Truth
- Honesty
- **Trust**
- Respect for others and the environment
- Fairness
- Respect for the concerns and interests of others
- Making what we do enjoyable for those with whom we interact
- Openness
- Competence
- Sustainability
- Balance
- Harmony
- Reasonableness

Based on a reading of many professional codes of conduct the responsible construction player should always, as a minimum, be clear about the issues shown in Box 6.25.

Box 6.25   **Principle**

Construction players should:

- be clear about what their own values are;
- be informed about the projects in which they are involved;
- think about the consequences of what they do and in particular try to anticipate the unwanted and unintended consequences;
- be up-to-date in professional skills;
- act professionally only in their areas of competence;
- keep health and safety and public welfare paramount;
- communicate openly with the public about technological developments;
- be honest;
- disclose circumstances where there may be a conflict of interest;
- neither offer nor accept bribes;
- treat all others fairly in respect of race, religion, sex, age, ethnic background or disability;
- help colleagues promote growth of skills and competence.

We believe that business ethics is an underdeveloped subject in the construction industry and the value systems that players use are not often explicitly discussed. While most professional institutions have practical codes of conduct and guidelines of behaviour, these vary in detail. Most of the general principles mentioned so far here are included and are applied by most construction players, whether they belong to a professional institution or not. The problem is that where difficult dilemmas involve a clash in some of the basic values there is little guidance — the individual has to make a judgement. Classical cases are those such as when to decide to 'blow the whistle' on a situation which involves setting the needs of one's family against those of the wider community (Blockley, 1998). Box 6.26 sets out some of the consideration that should be made when deciding whether or not to 'blow the whistle'.

Box 6.26   Factors to consider before   Explanation
**   'blowing the whistle'**

- Is there a serious threat to the safety of the public?
- Has no satisfaction been obtained from one's immediate bosses or for whistle blowing to people outside of the organisation, from a higher level of bosses including the Board of Directors?
- Is convincing documented evidence available?
- Is there evidence that by blowing the whistle, public safety will be maintained?
- How can I avoid breaking my duty to maintain confidentiality to my employer or client?
- Have I sought legal and professional advice and guidance?
- How can I avoid unacceptable harm in fulfilling responsibilities to my family?

Guidance is available from the Codes of Conduct of the professional institutions and the Engineering Council's *Guidelines on risk issues*, 1993 (particularly the section entitled 'Resolving a risk concern') or the Royal Academy of Engineering's *Guidelines on warnings of preventable disasters*, 1991.

Build trust

Trust is a fragile commodity. You either have it about someone or something or you do not. It is easy to break and hard to build. Trust between construction players is essential for the *Rethinking Construction* initiative. This is why clear ethical values are so important. Trust depends upon honesty, openness and fairness. It depends on agreed ways of doing things to develop a win–win for all. It depends upon measurement and agreed objective criteria (remember Popper's World 3 is where we share things — Chapter 4). That is why measurement is crucial to building trust.

6.9 Understanding the risks

We want to deliver quality. If we have decided on our values and we have identified our success targets, if we have summoned up the resources and we have planned what we want to do, then just what can prevent us from reaching our goals? The answer is, of course, **almost anything**. There are many hazards that can get in the way.

We want to add value by controlling risk and hazard well and by making new opportunities (Fig. 6.19).

If you look again at Fig. 2.14, you will see that it shows a process at a point in time part way through the process. At this moment the process owner and all

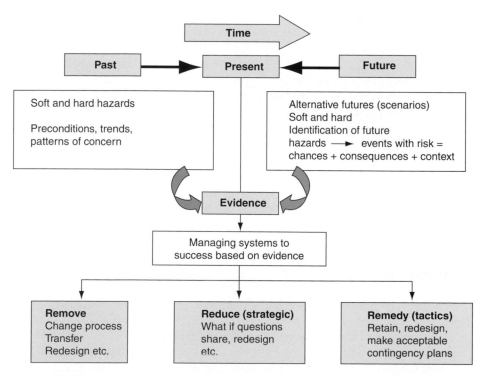

Fig. 6.19. Management of risk and opportunity for success

of the other parties to the process will be concerned to know whether quality is being delivered. This means that they want to know if the process is on track to success. In order to decide, we need to look at the *evidence*. All too often there is very little formal consideration of the risks to a project to provide such evidence and that, of course, is in itself a risk!

Evidence of progress to success comes from the past, present and future

Evidence comes from **past** performance, **present** performance and possible **future** performances (scenarios).

Of course, we have to include in that evidence an estimate of the chance that these future scenarios will actually come about. Unfortunately, present published guidance on risk management tends to focus almost entirely on these chance predictions. That is not to say that evidence from prediction is not useful — it is essential — but there does need to be more credence given to evidence from a more detailed analysis of past and present performance. In this we seem to fail to learn from the practical experience of the people at the front line doing the work. We find it difficult to synthesise knowledge from a series of projects.

The type and amount of evidence that can be collected will depend on whether or not the resources have been justified in the earlier decisions about the management of the process. For example, the observational method in geotechnical projects has produced significant benefits. Extra expenditure on monitoring particular technical parameters (such as the deflection of a retaining wall) has resulted in cost savings (Box 9.9).

Evidence for risk management derives from hard and soft systems. However, it is important to remember, as we discussed in Chapter 4, that all hard systems are embedded in soft ones.

Clearly, evidence will be from both the hard and the soft systems attributes of the process. For those attributes that are easily measurable, there may be easy and obvious measures of progress. Thus progress on a bridge that is being constructed according to a particular plan (as expressed through a timebox, a critical path analysis or just simple bar chart) may be measured through a number of parameters or just simply as a percentage completion. The expenditure against the spending plan may be similarly expressed. Soft systems attributes will be more difficult — however, they are taken into account on a daily basis in current construction but perhaps in not such a formal way as indicated here. Site meetings and management meetings should routinely consider such matters, although often they do not.

There is a need to face up to issues positively and to solve them as a team for the benefit of all. This requires people to have the courage and support to enter a zone of discomfort (Box 6.27) as they realise the problems and proceed to solve them. A process owner should try to establish the principle that it is legitimate to do it provided that it is done from principle and not for personal reasons.

Hazards are 'banana skins'

A hazard is commonly defined as the potential for adverse consequences of some event or sequence of events. It is more generally, therefore, a situation that could occur during the lifetime of a system that has the potential for human injury, damage to property, damage to the environment, economic loss or, in a word, harm.

Hazards are banana skins, some fairly obvious and some hidden, on which a process could 'slip' — with some consequent damage to the process.

> **Box 6.27 Zones of discomfort**   **Explanation**
>
> Most issues carrying a risk are known to at least one member of the team. Unfortunately, the issues are often not brought out into the open. The reasons for this include:
>
> - the possibility of a future claim and a potentially better case for that claim if the problem gets worse;
> - self-protection;
> - a culture of blaming, rather than addressing the real issues;
> - a tendency to 'shoot the messenger';
> - competitive pressures between teams, e.g. sales team, design team, procurement team, construction team;
> - a sense of loyalty to one's client, colleagues, team or employers;
> - people just do not want to jeopardise personal relationships by opening them up.

Hazard analysis is about identifying these banana skins, the hazards and the consequential events. Hazard management is about dealing with them. Some can simply be **R**emoved, some can be **R**educed and others have to be **R**emedied so that the risk is acceptable. We shall refer to these later as the 3**R**s of risk management response.

Hazards exist in the past, present and the future

It is important to realise that hazards may have existed in your systems for some time and gone unrecognised. There has therefore been a potential for failure that we did not know about. For example, we should always think of welds as having cracks — even though they may be very small at the moment. (There is always a potential for the cracks to grow, and in situations where that is important — such as a nuclear pressure vessel —we have a duty to monitor the possibility of crack growth.) Likewise, we should think of computer programmes as having bugs (even if they have not yet manifested themselves). Fortunately, if failure has not occurred then the hazards are not yet at the level to cause damage. However, it may be that events of past history may be more easily explained when we realise that a hazard existed. It is analogous to you going to the doctor feeling 'one degree under' and learning that you have been suffering sometime with a specific illness you did not know you had and have never heard of before.

Hazards may also exist in the future — but there are many possible ones forming many possible future scenarios. Therefore, we have to attempt to predict which ones are the most likely to occur. These hazards are the source of risk. These hazards are the continuation (through the process) of current conditions into future ones. The way the process continues can only be a matter of projection into the future. For hard systems that we understand well we can project well. We can use our models to predict and possibly to simulate future scenarios. For some hard systems (e.g. soils and foundations) and for most soft systems our projections are much less certain.

It is obvious, therefore, that we will only be able to predict future hazards that we understand. Nevertheless, the number of possible futures is infinite especially when people are in the system. We will return to this issue later when we discuss the nature of risk.

Hazards are hard and soft

We can classify hazards into four dependent kinds: physical; environmental; individual human; social. The first two are traditionally categorised as hard and the last two as soft — although there are elements of both hard and soft in all four.

Physical hazards are the most obvious. There is a fire without a safety guard and a child playing nearby. There is a trailing wire across the floor just waiting for someone to trip over. The typical hazards on a construction site, such as unprotected trenches or inadequate scaffolding, are well known and will not be discussed further here.

There are more subtle hard physical hazards such as leaking joints or cracks in welds that exist whether we have noticed them or not. They may allow corrosion to develop or grow in size under repeated loading into significant sources of damage. For example, nuclear pressure vessels are constantly examined for the presence of weld cracks through high temperature loads as well as the normal gravity forces. The steel not only fatigues but it also creeps in a very complex manner. There are other unusual ways in which physical systems can be damaged from as yet unknown or poorly understood phenomena. Condition monitoring processes are increasingly being adopted to monitor these incubating hazards.

Likewise, environmental hazards are well known. They are the weather hazards such as snow loading and wind loading as well as the hazards more unusual for the UK but important worldwide such as earthquakes and tornadoes. Hazards that are much more difficult to assess over the long term are global warming and damage to the ozone layer.

The third category of individual human hazards are those created by people on their own such as errors, mistakes and other unsafe behaviours. An undetected calculation error in a design would be an **error** — since the intention was correct but the execution was faulty. A **mistake** is made when the intention itself was faulty — e.g. the use of a wrong design concept. The problem here is that human beings have an almost infinite capacity to change their minds or to make errors and mistakes, so it is difficult to anticipate under what circumstances individual human hazards will occur. The attitude and behaviour of individuals could also be a hazard. For example, a 'macho' attitude to personal safety causes many construction accidents.

Likewise, but even more difficult to detect, are social hazards. These are subtle and deeply difficult to identify and manage. If there is an inadequate safety culture, if communications are poor or if difficult issues are commonly ducked, then we have a social hazard. We will return to this fourth category of hazard in the next section.

Box 6.28 shows a more detailed hazard classification for risk to a client's business from construction (Godfrey, 1995). There are many texts now available to help you deal with the relatively clear hazards that can be anticipated. The standard way to deal with these is to draw up a risk register (Godfrey, 1995). However, it is important to remember that risks are dynamic and continuously changing and need to be constantly managed. Some of them are very difficult to spot.

However, it is the **subtle and difficult to identify hazards** that incubate in the system that pose the real challenge.

Hazards are incubating preconditions for failure

In 1978, Barry Turner, a sociologist, wrote a book in which he noted that certain regularities occur in disasters (Turner and Pidgeon, 1998, 2nd edn). The first edi-

Box 6.28	Enhanced list of hazards from CIRIA	Example
Political	government policy, public opinion, change in ideology, legislation, disorder (war, terrorism, riots)	
Environmental	contaminated land, pollution liability, nuisance, permissions, public opinion, internal/corporate policy, environmental law or regulations or practice or impact requirements	
Planning	permission requirements, policy and practice, land use, socio-economic impacts, public opinion	
Market	demand (forecasts), competition, obsolescence, customer satisfaction, fashion	
Economic	Treasury policy, taxation, cost inflation, interest rates, exchange rates	
Financial	bankruptcy, margins, insurance, risk share	
Natural	unforeseen ground conditions, weather, earthquake, fire or explosion, archaeological discovery	
Project	definition, procurement strategy, performance requirements, standards, leadership, organisation, (maturity, commitment, competence, experience), planning, quality control, programme, labour and resources, communications and culture	
Technical	design adequacy, operational efficiency, reliability	
Human	error, incompetence, ignorance, tiredness, communication ability, culture, work in dark or night or difficult conditions	
Criminal	lack of security, vandalism, theft, fraud, corruption	
Safety	regulations (e.g. CDM, Health and Safety at Work), hazardous substances, (COSSH), collisions, collapse, flooding, fire, explosions	
Legal	land ownership, interpretation of contracts, court actions, constrained relationships	
Process	lack of process owner, clear roles, competent players, success measures and targets, customer focus, risk management, etc.	

(Godfrey, 1995)

tion of the book was way before its time and only in recent years has the essential message begun to be more widely appreciated (e.g *J. Contingency Management*, 1998, Vol. 6, No. 2) (Box 6.29).

Some of the social hazards are **very difficult to identify** because there is no understanding of a **causal connection** between present conditions and future conditions. To illustrate the difficulty, let us consider an example from a different issue. Is there a causal connection between violence on the TV and violence among certain teenagers? Many people would believe that such a connection (i.e. that violence on TV influences some teenagers to be violent) is a simple matter of commonsense. However, it is very difficult to establish a causal connection — particularly one that is testable in a scientific way. Therefore, it is possible for people to argue that it is perfectly acceptable to continue to make and to show violent films because there is no evidence of any connection with teenage behaviour patterns. However, as a parent, many people would want to limit the

---

Box 6.29   Hazards as incubating preconditions   Explanation
**   for failure**

In 1978, Turner argued that the potential for unintended and unwanted consequences of human actions can develop over time. He showed that large-
scale accidents usually have multiple preconditions with factors which
accumulate over a considerable period of time (which he called an incuba-
tion period of an accident). For example, events may be unnoticed or mis-
understood because of wrong assumptions about their significance.
Dangerous preconditions may be unnoticed because of the difficulty of handling information in complex situations. There may be uncertainty about how
to deal with formal violations of safety regulations. When things do start to
go wrong the outcomes are typically worse because people tend to minimise
the danger as it emerges, or to believe that the failure will not happen. As a
result, events accumulate to increase the predisposition to failure. The size
of a trigger event (e.g. a high wind or snow fall, an earthquake or human
error) which releases the pent-up energy in the system is not the only important cause of the accident; rather, one of the main tasks following an accident is to identify the preconditions of the accident waiting to happen. These
preconditions are the hazard and they represent the developing potential for
failures and accidents.

Box 6.30   The balloon model   Explanation

Imagine the development of an accident (failure, disaster) as analogous to
the inflation of a balloon. The start of the process is when air is first blown
into the balloon, when the first preconditions for the accident are established.
Consider the pressure of air in the balloon as analogous to the 'proneness to
failure' of the process. As the balloon grows in size, so does the 'proneness
to failure' of the process. Events accumulate to increase the predisposition
to failure. The size of the balloon can be reduced by letting air out and this
parallels the effects of management decisions that remove some of the pre-
disposing events and reduce the proneness to failure. If the pressure of events
builds up until the balloon is very stretched, then only a small trigger event,
such as a pin or lighted match, is needed to release the energy pent up in
the system. The trigger is often confused with the cause of the accident. The
trigger is not the cause — the over-stretched balloon represents an accident
waiting to happen. In accident prevention, it is important to recognise the
preconditions — to recognise the development of the pressure in the balloon.
Indeed, if you prick a balloon before you blow it up, it will leak not burst!

   One of the responsibilities of all of the players in any process (led by the
process owner) is to look for evidence of the building pressure in the balloon
— to spot the accident waiting to happen — and to diagnose the necessary
actions to manage the problems away.

---

viewing of such films by their children — because they judge it to be commonsense to do so.

   Many of the social hazards that Turner identified are of this type — hazards
where a causal connection is difficult to argue — but nevertheless there seemed
to be patterns of commonsense reasons why these hazards are preconditions to
accidents. These patterns form evidence for decision makers who want to steer
their projects away from hazard to ultimate success.

There are tools to audit hazards in the past and present

ISRS

Evidence of past and present performance can be examined by formal audits. For example, the ISRS (International Safety Rating System, Box 6.31) is widely used to audit management systems, and was used on the Channel Tunnel and by British Rail to monitor safety systems.

Box 6.31   The International Safety Rating   **Explanation**
System (ISRS)

The ISRS is an audit of safety management. In each of 20 major categories there are questions with associated points scores. The accumulated score is the measure of the safety effort of the organisation.

The categories are:
  leadership and administration
  management training
  planned inspections
  task analysis and procedures
  accident/incident investigations
  task observation
  emergency preparedness
  organisational rules
  accident/incident analysis
  employee training
  personal protective equipment
  health control
  program evaluation system
  engineering controls
  personal communications
  group meetings
  general promotion
  hiring and replacement
  purchasing controls
  off the job safety

MARIUN

MARIUN (MAnaging RIsk and UNcertainty), Box 6.32, was developed by the first author, based on the systems process ideas of this book, precisely to tackle these difficult to identify hazards that are not understood as causal but nevertheless have been found to be important in failure case histories. MARIUN enables us to interrogate a process to discover soft hazards in a way that allows the results to be linked directly to what we do, i.e. the process. Thus a diagnosis of remedial action is possible.

MARIUN also creates a dialogue between the players in a process which in itself adds value. It increases understanding of hazards and future risks and it directly informs decision making.

MARIUN is presently undergoing trials. The basic idea is that it is possible to assess whether a process holon is, at any stage of development from inception to completion, proceeding towards eventual success.

The process owner, or an auditor of a process, looks for evidence that the process will be successful. The evidence will ideally come from the past, present and future. Evidence from the past and present comes from a detailed audit.

> **Box 6.32   MAnaging RIsk and UNcertainty (MARIUN)   Explanation**
>
> MARIUN is a tool for life cycle process and product management which is designed to help manage away the complex technical, human and organisational factors that have been found to be important in case studies of technical and business failures. Failure is defined as lack of success in reaching stated objectives. Examples are accidents, disasters and business failures, whether large or small.
>
> The factors that MARIUN is designed to detect may be difficult to foresee and hence control since none of them may be a direct cause of failure — rather they contribute to a process through which accidents develop. Research has shown that when these factors occur together there is a potential to 'incubate' a failure. These factors may be the preconditions of an 'accident waiting to happen' and hence need to be identified and controlled.
>
> MARIUN can be used to examine projects such as: a construction process or the operations of a construction company; the operation of a piece of equipment or a power station or a power generating company; the operation of a school, financial or public institution; processes of engineering, design, management or administration.
>
> At the heart of MARIUN is the idea that hazard is a much more general concept than is commonly perceived. In MARIUN, a hazard is an incubating set of pre-conditions to failure.
>
> MARIUN is a methodology for the rigorous assessment of proneness to failure as a measure of the hazard content of a process — the capacity for the development of a failure. MARIUN is a high-level description of hazards and can be developed in specific ways for specific projects.
>
> The assessment is made through a rigorous examination of all processes including technical and business processes both hard and soft.
>
> The hazard content is described through a set of attributes that are descriptors of the state of the process. They are shown in Box 6.34. The analysis can be qualitative or quantitative using the Italian Flag and Interval Probability Theory (Cui and Blockley, 1990).

Evidence of future performance is more difficult because it involves predicting the future. However, that is exactly what almost all of engineering science is about.

Box 6.34 shows the seven process attributes to be assessed for evidence of these subtle hazards that are the pressure in the balloon of Box 6.30. The evidence collected by assessing these attributes represents the proneness to failure in a possible accident waiting to happen or, in other words, threaten the success of the process.

The first and sixth attributes are the process and sub-process names. As we have seen, one of the most difficult phases of process modelling is naming them. In the system we are examining there may well be processes happening that are completely unrecognised. However, once named you have a handle on them. We want to ensure that there are no unrecognised processes. We have to search for them systematically, using the same logic we have used in building process models. If we find processes with no process owner, and hence no means by which success is defined and delivered, then we have evidence of a hazard. Such processes are usually across functional departments. They are often dysfunctional and yet no one notices until some more major failure occurs. They can be a major source of waste and can sometimes cause consequential failure of processes that depend on them (Box 6.33).

The second attribute is a statement of one or more of the major issues which have to be resolved within the process before success can be reached. These are simply the blocks to progress that must be overcome. The hazard is not simply that such issues or blocks exist but whether they are being tackled appropriately.

For example, does the issue concern something where the state of the art is poor or is it something familiar and well known? The issues have to be clearly understood, there has to be enough knowledge and information, and control procedures should be in place. MARIUN provides a whole range of questions to collect evidence about these hazards.

Box 6.33   A process with no owner is a hazard   Example

In a company that is organised around functional departments, some processes inevitably cross departmental boundaries. Employees have access to sports facilities of the company but they have to pay for the privilege. The process of payment involves the employee registering a wish to use the facilities with one department and then paying a fee to another (finance) department. The process takes each employee about 30 minutes. No-one is responsible for the total process except the departmental heads who are responsible for their part of the process. However, they are too remote to take an interest in such a seemingly trivial process. Nevertheless, the number of hours wasted by staff going through a two-stage process and having to attend in person is considerable and important to them. A simple re-engineering of the process with a clear process owner responsible for delivering significant savings requires management to see the opportunity and to grasp it. However, in a functionally organised company the incentives to individual managers to do this are small.

Risk is in the future

Risk is the chance that a particular set of conditions will happen in a stated context. This latter aspect to risk, the context, is almost invariably forgotten yet it is critical to proper assessment. The hazards in the past and present have happened and therefore are not part of risk — **risk is in the future**. The problem about risk is that the number of possible futures is infinite — particularly where human beings are involved.

Predictions about hard risks are possible within a clearly stated context. The problem is that the soft systems in which the hard system is embedded can bring all sorts of unintended and unwanted consequences (Box 6.35). It is also difficult to model the uncertainties in the modelling of system behaviour (Boxes 6.36, 6.38).

People have a propensity to do the unexpected that is almost infinite — it certainly is not predictable with certainty. Probabilistic analysis is 'closed' and so applicable to tame problems. We need an 'open' world theory applicable to wicked problems. The Italian flag of evidence (Box 4.16) was developed for this very purpose.

Box 6.34	Process attributes and associated hazards	Explanation
Attribute	Definition or frame of reference	Example hazard
Label	The name of a particular process.	Unnamed and hence unrecognised
Issues to be Resolved	The issues or matters that need to be resolved if a process is to be implemented successfully. This covers the development of problems and solutions and the taking of opportunities.	Objectives not well defined. Roles not well defined. No process owner role
Control	The controls on the development and application of all activities and procedures for implementing the process.	Poor culture Inadequate policy Poor cost control
Knowledge	The knowledge products and methods that are the basis for development of all activities and procedures for implementing the process including the resolving of issues and controls. It includes the capability to use knowledge, products and methods.	Difficult and poorly understood technical knowledge. Regulations complex and not well understood
Performance	The performance of a process past and present and projected future.	Poor accident record
Sub-processes	The sub-processes that have been delegated to other roles.	Poor performance, accountability
Environment	That which is outside appropriate process boundaries but which can influence or be influenced by a process.	Financial pressures

Box 6.35 Roof collapse	Example

A factory roof collapsed under snow loading in the UK in 1982. The mode of failure was repeated in a number of similar structures. The failures were due to an increased sensitivity of this class of structures to snow drifting. It was demonstrated that the failure occurred from the unintended consequences of progress in our understanding of the structural behaviour of cold formed purlins. As safety margins had been reduced by technically more efficient designs, the hidden assumptions in the then design code for loading were no longer acceptable. The failure was the fault of no-one and no legal action was taken. Everyone acted with proper duty of care. Nevertheless, failure occurred because of the lack of foresight concerning subtle trends in the design of a particular type of structure.
Pidgeon, Turner and Blockley, *Structural Engineer*, 1986, Vol. 64A, No. 3, March.

Box 6.36   There is a certain poverty of prediction   Theory

In Chapter 4, we talked of four types of analytical problem. Let us now examine them from the point of view of the predictive capability. A Type 1 problem is determinism. Although we assume determinism quite readily in engineering science it has a limited place in the everyday management of systems. This is simply because there is a theoretical assumption in Type 1 problems that the future is determined *exactly* by the past and present. All that we need to do, therefore, is to discover the *model* that represents that determination. These models are the stuff of basic engineering science. At the end of the last century, everyone thought that Newtonian mechanics was the ultimate deterministic model of the universe. However, through a number of scientific developments this century, we have realised that is not the case. In fact, Godel's Theorems in mathematics, Heisenburg's uncertainty principle in physics and the more recent discoveries of deterministic chaos in non-linear dynamics have dented our confidence in being able to predict the future exactly. However, that does not mean necessarily that we cannot predict it probabilistically as in quantum mechanics. Unfortunately, as we discussed in Chapter 3, we have, in both everyday and construction processes, to allow for rather imprecise notions, particularly in soft systems. Unfortunately, we need vague and imprecise fuzzy concepts in our predictive models.

Box 6.37   **Principle**

Failure often occurs because of the unintended and unwanted consequences of our actions

---

Box 6.38   Probabilistic Risk Analysis (PRA)   Theory

Probabilistic Risk Analysis (PRA) is based on an assumption that problems are of Type 2 in Box 4.12. There is an implicit assumption that all possible future behaviour scenarios for a system can be identified as the sample space and that a measure of probability can be associated with each one. The sum of all of these probabilities is 1. Thus if we calculate that the probability of failure of a structure in a certain limit state is 10^{-5}, we are explicitly comparing the chance of that limit state exceedence relative to all other possible states of the structure.

In Fig. 2.15, we show the trajectory of a process at a point in time with respect to two performance measures or state variables. If we do not know precisely the position of the point, we can estimate the probability that the point is in a certain location. This is modelled by a joint probability density function that expresses the probability that a point is in a certain region of the space. Clearly, that part of the space of possible positions of the point that is within the failure region represents all of the scenarios of failure. Thus the union of all of the probabilities for all of the points is the total probability of failure. This is the volume of the joint density function in the failure region as shown in Fig. 6.20. The mathematics of PRA is about calculating that volume for various circumstances.

The important point to recognise is that the calculation is about the hard system. What is more, the uncertainties are entirely in the parameters that represent the system — the uncertainties in the modelling are not included. Secondly, the calculation does not include the probabilities of soft system failure.

Responding to risk — the 3 Rs

Figure 6.19 shows how we may respond to risk as Remove, Reduce and Remedy. Figure 6.21 shows how we may respond to the three aspects of uncertainty i.e. fuzziness, incompleteness and randomness.

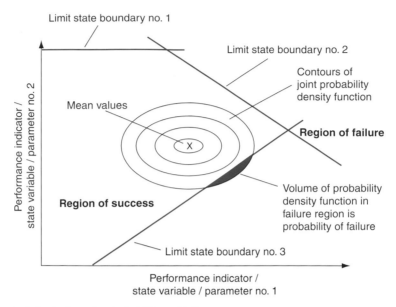

Fig. 6.20. Calculating the probability of failure

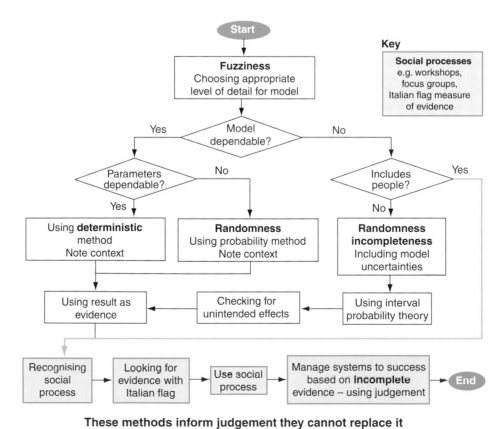

Fig. 6.21. Responding to uncertainty

Remove

Clearly, it is sensible to remove a hazard (both now and by redesign in the future) if that is feasible. If the hazard were indeed a banana skin one could simply pick it up and throw it in the bin! It is worth noting that a person devoted to risk analysis will want to calculate the chance that someone will slip on the banana skin and injure himself — even kill himself — but such a calculation is unnecessary at this stage!

The Remove option really is about thinking through all of the ways in which the hazard can be removed. This is achieved by changing the processes, **both hard and soft**, and then **redesigning** them.

Often this remove alternative is not available or even desirable. An example of the former is an earthquake risk for a structure in Japan — that hazard simply cannot be removed. An example of the latter is the transfer of a risk to a third party who cannot actually bear it. Indeed, by transferring the risk an unintended consequence may well rebound right back on you at a later date.

Three questions that might be asked of a process are as follows.

1. Is there evidence of an 'incubating' hazard that can be removed, such as:
    too much being asked of inexperienced people;
    poor communications;
    common place breaking of safety rules;
    wrong assumptions about emerging events;
    poor quality information?
2. Is there a link in a chain of processes that if removed will eliminate a hazard? For an example, see Section 9.8.
3. Are there physical system details that can be redesigned since they are not robust to variations in load/capacity/construction/operations? Are there details that:
    are not fail safe;
    will fail in a brittle not ductile manner;
    have hidden critical members that cannot be inspected;
    are lacking in continuity;
    are too sensitive to construction method;
    lack adequate strength or stiffness;
    are sensitive to changes in weather patterns;
    are sensitive to cyclic loading;
    etc.?

Reduce

After the Remove option has been explored the process team can examine each part of the process and product (as a process) asking 'What if?' type **strategic** questions. Certain key words can be developed as appropriate (as in HAZOP as used in the chemical process industries — see Kletz, Chapter 15, in Blockley, 1992) such as 'What happens if more of ... less of ... etc.?

What happens if:
    the capacity is degraded by some damage ... total damage?

What happens if:
    a pin moves?
    a pin forms here?
    this member fails?

stiffness is lost here?
loads are shed there?
there is dilatation?
   swelling?
   shrinking?
   creep?
   cracking?
   water ingress?
   corrosion?
   erosion?
maintenance is neglected?
contractor is inexperienced?
There is unusual demand (through):
   repeated loadings?
   a hole is cut in the wrong place?
   sudden crowding of people?
   sudden impact?
   load in different direction?
   different erection sequence?
   earthquake?
   extreme political pressure?
   no competent people to do it?

Remedy

This is the final **tactical** option after the other two have been explored. Hazards are identified as before. The emphasis is on attempting to predict the likely consequences, to estimate chances of failure. Judgements about these must be made in the context. Necessary redesign must be made after a similar series of questions to the Reduce option. It is at this stage that contingency planning (see next section) and protection systems may most often be designed. Commonplace examples of protection systems are fire sprinklers and fire compartments. A philosophy of nuclear systems is defence in depth. This means that if one system should fail then there is another there to provide cover. Such systems may be four or five deep. In other words, five protection systems may have to fail before there is total failure. Ideally, these systems should be independent. But this is virtually impossible to guarantee. There are many possible failures from 'common causes'. These include, for example:

- a failure in the power supply (protected by emergency back up systems);
- bugs in computer chips in COTS (Commercial Off The Shelf software protected by contingency plans); and more subtly
- the common educational background and thinking characteristics of designers that will influence them to design in similar ways.

Plan for contingencies

Thus the process of looking forward into the future of the process is to examine various possible future scenarios and to decide how likely each one is and how seriously we need to consider each one. We need to make contingency plans to allow for as many credible futures as we can imagine. From the totality of that consideration, we derive evidence of the possible future performance of our process which we combine with evidence of the past and present to come up with a combined judgement about the evidence that our process will succeed or fail.

One major method of contingency planning is the Observational Method in geotechnics and the basis of the New Austrian Tunnelling Method. We shall look at this method in more detail in Chapter 9.

Clearly, any evidence expressed as failure probabilities against hard limit states as in structural reliability theory (Blockley, 1980, 1999) is partial. It deals with only one aspect of the total safety and the total quality of the systems. It has to be absorbed into a more general assessment of the state of the process.

Engineering scientific knowledge and its use in prediction has been and will always be extremely important. However, we need to learn to deal with it for what it is and more importantly for what it is not. It is not a truth about a certain future as the deterministic philosophy would have us believe. It is not a truth about a closed set of possible futures with varying degrees in their chance of occurrence, as the probabilists would have us believe. However, in an uncertain and complex world of constant change and infinite variety of human behaviour it provides us with some evidence. It tells us that in a certain set of circumstances then this is some evidence about what may happen.

Risk and opportunity are two sides of the same coin

There is an old story that a boy in the garden with a ball presents, to his father, a risk that a window will be broken. However to the glazier such a situation is a business opportunity! The misery created by war is very unfortunate — but after the war is over there may well be business opportunities. Every problem hides an opportunity if only we are creative enough to find it (Godfrey, 1995).

Box 6.39   There are good risks   Example

The share price of a company did not change materially for a decade in spite of the fact that it was going through a bonanza period of trading. The new CEO realised that the company was particularly good at managing risk — outstanding in fact. He therefore sold off all those parts of the business which held low risk and bought new high risk businesses. The share prices soared and the profits increased even more dramatically in spite of poor trading conditions. They have actually increased by a factor of 5 in the subsequent decade.

If we do too much to avoid risk we may perversely actually increase risk. Taking risks creates opportunities. Averting risks will lead to stagnation at best but could actually result in loss and excessive costs as we actually avoid taking the steps necessary to get to success. As individuals we enjoy taking risks as long as we think we are in control and can manage the risks without undue harm to ourselves. Such challenges are exciting and invigorating.

Consider robustness and vulnerability

A robust system is one where the consequences of any possible damage to the system is not out of proportion to the magnitude of that damage. In other words, if some small damage, such as that cause by a minor vehicle impact on a bridge abutment, results in total collapse of the bridge, then that bridge is not robust

— it is vulnerable to minor vehicle impact. Clearly there are commonsense ways in which robustness can be built in to a system through redundancy.

There is as yet no theory of system robustness; in fact, there is not even a generally agreed definition of it. In every day language, concerning a structure for example, robustness implies strength and sturdiness in all possible failure modes or limit states. Structural engineers are totally familiar with the consideration of the strength of a structure in various limit states — however, the idea of sturdiness is not so familiar. Sturdiness implies a consideration of all reasonable limit states and it implies that the response of the structure is not disproportionate to the actions and loads on the structure.

The water company team, who learned to use the Italian Flag in Section 2.7, also learned about the difference between vulnerability and risk.

Box 6.40   Practical robustness   Example

Early in the development of the North Sea, the *Sea Gem* collapsed owing to brittle failure of one of its high tensile steel legs. As a result during later platform design development, engineers were empowered to insist on sufficient ductility and through-thickness quality of the steel. Brittle high performance steels were avoided in fixed platforms, in spite of the need for high strength to weight ratios. The robustness imparted by these limitations was very fortunate when unintended fatigue cracks began to appear. It allowed time for remedial measures to be taken. Had brittle failure occurred in primary members the consequence could have been catastrophic collapse, substantial economic loss and environmental damage.

6.10   Establishing a quality culture

There has been much talk in recent years about the notion of a quality culture and, more particularly, about one aspect of that which is safety culture. A simple commonsense view of culture is summed up in the phrase 'the way we do things around here'. There may be an agreed part (that which we take for granted) and a questioned part (which is problematic). Too often compliance cultures and efficacy rule the day. Many of the ideas discussed in this book are important in a quality culture. It is important to realise that culture is not about techniques, morale or even good management —although it depends upon these things — rather it is about the indefinable emergent property of the way things are done in a team or organisation. Box 6.41 represents an attempt to set out the ingredients from which a quality culture emerges. An important property that emerges from a quality culture is trust.

Box 6.41	The ingredients of a good quality and safety culture	Explanation

P	Point of view	remember we all have one and we should respect those of others
R	Responsibility	ensure responsibility and accountability are clearly defined
A	Attitude	encourage positive attitude
C	Communications	have good communications — both formal and informal
T	Technology	ensure technology is appropriate
I	Intentions	have clear objectives
C	Caring	show a caring approach (especially senior management)
A	Awareness	keep people aware of issues and stakeholder interests
L	Learning	encourage a learning approach — see failure as an opportunity to learn not to blame
L	Listening	encourage active listening — talk with people not at them
E	Encouragement	give praise at every *genuine* opportunity
A	Auditing	keep testing the processes, measure and check
R	Reality	keep a firm grip on it, face facts
N	New ideas	encourage new ideas
I	Information	make it as clear and unambiguous as possible
N	No 'yes' men	truth derives from honest disagreement among friends
G	Genuine	be genuine, honest and open

Notice that a quality culture depends very clearly on the ethical stance of the players taking part in the process.

6.11 Checking for success

The success targets for this chapter set out at the beginning were that, at this stage, you will be able to:

Success target	Review
• describe how quality depends upon values;	quality is a measure of how good the totality of what we are getting is relative to what we want from any process. We have to decide that we prefer one option to another. In order to do that we ascribe a 'worth' to something. A value is quite simply that worth;
• write down many different values;	customer satisfaction, shareholder value, customer loyalty, profit, return on capital, health and safety, quality of life, functionality, elegance, pollution, waste, sustainability, energy consumption, future generations;

• realise the importance of measuring worth;	in all of our attempts to measure worth, it is the listening, observing and understanding that follows that creates the added value. The dependability of soft measures cannot be the same as for traditional hard values — but that does not mean they cannot be useful as long as they are used appropriately. Worth is expressed in people through preferential choice and therefore all of the ways of measuring it are based on observing and recording such choices. Examples are betting and voting. The Italian Flag can be used in this way.
• set out how companies and individuals can add value;	the totality of value making quality is clearly considered and decided by those involved in a process;
• describe a hierarchy of needs;	from safety to self-fulfilment;
• describe how ethics underpins our values;	ethics is about deciding what is good — it defines our values;
• be clear that you need to be clear about your own values;	from honesty to reasonableness;
• see hazards as both hard and soft system 'banana skins' and that risk is in the future;	hazards are the banana skins that get in the way of success. They have to be actively managed by collecting evidence from the past, present and future and using the understanding so gained to keep the process on track; risk is essentially in the future — it concerns the chance of an unwanted event in a stated future context;
• describe hazard as a set of incubating preconditions to failure;	the balloon model illustrates the pressure within an **accident waiting to happen**;
• describe how to collect evidence from the past, present and future about the success of a process;	either informally from past, present and future projections or by formal audits such as ISRS or MARIUN. Use the 3 Rs of risk management, Remove, Reduce (strategy) and Remedy (tactics);
• describe robustness and vulnerability as a property of the form of a system;	a robust system is one where the consequences of damage are not out of proportion to the magnitude of that damage;
• set out the essential ingredients of a quality and safety culture.	culture emerges from ingredients such as good communications and a caring approach from senior management.

We hope that we have reached the success targets for this chapter — please use the feedback form at the end of the book.

7. Maintaining the business case

7.1 Needs, desires and demands of customers

Our success is driven ultimately by the needs, wants and demands of the customers of our clients. It is they who pay for our services — but, of course, indirectly through our clients. The needs of customers are converted into intentions and desires that, in turn, are converted to demand through a willingness to pay our clients. In turn, that drives the expectations of our clients. Their willingness to pay us depends upon our ability to satisfy them as they strive to satisfy their customers.

It is clear from the Egan report that many of our clients are dissatisfied. This is a serious opportunity for those who can find a way of changing the view of these clients from one of dissatisfaction to one of delight. In practice, the margin between these two states is small in comparison with all that we do. However, it is just this margin that will *make the difference*.

One of the best ways to delight the client is to offer him an improvement in his business case as an outcome of what we do. This is the point of view we take in this chapter (Fig. 7.1).

Fig. 7.1. Maintaining the business case

195

7.2 Targeting success for this chapter

The success targets for this chapter are that, after reading, it you will:

- see the importance of focusing on the needs and values of the client and his customers;
- know how to move from an impelling proposition to the processes that will deliver it by adding value;
- be able to interpret the essentials of a business plan;
- be able to use the client's business plan to understand his needs and values;
- be able to identify relevant sources of finance;
- be able to contribute to achieving competitive edge;
- know how to manage time to deliver a plan;
- know how to prepare a team to deliver on the plan and provide customer focus.

7.3 Delighting the client

Add value that exceeds expectations

A product is anything that can be offered to a customer to satisfy a need or want in exchange for a consideration — usually money. This is, at root, the process of business. Of course certain new products, particularly in manufacturing and retailing, are designed actually to generate a need or want in the customer. For example, no one could need or want a mobile phone until they became available. However, the need or want to communicate flexibly and easily from any location meant that, as soon as the new product became technically possible, the business could develop. In this chapter, we will consider the business case for a construction project in relationship to the business of the client.

In Box 2.8 we set out some of the products of the construction industry. The needs and wants of clients from the industry are indeed very rich and very varied. Construction touches the lives of everyone in a very basic way because it provides, among other things, the fundamental human need of shelter and transport.

Unfortunately, as we have said, cost often so dominates our thinking about these products that we neglect the other needs and wants of the client. Of course, no one would deny that costs are important but reducing cost is only one way of delighting clients and gaining competitive edge. We believe that construction professionals have to pay more attention to understanding as far as possible the needs and wants of clients and their customers both now and in the future. This will enable us to think of various ways in which we can generate competitive advantage. We have to look for opportunities to add value both to clients and to ourselves. We have to do this in current projects by building on the unanticipated consequences of decisions we make that are fortuitous and positive and can lead to benefits for all involved. We also have to explore proactively new business developments (the construction equivalent of the mobile phone). Many companies are becoming more active in this area. This will require a bigger spend on research and development funded from the increased share of the value added.

Thus if we have it constantly in mind to delight the client, his customers and our stakeholders — and furthermore if we can exceed their expectations — then we have a major source of competitive advantage. This is **the** major challenge to our creative thinking skills.

The business case is the expression of how the client's needs will be met with some reward for all involved.

> **Box 7.1   The purpose of the business case   Explanation**
>
> The business case is a statement that presents the case for investment in the project.
>
> The business plan is a tool for communicating understanding of how value is to be added to people, e.g. investors, directors, staff, providers. It is also usually needed to get regulatory approval.
>
> To understand how a process adds value we must first understand its *purpose*. The highest level purpose of most large business organisations is to add shareholder value. This they do by fulfilling many lower level purposes.

7.4   Identifying the processes

Understand the needs of the client

In order to understand better the needs and wants of clients we need to think more about the earnings side of their businesses. We need to be aware of their overall business values. Construction industry clients run businesses with customers to whom they are providing a service or product. For example, a supermarket chain sells household products to the public who are the customers. It is these customers that head up the value chain of which the construction companies involved are a part. The supermarket chain knows that without customers it has no business. Its key processes are designed to attract and keep those customers. It looks for competitive advantage in what is a hugely competitive retail sector. The most successful are integrating processes and teams and eliminating waste (Womack and Jones, 1990) by examining every process in their supply chains right down to the most detailed level.

So, for example, a large retail company which wants a new store will be significantly concerned about the cost of the building. However, it will also have other important concerns too. Examples are time to opening, noise and inconvenience to its customers, potential embarrassments from environmental damage, loss of revenue due to a hygiene scare, etc. If the construction industry professionals focus exclusively on the cost of the work then they should not be surprised if their clients, who have these other agendas to pursue in their total businesses, reject them or try to screw down construction costs to the absolute minimum. This then makes life difficult for the construction process.

Drive a business by adding value

A *values driven business* is one that is devoted to adding value to its customers and in doing so adds value to itself and its staff, Box 7.2. Figure 1.5 shows some of the measures and KPIs under the generic headings of BCIOD+R — see also Boxes 6.4. and 9.11. Clearly, individual companies (both construction and client) will have various 'mixes' of measures for their own purposes but the figures indicate some important ones. Figure 7.2 shows some of the processes that an organisation may go through in order to decide its business strategy.

Figure 7.3 sets out the essential processes of making the business case.

Box 7.2   Adding value together   Principle

Delight clients by *exceeding* their expectations.

Exceed expectations by focusing on *adding value* and not just on reducing costs.

Recognise that *interdependence* and *co-operation* are needed in order to *add value* effectively.

Recognise that to *co-operate* all players have to have a *share* in the *added value*.

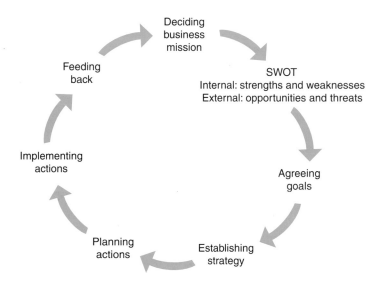

Fig. 7.2. Strategic business planning process

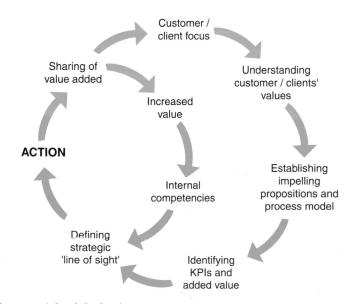

Fig. 7.3. The essentials of the business case

Starting with the impelling vision about a success target

We can create a vision for all involved in a project by developing an impelling proposition mind map which answers the *why* questions and provides the vision of high level added value to drive the business case — see Chapter 2.

Clearly, the impelling proposition has to be owned completely by the client but can be explored and developed by the supply team with the client. *Shared vision* is very important in team building. The impelling proposition should be inspirational rather than factual. The idea is to appeal more to the emotional (limbic) region of the brain than the cognitive and rational brain in order to motivate people. Hence it will be not very specific and could therefore be quickly dismissed by many practitioners as worthless unless there is a connection with delivery processes. So if the impelling proposition gives added purpose to what is done then the process model map needs to be developed from it early in the project. That will then help the client to create competitive advantage through the focus that the impelling proposition brings. The team thinking about air conditioning in the healthy pub example of Chapter 1 illustrates this point.

Defining the success target clearly

So often with the predict and provide way of organising projects (Fig. 1.7), success is not as clearly defined and agreed as it could be because many of the parties to the project have their own agendas which are not shared with the others. Thus the result is uncertain and progress can often end up in 'uncharted waters' — especially after prolonged claims, disputes and litigation. Figure. 1.9 illustrates this situation as 'success is where you get to!'

We need to move to a situation where success is agreed before we start and everyone in the team works towards the same goal as in Fig. 1.10. The success targeted approach starts with a very clear idea of success and then works backwards to devise a strategy for getting there. In order that we can do that, we have to make sure that the appropriate 'carrots and sticks' are in place. The major 'carrots' are a clear 'line of sight' and fair rewards to everyone. The 'sticks' should ideally be minimalist. Present examples of 'sticks' are laws and statutory regulations and the risk part of risk and reward agreements. The biggest stick, however, is the possibility of being passed over in favour of a competitor who is believed to be better able to add value.

Process models are the line of sight

Construction players are often suspicious of soft ideas that may seem to be all 'motherhood and apple pie'. They may therefore condemn an impelling proposition as being worthless unless there is a *direct link* between it and more specific notions of the *processes by which success can be delivered.*

Faced with the wicked problem of developing a strategic connection between these very high-level ideas and the practical reality of running a business, there is a strong need for any company to have a strong 'line of sight' from one to the other. This has to be so clear that it can be communicated to all concerned.

We use mind mapping and the process model in Chapter 2 to provide this 'line of sight'.

To recap, we create, with the client, a mind map to develop the implications of the impelling proposition. Again, at first, even the mind map may still seem rather vague. However, as the mind map develops, we begin to see the more specific ideas on which the top level impelling proposition depends. From the mind map we then create a process mind map that sets out all of the processes needed to deliver the vision — this is the product process mind map. We use the generic processes of BCIOD+R to guide our thinking and to help us generate the success measures we need.

Using the Italian Flag to monitor progress

The business case requires that progress through the work is monitored appropriately. There will often be no obvious key performance indicators for us to recognise successful delivery of the top level impelling proposition. Nevertheless, high-level management has to make decisions about such matters. If there are KPIs then we may choose to summarise them by a single judgement, i.e. to what extent do we have evidence that the process will be successful? We can collectively, and hence inter-subjectively, at any stage during the life cycle of the project, assess the evidence that the processes of delivering the impelling proposition will be successful by using an Italian Flag (Box 4.16) with it.

Of course, the evidence of success of the very top level process (as assessed by the Italian Flag) is the accumulation of the evidence of the delivery of success at the second level down. This is because those processes are, as far as is possible, necessary and sufficient (but hardly ever complete) for the top level process. This is the major criterion used to build the process model.

Again, those processes may be rather vague with no obvious key performance indicators. We can in the same way associate an Italian Flag with each one to measure the evidence that the process will be successful. Then we drop down to a third level in the hierarchy to another set of processes that are necessary and sufficient for the second level process. We can continue digging down into the hierarchy as far as we wish. Each time we assess the evidence to determine an Italian Flag we can also look for appropriate key performance indicators to help us assess the evidence. The lower the level of process, the more detailed and less vaguely defined it is and the easier it is to find performance indicators.

Of course, the best evidence, the most dependable evidence, in the limit, is when each performance indicator is connected by a highly dependable predictive mathematical function as in, say, a calculation of the response of a structure to a set of loads. These are Type 1 and Type 2 problems of Box 4.12. In that case, our assessment of the evidence will be with total confidence and the white part of the Italian Flag will not be present. These are classical deterministic and probabilistic methods with an Italian Flag entirely of green and red with no uncertain white.

The power of the methodology here is that the combined effect of all of the indicators is expressed in the Italian Flag for the top level process. In fact, there is a whole set of Italian Flags for every process in the model as contributed by all of the various process owners. Inconsistencies are easily spotted. The reasons for them reveal the need for actions that quickly add value. In other words the Italian Flags can facilitate discussion between players about the reasons for their assessments and to iron out those differences to gain understanding. The aim is to produce a consistent set of Italian Flags for all appropriate processes right up to the very top level process. In this way, new actions are diagnosed that will add new value to the process.

Building trust — address BCIOD+R

This approach addresses all aspects of BCIOD + R (Business, Customer Integration, Operations, Delivery, + Regulation). It addresses the way in which a balance is drawn between various aspects of the business (see Chapter 2 and the Balanced Scorecard approach Box 6.19). All of these issues are part of a strong business case.

Naturally, the client will have commercially sensitive material which he will want to be part of these considerations. However, he may well withhold them from the design team and, in doing so, damage the potential success of the project. It is crucial that construction professionals do everything to develop the *trust* of their clients so that they get involved early enough for these confidences to be shared within the developing business case. In this way, the construction process will be able to add even greater value to the client since those issues will be integrated into the project and not kept separate.

This emphasises the importance of explicitly stated and clear *ethical* values for the companies and for the individuals involved as discussed in Chapter 6.

7.5 Writing the business case

Understand why

As we have said the business case for the project is the answer to the 'why' question. Why is this project going forward? It has to develop confidence in the proposal — it is the basis for the delivery of the *shared vision* about the project or the 'line of sight' through the wicked problems yet to be faced.

The business case is developed by the client often with the construction professionals as part of the team. If you are not involved then at the very least you should understand the client's business and his needs and values. The business case often needs more research effort than is presently the norm — especially for smaller projects.

Be convincing

The business plan is an essential part of the case. It has to be used to obtain approval and that will normally mean making convincing presentations to potential clients, customers, funders and stakeholders. The requirement is to convince them that you know what you are doing and how it will work — that you have a good plan and you are capable of delivering it.

The business case is used to:

- seek approval for a proposed activity, e.g. from regulators
- raise finance from banks and investors
- sell or value a business
- protect the author and recipients by honestly considering the risks.

A successful business case has to demonstrate:

- sufficient market or need exists
- that management are capable and efficient
- the service or product is good and meets objectives
- risks have been recognised and will be controlled
- finance will be adequate to meet requirements and contingencies.

The processes of 'Making and maintaining the business plan' are shown in Fig. 7.4.

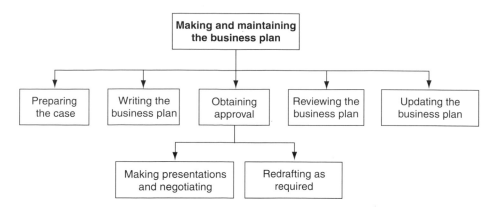

Fig. 7.4 Making and maintaining the business plan

The plan is itself a process

The writing of the business plan is a major sub-process, the output of which is the plan itself. The plan then, in turn, is a process that will be subject to change as the project develops. Clearly, as the project process advances the actions that are possible are reduced and the cost of change increases. A change in concept in the process of developing the feasibility of a scheme can cost almost nothing (Box 7.3) when the players are still considering conceptual options — whereas a change in concept during construction could not really be considered since it might well involve massive reconstruction costs.

Box 7.3 Escalating cost of change	Explanation
To alter concept	£10
To alter preliminary design	£100
To alter detailed design	£1000
To alter during construction	£10000
After a major accident	£100000

Note: Figures are indicative only.

Box 7.4 shows some of the basic questions that must be addressed to make and maintain the business case for any project.

As the process of 'Delivering the project' actually happens (designing, constructing and operating processes) then the business case must be maintained so that the basic reasons for the process are constantly being addressed and updated as necessary The basic questions of Box 7.4 are always relevant.

Box 7.5 shows a typical index for a business plan. The first background section will describe what the organisations involved do and the context they are working in.

What existing business are they in? Where they are located? What service or product do they sell? How big are they? The key issues, the market and the competition need to be outlined. If the business is regulated (and all are to a greater or lesser degree) then the relevance and constraints imposed by that regulation should be stated. The people and the management teams should be described, together with the relevant track records.

Box 7.4   The six honest serving men   **Explanation**
and a business plan

- *Why* is this proposal being made?
- *What* is the need to be met? *What* is the purpose of the proposal?
- *Why* is it different?
- *What* is the proposal — what do you/does the organisation want to do?
- *What* is the product or service, the end product?
- *Who* wants to do it with you?
- *What* is the background and context, i.e. the existing organisations, the market?
- *Where* do you want to do it?
- *When* do you want to do it?
- *How* do you propose to do it?
- *Who* wants this product or service, i.e. is there a market?
- *Who* will supply you?
- *What* are the benefits the proposal will bring?
- *What* are the constraints, regulations, laws, etc?
- *What* can go wrong? *What* are the risks we run?
- *What* do you want to do next?
- *What* is important to you?
- *What* is not important to you?
- etc.

Box 7.5   An index for a business plan   **Explanation**

Executive summary
1. Background
2. The need, market objectives
3. Options considered
4. Risk to objectives
5. Preferred approach
6. Finance, costs and benefits
7. Operations
8. Management
9. Finance
Appendices
   – research reports
   – outline designs — supporting documents

The business plan can be based on a process model. Through it, various objectives can be integrated. The needs of the customer, the objectives of the project and the overall objectives of all of the organisations involved — including the recipients of the plan — can be linked. The recipients, of course, are extremely important and the plan has to be written in a way that will convince them. Thus the writers need to know who they are and what they want and should use a language that they will understand.

Analyse stakeholder needs

As we have said, the stakeholders are those people and organisations who are not players in a process but who have an interest in its success. They, of course, vary greatly from project to project and include shareholders, government and the general public (Fig. 7.5). In some projects, all three of these may be the customer at the top of the value chain. We need to think about stakeholders, particularly when considering competitive advantage (Section 7.8) and building the team ready for the contract (Section 7.10) and managing it (Chapter 8).

Company shareholders are primarily interested in the market value of their investments, the size and stability of the dividends. Other important factors may be requirements for an ethical business that is safe, sustainable and environmentally friendly. The annual report of the directors together with balance sheets, profit and loss accounts and cash flows indicate what the company is about, and the notes to those accounts may or may not reveal some deeper insights.

Government is also a regulator

The Government has an interest sometimes as a client and always as a regulator. The health and safety regulations, for example, are well known and will not be discussed here except in general terms. The interested reader is referred to the many books on the subject (e.g. Barnard, 1998; Blockley, 1992). Traditionally, safety and cost are seen to be in competition. By this view one has to be traded off against the other so safety therefore costs money. However, studies by the Health and Safety Executive show that safety is good business (Health & Safety Executive, 1993). They have demonstrated that the costs of accidents at work are considerable (Box 7.6). The UK construction industry has a poor but slowly improving record on safety, and a systems approach would suggest that almost all that a company should do to manage quality is what one should also do to manage and promote safety. This is an example of one of Senge's 'laws of systems' as described in Chapter 3, i.e. that one can have the cake and eat it — but not at once. You can deliver safety with reduced costs but not without a significant culture change.

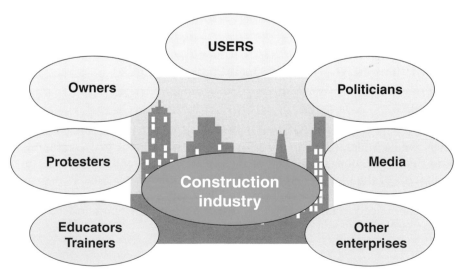

Fig. 7.5. Stakeholders in construction

Box 7.6   Safety is good business   **Explanation**

UK experience 1990–91

1 600 000 accidents at work per year resulting in injury

30 000 000 working days lost costing £700 000 000

Total cost of accidents at work:
£10bn to £15bn or 1.75–2.75% of GDP

Examples studied in detail were:

Situation   Cost of accidents

Construction site   8.5% tender price
Creamery   1.4% operating costs
Transport company   37% profits
Oil platform   14% output
Hospital   5% running costs

Costs of accidents at work, HSE, HMSO, London, 1993

The general public has a stake in safety too as the user of major construction facilities. When major accidents happen such as the collapse of a bridge or building then the industry has to account for itself. The Construction (Design and Management) Regulations 1994 (CDM) and the Health and Safety at Work Act require that safety be demonstrated throughout the life cycle. If the regulatory issues are critical to business success, they have to be included in the business case. Indeed, the Hampel Committee Report (1998) on corporate governance requires directors to control all risks to the business.

7.6   Driving in value and driving out waste

We have described how we can use an impelling proposition to identify processes that, in turn, define what has to be done. It is important in defining success for each process that, wherever possible, the key performance indicators reflect appropriate values. If the human individual and team cultures are right then the risks can often be turned into opportunities using the creative thinking skills referred to in Chapter 5.

Driving out waste is, of course, the aim of lean construction. To do this requires a clear view of the value chain. The value chain is a sequence of key processes to deliver value to the client. Figure 7.6 shows a value creation process in which the business case is connected to the delivery process by way of a unifying impelling proposition. The first part of the process (up to the impelling proposition) is the strategy and the second part of the chain is the delivering of value through a specific product.

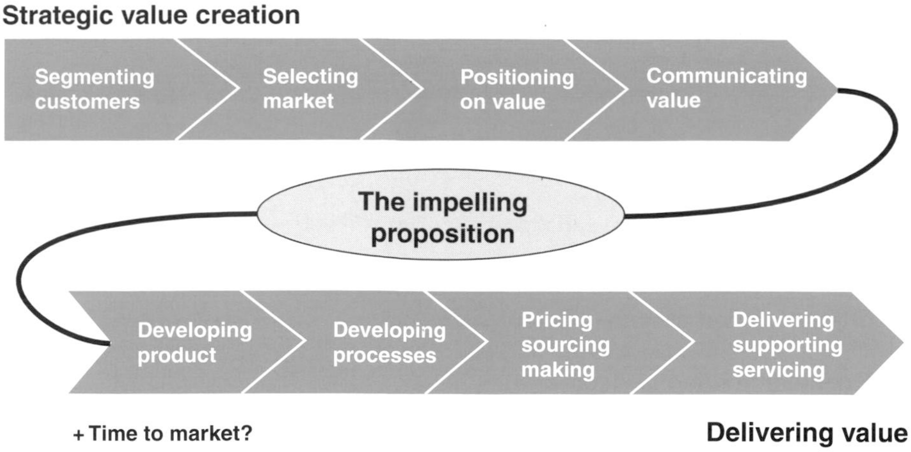

Strategic value creation

Fig. 7.6. Creating business value

7.7 Finding the finance

Finding finance is seldom the problem — the issues are affordability, risk and cash flow and confidence

It is important that construction professionals have some understanding of not only where the finance for their project is coming from but also how the client is financed from the top. While the detail of these arrangements must be the province of a financial expert the construction professional should at least be able to appreciate the major issues that are involved. For example, the information about client company finance can be found from company accounts. The financial measurements are usually translated into some key performance indicators (KPIs). The profiles of these indicators and data about the company, including the balance sheet, the accounts, share price movement as well as much other information, are usually directly available from Companies House or on the internet or from the company itself.

Box 7.7 Ask about SORM		Principle
Strategy	What is the company's strategy?	
Opportunity	What opportunities do they have?	
Risk	What risks do they face?	
Management	How are they managing them?	

Be careful about cross-industry comparisons

One has to be very careful about the interpretation of data from one company to another as profiles vary between sectors. The financial profile of a water utility will be quite different from that of a manufacturer of widgets. For example, the stock control of a widget manufacturer is crucial and has led to just-in-time manufacture, while stock control is not a major issue for a water utility company except for the crucial distribution of the water itself. Utilities in the UK compete in a pseudo-market as regulated by, for example, Ofwat for the water industry and this makes their business have special characteristics that have to be appreciated by construction players working with them. It is therefore not a simple matter to transfer techniques successful in one sector of industry to another.

An analysis of what drives the client from top down is invaluable evidence in the preparation of the project business plan. It enables the whole project to be targeted towards helping in that success and, subsequently, *identifying opportunities to add value to the client*. Confidence and trust between the parties adds potential value because many ideas for opportunities fall by the wayside without it. If issues are not faced up to because of a lack of trust then the problems are built in to the project and will emerge later to cause losses.

Are you adding value?

All construction players may from time to time find it helpful to ask of themselves the following question on a project on which they are currently engaged.

How are we *adding value* to the client's *business*? Is that value sufficient for the rewards we receive? If not why not and *how can we change our behaviour* so that the value is recognised?

Sources of finance can set the risk culture

The needs and behaviour of the client will be conditioned by his source of finance for the project. Investigations for the CIRIA guide '*Control of risk*' (Godfrey, 1995) showed that clients funded by the tax payer were far more averse to risk than those clients funded privately.

Sources of finance

The client's source of finance can be:

— from taxes
— out of income
— out of reserves/savings
— commercial loan
— selling shares (equity)
— selling stock/bonds.

Box 7.8 shows sources of finance from taxes or from commerce.

Box 7.8 Sources of finance	Explanation
Taxpayer	**Commercial**
– own finance	– private entities
– multilateral financiers	– developers
– bilateral aid	– Build, Operate, Transfer (BOT) etc.
– commercial loan	– Design, Build, Finance, Operate (DBFO)
– ECGD	– Private Finance Initiative (PFI)
	– Public Private Partnership (PPP)
– other	– contractors (Design & Build)
	Lottery

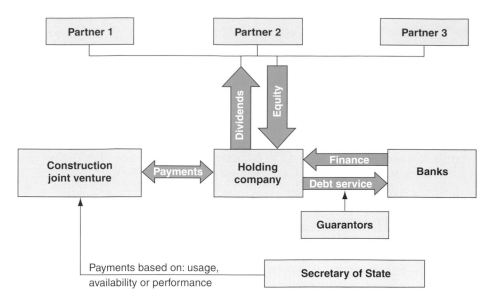

Fig. 7.7. Private funding for a concession contract

Figure 7.7 shows an example of a financial structure for a PFI construction project. The business structure informs the other processes (CIOD+R) and can change the outcome for all the players including the client. By focusing on success right from the start, a road construction project was brought in 18 months ahead of schedule while another traditional project, where there was a confrontation culture, went twice over budget. In the successful scheme the PFI enabled early income from shadow tolls that allowed extra investment during the project. The customers benefited from excellent traffic management and the scheme adopted was managed well.

At the early stages of pre-project planning, where decisions are being made about what is wanted, there is cash outflow (see Fig. 6.18). This continues through design and construction and into operations. The effect of cost savings or delays and cost overruns are shown to demonstrate the effect on the payback period. The figure demonstrates quite clearly the need to project the whole life cycle of the project in the business case.

7.8 Gaining a competitive edge

Differentiate yourself and your company

To have any competitive advantage a business has to be differentiated from others. This has to be done in terms of the values that the customers have about the business since that is why they are willing to pay. If that willingness to buy is not there then the business fails.

Cost is a basic part of any person's value system — very few people can disregard the cost of something. It is worth separating cost from other values therefore. Porter (1985) has argued that competitive advantage is either a cost advantage or a differentiation in terms of the other values such as overall quality for the same product, service levels or niche leadership in technical expertise, safety, reliability, service, etc. (Fig. 7.8.). A difficulty is that the behaviour required for each of these values may be quite different and so a company needs to focus quite sharply. However, basic levels of provision of each value are required just to stay in business whatever the particular focus.

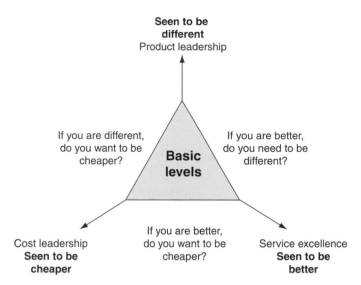

Fig. 7.8. Strategic sources of competitive advantage

Cost leadership requires tight controls

This strategy requires sustained investment with tight cost control. Delivery processes have to be efficient with intense supervision to get the quantity of work which can be delivered with adequate quality.

Leadership through differentiation

Service leadership may depend on developing a 'comfort level' for the client such as the feeling of a 'safe pair of hands'. Differentiation in terms of technical expertise requires creative flair and research skills with co-operative relationships between client and construction professionals to take opportunities and develop new products. It requires the ability to attract highly skilled creative people who have the reputation and self-belief to deliver.

Differentiation in the construction industry is swamped by focus on cost

While there is differentiation in the industry, it is often swamped by the focus on cost with insufficient regard by construction players and client representatives alike to the added value that is brought by these specialists.

Doing it differently will require creative people to develop the processes which are important to business success and meeting the Egan Challenge. In the past, this type of creativity has not been valued in the industry.

Porter defined five forces

Porter identified five forces on competitive advantage (Fig. 7.9). First the buyer or client has to value the product of the business sufficiently to want to buy it. However, while this is necessary, it is not sufficient. There are threats from competitors within the industry or of substitutes from outside — the client may decide

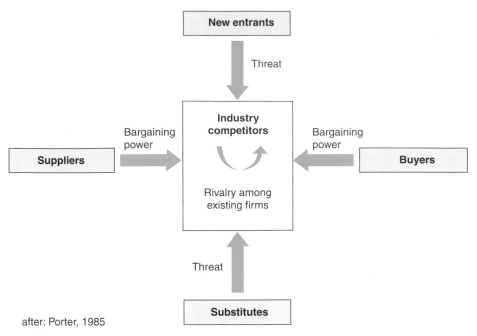

Fig. 7.9. The five competitive forces that determine industry profitability

to buy something else entirely. There is a threat from new businesses coming in to take the business. The suppliers may keep all of the value to themselves so that the margins available for the business are too small.

Currently, the construction industry is a set of businesses with low profit margins, low investment and low research and development. Compare it with the pharmaceutical industry or the computer software industry where margins on new products are much higher. These are industries with higher investment levels and large research and development budgets. Why is this? One reason is because the perceived value added is much higher than it is for the construction industry.

So how can the construction industry, with an output of some £58 billions in 1998 (equivalent to 10% GDP) move towards higher profitability? The answer is simple to diagnose — but not simple to implement. The answer has to lie in delivering higher added value to the client. This way everyone wins. However, to do this requires an analysis of the value chain and this requires an understanding of process. Further, the ruthless elimination of waste (processes that do not add value) requires a total culture change. These essential ideas of Lean Construction and Value Management will be effective when underpinned by systems thinking. Otherwise they will go the way of QA and end up as bureaucratic box ticking exercises generating massive amounts of paperwork adding little value but a lot of frustration.

7.9 Managing time

Managing time is a wicked problem

Wicked problems can cause cries of desperation such as 'Why does everything take so long these days?' or 'I seem to be working harder to stand still!'

Time is unique — it is the one resource that is the same every day. It cannot be collected and turned on or off at will — it just clicks by at a constant rate day by day by day. Yet our perception of time is not at all a constant. Some days just rush by and others seem to drag. As one gets older time seems to pass at an ever increasing rate! It is amazing that a journey always seems quicker coming back!

Clearly projects and hence processes have to be delivered on time. The challenge is to manage time so well that the client is delighted.

The project programme times are an emergent property of the times of all of the players carrying out their particular roles in a process. It also emerges from the interactions between the time keeping on all sub-processes. If a sub-process gets behind programme then things may well be delayed if it is on the critical path.

Are you a good time manager?

Some people manage time well and others badly. Most of us are somewhere in the middle. There are many books written on personal time management. Clearly, the players in any process must be helped, by the managers to whom they are responsible, to identify difficulties and to overcome them by suitable training and mentoring. Personal time management rests on a number of simple principles such as:

* understanding how you use time
* understanding what problems you encounter
* understanding what causes them
* deciding how to put them right
* focusing on what is important
* anticipating the future by thinking long term
* delegating effectively and co-operating.

There is a need to prioritise

Thus prioritising what we must do is crucial. To do this we must make choices and to do that we must be clear about our values. Tasks have to be classified into those that are necessary (must be done), those that should be done (ought to do) and those that are desirable (nice to do) — the MoSCoW rule of Box 6.7. Of course the problems start when there are too many tasks of the 'must be done' category to fit into the time available. Time should not be wasted but that is easily remedied if there is a will to identify the causes and to put them right. The real key to personal time management is planning. If one is thinking days or even weeks ahead of what is coming up then you have the capacity to fit in contributions to the task at odd moments. The good personal time manager is dealing with the immediate tasks but is also thinking about the long-term ones.

Be clear, in the business case, about how time will be managed. Time management for projects and for large organisations is obviously much more difficult because the time factors are an emergent property of the many interactions in all of the processes involved.

7.10 Preparing the team

Teams form and reform

Project teams, in the construction industry, are constantly forming, reforming and disbanding. People come together from one organisation or company, or more usually from different organisations and companies, to run a project. Quite naturally all of the people involved have their own individual agendas and all of the organisations and companies have their own business agendas.

They have agreed to come together because they see benefit — they know there are also risks but they are making a judgement about risk and reward. They are brought together by the convenor of the group for a common purpose — but do they have a common vision? On the face of it, the answer is obvious — of course they have a common purpose — it is to design, or to build, or to operate, or to do whatever, for this construction project whether it is a building, bridge, dam, pipeline, etc. However, as we have said, there is more to having a common vision than having a common purpose — it involves a wide consideration of what success means to all involved and how to co-operate to achieve it for all. A colleague was appointed commercial manager for a major contractor to build a rail link to an airport outside the UK. When he arrived, the team members thought they were delivering a tunnel but by the time he had finished briefing them they knew they were delivering a railway business.

Being clear what success is for everyone in the team

What precisely is success for all the parties involved including, quite crucially, **the client**? The team has to develop a common vision of the answers to these questions.

- **Why** is this project different from anything else on offer to the client? What is the **purpose**?
- **What** is to be done? What is needed? What is the context and what are the constraints?
- **Who** is to do what? What roles will each of the players take on?

In short many of the major attributes of process.

In construction culture, there is, more often than not, an in-built tendency to approach the new project with some apprehension because the past history has shown that there is likely to be expectation of confrontation. The designers and the contractors think that the client is likely to be trying to minimise costs and will screw them down tightly to a price, which will not be adequate to fulfil his purpose. The expectation from the outset is of claims and dissatisfied customers.

The client expects claims — so he puts all his effort into establishing a watertight contract often when he is uncertain what he wants in detail and in the face of risks that he has not understood. Perhaps his past experience is of projects overrunning budgets and overrunning programme. This may not be surprising where projects have to be bid at below cost and claims are an essential requirement for supplier success. Such a confrontational approach motivates failure and disappointment.

Thus we often have an in-built set of issues that lead to conflict — but they do not have to do so. There has never been any activity of any significance that has not had problems of this sort. The important thing is not that there are problems but rather the way in which the problems are dealt with (Box 7.9).

Box 7.9	Principle

Truth arises from honest disagreement among friends

If the attitude is one which is ready for confrontation then that is likely to lead to litigation, delays and all sorts of problems affecting the quality of the work. It is these issues that have to be overcome at the very start (Box 7.10).

<table>
<tr><td>Box 7.10   The Heathrow Express</td><td>Example</td></tr>
</table>

In June 1998, the Heathrow Express opened to the public only six months late. The members of the construction team had recovered from an enormous and embarrassing setback, when a tunnel at Heathrow airport collapsed in 1994 — Box 9.10.

They took an approach to teamwork which was simple but which turned convention on its head. They invested in the development of people. They recognised that individuals often need help rather than set programmes. The senior management team adopted an attitude to leadership which required a huge investment of time, effort and personal involvement. They gave personal support to a change programme that recognised that the human reality is that we do not all possess exactly the right skills at exactly the optimum level. Some members of the team will not be able to deliver all of the time — so they planned for this and covered for each other.

(Lownds S., 1998)

So how *collectively* do we get out of this situation?

Perhaps one of the first things that we need to ask ourselves is what can we do *individually* to help get out of this cycle? The first thing to realise is that we cannot change the other players in the team directly, we can only change our behaviour towards those people (Box 7.11). We will explore that idea in the next chapter.

Box 7.11	Principle

- **We cannot change other people**
- **We can only change our behaviour towards those people**
- **By so doing people will respond**
- **Don't wait for the world to change towards you — it won't**
- **You can only bring about change by changing yourself**

Focus on the customer

The essential business strategy is that the project team should *focus on the customer* and the stakeholders and should *understand their values* and how they are monitored and measured. The team can then, through that understanding, work out how to *add value to the client* and to the stakeholders. This then defines the essential strategy of the processes and the detailed actions for delivery of the end process/product of the project. It enables the team to manage and change its behaviour so as to deliver added value to all involved. If the team gives the client what he wants then the client is more likely to give the team what it wants — it is a *win-win* strategy (Fisher and Ury, 1981).

Box 7.12 sets out one way of describing the positioning of individuals/ groups/ organisations/companies towards others.

What is the focus of your current project teams?

Those teams who are inside a system looking in are introverted. They are preoccupied with their own needs and concerns with little time for others. They have great difficulty in understanding the needs of others and seem not to be interested, perhaps because they see no benefit to themselves from doing so. They are concerned only about themselves and will tend to see others as the ones to blame when things do not go as well.

Box 7.12   Focus of project teams   Explanation

Inside looking in —   introverted navel gazing, focusing on the team's own needs not on those of the customer — who barely gets a mention!

Inside looking out —   realising there are others out there, but still focusing on the team's needs rather than those of the customer.

Outside looking in —   getting outside of the group and attempting to 'step into the shoes' of others — particularly the customer, to see the team as others see it. Recognising the primary source of value is the customer.

The second group have a more outgoing attitude but are still only able to see others from within their perspective. They relate the actions of others to their own needs, they interpret the actions of others in terms of their own attitudes and beliefs. They cannot see themselves as others see them.

The third group is the one where people are able to stand outside and look at themselves or the group/organisation as others, even strangers, might (Box 7.13).

Box 7.13   Teams with 'outside looking in' focus   Principle

They understand that their attitude to life does not affect the world nearly as much as it affects them.

Companies and teams in the construction industry which operate in the first two modes of Box 7.12 are actually incapable of working through their needs and problems with the client because the client will not be able to respond in a useful way to them — there is no common language. Clients are almost bound to be dissatisfied with the company performance. Construction companies that operate in the third mode can delight clients and customers. They will focus on the customer needs and understand where the client is coming from. They will find out how that client views that construction company. The essentials of this customer/client focus are set out in Box 7.14.

Focus on stakeholders

The team should be prepared so that it can also begin to think about its stakeholders as soon as any process starts. The stance of every stakeholder should be assessed by the team using Fig. 6.12. This assessment could also include a judgement about the power and interest of the stakeholder in the process. Figure 7.10(a) is a repeat of that diagram with four stakeholders A, B, C, D marked on the axes with a + if they are judged to be supportive, 0 if indifferent and – if they show opposition. It is possible also to associate Italian Flags with the evidence for each of these judgements. One could then devise a strategy to influence the stance of the stakeholder towards that which is desired as shown for Stakeholder C in Fig. 7.10(b). It is the process illustrated in Fig. 6.4(c).

Box 7.14   Essentials of customer focus   Principle

- Understand the values of your customer (e.g. start with the Business Plan).

- Recognise that he may have various values:
  - stated: the lowest capital cost,
  - actual: an affordable capital cost,
  - undeclared: feeling of value for money,
  - secret: to be admired,
  - delighted: if you exceed his expectations.

- Know and monitor the Key Performance Indicators (KPIs) of your customer throughout the project.

- Identify how to add value to the KPIs of your customer.

- Change team behaviour to deliver added value to the KPIs of your customer.

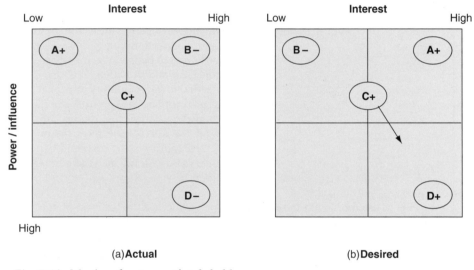

(a) **Actual**   (b) **Desired**

Fig. 7.10. Moving the stance of stakeholders

A more detailed set of assessments that could be used is shown in Box 7.15.

Box 7.15   Stakeholder stances   Explanation

- Partners: actively support you
- Allies: support you but need motivating
- Fellow travellers: passively support you
- Fence sitters: allegiance is unclear
- Loose cannons: are on another agenda
- Opponents: oppose the agenda
- Adversaries: oppose the agenda and the sponsor
- Bedfellows: support the sponsor but not the agenda
- Voiceless: powerless but may be used by opposition

7.11 Checking for success

The success targets for this chapter set out at the beginning were that after reading it, you will:

Success target	Review
• see the importance of focusing on the needs and values of the client and his customers;	construction players need to think more about the earnings side of the business of their clients. They need to concern themselves with the overall business needs and values of their clients;
• know how to move from an impelling proposition to the processes that will deliver it by adding value;	a *values driven business* is one that is devoted to adding value to its customers and, in doing so, adds value to itself and its staff. We create, with the client, a mind map to develop the implications of that proposition. From the mind map we then create a process mind map that sets out all of the processes needed to deliver the vision. The success target is to deliver the impelling proposition;
• be able to interpret the essentials of a business plan;	the business plan is a tool for communicating understanding of how value is to be added to people, e.g. investors, directors, staff and providers. It is also usually needed to get regulatory approval. It should contain background, the need, market objectives, the options considered, the risks to objectives, the preferred approach, the costs and benefits, the operations, the management and the finance;
• be able to use the client's business plan to understand his needs and values;	we should use the business plan to investigate the company's strategy, the opportunities that they have, the risks that they face and the way they are managing them;
• be able to identify relevant sources of finance;	the client's source of finance can be from taxes, from income, from reserves/savings, from commercial loans, from selling shares or stock/bonds;
• be able to contribute to achieving competitive edge;	if we have it in mind to delight the client and to exceed his expectations then we have a major source of competitive advantage. To have any competitive advantage, a business has to be differentiated from others. This has to be done in terms of the values that the customers have about the business since that is why they are willing to pay for the outputs of the business. If that willingness to buy is not there then the business fails;

• know how to manage time to deliver a plan;	time management rests on a number of simple principles such as understanding how you use time, what problems you encounter, what causes them and deciding how to put them right. Thus prioritising is crucial and to do that you must be clear about your values. Use the MoSCoW rule. Consider using timeboxes;
• know how to prepare a team to deliver on the plan and provide 'customer focus'.	decide if your team is inside looking in, inside looking out or, best of all, outside looking in and recognising that the primary source of value is the customer. A team should work out how to add value to the client and to the stakeholders. This then defines the essential strategy of the processes and the detailed actions for delivery of the end process/product of the project. It enables the team to manage and change its behaviour so as to deliver added value to all involved. If the team gives the client what he wants then the client is more likely to give the team what it wants — it is a *win–win* strategy.

We hope we have reached our success targets for this chapter — please use the feedback form at the end of the book.

8. Managing the team

8.1 Team working

People are the root of success and failure

Groups of people are regularly brought together in construction projects for specific purposes. Teams are constantly being formed and reformed. Individuals are asked or chosen to take part for all sorts of reasons. Two common ones are the relevance of a skill or a functional role. If we want to improve the way people work together then we need to attend to the way in which teams work together to add value and to generate competitive advantage (Fig. 8.1).

Likewise, if the culture of the construction industry is to move from one of confrontation to co-operation as suggested by *Rethinking Construction*, then there has to be a much greater emphasis on understanding how teams work across organisations. We need to put teams together to add value for all involved to obtain a holistic gain from improved interaction between process holons. The rewards are potentially very large.

Fig. 8.1. Managing the team

8.2   Targeting success for this chapter

The success targets for this chapter are that, after reading, it you will be able to:

- play an active role in building and developing a team;
- describe what makes a good leader;
- describe the various states of team dependency;
- describe the importance of shared vision;
- decide how to develop your own skills for personal success;
- use win–win strategies to improve performance.

8.3   Building and motivating the team

Benefit of team working

What is it that makes a team great? The easiest comparison is with sport. Many people have experienced or observed what it is like to be part of a soccer or cricket team which is doing badly and, at a different time, one that is doing really well. Occasionally, one is fortunate to be part of, or a supporter of, a truly exceptional team. The varying performances of club and national teams are cases in point.

Box 8.1   The importance of personal 'chemistry'   Example

A small structural engineering consulting practice foundered when the 'chemistry' between the principal partner and his new colleague did not work. They were too alike. Eventually they parted company and the second partner went to work separately. A new partner came in to the practice who fitted like a glove — the 'chemistry' worked incredibly well and the practice flourished unrecognisably from what it had been before.

To see a successful team in action is awe inspiring. The way they think together, anticipate the moves of the opposition and support each other can look so effortless that we may forget the training and coaching that has brought them to this level. The team has an **emergent property** of co-operation which would not be there if each of the players was selected only for his star quality or if they had met for the first time at the match.

Some people shine when working in teams

There is then a rather surprising effect. A group of fairly ordinary players at the individual level can play exceptionally well together as a group. They realise that while hard work is necessary (perspiration), they need (inspiration) to create remarkable teams. They can easily outperform a group of individually talented players who do not work together as a team. It is a classic case of a systems emergent property where the sum is greater than the parts — there is holistic gain.

Team working can get suppressed in construction

In an industry where professional skills, technical discipline, trade skills and industry experience are key criteria, the importance of co-operative skills and team working can get suppressed. This tendency can be reinforced where activities are based upon a large number of adversarial contracts. Construction companies are becoming more aware of the benefits of working to improve team performance. Those companies that do recognise it are the ones that are doing well. The habits have to be extended beyond those successful individual companies to teams drawn from the whole supply chain from client to material supplier. A remarkable example was the construction of the Heathrow Express as reported in Box 7.10.

Box 8.2   Learning to work in teams   Example

One of the authors asked first-year civil engineering students about teamwork in sport. They recognised the idea and the need for it immediately. However, when asked about it with respect to themselves and their own studies (e.g. project work for their degrees) then the recognition was almost completely absent.

8.4   Team learning

When a group of people function effectively as a whole, it is as though personal agendas and personal objectives have moved from being randomly oriented, with people pulling in all directions, to being aligned (Fig. 8.2). There is less wasted energy — people are pulling together — so it is rather like a coherent light source such as a laser.

There is a commonality of vision of purpose or mission and an understanding of how to complement each other in the team. It is important to stress that this does not imply that individuals are giving up their individuality and becoming automatons — it is not command and control. It is an alignment of individuals who want to play their part in the team. This alignment is a necessary condition for empowerment, since an empowered group which is pulling in different directions will descend into chaos. The alignment is achieved through agreement to a common purpose to which each individual contributes.

Dialogue and discussion are different

Senge (1990), following the physicist Bohm, distinguishes between dialogue and discussion. The latter, he says, has the same root as percussion and concussion. It suggests a sort of tennis game where a ball is being hit backwards and forwards between us. The purpose of this game is to win — which means to have your views accepted by the other party. The winner's view must prevail — it is a win–lose game. By contrast a dialogue is a win–win game. It is a systems notion

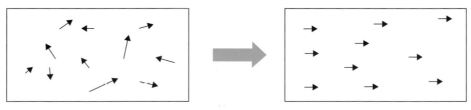

Fig. 8.2. Getting people to pull together

of the outcome of the dialogue being greater than the parts. The purpose is not to win but to enlighten and to go beyond the understanding of any individual to some greater collective understanding that **emerges** from the dialogue. The purpose is to reveal the incoherence in our thoughts, while quite often people are reluctant to admit their difficulties of understanding. For example, prejudice about a certain issue can shape all that a person thinks and sees. A discussion often finishes with that prejudice even further entrenched. The purpose of a dialogue should be to bring that prejudice out without loss of face for the benefit of all concerned — particularly the person concerned. The outcome should be an accumulation of collective understanding, not a division of it.

Box 8.3   Dialogue   **Principle**

In dialogue, people become observers of their own thinking.

(Senge, 1990)

In Box 8.4 (taken from Senge, 1990) three suggested ground rules for a dialogue are given. Notice that suspending assumptions does not mean abandoning them nor does it imply that they are bad — rather it means that you are prepared to examine them honestly.

Box 8.4   Suggested ground rules for dialogue   **Explanation**

1. *Suspension of assumptions.* Typically people take a position and defend it, holding on to it. Others take up opposite positions and polarisation results. In a dialogue we should try to examine some of our assumptions underlying our direction and strategy and not seek to defend them.

2. *Acting as colleagues.* We ask everyone to leave his or her position at the door. We have no particular hierarchy in a dialogue except for the facilitator, who will hopefully keep us on track.

3. *Spirit of enquiry.* We should encourage people to explore the thinking behind their views, the deeper assumptions they may hold and the evidence they have that leads then to these views. So it will be fair to begin to ask other questions such as 'What leads you to say or believe this?' or 'What makes you ask this?'

Likewise, seeing each other as colleagues and suspending positional power, does not imply that you must agree with everything that others say. The real power is to attain honest disagreement among friends. In some teams in which we have worked it has been deliberately made legitimate to 'challenge' an issue or view. This is regarded as a test rather than a disagreement or trial of power.

There will need to be a final discussion as a counterpart to the dialogue. In a discussion, different views are presented and defended and this allows diagnosis of what needs to be done and the decisions and actions to be taken. A learning team moves backwards and forwards between dialogues and discussion.

Deal with conflict and learn together

Senge notes that Argyris has studied the dilemma of why bright capable managers often fail to learn effectively in teams. The difference between great teams and mediocre teams, it is suggested, is how they face and deal with conflict. Defensive routines form a sort of protective shell around our deepest assumptions, defending us from the pain of exposing the weaknesses in our reasoning, but also preventing us from learning. Defensive routines are all pervasive and pernicious. They cannot be challenged directly because that will cause further negative reaction. Skilled facilitators will offer help by disclosing the reasons for their own feelings of defensiveness by saying 'Does what I say make sense or am I talking nonsense?' It is an invitation to share the reflective collective process. With genuine shared vision, defensive routines are another part of the current reality that must be faced.

Box 8.5   Improving the effectiveness of seminars   Example

University research groups traditionally develop their collective understanding of each other's work through seminar programmes. The traditional seminar lecturer talks for about 45 minutes, followed by questions and discussion around a few points raised by members of the audience. Often the understanding of the audience is partial and the deeper difficulties are not brought into the open. Junior members are often reluctant to expose their views to senior colleagues in open fora since they may feel intimidated by the latter's reputation and scholarship. In research meetings in the Civil Engineering Systems group at the University of Bristol a dialogue format very similar to that suggested by Senge has been used for about 10 years very successfully. In each session, a speaker introduces a topic for about 10 minutes after which a dialogue is encouraged to allow members of the group to bring out issues that concern them without fear of undue criticism if the points are felt by others to be naive. In this way, newer researchers are encouraged to bring a new point of view to basic issues as well as advancing the understanding of the group as a whole.

We suspect that construction project teams would do well to practise team learning. It will improve effectiveness when the team are convinced that learning to learn as a group is important enough to be practised.

Stages of team development

As we have said, construction projects are often characterised by the need to build a new team rapidly from an assembly of organisations often picked for their ability to offer the lowest price!

There are two aspects to any group interaction. They are the 'what' of the process, i.e. the content or the task and the 'how', the method or the way in which the group works. Many of us focus so much on the task that we are only dimly aware of the group behaviour. The interactions can be examined by noticing the answers to a number of questions. Who talks the most? Who is left out? How are decisions taken? Is there an attempt to get a consensus? How is lack of response handled? Is conflict avoided? Is there competition or compromise? Who is influencing whom — where is the leadership? What roles do people take? How are the objectives decided? What are the ground rules — the norms of behaviour? What is the atmosphere, feeling or tone of the group?

When groups come together for some reason there seem to be four stages that they go through (Blanchard K., Carew D., Parisi-Carew E., 1994), namely, orientation, dissatisfaction, resolution and production. No stage is bad but is an almost inevitable part of the journey towards success. The stages correspond to the four stages of running a workshop (Box 5.14) of forming, storming, norming and performing

Stage 1. Orientation

When people come together, they have some eagerness, some tentativeness and some anxieties. They are needing and wanting to find and establish a place or a role for themselves. They have to find out about each other perhaps and to understand where people are coming from and what contribution they can make. In this stage, the vision, mission and objectives will be aired and, after the first flush of exchange, the group may move into the second stage.

Stage 2. Dissatisfaction

Here people begin to feel frustrated. Perhaps the task is harder than was realised. Maybe some members of the group are hard to accommodate. Maybe the chairperson is unsatisfactory. As a result, feelings and morale commonly take a dip. If the task is not especially pleasant it is possible the group morale is low right from the start. The members of the group should be encouraged to express their feelings so that those feelings can be dealt with. This is the beginning of the next stage when members of the group begin to work through these blocks to the final production stage when the group begins to hum like a real team.

Stage 3. Resolution

This stage depends crucially on the leadership given to it to work through the issues and to find some accommodation. The different styles of leadership discussed in the next section need to be used as appropriate. If this crucial stage is successful, then the issues are brought out, thoroughly examined and people begin to feel they are making progress. They begin to feel good because they have struggled through the issues together and, while they may never see exactly eye to eye, they see a way of working which will help get through the issues in a way all can own.

Stage 4. Production

The last stage is then the real success stage because the group really starts to deliver on the task in hand. The blocks to progress have been cleared away in the earlier processes and the task in hand is being dealt with hopefully in a constructive way that all can be part of. It is the stage to which all groups need to aspire. It is the stage where there is real action.

8.5 Understanding leadership

Rethinking Construction calls for committed leadership. This is about management (i.e. process owners and players from the top to the bottom of the process hierarchy) believing in, and being totally committed to, driving in improvements and communicating the required cultural changes. This vision of committed leadership at all levels and throughout the supply chain is far more powerful than a command and control model

We worked with a manufacturing company that, owing to changes in political policy, was faced with a sudden loss of market. Most companies would have been overwhelmed. This company simultaneously repositioned itself in the market and developed new skills. It is thriving now seven years later. The leadership model before the change was exactly as described above. Everyone owned their part and co-operated to deliver success. The pride in what they were doing could be felt.

Management and leadership are different

Box 8.6	Principle
Management is doing things right	
Leadership is doing the right things	
(Covey, 1992)	

Many senior executives manage rather than lead their organisations. They are buried in the day-to-day rough and tumble of getting things done. Clearly, companies need managers to manage — to get done what is required — but it is worth asking if there is any real leadership. Leadership sets the whole direction of the company — agrees just what markets to be in and provides the ethos of how things will be done. It generates quality in the whole sense through establishing values. Above all, leaders listen and recognise that the real basis for decision derives from the people who are adding the value.

There are types of leadership

Blanchard *et al.* following Lacoursiere describe four types of leadership, as shown in Fig. 8.3

The most important function of a team leader is to help the team through the four stages of development. Directing behaviour is probably best during the first stage of team orientation because the role of the leader is to ensure information is shared, initial goals explained and direct suggestions made. Like the new conductor of an orchestra, when setting out what he wants to do and how he wants to do it, the leader sets the stage for the later processes. He has to establish the vision with them by being reasonably directive at first. However, if this directing style goes on too long the members will become resentful about being told what to do. Of course, this explanation must be seen in the context of the norms of behaviour of the group. In a military culture of command and control, it is clearly expected that the officer will order the junior to do certain tasks. In a university, at the other end of the scale, colleagues often find it difficult to take any instructions from a head of department because the norm is to expect that discussion and consensus decide all issues. The conductor of the orchestra is now beginning to listen to the performance of the orchestra in rehearsal and is helping the members to sort out how to play together to reach the sound that they have agreed that they want. Thus the style of leadership in Stage 2, dissatisfaction, moves to one of coaching the group. It is a facilitating role to ask questions,

---

Box 8.7   Administration is an inadequate word   Example

It is typical in universities for academics to refer to anything which is not the core business of teaching and research as *administration*. Administration is a 'dirty' word which is despised by nearly all academics and seen to be a chore to be only tolerated since it is not properly academic. The word administration, however, is a totally inadequate word in the running of a modern university. A modern university is at the same time a community of scholars and a multi-million pound business. Clearly that means that there is administration (implying paper pushing) to be done — but the word is lacking as a description of running such an organisation. Even the word management is not enough since it does not include the understanding of the need for inspired and inspiring leadership. The traditional professor will be reluctant to take on the role of a Head of Department or Dean and when required to do so will complain loudly about it, typically saying in public that this is a chore that he must do and does not enjoy — it is administration. This is debilitating to younger staff when universities are having to fight for recognition for their role and for proper funding — the culture of the team is then driven downwards. If, however, management and leadership are clearly separated then the leading professor can focus on leadership to identify new directions and exciting developments. This requires proper administrative support to take away the management 'chores' and to leave him free to lead. Then the department and the university as a whole can progress in a way undreamed of previously.

---

to bring out issues and have them aired, and then to begin to tease out suggestions for resolution. This supporting style is very much a part of coaching and the two are used together to work through the issues and to resolve them. The conductor is explaining why the woodwind should take one passage a little more quietly than before, perhaps so the blend of sound is achieved in the way he wants. Once the team reaches Stage 4, production, then the leader can delegate and almost leave the group to itself. The orchestra now knows what it is play-

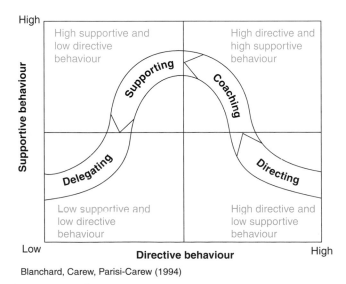

Blanchard, Carew, Parisi-Carew (1994)

Fig. 8.3. Four leadership styles

ing and how it should be played and will produce the results. On occasions, it will play in an inspirational way as all of the factors come together and the chemistry works. In an exactly similar way the sports team coach works through the team's problems to get the members to play together in an inspirational way. This is empowerment when the leader can let go so the team members can get going (Blanchard K., Carew D., Parisi-Carew E., 1994).

Undertand influence, power and authority

As we mentioned in Chapter 2, any player in a process, and especially the process owner and the leader, should understand how people attain and exert power and influence, Box 8.8.

Box 8.8   Influence, power and authority   Explanation

- **Influence** is the process whereby one person modifies the attitudes or behaviour of another.
- **Power** is the capacity to be able to influence another.
- **Authority** is legitimate power.

(Handy, 1985)

Three general points about the nature of power are worth noting

Firstly, power is relative. A source of power in one situation may not be so in another. For example, bribes will sway some but repulse others since they are unethical. Guns will silence one but may stimulate another, as we see in the raw conflict of war. The effective power may ebb and flow with circumstances — it is rarely constant

Secondly, power is rarely one-sided — even a prisoner can get back at the warder. Negative power is the power to disrupt. The possession of a source of power does not necessarily mean that you can influence someone.

Thirdly, power is valid in context and few sources of power are universally valid.

To understand power is to begin to be able to harness it

The categories of power are (following Handy, 1985) *physical, resource, position, expert, personal* and *negative.*

Physical power is the self-evidently primitive and, unfortunately, often ultimate power, as expressed in fighting and in war.

Resource power is that which derives from one person having a resource that the other wants or needs — usually but not always money. The construction industry has focused on cost as power whereas it should seek to understand the values of the client to enhance its resourcefulness and so dig itself out of its relatively 'powerless' state.

Positional power is that which the boss has because he is the boss — it is an authority awarded to him by the organisation.

Expert power is that which derives because you have knowledge or a skill that is needed.

Personal power is that which derives from the personality of an individual who has charisma and popularity. It is often associated with positional power since the star performer seems to lose charisma when sacked from the star team.

In different team cultures, different mixes of categories of power are needed. In a professional team if positional power is given to someone who does not have at least some expert power in one area of the work, then he is likely not to be effective. In organisations that have a culture of hierarchical 'command and control' positional power is often all. As we have said earlier, by rapidly creating new teams from organisations and people who are selected on the basis of cost alone, a hierarchical form of positional power is encouraged which suppresses the ability of the team to enhance value co-operatively.

8.6 Recognising interdependence

Teams are holons: looking inwards, they are made up of individuals; looking outwards, they are part of other groups and organisations. Team success is best achieved through harmonising individual and collective needs.

Distinguish dependence, independence and interdependence

Covey (1992) points out that we all start our lives being totally dependent on those people (usually our parents) who feed us and look after us. As we grow older, we seek independence to make our own decisions and to look after ourselves. As we grow older still, we become aware that all of nature is interdependent. We also discover that our higher needs are reached through others.

The **dependency** phase is one of *you*. *You* take care of me — it is *your* fault that this happened to me — I blame *you*.

The **independence** phase is one of *I*. *I* can do this on my own — *I* am responsible — *I* can choose — *I* blame myself.

The **interdependence** is one of *we*. *We* can do it — *we* can co-operate — *we* can create something together.

The current social climate is one that seems to value independence the most highly — many speak of it as though it is superior to interdependence. Much of the material on self improvement puts independence as a major achievement in itself. We suspect that much of the talk of independence is a reaction to dependence — of having others control us. Interdependence seems to be little understood and appears to be too like dependence. We therefore find people — for selfish reasons — leaving partners, abandoning children, giving up all sorts of responsibilities in the name of independence. Quality derives from a duty of care to act responsibly and co-operatively for mutual added value.

Interdependence is a mature advanced concept. It is a choice that only independent people can make. If we are self-reliant and capable, we can choose to work with others to accomplish more than we can on our own. If we have good self-esteem, we may grow and derive even greater joy through caring for others. If we have intellectual independence, we may do even better thinking when working with others.

Interdependence is about working in teams and is the theme of this chapter.

Process owners lead the process teams

The process roles, introduced in Chapter 2, are process owner, client, players and stakeholders. A role is in this sense a set of responsibilities that will normally be written down in QA documents or as a function for a hard process. A role is enacted by a player who is a person, machine or artefact.

The human process owner role has the responsibility to initiate a process and is accountable to another role for delivering success. The process owner, therefore, is the convenor, the chairperson or facilitator and will lead the team. The player enacting the process owner role may well have other roles in the process. These player roles are specific tasks, duties or sub-processes that have to be done to attain the success of the process in question. Players, therefore, will have functional roles as well in an organisation and may well come from functional departments. Examples are all specialists such as engineers, architects, accountants, quantity surveyors, etc. These players need a functional department in order to progress their training and careers and to have access to specialised knowledge, but in a process-oriented organisation they will act as the specialist in taking roles in process teams. Hammer (1996) argues that functional departments should be closed and replaced by centres of excellence (see also Chapter 9).

Belbin defined some team roles

As we have said, we suspect that most of us are aware that different people behave differently in meetings. Some seem to talk all of the time. Some remain quiet but when they speak their contribution is valuable. Some are good at summarising and some are good at generating ideas but are not so good at picking out the important or effective ones.

Belbin, after studying the behaviour of teams over a number of years, described nine team roles that people tend to play quite independently of their functional or process roles. These roles are more to do with the personalities and abilities of the players than with their level of seniority or professional job. The success of a team depends on the way in which these roles interrelate. Most of us are a mixture of these characteristic roles and prefer to play the roles where we perceive we can be most successful.

Belbin (1981, 1993) has designed a questionnaire that allows people to assess their Belbin role profile such as that shown in Fig. 8.4.

Groups where the Belbin role profiles do not fit well together will often be unsuccessful teams. For example, if all members are Shapers then it is quite likely that the players will fall out as they get impatient with each other. In practice, you would be unlucky to find yourself in a team where all of the players are of one Belbin type.

Generally, you will be part of a team which you cannot change for many other practical reasons than the Belbin profiles. There is little one can do purposely to

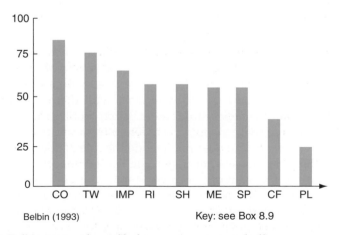

Belbin (1993)　　　　　　　　　　Key: see Box 8.9

Fig. 8.4. A Belbin team role profile for a senior personnel officer

Box 8.9 Belbin's team roles				Explanation
Type	Symbol	Typical features	Positive qualities	Allowable weaknesses
Company worker	CO	Conservative, dutiful, predictable	Organising ability, practical commonsense, hard-working, self-discipline	Lack of flexibility, unresponsiveness to unproven ideas
Chairman	CH	Calm, self-confident, controlled	A capacity for welcoming contributors; strong sense of objectives	No more than ordinary intellectually or creatively
Shaper	SH	Highly strung, dynamic	Drive, readiness to challenge inertia and complacency	Proneness to provocation, impatience
Plant	PL	Individualistic, unorthodox, serious-minded	Imagination, intellect, knowledge	Up in the clouds, inclined to disregard practical details
Resource investigator	RI	Extroverted, enthusiastic, curious	Capacity for contacting people; able to respond to challenges	Liable to lose interest
Monitor evaluator	ME	Sober, unemotional, prudent	Judgement, discretion hard-headedness	Lacks inspiration to motivate others
Team worker	TW	Socially oriented, rather mild, sensitive	Able to respond to people, situations; able to promote team spirit	Indecisive in crisis
Completer finisher	CF	Painstaking, orderly, conscientious, anxious	Capacity to follow through, perfectionism	Tendency to worry about small things

design a team from the point of view of Belbin profiles unless there are competing choices of people who could fulfil the process and functional role or where you are recruiting to a new job. Generally, you are faced with a situation where the players are as they are and you have to work with them. Clearly, an understanding of the team dynamics through the Belbin profiles can help the team to work better, and that understanding can derive from understanding what the design principles are. Belbin does not include the role of specialist in his general categories (Box 8.9). However he does recognise the important role of the technical specialist and the team players around him when he writes:

There are occasions where the key man in a technical sense is neither creative nor particularly clever; it is just that he possesses unsurpassed technical knowledge and experience. He is indispensable to a project team although he has none of the qualities of team members. These individuals we have referred to as specialists for which we use 'SP' to denote the team type — we can scarcely talk of SPs as having a recognised team role. SPs have characteristic psychometric test scores, being highly introverted and anxious. The first requirement of a manager, or in the case of a team a CH, is whether he can relate to and manage the SP. If the SP were a man of exceptionally difficult disposition or outlook, a suitable team leader might be someone in the CH/TW mould. There is then a danger that the sort of manager who can humour a SP and underpin his failure to communicate effectively with his fellows will end up making too many concessions to him. The SPs experience may be overvalued and begin to distort the strategies that are pursued. The safeguard is to introduce as a third member into the team someone in the PL/ME mould who could challenge the SP where necessary on fundamental issues and put forward alternative proposals. The price that might have to be paid is a rise in the temperature of disagreements. Creative conflict can be very rewarding but only a thin line of demarcation separates conflict which can have positive effects from that which becomes seriously disruptive. Therefore to create a final balance one could recommend for such a team a fourth member who could hold the team together. Here a TW/CW might be an excellent choice. The team would now have the following design:

Specialist	*Chairman/Team Worker*
Team Worker/Company Worker	*Plant/Monitor/Evaluator*

Belbin says *that this team might be well equipped to tackle a technically very difficult project in a practical way and that whilst disagreements would be likely to break out, the team has the resources to settle its differences and to reach its goal.*

What happens when some roles are missing?

We have found the Belbin roles are a useful check to ensure all the necessary team roles are being fulfilled. It is not uncommon for team players to choose naturally to play in their preferred positions and for some roles to be weakly supported. For example, concept design teams can lack Completer Finishers because their painstaking approach holds back the development of the big picture thinking needed at this stage. Nevertheless, they can have an important part to play in ensuring that the report produced is complete and avoids the minor errors that diminish its credibility. If the absence of such a player is recognised then somebody can take the role — even if playing 'out of position'. The absence of a Plant in the construction phase may similarly weaken a team when something has gone wrong and a really bright idea is urgently needed.

8.7 Sharing the vision

Shared vision must be built bottom up by strong leadership not imposed top down by weak leadership

In Chapter 7, we referred to the business case and the need to understand the values and needs of the various organisations participating in a construction project. The first step, we said, in reaching that understanding is to read the vision and mission statements — but many would say that vision and mission statements, in themselves, are a waste of time. They are very limited because they are usually so very vague and uninformative. As many people say such mission statements are mere examples of 'motherhood and apple pie', i.e. statements that everyone agrees — but have no real substance.

However, we believe that good vision and mission statements can be highly effective as the impelling propositions that we saw in Chapter 1. Their value lies less in the actual words but rather more in the process by which they were reached and how they are used. If they are imposed from above on the rest of the organisation by a few senior managers then they will have little effect and be largely rejected by the rest of the organisation. They can even be counterproductive where their imposition reinforces the lack of two-way communication. The importance of a vision statement is not what is — but what it does! (Box 8.10).

Box 8.10   **Principle**

It is not what the vision is — it is what the vision does that is important

---

We live in a world where change is constant. Organisations change and people change. However, even though an organisation will change, the vision will not — or at least only slowly.

Shared values are the constancy of the organisation

Thus in trying to understand the values of an organisation we need to know how the vision and mission statements were reached. We need to dig down deeper into the organisation in order to observe how people behave — this is a complex matter. However, in this chapter we are concerned with the making of a team. To do that we need to develop a shared vision and within that vision will be shared values.

Shared values provide control of the team or organisation because they guide behaviour. They work because people believe in them. They state what it is that is expected of people. Within companies with strong shared vision, it is common for those who can 'buy in' to that vision to flourish and for those that cannot to not do so well, to be unhappy and eventually leave to work elsewhere.

Box 8.11   **Mission statement**   **Principle**

**No involvement
causes low commitment,
and promotes loss of communication and trust**

This does not mean that everybody has to attend workshops at every stage. It does mean that they have to feel they **have had the chance** to contribute. The process used has to be **accepted** as open, honest and representative. Perhaps a dialogue at regular communications sessions is sufficient to selected or elected representatives who participate and provide feedback into the process. Best of all are companies where there is a culture of listening up and down the organisation.

The shared vision should express the beliefs that everyone in the organisation should hold, and with leadership shared vision helps to drive in the necessary commitment to make it work in practice. It can begin with an ethical framework such as *having respect for the individual* and continue to business principles such as *putting the customer first* or *never knowingly undersold* and quality issues such as *delivering it right first time*. It should include a statement as to how the organisation adds value to itself such as *providing sustainable profit*. It also needs to have a statement about commitment to its staff such as *investing in the con-*

Box 8.12	Principle
Vision:	Our shared mental picture of the future we seek to create.
Mission:	The impelling purpose that drives us to create it.
Core values:	The shared values that will drive the organisation to success (often expressed as a charter).

tinued development off our staff. However, if the people on the ground working with customers and who are doing the actual work do not believe in these ideas, then no vision or mission statement will work. Thus they have to be consulted, the leadership has to spend time genuinely listening, talking, persuading and focusing lots of different views into something that people can *own*. The leadership should 'walk the talk' — belief is created by action not words. Box 8.13 shows various attitudes to the company vision.

Box 8.13	A scale for testing attitudes to a vision: mission statement	Explanation
Commitment:		Wants it. Will make it happen. Creates whatever is needed to get it.
Enrolment:		Wants it. Will do whatever can be done within the existing structures.
Genuine compliance		Sees the benefit. Does everything expected and more. 'Good soldier'.
Formal compliance:		On the whole sees the benefit. Does what is expected and no more.
Grudging compliance:		Does not see the benefit — but does not want to lose job. Does enough of what is expected because he has to.
Noncompliance:		Does not see the benefits and will not do what is expected. I won't do it — you can't make me.
Apathy:		Neither for, nor against. Is it five o'clock yet?

Shared visions derive from personal visions

As we have said when a new project team comes together there will be a process of getting to know each other and settling into a working pattern. However, shared visions emerge from personal visions. In order to get genuine commitment to shared vision, it has to be rooted in personal visions. Personal excellence, as we shall see in the next section, is the basis for developing shared visions through a commitment to honesty and co-operation.

Indeed the vision statement for a process team at all levels in the process hierarchy is the big *what*. On the grand scale it expresses the future we want for ourselves with respect to the team activities. The mission or purpose is the *why* — why do we exist? The team needs to develop a larger sense of purpose than the immediate needs of the shareholders (for a company). They need to contribute to the world in some way, to add a distinctive source of value. The values should express how we want to act and might include honesty, integrity, openness, leanness — they are what the team believes in. The vision and mission statements for each process at each process level need to be integrated through the responsibility and accountability of the process owners.

Aims are expressions of the mission at a more detailed, but still quite overall and fairly broadly stated level. Objectives are precise statements that might follow the well-known acronym SMART, Box 8.14.

Box 8.14   SMART objectives   Explanation

An objective should be specific. You should know clearly when you have reached it. Five criteria for this are that objectives should be:

S   Specific
M   Measurable, Memorable
A   Achievable
R   Realistic
T   Timed

Objectives are the statements of what will be achieved in detail in order to attain success. Objectives are the success targets. The relationships between vision, mission, aims and objectives are shown in Fig. 8.5.

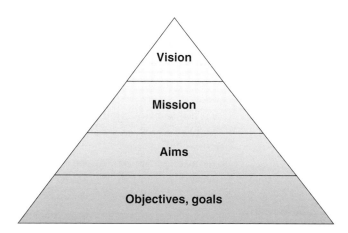

Fig. 8.5. A hierarchy of purpose

8.8   Developing personal excellence

Perception is what we bring to it

In Chapter 4, we referred to subjective and objective information and the importance of measurement. We referred to the confusion in the common usage of the term *objective* when we really mean dependable. The most dependable information is that which derives from a testable experiment such as a standard measurement.

When we are dealing with the soft issues such as personal development and team behaviour, we need to understand the importance of individual perception and our own point of view.

Probably the most famous example of how perception can be affected is the picture of the woman in Fig. 8.6 (Box 8.16). The lesson is that many of the differences of opinion that we have in group discussions are in fact attributable

---

Box 8.15   **Perception**   Explanation

We see in a face what we bring to it

Alistair Cooke, *Letter from America*

---

to differences in what we perceive as individuals. If we can understand those differences, we can eliminate some of them, agree to tolerate others (or at least agree on the reason for the difference of view and put it on one side for the moment) and take our discussion forward towards a decision.

Box 8.16   **Perception and point of view**   Explanation

Look at the picture in Fig. 8.6. Now look at the picture in Fig. 8.7. What do you see? Probably you can see a young woman of about 25 years old. Now look at the picture in Fig. 8.8 and look back at the picture in Fig. 8.7. What do you see now? Look hard — it may be difficult at first but you will see an old lady with a hook nose — she must be at least 80 years old.

   You can try this experiment with a group of people. Before they look at the picture in Fig. 8.7, get half of them to look at the picture in Fig. 8.6 first and half to look at the picture in Fig. 8.8 first. Get them to discuss what they see in Fig. 8.7. Help them to see each other's perspective.

Fig. 8.6. Picture of woman

Fig. 8.7. Picture of woman

In Fig. 8.9, we have a difference of perception that we can measure. If we think that the upper line is the shorter then we can at least get out a ruler and measure it — the lines are actually the same length. We can discuss the relevance of the perspective on the decision that we have to take based on that information.

Box 8.17   The importance of context   **Explanation**

Three men are holding sticks. The first man lets go of the stick and it falls. The second man lets go of the stick and it rises. The third man lets go of the stick and it stays where it is. How can this be?

The first man is on the surface of the earth.
The second man is under water.
The third man is in outer space.

(from a lecture by Edward de Bono)

We see the world not as it is but as we perceive it. We perceive it through what we are. As we shall discuss, our habits form what we are.

It is important to note that all of this talk about perception does not imply there are no facts. Facts are perceptions that we all agree about. They are *dependable* pieces of information that lie in Popper's World 3 of shared objective knowledge.

Practical tips for working in teams

Working in a team requires that all members have a dependable perception of each other and mutual recognition that the outcome will be better than working separately in competition. To achieve this it is necessary to:

- take an interest in each other
- work together to earn trust
- share knowledge and information
- understand and measure as dependably as possible the benefits of sharing.

Personal excellence is more than competence

There is much talk about competence and commitment from chartered engineers. If we are collectively to improve the performance of the construction industry we need to harness the commitment of all who are involved. This is where the real systems leverage will come from. Personal mastery is the phrase used by Senge (1990) for the discipline of personal growth and learning that we hope all of us can attain and which goes beyond competence and skills, although it is grounded in them. You may prefer to use the phrase *personal excellence* because it derives from our personal habits. It involves continually clarifying what is important to us and continually learning to see our current reality more clearly. It involves behaving in a manner aligned with our personal and shared vision, mission, aims and objectives.

We often spend so much time coping with problems along a particular path that we forget why we are on that path in the first place. We all have been in situations or have observed situations where an honest appraisal of what is being said or agreed is not how the reality is. The juxtaposition of vision (where we want to be) with a clear picture of the current reality (where we are relative to where we want to be) generates what Senge describes as 'creative tension' (Box 8.18).

Box 8.18   **Principle**

**Creative tension is the force bringing together
vision and current reality.**

**The essence of personal mastery is learning
how to generate and sustain creative tension in our lives.**

(Senge, 1990)

As Senge writes: *'People with a high level of personal mastery share several basic characteristics. They have a special sense of purpose that lies behind their visions and goals. For such a person a vision is a calling rather than simply a good idea. They see 'current reality' as an ally, not an enemy. They have learned how to perceive and work with forces of change rather than resist those forces. They are deeply inquisitive, committed to continually seeing reality more and more accurately. They feel connected to others and to life itself. Yet they sacrifice none of their uniqueness. They feel as if they are part of a larger creative process, which they can influence but cannot unilaterally control ... they live in a continual learning mode. They never 'arrive' ... . They are acutely aware of their ignorance, their incompetence, their growth areas but they are deeply self confident.'*

Fig. 8.8. Picture of woman

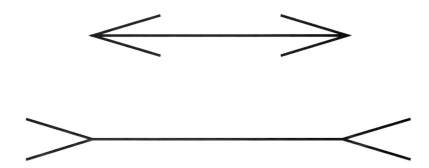

Fig. 8.9. Which line is the longest?

So helping all of us involved in the construction industry to achieve some level of personal excellence is one of the keys to *Rethinking Construction*. We will see in a later part of the chapter how this applies in particular to taking advantage of opportunities and removing blame in preventing mistakes. Meantime how many of us would see a mistake as a genuine learning opportunity (Box 8.19)? The important thing about mistakes is to try never to make the same one twice.

Box 8.19 The benefit of mistakes	Principle
A mistake is an event, the full benefit of which has not yet been turned to your advantage.	

Some fear that personal mastery will threaten the established order of a well-managed company. If people in a company have no shared vision this could well be the case. Personal excellence must go hand in hand with, indeed must be the basis of, shared vision. Personal excellence leads to a quite different view of reality than many people have. Personal excellence and corporate excellence are aligned in successful organisations. Sometimes the spin that each of us puts on reality inhibits us from behaving effectively. If we are able to see the current reality as our ally and not our enemy then we can diagnose very much better what we need to do. We have to be true to our own vision.

Senge describes three ways in which we allow our true vision to be compromised if we have less than personal excellence. The first is that we allow the vision to erode, to degrade so that we degenerate into dissatisfaction. The second is that we engage in conflict manipulation where we focus on what we want to avoid rather than what we actually positively want. Thirdly, we jack up the effort and aim at the objectives through sheer willpower. We consume enormous energy to get what we want with dogged determination. Many successful people who work this way still find areas of their lives where there is deep dissatisfaction because it just cannot work for all objectives.

8.9 Looking for personal success

When things are not as we would wish, people often ask for a technique to solve the problem. Engineers are especially prone to this way of setting out an issue — find a technique and we can solve it. Sometimes this is the case and we have success. However, often there are deeper issues that require us to look at an issue in a different way. Frequently, it is the way that we see the problem that is the problem (Box 8.20).

Box 8.20   **Principle**

Frequently it is the way that we see the problem that is the problem.

In order to obtain personal excellence, Covey (1992) argues that we have to adopt certain habits to improve our *effectiveness*. He defines a habit as something that we do repeatedly and argues that personal excellence is therefore not an act but a habit. Collective habits emerge (in systems terms) as a *culture* and personally excellent habits emerge as a *quality culture*. A habit is the intersection of why, what, and how:

- an ethic of why to do it (purpose)
- knowledge of what to do (action)
- and a skill of how to do it (resource).

When we open our mouths we reflect not the world as it is but as we perceive it. *What we say is a reflection of who we are.* We effectively describe ourselves in what we say and do. Clearly, if the construction industry is to change then we have to change ourselves.

If we think of ourselves as a holon then the first three habits (of Box 8.21) are to do with us looking inwards to ourselves as a whole dealing with personal mastery. The second three are to do with us looking outwards to others as a part — with teamwork, co-operation and communication. Habit 7 is about learning and renewal for continuous improvement.

Box 8.21	The seven habits for personal success	Explanation

Habit 1. Take personal active responsibility for all that you do — be proactive.

Habit 2. Be purposeful — begin with an end in mind.

Habit 3. Put first things first — prioritise what you do.

Habit 4 Think win–win — understand principles and mutual interests.

Habit 5. Seek first to understand, then to be understood.

Habit 6. Look to complement and reinforce — synergise.

Habit 7. Sharpen the saw (continuous learning and improvement).

(Covey, 1992)

Be proactive

The *first habit* of being proactive is to take active responsibility for our own lives. It means more than taking the initiative, it implies making things happen that depend on our values, our decisions and not on our conditions — although commonsense tells us that our conditions must be dealt with. Highly proactive people do not blame others or their circumstances, conditions or conditioning for their behaviour. They make conscious choices based on their values, rather than a product of their conditions and their feelings in those conditions. Reactive people are affected by their circumstances and their physical environment — if other people treat them well or the sun is shining then they feel good and vice versa. Of course, proactive people are influenced by these things but still base their decisions on their values and not just their feelings. Nevertheless, they do not ignore their feelings.

Be purposeful

The *second habit* is about defining ones own values and principles of behaviour. Covey argues that there are four interdependent strands that we all need to get into balance, namely *security, guidance, wisdom* and *power*. Security is about our sense of worth and self-esteem. It lies somewhere between extreme insecurity at one end and a deep sense of intrinsic worth at the other. Guidance is about our source of direction in life. It lies between dependence on all around you to strong inner direction. Wisdom is about our perspective on life and our sense of balance, our understanding how the parts of our lives fit together. It lies between a totally undependable map of what the world is like to one that is very dependable. Power is the capacity to act, including the capacity to overcome deeply ingrained habits and to build newer better ones. It lies between being a puppet with strings pulled by others to being highly proactive where you act entirely through your own thought through values.

First things first

If the second habit is about setting the scene, about personal leadership, the *third habit* is about personal management. It is about achieving what we set out to achieve; it is about the will to achieve what we want. Personal leadership decides what the first things are — personal management is about putting first things first. Habit 3 is about achieving effective time management through effective priority management, it is about being clear about roles and purposes and the setting of objectives. However, it is not so much about notes, checklists, diary keeping, or even priority setting as it is about managing ourselves. Rather than focusing on time and things, it is about preserving and enhancing relationships and focusing on accomplishing results.

Box 8.22   **Principle**

Effective people are not problem minded,

they are opportunity minded

(Covey, 1992)

Earning trust

While habits 1, 2 and 3 are about the whole individual, habits 4, 5 and 6 are about the individual as a part of a group. They are about trust between people and about personal integrity. Covey speaks of the *emotional bank account* we each have with others. If the balance of the account, the reserve, is high then even quite large difficulties can be overcome — there is trust which is deep and meaningful. If the reserve is low then even the smallest of difficulties will cause major losses in effectiveness. We make deposits into this emotional bank account by showing that we recognise the feelings of others through acts of courtesy, kindness, honesty and keeping our commitments. We withdraw from the account each time we are discourteous, unkind, dishonest do not keep to our commitments. Our accounts with all of those we interact with need to be examined constantly.

One of the very difficult issues is the implicit expectations that we all have about each other. It is crucial to get all of the important expectations out into the open. *People do judge each other through their expectations of the relationship and if their expectations are not met then the reserve of trust is diminished even though you may not realise it.* We cannot anticipate all that people think and do — but we can attempt to bring out the important elements of their expectations and of future scenarios. There are frequently unanticipated consequences from our actions. Our ability to see into the future is limited. The times when we fail to foresee these unanticipated consequences are the very times we need a reserve of trust in our emotional bank account with the players in that process.

One of the most important personal attributes is personal integrity. As Covey states integrity is more than honesty. Honesty is telling the truth i.e. conforming our words to reality. Integrity is conforming reality to our words i.e. keeping promises, honouring commitments and fulfilling expectations. One of the important ways of doing this is being loyal to those who are not present because by doing so you build the trust of those who are present. One way to withdraw large reserves from the emotional bank account is to criticise those who are not present in a way you would not do if they were present.

8.10 Looking for win–win

Think win–win

The *fourth* habit is to think win–win. Fixed lump sum contracting awarded to the lowest bidder has promoted an adversarial approach to establishing a contract. The assumption is that there are sufficient contractors all equally capable of doing the job specified. While this may be true, it misses the point that it tends to eliminate the contractor's incentive to add value through his ability to work with the owner to meet his objectives. How can he seek to find a win–win if the negotiation process assumes it does not exist (Box 8.23).

Box 8.23   A value-based selection process   Example

Tenders had been received from five contractors to provide a project control tool. All five had met the pre-qualification criteria. They had been told the level of the affordable cost. The evaluation of the tenders was a competitive process to discover who offered most value.

Teams for three of the tenders were invited to interview by a panel which was made up of:

- a representative of the prime contractor's business (business process owner)
- their project manager (development process owner)
- a construction industry client (end customer)
- a contractor (potential user)
- and the chairman of the selection panel (selection and integration process owner).

The BCOD dimensions (Chapter 1) were thus represented in the meeting and were empowered to make the decision subject to a prime contractor's corporate audit check.

Each team had been asked to prepare a 25 minute presentation as part of a 75 minute interview process. In each case, the agenda was strictly timed as shown in the table below.

Duration minutes	Agenda item	Observations of process
5	Set up	Selection panel not present (not part of the evaluation.)
25	Presentation	**Tenderer 1** devoted 80% of his time to demonstrating he was good at controlling projects and 20% to the needs of the client, the product and its production.
		Tenderer 2 made an excellent presentation driven off his understanding of business strategy and then explained there was not sufficient funds to develop the product he considered the client needed.
		Tenderer 3 made a Team presentation in which he demonstrated that he understood the process of producing the product and had a range of skills and experience from inside and outside the industry and needed to work with the client to cut the cloth to fit the budget.

continued

Box 8.23 continued		
10	Questions and answers	**Tenderer 1** turned all questions to expanding on his presentation. **Tenderer 2** demonstrated that he did not understand that the client needed to have a product that could at least be used in prototype mode and improved by the funders. **Tenderer 3** used the questions to explore the client's priorities.
25	Structured questions	The same three questions were used to probe the potential contractor's approach. The first explored his understanding of how the product added value to him and to its users. The second addressed his view of the sources of knowledge he would use. The third challenged him to show how he was able to deliver a team outcome that exceeded the expectations of the specification. The differentiation on value offered by the tenderers was easy to assess by comparing the responses.
10	Tenderer to ask panel questions	Two contractors asked polite questions. The third used the time to get a better understanding of the customer, his needs and concerns that were driving such a testing evaluation process.
5	Tenderer to sum up	Two used this to consolidate their original strategies. The third used it to explore the opportunity for an early partnering workshop with the panel to get a better understanding of need and project process.

As Covey says, thinking win–win is not a technique it is a total philosophy of human interaction. It means that agreements and solutions to problems are mutually beneficial, mutually satisfying so that all parties feel good about the decision and feel committed to the actions agreed.

Unfortunately, the construction industry has been locked in to a win–lose strategy. It is not unnatural in the sense that win–lose is all pervading in society. If one football team wins then the other must lose — it is obvious! That may be so in sport but in life we need to look longer term and for sustainability. If you screw someone into the ground over one deal they are unlikely to trust you on the next. Win–lose is not a sustainable policy.

Fisher and Ury (1981) suggest that negotiations should be based on a principled approach rather than a positional approach. The essence of principled negotiation is to separate the people from the problem, to focus on interest and not on positions, to identify options for mutual gain and to insist on objective criteria — some external standard that all parties can buy into.

Seek first to understand, then to be understood

The *fifth habit* follows naturally on from the negotiating process of Box 8.25. It is to seek to understand before deciding and acting. We live in a society where listening is not generally well done either at an individual, personal and private

---

Box 8.24   Win–Win   Explanation

Hard on the problem, soft on the people

If negotiation is adversarial and based on who has the most power, the opportunity to find win–wins can be missed. Co-operation will be devalued and each party will be seeking to put one over on the other.

    The alternative is to focus on principles, a co-operative relationship and mutual benefit. By this means win–wins can be identified, interdependence realised and mutual benefit shared. The outcome has to be demonstrably better than the adversarial approach to avoid accusations of cosiness. We have to be seen to be hard on the problem and demonstrating the benefit of co-operation with our Key Performance Indicators.

Fisher and Ury (1997), *Getting to yes*

Box 8.25   Steps in a win–win negotiating process   Explanation

1. See the problem from the other point of view. Understand and express the needs and concerns of the other party.

2. Identify the key issues and concerns (not positions) involved.

3. Determine what results would be a fully acceptable solution.

4. Identify possible new directions to achieve those results.

(Covey, 1992)

---

level or in business where people tend to talk at each other rather than with each other. They take positions determined before the meeting and are reluctant to take time to listen to other points of view and hold a dialogue in the sense promoted by Senge. People seem to be waiting to talk about *their* issues rather than to understand and relate to the needs of the other person. It is rare to be in a situation where, what Covey calls empathic listening takes place. This is more than active listening where the listener repeats what the speaker is saying, but is genuinely seeking to understand the speaker by rephrasing what is being said in a genuinely empathetic way. Note that empathy and sympathy are different. Being an empathetic listener does not mean that you have to agree with everything that is said — rather it is seeking to understand.

Look to complement and reinforce

The *sixth habit* is to look to how integration of processes and teams delivers more value than the normal compartmentalised approach. This is another example of holistic gain. It is to recognise that if the parts of a system co-operate then the whole can achieve more. As Senge puts it *you can have your cake and eat it — but not at once* (Boxes 3.7 and 3.8). As we said in Chapter 3, it is often asserted that quality and cost are in opposition. In other words to increase quality costs more. At a superficial level that is true. If you have to do extra work to make some-

> **Box 8.26   Seek first to understand then be understood   Example**
>
> One simple practical example where this fifth habit has been important is in bringing an initially interested but unconvinced company to understand the benefits in a partnership arrangement with the university. The approach of a typical academic is to talk enthusiastically about his own interest whenever given an opportunity to do so. This he will often do without understanding first the needs of the listener. The unintentional effect of this on the listeners is to feel that this is a take it or leave it deal with no potential mutual benefit. In negotiations to set up partnership support for two academic posts and research centres these natural inclinations of the academic partners were deliberately restrained until after the needs of the potential industrial partners were understood. By this simple act the academics were then able to present the opportunities to potential partners in a very much more clear and convincing way.

thing better then that work costs money. However, when one examines this much more deeply, it is evident that you can increase quality and reduce cost together. What is not obvious is that by improving work processes, rework can be eliminated. We can reduce the need for quality inspections, the number and cost of accidents and complaints to improve client satisfaction. Of course, investing time and money into improving work processes is an up-front cost, and quality improvements may take some time to come through. However, if one considers the whole process from a systems perspective then the savings can be real and significant over a period. Many apparently opposing strategies such as central versus local control, investing in employees versus competitive labour costs, are products of thinking statically about a point in time. The real leverage is in thinking these issues through within a process and seeing how both can improve in time.

> **Box 8.27   Adding value by integrating processes and teams   Example**
>
> One strategy for selling the chairs of Fig. 2.6 is to market them through the internet. The communication between customer and provider is then direct. The provider has lower marketing costs by cutting out the middleman and better feedback to improve comfort levels. He is also able to offer his customers the option to participate in the creation of their own product. The chair can be designed to fit the customer 'bottom'.
>
> Airline alliances at hub airports integrate the journey for more passengers. This results in a greater choice of routes and reduced door to door journey times. It also creates the opportunity to better segment the needs of customers and to offer a greater choice of service.
>
> Pubs provide bar food so as to increase the value per hour they add for their customers. Flexible working is achieved when staff take the roles of bar person, waiting at table and kitchen assistant depending on need. The outcome is increased turnover at less unit cost per setting than competitive restaurants. Customers who acquired an appetite while having a drink, extend their stay. The service is so responsive that customers are more likely to return.
>
> The joint marketing of electricity, water and gas is a possible opportunity for the supplier to reduce sale costs per unit and to increase knowledge of customer needs. The customer benefits through lower costs and hassle.

Learn to improve

The *seventh* habit is one of continuous investment in improving oneself. It is about sharpening the axes to cut down the trees. To make the changes needed to *Rethink Construction* we have to learn to learn from ourselves and from others. This is as true personally, as it is in each layer of our organisations. The idea that organisations are 'investors in people' has to be matched with the idea that people want to invest in themselves and that the outcome will add value to people and organisations. As an industry we have been talking about this for a long time. As professionals we have been exhorted to plan and to record our continuous professional development (CPD).

An understanding of the processes that add value should help us to understand where we want to focus our effort to add value to ourselves. There is no doubt that the knowledge that an MBA provides opportunities for engineers to increase their income has induced many to invest in themselves. There the route to adding value is easy to see and the motivation is strong. The outcome is high levels of commitment to learning new skills.

Systems thinking provides us with an opportunity to understand and share the processes and skills needed for success. It provides an explicit means of understanding the key performance measures and the creative tensions — the gaps between 'where we are now' and 'where we want to be'. The benefit in closing that gap should be evident. We now have in place the means for people to motivate themselves and realise mutual value by investment by their employer in them and by them in themselves.

The *seventh habit* is therefore also about self-renewal — preserving and enhancing the greatest asset that each of us has — yourself. It is a habit of continuous improvement. Covey talks of four areas of personal self-renewal as in Fig. 8.10. If any of these areas are damaged then so are you damaged — just as junk food and lack of exercise damage physical health (Box 8.28).

The equivalent idea at a group level is that of a *learning organisation*. The idea here is that individuals do actually want to learn. The organisations that can discover how to tap people's commitment and capacity to learn at all levels in an organisation will be the ones that excel in the future. Learning organisations will move us from an *instrumental* view of work — where work is a means to an end

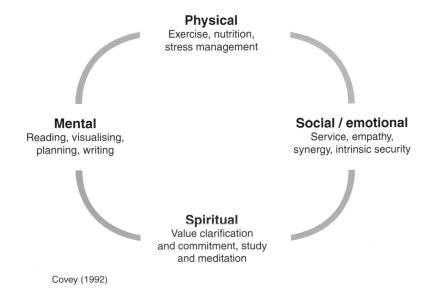

Covey (1992)

Fig. 8.10. The four dimensions of renewal

Box 8.28   Explanation

You cannot play with the animal in you without becoming wholly animal, play with falsehood without forfeiting your right to truth, play with cruelty without losing your sensitivity of mind. He who wants to keep his garden tidy does not reserve a plot for weeds.

Dag Hammarskjold

— to a view of work which is more in tune with man's higher aspirations beyond food, shelter and belonging. It is a view based on bringing worth to as wide a set of people as possible. A learning organisation will make mistakes but will not repeat them. It will have a corporate memory. Most of all, it will have a clear view of the values that sustain it and the world around it. A learning organisation will understand what makes a team great.

8.11 Training, mentoring and coaching

Awareness training — nurture a culture of self-improvement

The integration of processes and teams is not simply about meeting at an interface. It is necessary for players to understand where each is coming from and be empowered to ask questions. It is all too common, particularly at the interface between client and provider, that the integrating process is inhibited by a lack of team awareness of what is being integrated.

This is particularly true where unfamiliar or specialist skills are a key requirement for success. The spider diagram in Fig. 8.11 illustrates the point. In many risk and value management workshops, these diagrams have raised awareness levels and promoted mutual understanding.

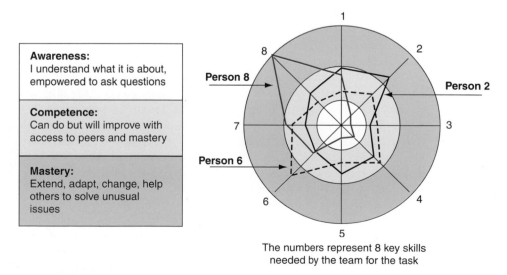

Awareness:
I understand what it is about, empowered to ask questions

Competence:
Can do but will improve with access to peers and mastery

Mastery:
Extend, adapt, change, help others to solve unusual issues

The numbers represent 8 key skills needed by the team for the task

Fig. 8.11. Spider diagram of team competence

Box 8.29   When will we ever learn?   Example

A client wants to ensure that his designers and contractors will co-operate with him to add value. He is, however, concerned that if he reveals the source of value in the project to them, they will get greedy and hold him to ransom. He adopts a posture whereby they are required to co-operate with him but he will communicate only what he wants them to know. They do what they are told but are only able to reduce cost or generate claims because they are deliberately excluded from the awareness level of knowledge that would have allowed them to proffer genuine value adding options.

Recognising the problem, a client encouraged each member of his team to give lunchtime seminars on what he is doing, why he is doing it and to promote discussion of emergent ideas. Initially, a facilitator was used to establish the rules of play. It was interesting to observe how this promoted day to day dialogue. This project delivered early with several operational improvement at less than budget. It was regarded as a good job to have been on for career advancement as well as having been fun. The client paid for the lunches and the facilitator.

Rapid improvement through targeted training

'With people power everyone's a winner.' 'Only workers willing to adapt and retrain will have a future.' These headlines from *The Times*, December 1998, introducing an article on national training awards, illustrate the importance of training. The chair of the judging panel, Geoff Armstrong of the UK Institute of Personnel & Development, said that training is the only way to make a breakthrough in a new market or with a new product. He is quoted as saying that research at the University of Sheffield showed that, on a like-for-like basis, development of people contributes most to improvements in performance. It was three times more significant than research and development and many times more significant than the introduction of quality systems.

Box 8.30   UK National Training Awards 1998   Examples

The 1998 winner RHP is a small bearings manufacturer in Nottinghamshire which succeeded dramatically in reducing its level of rework from 20% to just over 1% while also increasing output. This was achieved with the same work force and the same machinery. The difference lay in a carefully targeted training exercise. They moved from a blaming culture to one of supporting each other and a better team spirit took hold. A similar story came from Scottish Power that achieved dramatic business improvements after a significant investment in training. Du Pont commissioned a new plant in Dumfries, Scotland, in one third of the time taken by the company's previous best performance. This was achieved with no injuries and using new recruits with no previous experience. The success was attributed to an intensive training programme.

In 1994, Clamason Industries Ltd, a firm of automotive engineers, was threatened by overdependence on one customer and disruption caused by the introduction of new processes and products. The Chairman said: 'Many
continued

Box 8.30 continued

organisations would have responded to the crisis we faced by slashing their training budget. We did the opposite'. A new programme of training was launched to reduce the hierarchy, introduce new management controls, improve marketing and abandon the piecework approach. The company has since won several contracts and received an award for manufacturing excellence.

Galliford UK, a construction company, has trained 120 of its workforce in customer relations. One of the directors is quoted as saying, 'We have been genuinely stunned at the extent of our success'.

Training works across all work places. In 1995, Shaw Park Primary School in Hull failed its Ofsted inspection. Standards and morale were so low that staff were issued with alarms to guard against attack by angry parents! Then the American system 'assertive discipline' was introduced and staff were trained to deal with disruptive behaviour. Pupils were given a set of rules, rewards and sanctions while parents were asked to pledge support. In 1998 it was reported that the school is a happy place to work, with a rising student intake and much happier inspectors.

The Times, December 1998

8.12 Checking for success

The success targets for this chapter set out at the beginning were that, after reading, it you will be able to:

Success target	Review
• play an active role in building and developing a team;	the distinction between discussion and dialogue is significant in bringing some of the hidden assumptions and pre-judgements that people hold about an issue. People have to be encouraged to become observers of their own thinking. Learning together is a key element of team development and the four common stages through which teams grow are orientation, dissatisfaction, resolution and production. A group of fairly ordinary players at the individual level can out-perform a group of individually talented players who do not work together as a team — there is holistic gain;
• describe what makes a good leader;	management is about doing things right; leadership is about doing the right things;
• describe the various states of team dependency;	the dependency phase is one of *you* — its *your* fault and I blame *you*. The independence phase is one of *I*. *I* am responsible and *I* blame myself. The interdependence phase is one of *we*. We can co-operate — *we* can create something together. Interdependence is a choice that only independent people can make;

• describe the importance of shared vision;	shared values are the constancy of the organisation. The mission is the impelling purpose that drives us to create it. It is not what the vision is — it is what the vision does that is important. If there is no involvement then there will be low commitment, which will promote loss of communication and trust;
• decide how to develop your own skills for personal success;	creative tension is the force bringing together vision and current reality and the essence of personal excellence is learning how to generate and sustain creative tension in our lives. A mistake is an event, the full benefit of which has not yet been turned to your advantage. Covey's seven habits for personal success are: be proactive; be purposeful; prioritise; think win–win; seek first to understand, then to be understood; synergise; and learn and improve continuously;
• use win–win strategies to improve performance.	if negotiation is adversarial and based on who has the most power, the opportunity to find win–wins can be missed. Co-operation will be devalued and each party will be seeking to put one over on the other. The alternative is to focus on principles, a co-operative relationship and mutual benefit. By this means, win–wins can be identified, interdependence realised and mutual benefit shared. Thinking win–win is not a technique, it is a total philosophy of human interaction. It means that agreements and solutions to problems are mutually beneficial and mutually satisfying so that all parties feel good about the decision and feel committed to the actions agreed.

We hope that we have reached our success targets for this chapter — please use the feedback form at the end of the book.

9. Managing the life cycle

9.1 The pressures

We are all under pressure to:

- identify markets quicker than anyone else;
- develop products faster than before;
- produce higher quality than before;
- do it at a lower price than ever before.

This is true for all industries and businesses. We will make a substantial difference if we can go beyond thinking only about the construction project. We can do it if we think about how we can improve the process **as a whole** to deliver maximum holistic gain for clients, their customers and all of the businesses that support them and us. This total process will be sustainable if we have considered the whole **life cycle** from first vision through development, definition, delivery, operation and through to eventual removal. None of us can do this alone — it has to be done together.

These are the things that we can strive for — but we have to start from where we are now. We need a process of change. The tools we have been describing are generic to this process and they can be applied at any level in any system with which we are each concerned. We just have to be clear what is inside and what is outside **our processes** — the processes we own. We have to describe the

Fig. 9.1. Managing the life cycle

why, what, who, how, when and where for us. We have to develop an understanding of how our process communicates with other processes.

Remember that process has the form of the snowflake so that whatever the scale, part or at whole, the basic shape is the same. People govern soft process behaviour at every level. If the processes, hard or soft, are aligned to a common purpose, within the commercial world of construction, the drivers are basically similar. There are well-tried and successful methods to manage success inside tame processes. We need not dwell on them here. We need to focus on the problems that arise from:

- what we do **not** know about the future;
- the lack of relationships — with consequentially **inadequate communications** between processes;
- the lack of recognition of **interdependence** — where process players have to work together and co-operate;
- **clashes of culture** — whereby one process player makes inappropriate assumptions or has unjustified expectations about another.

In other words problems that are seriously **wicked**.

9.2 Targeting success for this chapter

The success targets for this chapter are that after reading it you will be able to:

- describe the importance of the whole life cycle to the client;
- state how a process model may be developed with practical rigour;
- decide on appropriate attributes for each process;
- show how a process model contains all supply and value chains and how specific chains can be picked out;
- describe the importance of planning to learn;
- discuss the generalisation of the Observational Method in geotechnics into the Observational approach;
- describe how lean construction, value management and partnering relate to the systems approach.

Figure 9.1 sets out the loopy logical processes for this chapter.

9.3 Thinking about whole life cycles of our products

Generally, during the total life cycle of our infrastructure products, our **clients** or their products add, through their use of the product, far greater value than is represented by the first construction cost. Our products must help to add that value to our clients, otherwise they will not be willing to pay.

Consider the value of the time users and their vehicles spend on a motorway compared with its infrastructure cost. Consider the value of the product that passes through a factory or depot compared with its infrastructure cost. Consider the turnover of a supermarket compared with its infrastructure cost. Consider the duration of the construction programme in proportion to the usable life of the infrastructure. In each case, the life cycle value is dominated by the **purpose** of the product.

Such thinking takes us away from a focus on a whole life cost dominated by construction and maintenance projects to one driven by the **purpose** of the construction product. It demonstrates the need for the holistic dimensions of success, BCIOD+R (i.e. Business, Customer, Integrating, Operating, Delivering and

Regulating processes) to generate understanding of value. It helps us to understand what we can do, in the construction process, **to improve** the value we add and what we can **stop doing** because it is not adding value.

However, our willingness to invest in improving the delivery of this total purpose is constrained by:

- the realities of business value, affordability and in some cases commercial regulation;
- a predict and provide approach in which we co-ordinate activities — but then prevent players from co-operating to manage uncertainty through the way in which we organise ourselves and make contracts;
- perceptions that set a context in which many of us are not appalled (or even surprised) by waste and substantial cost and time overruns.

Develop the supply network

These constraints are not restricted to clients and their primary suppliers. It pervades the supply chain, with increasing levels of frustration as the relationship between ultimate customer and supplier becomes more and more distant. This diminishes the power of the supplier to invest in his process, his future, and the future of the industry. Concepts of take-it or leave-it outsourcing, which increase efficiencies where problems are tame, may well be counter-productive when they are wicked. The chair manufacturing business described in Chapter 1 not only depended on its having BCIOD + R dimensions of success for its competitive advantage *hand-crafted for comfort*, it needed a line of sight between the processes, *being comfortable* and *hand-crafted* and *customer needs*. The same sort of line of sight is required for the air-conditioning supplier for the healthy pub example (Chapter 1) and for the water plc (Chapter 2).

Many people agree that there is a need to improve the business process up and down the supply chain. The supply chain consists of processes along which components and payments are passed to deliver the ultimate product. This is necessary but it will not be sufficient because many of our processes need a line of sight across the dimensions of success BCIOD+R to improve them. It is not just a chain of communication that is needed, it is an **open network**.

Promote openness

People working at the front line hold most of the knowledge and information that is required to improve the processes. For example, these are people who:

- deal with the endless, costly and time wasting frustrations of getting an invoice paid;
- deal with angry residents or disappointed customers;
- struggle to control compensation grouting from within a saturated hole where the primary objective is to remove earth and anything that gets in the way as fast as possible;
- have to try to fit reinforcement bars into an over-congested shutter;
- have to fix bolts through misaligned holes 20 m above the ground;
- continue to deal with signal failures in the snow at the end of a shift because the relief has not turned up.

Many construction players seem to have lost touch with this knowledge. We have interviewed people at the front line as a part of various risk assessments. Frequently, we have seen that the knowledge to improve exists. However, it is not communicated dependably to the process owners in a way that they can use it when it is needed. We have become all too familiar, through these interviews, with the impediments of layered management that in the name of control, frustrates the communication. Typical comments are: 'You must talk to me before you talk to my staff', 'I have to know what is going on otherwise somebody will think I am not doing my job', 'I am so busy that I will deal with your request when I get round to it'.

If you are one of these people, then we are entirely sympathetic with you. You are probably overworked, pressured from above to perform and pressured from below by frustrations that are usually not of your own making. In our experience, when people in that position realise that we are genuinely there to improve things and operate a trustworthy blame-free reporting approach, they could not be more helpful. However, the knowledge gained by interviews is the tip of an iceberg of possible improvements. If this knowledge were highly valued and genuinely recognised, then the motivation for improvement would be very strong.

One of the authors, working in the oil industry in the USA, found the freedom of access to people there most refreshing. His experience was that doors are readily opened but if you waste people's time then meetings or telephone calls are brief. Recently, a colleague needed to specify a type of glass fibre fabric in the design of a refrigerated air transport container. A combination of the use of the internet and telephone to the USA provided a wealth of knowledge backed up by an e-mail of relevant data. Suppliers want to talk to customers if they sense a business opportunity. Direct dialogue at any BCOD dimension seems to be valued.

Too often suppliers in the UK seem to filter the exchange through a less than well-informed sales force. Clients too often seem to filter exchanges through a less than well-briefed procurement department. The more open the system the more helpful the exchange. The more helpful the exchange the better the relationship. The better the relationship the less time it takes to get to the point and add value. A competent person knows when he is talking to another.

An internet site can be used to provide channels to competent advice and knowledge. The internet now represents a real opportunity for improving competitive advantage. It allows an organisation to have a new kind of relationship with its clients and customers (old and new), as well as with stakeholders and, through an intranet, with process players.

9.4 Starting with the whole and drilling down

There are processes within processes

In Chapter 2, we set out the high-level processes for the life cycle of some construction projects. The life cycle is the process of 'being' which begins with the conception of the idea and ends with decommissioning — it therefore includes all aspects of BCIOD+R as shown in Fig. 2.6. In Fig. 9.2, we show some processes that could be used for delivering a project as an alternative to the process of **being**. We will now rehearse and build on the methods described in Chapter 2, using the systems ideas set out in Chapters 3 to 8.

To recap briefly: in Chapter 3 we introduced process holons. We said that all holons are usefully conceived as processes in a hierarchy of parts and wholes. Each process has a rich set of attributes. We define and use these attributes to understand, predict and manage the process to success. In Chapter 4 we distinguished between hard and soft process holons. The intentions present in soft holons makes them difficult to understand, represent and hence simulate and

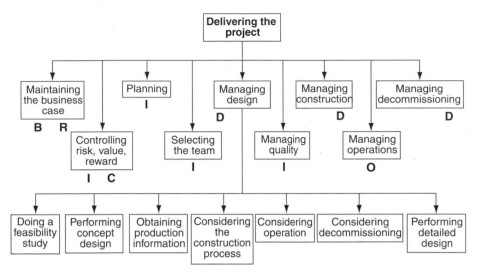

Fig. 9.2. Process model for delivering a project (partial)

predict. That is why progress in social sciences is so much slower than in the physical sciences. Nevertheless, soft issues tend to govern success since all hard physical holons are embedded in soft organisational ones. We all live with that in our daily lives, but the issues become particularly acute in professional practice based on science such as engineering and medicine when we have to justify everything that we do. It means that while prediction of hard system behaviour is an important resource, it is only that, namely a prediction in a limited context. It is information for use in managing the soft system (in which the hard system is embedded) to a successful conclusion. We have therefore to make judgements about the dependability of the prediction. In Chapter 5 we described the background to reflective practical action which is required to ensure that creativity and systems integration are combined with the scientific method. The practical requirement that we work in an *open* world in which we recognise what we do not know makes this approach essential for success. In Chapter 6 we saw how we need to be much clearer about our value systems and hence to manage the value chain (which is one perspective, one set of attributes, of the process model) more effectively. Through this clarity we are in a much better position to manage the expectations of our clients, stakeholders and, of course, all of the players in our various teams. This has to be done in a business framework where the case for a win–win strategy to enable all of us to find some success has to be agreed and made clear, as we saw in Chapter 7. Finally, in Chapter 8 we saw the importance of managing the team effectively. As construction players we need to consider the design of teams and our relationships with each other much more carefully than many of us do at present.

We have chosen to base our approach on a foundation of layered (hierarchical) process models because the construction industry is driven by the practical principle that value is added by purposeful actions, which, by definition, produce the outcomes of processes. In view of the complexity, we focus on key attributes of process such as purpose, owner, performance measures and risks. We can use the same approach to drill down into the detail of layers below as appropriate. By seeing things this way, we are able to focus on the interaction between processes as well. These interactions are often major source of opportunity and risk.

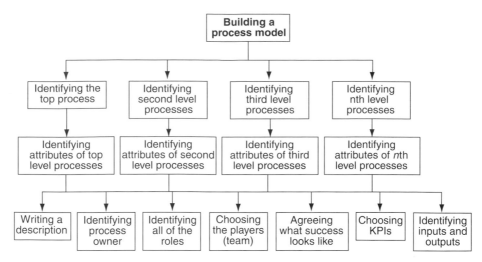

Fig. 9.3 Building a process model

Building a process hierarchy top down

So we start by identifying the top process. Every process is a holon, so every process can be thought of as a top process for those underneath. Where we start, the process we choose as the top one for our system, for our purposes, is a matter of where we decide to put the boundary of our system of processes. Thus a top level process for a smaller subset of a complete project might be *establishing the business case* or *designing the bridge deck* or *analysing the stresses in Girder X-42.*

We then proceed to build a model of the process hierarchy (in layers). Figure 9.3 shows a process hierarchy for building a process model.

It is worth noting at the outset that one of the critically important processes in the building of a process model, shown at the bottom of Fig. 9.3, is that of *agreeing success*. It is here that the values of all of the players and organisations involved (including stakeholders, clients and customers) have to be taken into account and appropriate commitment levels agreed. Without a realistic and rich set of values, it is not possible to find success for all through a mutually acceptable balance of interests. This is a key part of meeting *Rethinking Construction.*

Flush out waste through practical rigour

The next step is to identify those processes which are together necessary and/or sufficient for the success of that process. It is a top down process analysis and at this stage the process seems to be one of writing a flowchart. Of course, it is like a flowchart but it is much more than that because we can do so much with it — a process model can capture all the information that you wish, or are able, or it is appropriate, to capture. Thus we can, at any convenient time as we develop our model, attach any attributes to each process that are useful to us. Furthermore, we can manipulate and enhance those attributes by linking the process model with standard project management tools. For example, if we are concerned with how the processes will happen in real time, we can link to a critical path package and calculate latest start and finish times and then attach those times to the process in the process model.

These next level processes are still quite high level and perhaps rather vague but they will be important and useful and they are holons. Figure 9.2 shows a set of sub-process holons for the process *managing design.* The sub-process holons for the other processes are not shown just to keep the diagram simple. Likewise the sub-process holons for this third level which would make a fourth level are not shown. For example, the process *performing a concept design* could be made up of *deciding the overall form, choosing the materials, performing a concept analysis*.

At the top levels of an organisation and of project management the processes are generic and can be grouped into BCIOD+R, as we have said. Of course, they can be expressed in different ways according to taste. At the second level of an entire organisation the processes could be *achieving the mission of the core business* and *achieving the mission of the support infrastructure* or alternatively *maintaining the infrastructure to support the core business*. Generic lower level processes are *purchasing and procuring materials, tendering, estimating, setting the budget, marketing, managing the site* — the list of possible processes is very long. As one proceeds down the hierarchy, identifying more detailed processes, then the processes become more specific to a particular project or to a particular organisation. Once the technique is understood, it rapidly becomes quite easy to carry out.

Box 9.1   Fire fighting a joint venture   Example

A joint venture, involving two contractors, for facilities management ran into difficulties. It became apparent after a year of operation that accounts were running into deficit contrary to the business plan and expectations. Manning difficulties became apparent. Employees were leaving faster than they could be recruited and absentee ratios were rising alarmingly. Customers were complaining — but the complaints were not being reported.

When a process analysis was carried out, several misunderstandings about the way money should be handled and responsibilities defined were identified. A process map was developed in workshops with some of the employees. The organisation was simplified. Sponsoring directors took an interest in the people. Responsibilities and accountabilities based on need were agreed. Key performance indicators were established and reported regularly. The management was radically reduced. Access to support from either contractor was made available on call through sponsoring directors if necessary.

New process models are now helping to get to the root of the problem by focusing minds on principles and interests rather than positions. Improved customer and employee satisfaction is leading to smoother operations and a restoration of the business case. The reorganisation took about a month and required two outsiders as facilitators, one of whom maintained an occasional coaching role.

The clarity that the simple naming of processes and capturing them in a process model brings is significant in itself. The clarity comes from describing what is being done or what should be done. At this first stage, it is not about the six honest serving men of what, why, when, how, where and who — it is simply a **naming** of the process at a very high level. Then as we begin to break down this process into sub-processes, we begin to see how some of the parts fit together.

Of course, there are difficulties. A process analysis for an entire organisation is a daunting task and one not to be taken lightly. There are many points of view and much ambiguity in most organisations. A two-stage strategy is sensible for any large existing organisation (as distinct from a specific new project either within an organisation or across a number of organisations). Firstly, one chooses important and critical processes and examines them (Boxes 9.1 and 9.2 are of this type). Since the top process defines the system then it is desirable to aim as high as practicable in the process hierarchy and work down from there. You name

---

> **Box 9.2   Making a university leaner**   Example
>
> The registration process at a modern university is a highly concentrated set of processes carried out by a large number of support staff with around one thousand or more new undergraduate students in the space of a few days. As a result, long queues and frustrations were happening and questions were raised about the need to take the same information from the students for different purposes. For example, addresses should only be asked for once! Photographs need only be taken once! The principle of taking data only once was established by the process owner and a process analysis revealed many improvements very quickly. The result is a much smoother and leaner registration process, much shorter queues, fewer complaints, happier staff, less frustrated students. Photographs are taken digitally and available for authorised purposes through the university intranet.

processes by observing what is happening, or deciding what you intend to happen, and then modelling it faithfully. The **name for the process should indicate its primary purpose** and be expressed as the present participle (...**ing**). Improvements will suggest themselves very rapidly. Conflicts and ambiguities will become apparent so one quickly moves from a model that is as it is (a description) to one that is better fulfilling its purpose. This is **immediate added value**. Note that to do this exercise requires the **active support** of senior management — without that support you are unlikely to succeed in getting people to take the process seriously.

As noted in Chapter 3, the **process hierarchy** is **not** a hierarchy of authority (i.e. the structure through which legitimate power is exercised), except for that type of authority which is associated with higher levels of responsibility (Chapter 8). The hierarchy should not be seen as the setting up of an authoritarian power structure. The culture of the organisation is a separate issue largely set by senior management. At one extreme it may be hierarchical (as in the military), at the other it may be loose and flat in the sense that all workers are colleagues (as in universities). The hierarchy suggested here is one of delegated responsibilities that can be, but is often not in practice, set up independently of the organisational culture, Box 9.3.

> **Box 9.3   A story about organisations**   Example
>
> Some time ago an American colleague said to one of the authors: 'seek to understand how an organisation actually works. It will certainly be different from what is in the organisation charts and procedures. It will be different from how it is said to work. It will be different from how it ought to work. **It will often work in spite of itself**. You will know what makes it work by **observing** the actions of people' — and actions of people are the processes and they reveal the core values of the organisation.

9.5   Ordering the priorities of the attributes

The key attributes of process need to be understood and identified. In Chapter 2 we set out attributes of process in Box 2.12. Now we will review some of the important ones briefly in the light of Chapters 3 to 8.

Roles

As we said in Chapter 2, after naming a process the second requirement is to identify the key roles that have to be taken on by players who are people or things acting in each process. A process role is a set of responsibilities for people or set of functions for a thing, an artefact, or a physical system. The latter has a role in a process through its function — something that the players in the process ascribe to it — and they may not agree what it is. Systems thinking allows consensus to be built — but if that proves impossible then the process owner is responsible and makes the decision.

The player taking on a role will need appropriate capabilities and skills to fulfil that role and to be successfully accountable in specific and measurable ways. For example, he will need to be able to meet deadlines. The role description, as we shall see later, is different from a traditional job description in that it sets out the responsibilities and accountabilities but does not describe the tasks to be performed.

Roles of artefacts are functions

The door to your room is something everyone probably agrees about — doors are not usually problematical. It is most likely a piece of timber and that timber has the role of being a door — that is what a door is. The detail of what we each understand by a door is for individual interpretation, but we all agree certain objective criteria (Popper's World 3, Chapter 4), e.g. that it should open and close, be a space barrier and a heat barrier and so on. More generally a door could be seen as an opportunity to pass through a wall.

An artefact has no intentions, i.e. as we said in Chapter 2, the door to my room does not *know* it is a door. However, the system that loads bags on to the train in Hong Kong's 'in town' airport 'check in' has the capability of recognising a train door and lining itself up automatically to load containers of bags when the door is opened. In other words, it recognises, albeit in a limited way, a doorway when it sees one and is triggered into action by that recognition.

The timber of my door is itself a process in a hard physical system. The role of the door comes from the other players in the process — a soft social process in which the hard physical process of *behaving as a door* is part. The door's process is a process of **being**. The very fact of being brings risks. The risks are that the door will not be able to fulfil its role — its function. Maybe it is not secure enough, or sound passes through it too easily. All players, in their roles, contribute to the process of which they are part, to try to reach the success targets. Managing risk is about managing the uncertainties in the process, through the players, to steer the process to those targets.

The human players can be thought of as biological systems which have intentions at the human level and the characteristics of living systems in the lower level process holons — but ultimately some of the sub-systems are hard physical ones such as the molecules of which we are made. Life itself could be conceived as an emergent property of some systems in a way not yet properly understood — but even that issue may yield to scientific research eventually.

For an artefact, role and function are the same because the artefact cannot have intentions. Thus a role description for the artefact is a specification. An artefact cannot be a process owner because it does not have intentions and therefore cannot be held accountable. The **accountability** then passes upwards to the higher level process owner.

Roles for people include purpose

The role of a person in a process is more than function because it includes intentions and essential relationships. For example, the success of a role as leader depends not only on the leader's intentions but also on the willingness of the other people to be led. Where a hierarchy of process has been established then identification of process owner enables a better set of **responsibilities and accountabilities** to be established as part of the role description. The alignment of people, purpose, product and responsibility into a consistent framework helps to clarify what was complex. People begin to see their part, their contribution, to the big picture. We have already shown that the creation of the hierarchy of processes enables **efficiency and effectiveness** to be created by testing for **sufficiency and necessity**. By approaching the definition of roles from this framework, we encourage the implementation of an organisational structure to fulfil purpose and we provide a direct linkage to such process attributes as value, risk cost and time. We also encourage interactions between processes because the direct attachment of roles should promote communications between people, as we discussed in Chapter 8.

Roles are more than job descriptions

Job descriptions are usually written in terms of what a person in that job should do. The specification for an artefact should state what is required — delivering it is success. A role description for a person, in the way used here, is not a job description — but can serve as one in a suitable QA system. It is different because it sets out the **responsibilities of that role** and it is this that empowers the player taking on that role to act to fulfil those responsibilities. It also sets out how the player is accountable and so makes it clear how success is to be judged in that role. This is in itself **motivating** because it encourages the player to focus on what is needed and to eliminate what is not essential.

As a further help the role description can include some of the standard tasks such as attending certain meetings, responding to and reporting customer contacts, checking certain data or other everyday tasks. The emphasis in a role description is not on specifying tasks and activities (the how) but on purpose, responsibility (the why) and accountability (the measures of successful performance). In this way, the player is empowered to take responsibility against a very specific set of accountability measures. This allows the player to be creative and innovative. It is not without risk, however, and the player in the higher level role who has empowered the player needs consciously to manage that risk.

Every process needs a process owner

Someone must be responsible and accountable for every process — we have described the role of that person as the *process owner role*. It is likely that you will find in a typical organisation many processes that do not seem to have someone in charge of that process *specifically* at that level. Processes that are not locally owned tend to be where waste resides. Identifying such waste provides immediate added value. Often these processes are the ones that are in difficulty anyway. Normal functional departmental processes and reporting lines tend to be well owned — the waste often resides in the cross-functional departmental processes.

The player who agrees to be a process owner takes on the responsibility (from the owner of a higher level process) to initiate a process, to lead the team of players who enact the process and to account for the performance of the process to the higher level process owner. The process owner is also responsible for identifying and obtaining agreement for what is meant by success of the process and for delivering that success. This does not mean that the process owner has to do all of the work! The role is that of the leader, the **conductor of the orchestra** of that process as we described in Chapter 8, but the player may take on other roles too and therefore do other work, which contributes to the success of the team. Some common titles for a project process owner are project director, project manager or project leader or design leader. The process owner for an entire organisation may be the Chief Executive or Chairman. The Board of Directors is responsible for the delivery of the overall performance led by the Chairman. The actual titles used for the process owner are a matter of taste, the important matter is that in any process the role of process owner is clearly defined and understood. It is good practice for all of the roles in a process to be written down in the QA documents, as this should make the information more dependable and assist the formation of productive relationships.

The overall owning of process in a public institution may be split at the higher levels. For example, a chief executive may own the delivery of a process but a board, council or committee may be responsible for setting the strategy or indeed making choices on some detailed questions.

Some risk averse organisations deliberately create a fog of accountability to avoid the unwarranted attribution of blame. The well known television series 'Yes Minister' illustrates our point. However, in the authors' experiences, the behaviour is not restricted to government but is characteristic of many organisations. If there is no mechanism for recognising and accepting good risks, i.e. those that should be taken to enable overall success, then the organisation will only succeed in spite of itself — usually through the dedication of its staff.

A process owner is usually a person but not always

As we have said, a physical system without intentions, an artefact, cannot take responsibility and cannot therefore be a process owner. However, a computer is an interesting special case. A computer can be programmed to make choices from a finite set of rules and so effectively it seems to make decisions (see Chapter 10, multi-agent and process enactment systems). Thus it appears that a computer can effectively take on a responsibility — but it cannot be accountable since it is inanimate and without intentionality. Machines are already becoming process owners communicating directly to each other. In that case, the human higher level process owners may well have some interesting risk situations about which to make judgements. Box 9.4 sets out this way of thinking about safety critical systems such as automatic aircraft landing systems and power station control systems.

Match roles, skills and process

In every process there will be roles to be carried that require particular skills, education or experience. For example, in a typical company there will be finance, engineering, personnel, etc. Each of these roles will have players who see the process from a particular perspective and will use particular state variables or performance indicators. An accountant will describe it in terms of money and financial parameters. An engineer will use technical parameters and a personnel manager will use human resource attributes. An understanding of the process and its attributes should help in choosing people for the various roles and in

Box 9.4   Quality and safety critical systems   Explanation

A computer may have a role in a process such that choices are made by the machine in a time frame that does not allow human intervention (e.g. emergency control, landing an aeroplane in thick fog). If this is the case, such a process may be quality critical (safety critical systems are a well-known specific example).

In effect, the computer has been made the owner of the process. The process owner of the higher level process in which it is embedded has done this because there is an advantage. The process owners of the *even higher* processes will count that player responsible and call him to account. The process owner of the computer-owned process has effectively delegated a responsibility without accountability. That is a risk he probably must take where the benefits outweigh the risks — but he should do it knowingly.

An Airbus A300 came into land at Nagoya, Japan in January 1994 when the autopilot computer tried to abort the landing. The struggle between the pilot and the computer caused the plane to climb steeply, stall and crash, killing 264 people (*Sunday Times*, 27 June 1999).

analysing the creative tension — the gap between where we are now and where we want to be at some point in the future.

Hammer (1996) argues that organisations should actually close down functional departments (such as finance, engineering, etc.) and instead set up centres of excellence. These centres should not be responsible for any work directly other than for enhancing skills and developing their people (all Integrating I processes). In terms of BCIOD+R processes these centres provide players with specialist skills to take on specialist roles.

Processes interact

In Chapter 2, we recognised that processes, at the same level of the process model hierarchy, interact. We said that processes should be designated as 'friends' of other processes. This means that there is a defined and recognised link between two processes, with specific messages as files of information passing between them. The quality of the relationships between the players in the two processes determines the success of the transfer. The clarity with which a message is formulated and the willingness to receive it and work on it depend on the perception of the relationship of the sender and the receiver. For example, one process owner could be passing excellent messages to another who ignores them because he suspects his motives.

Figures 9.4 and 9.5 show one practical way of setting out the flow within a process. The lower levels of the diagrams can be called up in a computer by double clicking on a box — for example, double clicking on *Choosing beam sizes* will open up the window shown in the lower part of the figure. The solid line represents the delegation of responsibility and the dotted returning line represents the line of reporting accountability. The roles and players are shown in the diagram. The other process attributes may be obtained, for example, by right clicking on the appropriate process box.

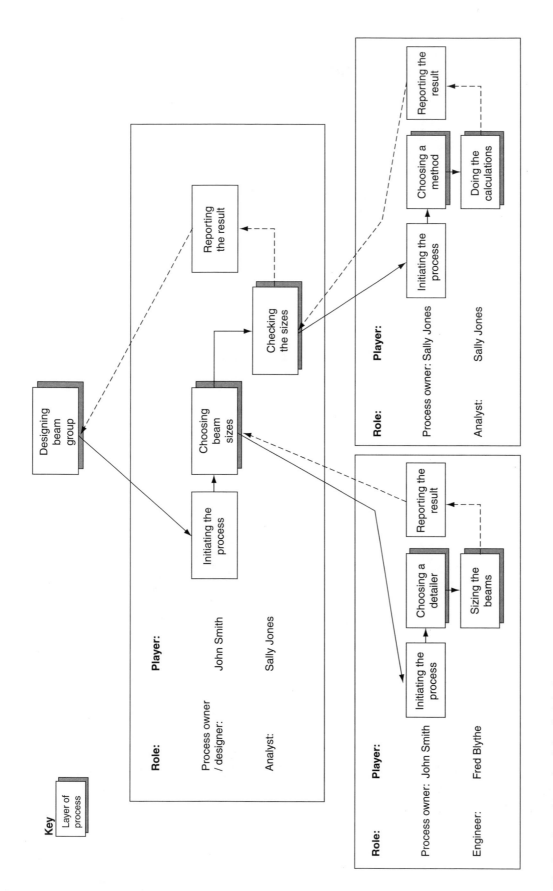

Fig. 9.4. Some lower level detailed design processes

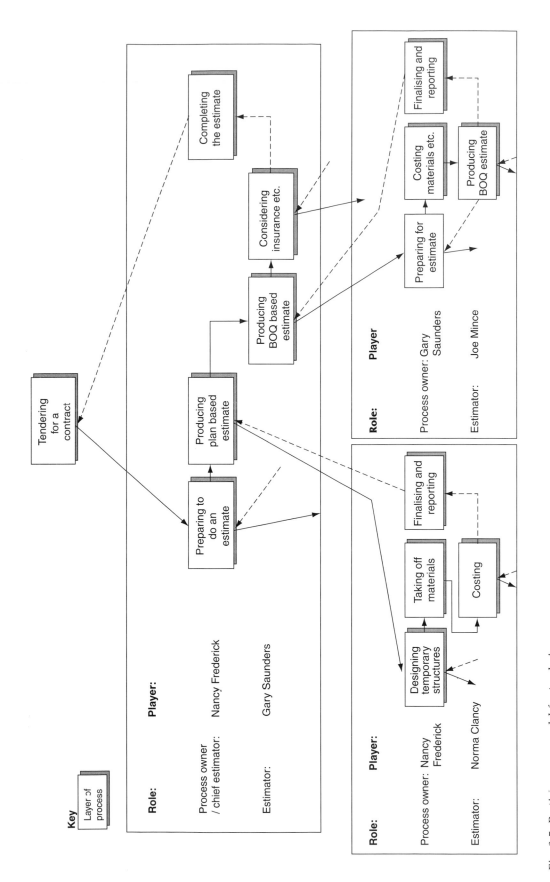

Key

Layer of process

Role:

Player:

Process owner / chief estimator: Nancy Frederick

Estimator: Gary Saunders

Role:

Player:

Process owner: Gary Saunders

Estimator: Joe Mince

Role:

Player:

Process owner: Nancy Frederick

Estimator: Norma Clancy

Tendering for a contract

Completing the estimate

Considering insurance etc.

Producing BOQ based estimate

Producing plan based estimate

Preparing to do an estimate

Preparing for estimate

Costing materials etc.

Producing BOQ estimate

Finalising and reporting

Designing temporary structures

Taking off materials

Costing

Finalising and reporting

Fig. 9.5. Partial process model for tendering

Delegate to sub-process ownership

When a process owner decides to delegate a role to a sub-process owner as in Figs. 9.4 and 9.5 then the responsibilities need to be negotiated with the new sub-process owner. Delegation does not mean abdication so the responsibilities and accountabilities remain — but they are executed through a sub-process. The accountability is expressed in terms of the extent to which agreed objectives (with performance measures as appropriate) are met. These performance measures must be **agreed at the start** of the process.

Of course, it is quite possible that the objectives agreed for any given role may not be met for various reasons. For example, it is possible that the objectives were inappropriate. In such a case the player in the delegating role needs to re-negotiate objectives in order to improve performance. The system is therefore one of a double loop learning where the delegating role not only monitors the performance of the sub-role but also evaluates its effectiveness and helps to diagnose remedial actions. This view of management and leadership is in accord with that set out in Chapter 8 where we discussed the new view of leaders as designers, coaches, stewards and teachers. They are responsible for building organisations where people continually expand their capabilities, clarify vision and improve team learning, i.e. they are responsible for organisational learning. They have a particularly important role in enabling knowledge to flow from the front line back to design and decision makers. This means they have to be skilled managers of change because this is usually not part of the existing culture.

Each role, therefore, has the potential to be responsible for many sub-roles, a one-to-many mapping through a tree of delegation. However, although this would be natural in an hierarchical organisational culture, in many organisations the situation may not be as simple. There may be many to many mappings of responsibilities in a flatter organisational culture. In this case a player in a role may be accountable to more than one superior role. For example, a role may be accountable to both a departmental (or centre of excellence) manager and a project manager. In this situation there exists a potential for conflict. The boundaries of each of the delegating roles will need to be defined rather carefully and if there is overlap a system needs to be established whereby conflict can be negotiated away. The defining of roles as sets of responsibilities is not a sufficient condition for success — but it is very important in reducing the chances of difficulties and failure. Committed leadership, recognition of interdependence and skilled change management will also be needed.

Customers are at the top of the value chain

The customer pays for the product or service. The customer is at the top of the value chain. Together, customers provide a revenue stream, either directly or indirectly through taxes. Where the costs are paid for or subsidised by taxation, the Government has a role to represent the customer by being the client or more indirectly through the role of regulators such as the Rail Regulator.

It is perhaps easiest to think of the value chain through an example. In each case the value chain is a chain of processes in which the values are the criteria used to make decisions. As a construction player your client may be, for example, a well-known chain of retail stores. They provide the revenue stream. The customers of this store are, for this purpose, the top of the value chain. The store, if it is successful, will know and value its customers — you perhaps do not. If you, during your contract, damage customer confidence in the store, you will have a problem with your client. In order to delight your client, you need to understand the values of his customers as he does. In one sense, it is simply a

Example

Figure 9.6 shows the structure of delegations for a typical Construction Director and a Project Controller extracted from the process model attributes. One of the responsibilities of the project management role in the figure is the initial setting up of the role of Contract Review for a specified project. In most cases it will be the same person who is responsible for both roles. The delegation structure is shown in Fig. 9.7. The mission and aims of the Contract Review role are 'To review the final contract as agreed with the client with a view to producing a strategy as to how the contract will be tackled and assessing the capabilities of the department to perform the task.' The objectives that follow are, for example, becoming familiar with the terms of the contract, paying particular attention to the client's letters of conditions and changes to the contract, nominating a Project Controller or identifying milestones and key deliverables. Some information requirements and deliverables are shown in Fig. 9.8.

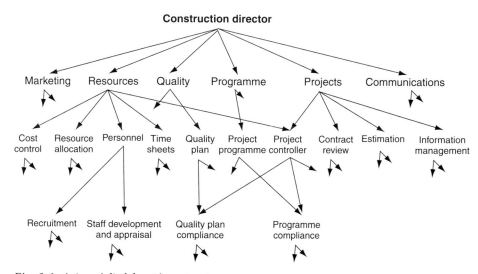

Fig. 9.6. A (partial) delegation structure

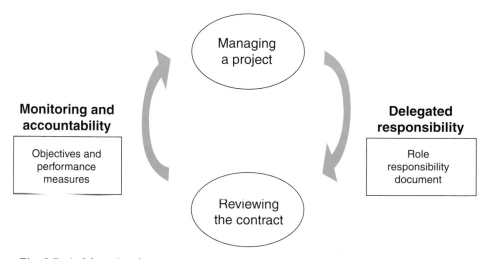

Fig. 9.7. A delegation for contract review

Information requirements

Description	Source
• All contract documentation	• Project database
• Letters issued and received while negotiating the contract	• Project database
• Changes made to contract	• Project database
• Changes made to pre-contract design	• Project database
• Agreed costs	• Contract
	• Client's brief
• Client's programme	• Contract
	• Pre-tender management role
	• Client's brief
• Regulatory requirements	• External sources
	• Local authority
• Resource availability	• Department resource management
• Other programmes	• Other disciplines

Deliverables

Description	Information content	Sent to
Report on the capability of the department with respect to the contract	• Nominated project controller • High level programme • Regulatory requirements • Identify need for assistance or special services • High level resource requirements	• Project director • Project manager • Regulatory requirements • Department resource manager • Project database

Fig. 9.8. Typical information requirements for contract review

matter of ensuring that you do not disturb the success of processes above you in which you take no part (wittingly). However, you can do more by looking for opportunities. For example, if you spot that by using a heavy lift crane you can open the car park three months earlier than previously planned at no extra cost then you could be adding value to the process. This might be particularly important if it means that the client catches the pre-Christmas trade.

This value chain continues right down through your partner companies — the suppliers to you and to your partners and to your client. In every case you do not wish to endanger success of the processes since you have a stake in their success.

The need is simple — it is worth finding out about the values of your client and your subcontractors and all who supply you and them. A typical value chain diagram, following Porter (1985), is shown in Fig. 9.9 — it can be extracted directly from the attributes of a process model. Fig. 9.10 shows, using Porter's notation, a typical value chain sequence of processes for a contractor. We will return to value and supply chain networks later in the chapter.

9.6 Planning processes

Value time

In the construction industry, time is usually taken along with cost to be the primary driver for our projects. Success is completion on time and on budget. Why is it that we so frequently fail to deliver on time and even when we claim to have done so, there is a long snagging list which indicates that we had not finished? How do our customers see this? They are certainly not impressed. The needs for reduced construction time, substantial reduction in defect rates and improved predictability of outcome are three of the seven Egan targets for improvement.

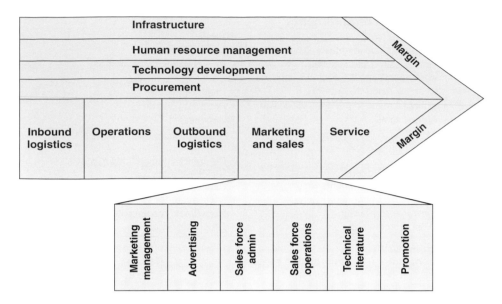

Porter (1985)

Fig. 9.9. A typical value chain

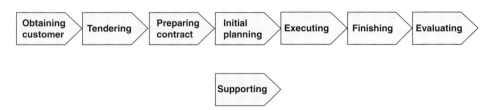

Fig. 9.10. A value chain for construction

Critical path planning has limits

We often fail to meet the expectations of our clients that we ourselves have generated. Yet in practice as construction players we are highly trained to plan what we do. Many construction players think about process solely in terms of **bar charts**. We need to do something so the automatic reaction is 'Draw a bar chart'. More detailed considerations might lead us to use a **critical path network**. The skills to think about and use these tools are **necessary but not sufficient** for managing time. Perhaps this is why we also have many players who are among the best in the world at responding to the unexpected, at fixing things and keeping the show on the road. We get a lot of practice but little thanks. Perhaps critical path planning does have its limitations because it:

- can fog understanding and communication of fundamental issues;
- does not represent learning processes well — it is a linear sequential view whereas learning is a continuous loopy process reinforced by practice and coaching;
- is not future proof — it works well for tame problems but can be misleading for wicked ones.

If we can address these issues then we can make a difference to time management. We need to focus more on what we do not know. We need to focus more on what is outside our system. We manage the processes to success in spite of the uncertainties.

Box 9.6   Critical path networks can sometimes fog   Example
           understanding

One of us was an expert witness for a contractor. We offered to provide a critical path network, from the project records, to demonstrate to the judge that
the argument of the other side was not practical. The reaction of our barris-
ter was that critical path networks are too complicated. In spite of many
attempts, he had never seen one yet convince a judge. He said that the other
side will use the network to fog the issue. They will talk about alternative
paths and alternative logic based on conjecture. The result will be stalemate.
The complexity of the network enables the issues to be fogged by the other
side.

   We therefore devised a set of rich pictures and demonstrated that the temporary support for the front of the building would be standing on the place
where the other side assumed a hole could be dug! The point was made simply and effectively. To achieve what the other side argued should have been
done, needed a radically different approach from the outset. The need for
the hole was only apparent after the building was opened up. The client had
not been prepared to invest in the prior site investigation. The opposition
then argued that the client's professional team should have told him what
they did not know. The client successfully claimed on professional indemnity insurance to the limit of its cover. Nevertheless the client went bankrupt
and the contractor was paid less than half what he had to pay to his subcontractors.

Plan to learn

Frequently, new teams are assembled for new projects in which what is done is
a new process adapted from previous methods and techniques. We see the team
begin to get its head round what it is doing and momentum gathers as they climb
the new learning curve. Just as they have got the hang of what is going on they
have finished and are on to another new process.

So the question is 'Do we, in the construction industry, invest enough in the
learning process?' We ask it as a practical question because we do not claim to
know the answer.

We can reflect on the opportunities in the learning curves we all experience.
It is also interesting that there seems, in our experience, to be some resistance to
learning new techniques. Perhaps learning as a process could be more highly
valued. It will certainly need to be, to do things differently. Just as communication of what success looks like enables the team to co-operate to achieve it, so a
vision of the skills required in the future enables them to be developed. A scheme
such as *Investors in People* is one approach that has a developing track record.
However, success depends on a culture of learning that includes everyone. In
this sense the more experienced staff sometimes have the greatest difficulty. Yet
they provide the greatest opportunity. If they are prepared to learn new techniques with younger less experienced staff the combination of experience and
energy can yield awesome results. The need is to understand what motivates
people to want to learn. It will not be achieved by continuing to 'beat people
until morale improves!' A dialogue about the needs for success of the company
and of the person can motivate and encourage in a way that changes the whole
perspective. We will fail to change if all we do is deliver another procedural bolt
on with shrink-wrapped training packages, supported by pep-talks from

management. For it to work we have to show we value the learning process. It has to be inspired and enjoyable. This is an area where we feel that our industry is firing on about one cylinder out of four. We can learn a great deal from others.

We have a culture in which it is often held that **to fail to plan is to plan to fail**. Perhaps this could be extended to **we will fail to learn unless we plan to learn**. Learning processes are loopy. Our concept of processes within process allows them to sit within our overall purpose — instead of languishing as a sideshow. The learning processes are the way we generate a lot of our key competencies. We can get better and better at them as we proceed. Some organisational roles will need redefining. We require less emphasis on supervisors and experts and more emphasis on coaches and mentors.

The learning processes are an essential requirement for sustainable business in a changing world. It may well be that organisations will be selected on the demonstrable effectiveness of their learning processes as well as their historical track record. Key performance indicators are needed and will be displayed in publicity material just as some companies are now reporting their progress towards environmental sustainability.

Learning curves are important

Learning curves have a substantial influence on cost and progress. For example, certain activities, such as the erection of a section of a bridge deck or of cast in-situ columns, may be repeated many times. The first time such an activity is performed may take some time but, after that, the cycle time reduces as the team learns. This process, as a one-off learning experience within the project, is generally well executed and valuable. However, there is an opportunity to extend that learning back into the design of the next project. If such learning is accumulated then the conditions become much more attractive for more investment in aids to the construction process. The move toward partnering and relationship contracts in which the contractor is appointed much earlier ought to facilitate this learning process. There should be consequent reductions in cycle times. There is plenty of evidence from other industries to demonstrate the benefit.

Try to standardise processes

The concept of investment in improved construction process is often rejected because of the 'one-off' prototype nature of what we produce. No two buildings are the same. Roads and bridges have to be fitted into constricted spaces. Our constructions needs to be in sympathy with their surroundings. Soil conditions vary. We frequently extend rather than renew. We reuse materials more and more. These are many of the realities that are seen as preventing effective standardisation. Many people claim that circumstances are unique and so are our products.

Standardisation of components and processes is often achieved project by project e.g. in motorways, bridges, railways and so on. However, standardisation between projects is rare except where the product is small and familiar such as a simple frame building. However, the concept of process mapping and co-operation promoted by BCIOD+R awareness offers opportunities to learn to standardise and automate parts of the process. It should encourage feedback from project to project; from the front line to design. In our healthy pub example of Chapter 1 the issue of standardisation was mulled over by the players. They saw that the examples of the systems building of the 1960s was not what this is really all about. In the construction industry the benefits will flow from standardised processes, thereby improving our ability to invest in learning.

Time boxes are useful if time is critical

As we saw in the healthy pub example of Chapter 1, where time is the critical resource, time box processes can be useful. We have to prioritise other values to achieve best value within the time constraint. This is particularly necessary in timing critical processes dictated by outside events such as weather, marketing windows, competitive time to market or the operational pressures within an organisation which tend to show short attention spans if benefit is not shown quickly. This behaviour is normally recognised by a tendency for managers to respond to pagers or mobile phones during meetings.

Whatever the reason, if time is critical it is important to ensure best use is made of it. Basic sequences of processes required for success are each assigned a time box (Fig. 9.11), as we saw in the healthy pub example of Chapter 1. The sum of the time boxes equals the available duration. Sometimes an extra box is allowed for a process repeat if an outcome is judged unacceptable but more commonly if this happens the subsequent time boxes are shortened proportionately.

The success targets for each time box can be prioritised using extended MoSCoW rules (Chapter 6). Tests can be established to determine whether 'must have' success targets have been achieved at each stage. Success depends upon having all of the necessary competencies. The process owners should have a high level of experience in its use. If they are over ambitious the outcome could be worse than useless.

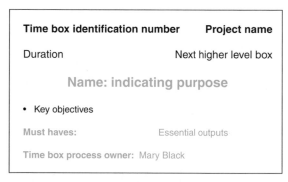

Fig. 9.11. Time boxes

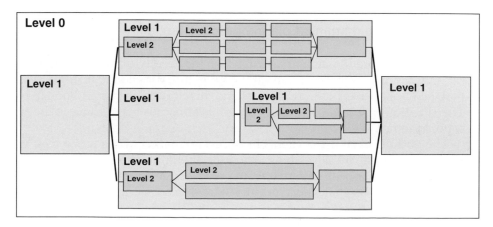

Fig. 9.12. Layered time boxes as processes

Box 9.7   Time boxes used for pre-qualification selection   Example

A team of three evaluators had exactly one hour to reduce eight suppliers, who had submitted pre-qualifications, to a shortlist of up to four. Each of the evaluators had read the submissions. They agreed that they would spend five minutes agreeing the process, five minutes assessing each supplier, ten minutes agreeing the shortlist and five minutes assessing if the process could have been misleading. The outcome was subject to corporate governance audit based on the written summary submitted. As well as agreeing the timings in the first five minutes the team reviewed the original success criteria. They also preferred to rely on their memories rather than spending time looking at their notes. In each five minutes they went round the table identifying issues, which revealed strengths and weaknesses in that submission. They immediately gave scores out of ten, which they did not change as they heard other people's scores. In the event they agreed the scores for each submission within a single point except in one case where all scores were very low when the variation was three points. Three of the bidders had scored well above the others and so were asked to submit bids. The highest scoring bidder had surprised them because he was not an expected choice. Incidentally, when bids were evaluated he was selected as offering substantially better value than the other two. All agree that the process had been effective, fair and efficient. The time pressure had also made it more fun than a normal selection meeting that could take half a day.

Try rapid prototyping using DSDM

We have already discussed the difficulty of transferring methods from one industry to another. It is important that industries learn from each other, and below we set out an example of a process that you might be interested in exploring.

In Chapter 7 we referred to DSDM (Dynamic Systems Development Method) as an attempt by another industry to create integrated process and teams. Actually, it was developed for use in the software industry. It is a time boxed method which could be prototyped for construction on a demonstration project. The learning could then be used more widely as appropriate (Box 9.8).

It is clear that DSDM has a systems based approach at its root and many of the ideas promoted here are a part of it.

Last responsible moment planning drives flexibility

The concept of predict and provide, in which the need is fully defined at the outset, means that, in theory, there can be no excuse for change justified claims. Inevitably, of course, there are changes and therefore claims for additional costs. The situation maximises the uncertainty faced because it maximises the time exposed to risk.

The businesses of many clients have several market cycles while their construction projects are developing. The expectation must be that the brief will change after it has been frozen. It would seem sensible to plan for change from the outset in a way that all players understand the consequences.

One solution for the client is to buy a speculative development instead of designing and building one. This is only possible in a reasonably dependable market such as housing or offices. It is not suitable for more specialised needs.

> **Box 9.8   DSDM Dynamic Systems Development Method   Example**
>
> DSDM derives from the pressure to deliver software support more quickly. It is funded by a UK based consortium. It provides a framework of controls and best practice for rapid application development of high quality business systems. There are nine key principles which are all necessary.
>
> 1. Users must be actively involved as part of process rather than as an external client.
> 2. DSDM teams must be empowered to make decisions and to prioritise using MoSCoW rules M(ust) S(hould)C(ould)W(ants) (Box 6.5).
> 3. Essential values must be focused on: e.g. affordability, meeting time constraints.
> 4. Fitness for purpose is the essential criteria.
> 5. Iterative and incremental development is necessary.
> 6. All changes during development are reversible.
> 7. Requirements are baselined (or frozen) at a high level.
> 8. Testing is integrated throughout the life cycle.
> 9. Co-operative approach between stakeholders is necessary.
>
> Note that this is a methodology for managing a process where there have been some serious failures to deliver, i.e. producing complex software for organisational processes. DSDM is about people not tools. It stresses the close involvement of all players, stakeholders and users. It requires frequent interactions to obtain views on requirements and to test intermediate prototype software products. Note that there is an implied hierarchy of requirements in principle no 7. DSDM is a process management methodology to manage risks. The proponents of DSDM realise that the method is more suitable for managing soft system processes than for hard systems.
>
> DSDM, J. Stapleton, Addison Wesley, 1997

An alternative is to drive in as much flexibility as possible for changes to be taken on board. In this case we have to establish the **last responsible moment** for freezing particular requirements. The criteria is that this moment is when the cost of change is greater than the benefit of change. The approach becomes much more practical if a relationship founded on understanding exists between the BCIOD+R process owners.

Use the observational approach to control risk

We can extend this thinking further to embrace the ideas of systematic observational risk control. There is nothing new in the basic idea — it is how we manage risk as individuals on a daily basis. The observational approach has grown out of the Observational Method (OM) as proposed by Peck (1969) for handling geotechnical uncertainty (Le Masurier, Muir Wood and Blockley, 1999a, 1999b). At the core of both ideas is the feedback loop of Reflective Practice as set out in Chapter 5. It is the idea that if we have to manage a process to success and if there is a great deal of uncertainty about the future, then the close involvement of all players and stakeholders is required. This has to be through a well understood and agreed process to review events as they evolve and to consider strategies and actions every step of the way. The top level process here derives from the definition of design due to Sir Alan Muir Wood which is that 'design is the process of *translating an idea into a reality'*.

Box 9.9   The Observational Method   Explanation

Design and construction are traditionally quite separate — predict and provide. Since there are often large uncertainties about ground conditions there is sense in delaying, where possible, some of the design decisions until construction on site. Not only is the necessary information much clearer but also other options might be pursued. This is the Observational Method (Peck, 1969). The idea is that a design scheme is drawn up based on the best available data but backed up with contingency plans. These are used only if required. Thus key performance parameters, such as ground settlement or pore pressure, are monitored, and decisions about contingency plans are made accordingly. These plans will cover situations where the design assumptions are found not to be justified and some redesign is needed or where unusual conditions that were anticipated but not expected are found. The OM requires a completely different set of contractual arrangements and a different way of working between designers and contractors. The rewards, however, are that large cost and time savings can be made (see below).

A case study — The Limehouse Link   Example

This was a £250m cut and cover highway tunnel started in 1989 and built in some of the most difficult and variable ground conditions in London. The OM was used to eliminate heavy temporary support works. The method was introduced progressively on a number of working fronts under a value engineering clause introduced into the contract after the start of construction. Without that clause it is unlikely that the savings of a total of 4900 t of temporary steelwork (91% of the original design) would have been possible. Wall movements, prop loads, ground movements and pore pressures were monitored and compared to three zones. The measurements that fell in the 'green zone' gave no concern, those in the 'amber zone' were a cause for concern and action had to be considered and those in the 'red zone' required immediate action.

(Glass P. R. and Powderham A. J., *Geotechnique*, 1994)

The traditional way of carrying out this translation is predict and provide, i.e. to complete the design based on a brief and then to construct it. In OM, some design decisions have to be made during construction. The motive for this approach is the high cost associated with designing to accommodate the uncertainty associated with ground conditions. We recall that uncertainty is FIR (Fuzziness, Incompleteness and Randomness, Chapter 4). In geotechnics, we may have a lot of incompleteness, i.e. we just do not know enough about what may be concealed in the ground. Hence designs may have to be very conservative using the traditional approach. Although there is high uncertainty, geotechnical engineers will know the range of what to expect. It simply costs too much to find out in precise detail before construction is underway. Instead of assuming the worst, it is possible to design quite enterprisingly, making reasonable assumptions together with *contingency plans* to cover situations where the design assumptions are found by observation not to be justified.

Of course, this way of thinking is not without its dangers. If due attention is not given to the process then things can go seriously wrong as was demonstrated by the collapse of the tunnel at Heathrow during the construction of the Heathrow Express line in 1994. (Box 9.10).

The accident provided an example of why it is essential to ensure that information available at the delivery end of our processes needs to be understood and fed back into our decision making process at a speed that reflects the reality of events.

Box 9.10   The Heathrow Tunnel collapse   Example

In 1994, a £60m contract was let to build the main tunnels and stations for the Heathrow Express from Paddington to the airport. Nine months into the work a major tunnelling collapse occurred. The total extra unplanned cost has been reported at £422.7m or seven times the original tunnelling contract price (*NCE*, 18 February 1999).

The method used to construct the tunnel was NATM (The New Austrian Tunnel Method) which is an OM (Observational Method) as described in Box 9.9. The problem was a weak tunnel invert. The contractor admitted that this was attributable to poor construction of the sprayed concrete lining. At the trial the subcontractor responsible for the monitoring was found to be guilty of failing to issue warnings when data from its monitoring instruments showed that collapse was imminent some weeks before the actual cave-in. However, the defence lawyer claimed that the readings were difficult to interpret and no one in any of the companies involved (including the clients) saw that there was a problem.

Controversy after the trial centred around interpretations of the New Engineering Contract (NEC) that was used. Any OM project requires close collaboration between design and construction because design continues through into the construction process. The issue was whether or not this is possible under the NEC.

However, the real hazards (pre-conditions to collapse Box 6.29) were the breakdown in the process of OM. Roles (i.e. sets of responsibilities) were either allocated inappropriately or else were insufficiently understood by those taking them on. The critical nature of the need to monitor the ground as the work progressed was not appreciated. The contractor admitted that everyone was inexperienced at self-certification and the use of that phrase indicated an ambiguity of responsibility within the process. There was no clear understanding of success for the team. The responsibility for quality assurance was not as clear as it should have been. As time pressures mounted the warning signs were not recognised and all of the factors combined to cause the collapse (Box 6.30).

Therefore, in summary, the central issues were that the roles in the various processes and the information to be passed between processes were not clearly set out. A process model, such as described in this book, would help to provide that clarity. It would set out the needs of OM and NATM as a method requiring the design role (responsibility and accountability) to continue actively through construction. It would provide a basis for success regardless of the conditions of contract (as long as the contract did not rule out or obstruct the collaboration required for OM, of course). An audit system such as MARIUN would have detected the warning signs.

Observational engineering is generic

The observational approach is generic — we have called it Observational Engineering (OE). However, it must be part of the thinking of the project team right from the start. It requires a co-operative relationship and a suitable set of contractual arrangements between designers and contractors Fig. 9.13. It is beyond the scope of this book to consider the detailed legal aspects of the actual contracts.

The OE approach is suitable for situations where the uncertainties are large and the dependability of the information is suspect. It is good for soft systems which is why it is at the root of the commonsense approach we use in our daily lives. A systematic use of OE will yield, we believe, large cost and time savings. Fig. 9.14 illustrates the relationship that OE could have with other initiatives such as partnering, value management and benchmarking.

9.7 Designing for delivery and use

We have defined the design process as that of moving from a vision to a reality. The design process therefore includes the design of the processes to achieve that. These include the physical artefacts that we normally associate with design — *the what* — the products as well as the softer processes such as the process teams. There will, therefore, be elements of BCIOD+R in all phases of the design process. There will be soft and hard systems to design.

It is important that players with expertise and knowledge from all of these process groups are part of the design team. The effort in integrating processes will remain pretty constant throughout. The emphasis of the other processes will change through the design cycle of pre-project phase followed by design, construction and operation. For example, in the pre-project phase the emphasis on delivery will be less than on the business. The customer processes will also be important and the actual balance will vary according to the purpose of the project. In the design phase the effort required may start with equal proportions between BCOD and will steadily develop so that at the construction phase, it will be largely delivery focused. In the operations phase (the use of the product where the client is now getting the payback) the customer, operations and business again dominate the effort. The delivery processes then are largely about maintaining and enhancing the infrastructure.

In order for the team to work effectively, the roles from BCIOD+R must be inside the process throughout. They must not just be brought in from outside

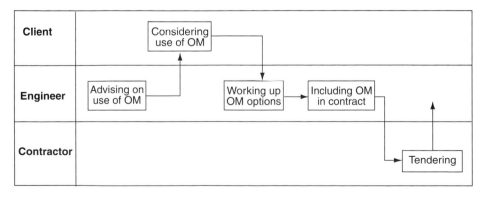

Fig. 9.13. Processes for introducing the observational approach

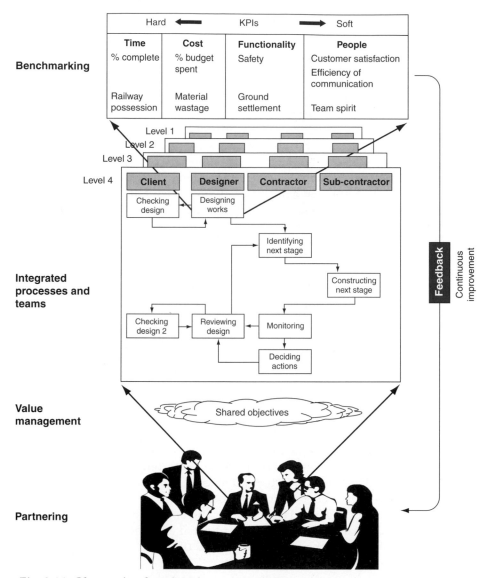

Fig. 9.14. Observational engineering

as the requirement is realised. That does not mean that the players must all be from one company. Rather it means that the team is empowered to design and manage the project and must act as a team throughout. The reason why this is important is that they need to understand each other's roles, each other's skills, each other's problems and each other's risks in order to be able to innovate and think creatively. They need to learn to build trust because they are inevitably interdependent.

A team put together in this way will provide significant added value.

Designers need to consider the supply chains

The design team needs to include players who understand the supply chains. In the past, they would have had the role of a procurement team. The role is now wider and more important. To achieve the feedback of construction process into design, a new role is needed. The aim of this new role should be to manage relationships and to build in incentives to add value. The team has to be the guardian of performance management and productive relationships. The outcome of this relationship has to be demonstrably better than from traditional competitive tendering. In some organisations, the supply chain manager is the integrating (I) process owner reporting to the programme or project manager.

A simple view of the supply chain is that it is a sequence of transactions to enable components to be assembled and delivered. The supply chain for a cladding panel may start with the subcontractor that blasts the granite in a quarry. He then supplies the granite to another subcontractor who takes it to another site. Here, another subcontractor cleans it and passes it to a company that polishes it. Still another company may cut it to size for another who makes the actual panel and supplies it to the building site. Here, another company erects it into a building.

In these many stages each company will be borrowing money. One client that looked at this supply chain noticed that the cost of borrowing money for many of the subcontractors was very high. The interest rates at which they were borrowing were high and they had to provide bonds to higher level process owners. The client therefore proposed a new set of relationships in the supply chain such that the client financed the whole operation. The result was a saving of about 15%. Of course, the client was taking extra risk (e.g. of a sub-contractor's failing) which needed to be explicitly managed.

In another supply chain for cladding, it was found that the fixings provided were not easy to attach to the actual building and a lot of rework was required. During the life of the building the fixings corroded because the rework had caused leakage at the joints. Finally, the panels failed with subsequent costs. In this instance the issue was not that the supply chain did not work well but that some of the processes between the supply chain and the operations process could have managed the risks that had been generated through the rework. For example, it was found later that, with a slight modification, the window cleaning system could have been used to monitor the performance of the cladding and, when necessary, the cladding could be replaced. The possibility of problems from the delivery supply chain had not been co-ordinated with the other BCOD processes. If that co-ordination had been in place the risks that had been generated by the rework could have been better managed.

Later, we will discuss the supply chain as a part of a supply network of interacting processes which are present in the overall process model.

Design leadership for success

Two of the most successful UK construction projects of recent years have been the construction of the main civil engineering works for Sizewell B Power station and the Second Severn Crossing near Bristol. In each case these major projects were delivered on time and within budget. The Project Director for these achievements was Norman Haste. His keys to delivery of a successful project are:

- clear direction
- positive leadership
- removal of complexity
- identification and management of uncertainty.

Every successful project he has been associated with has also had a single person driving it from the top level. All of these points are consistent with and reinforce many of the ideas presented in this book.

Design leadership is often fragmented and confusing

Various players regard themselves as having the role of leader of the design team. Typically for building projects the team leader is an architect. In recent years the QS (Quantity Surveyor) has often taken on that role. The real point is not that the team leader should be decided by the professional role in the team but by the skills that that player has in **being a design team leader**. In some projects there is an unfortunate lack of clarity about who is the team leader — the overall design process owner.

Design is a creative process that has to have a 'guiding mind'. The guiding mind is the **'conductor of the orchestra '** who provides a continuity of purpose from need to demolition. The fragmentation of roles and organisations can aggravate this problem and dissolve this sense of purpose. Sometimes, the client wants to provide the 'guiding mind but then wants to off-load all of the risks to others! Likewise, the other companies involved may be looking to transfer risk rather than participate in its good management by the team overall.

There are many differing skills required in the design team, e.g. creative and judgemental thinking, administrative and commercial skills, team leadership skills. These rarely reside in one person and so the team must be assembled with a clear idea in mind of the skills and roles required.

The process models with all of the useful attributes attached to each process enable a clarity of purpose and a focus on principle and interest.

A team can achieve what no individual can do. By appropriate design (see Belbin, Chapter 8) the team may have the competencies to achieve success, provided that it defines for itself what success is!

Innovation is essential

The rates of improvement targeted in *Rethinking Construction* will not be achieved by just delivering a steady stream of many small incremental improvements. Doing it differently means that we will have to innovate in order to take bigger steps. We use the word innovate to mean the successful implementation of new ideas. That can bring extra risks that have to be explicitly managed.

Innovation has to be supported by understanding, information and the right processes to manage the risks. This means more emphasis on prototype testing. It means more emphasis on research and development to inform risky decision making. It means that the impacts of the decisions we make have to be scrutinised more closely and the effects of what we do monitored more closely and actions taken to steer projects to success. Above all, it means that there has to be a return on the investment without threatening the business case for the project.

Excellent innovations are often rejected because it is much more comfortable when things go wrong to be able to say 'my decision to accept this approach is justified by the fact that it has been tried and tested'. This encourages claims that because systems have worked in one context they can be used confidently in another. Thus, the argument goes, the innovation risk has been dealt with and there is no need to concern ourselves with it in this new context. Such arguments are seriously misleading and complacency generated can lead to losses. It is clear that similarities in processes are useful and experiences in different contexts are informative. However, we have shown that the performance of processes are context dependent because they depend upon the purpose of the processes involved. Information and models of transformations in processes depend crucially on purpose for their effectiveness. These purposes are likely to be quite different in different industries. Similarly, the uncertainties in one context may be quite different from those in another.

It is clear that innovation is risky. We should always understand the intended benefit, challenge that it is real and then put in place explicit risk management processes. These include returning an adequate share of the value that is added. This generally means a continuity of return over several applications of the idea. Enabling construction players to achieve this is often an essential requirement for pre-investment.

There is a design spiral

Figure 9.15 illustrates the process of improvement as the design team discusses the various requirements from each point of view (BCIOD+R) and 'homes in' on a set of decisions which will define future success.

We have divided the design team into two sub-teams: one is the WHY team concerned with BCO; the other is the HOW team which is designing and delivering D. The I processes are those which help to drive the spiral towards success.

At the start of the process the two sub-teams will have a different views of need and cost and uncertainties will be large. This range is indicated by the scope of each spiral at the outset. The intersection of those ranges represents the area of agreement shown at the centre of the spiral. As the team discusses the issues they spiral around the values and move (in the diagram incrementally for the sake of illustration; but in reality the path will not be at all smooth) towards a final agreement. The diagram is included simply to illustrate the need for dialogue between the players in the design team to integrate and to cover all of the BCIOD+R dimensions of success and to converge together to the solution.

9.8   Delivering success together

Manage the supply network management

A process model is a network of inter-connected processes. Each process that sends information to a friend process is a supplier (of information or resource)

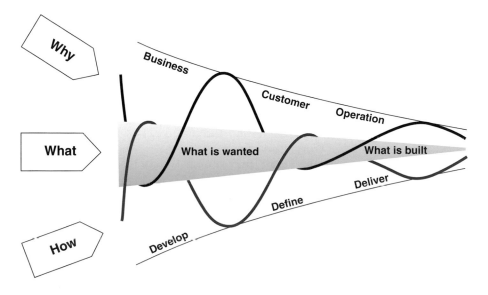

Fig. 9.15. Design spirals for construction

to another process. It is possible therefore to pick out specific chains of process-es for particular reasons (Fig. 9.16).

We will explain this through an illustration. Consider the delivery processes for a railway station. These involve maintenance and the development of new facilities. Let us move down the levels of detail and pick up some delivery process-es concerning the maintenance of a part of the roof. We will simplify the process-es, for the sake of providing a clear example, to that of painting a particular area of roof, as shown in Figs 9.17. We need eight processes which are: bringing in the scaffolding, erecting it, bringing in shot-blasting and other equipment, clean-ing off the steelwork, repairing it, painting it, removing equipment and scaf-folding, and cleaning up the site.

Clearly, such a sequence of processes is not independent of the main opera-tional processes of the station. Again, in simple terms there are also eight of these as, passengers arriving at the station, looking at display boards, buying tickets, waiting, buying from retail outlets, making way to platform, boarding train and train departing.

The processes that interact between the delivery and operational processes are potentially many. Again, for the purposes of illustration we will focus on one only, that of ensuring the safety and security of passengers (Fig. 9.17). When we consider that process, we see that the passengers may be required to take a dif-ferent and possibly more hazardous route. There is a greater risk of trips and falls. There is also a greater possibility of falling objects, particularly during the erection and dismantling of the scaffold.

The process of ensuring the safety of passengers is partially managed by removing the risk of objects falling on to passengers during erection of the scaf-fold. This is done simply by separating the two processes in time and space if possible. For example, the passenger route may be changed or the scaffold may be erected at night during a closedown period. Likewise the risks of falling objects such as paint brushes or paint splashes is prevented by sheeting up the work-ing area.

Figure 9.18 shows the process model as a chain for this example. The process-es in the suppliers to this chain are not shown but those processes could be mod-elled using the same technique. These include, for example, the scaffolding suppliers and the retail suppliers.

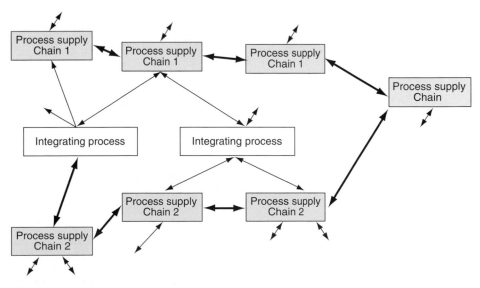

Fig. 9.16. Supply network processes

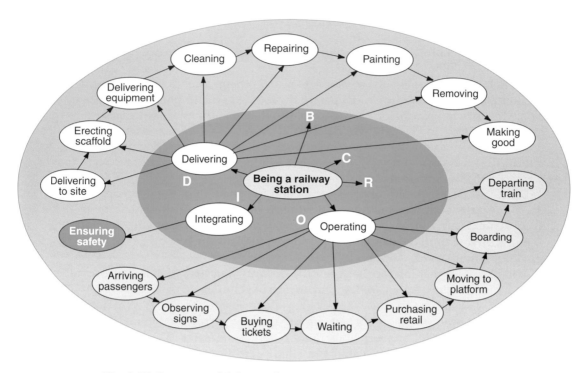

Fig. 9.17. Process model for a railway station example (partial)

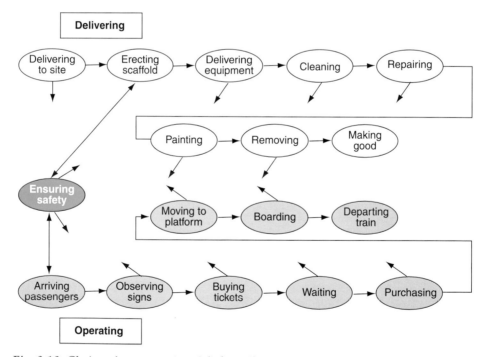

Fig. 9.18. Chains of processes (partial) for railway station example

Process models motivate

As we have said previously, the benefit of the process model is that it provides lines of sight between and across processes. Players can develop a clearer idea of their contribution to the bigger picture. One player can feel empowered to

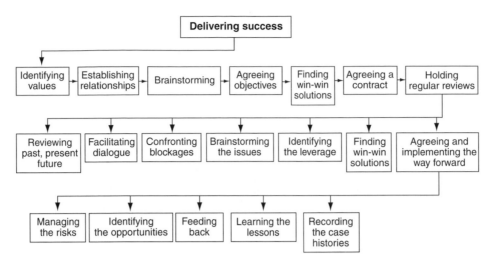

Fig. 9.19. Delivering a successful contract

communicate with another. The emphasis on team working presents many opportunities for joint skills training. There is a great potential for added value if we can motivate people to their work. This can happen if they feel an ownership of what they are doing and understand how their role is contributing to the whole.

Most improvements in process, particularly those that are innovative, benefit from being challenged from the outside. However, the challenge needs to be positive and co-operative to improve even more. Such opportunities can derive from, for example, cross-organisational mentoring, benchmarking and, most powerful of all, feedback about performance improvement from the people at the front line (Fig. 9.19).

Learn from measurement

In order to get to success we have to be able to recognise it. Personal achievements can remain private (Popper's World 2) if we wish. However, success in construction needs to be placed firmly in our world of shared perceptions (Popper's World 3). The best way for us all to agree about success is for it to be established by measurement both hard and soft. Such measurements will be objective — but as we saw when we were discussing the difficulties of measuring worth in Chapter 6 — some measures will be much more dependable than others.

Box 9.11 sets out some typical performance measures that are used to measure the progress of a construction project.

Clearly, hard systems measures tend to be more dependable than soft ones. Until recently, hard evidence about performance on site was difficult to find. CALIBRE (Box 9.12) has been developed for this very purpose.

Although CALIBRE has been implemented mainly on building sites with large clients who have large repeat business with the construction industry the message from the success of CALIBRE is clear. If you can measure your process performance dependably then you can identify what success looks like clearly. If you can perform those measurements quickly and dependably in real time so that you can feed back the results into the process performance, then you can steer the process to success and at the same time reduce waste dramatically.

CALIBRE is an example of the observational approach and is based on process.

Box 9.11   Some construction metrics (KPIs)   Example

Organisational performance

Time   Cost

Lead time   Cost of process
Process time   Labour cost
Waiting time   Material cost
Transfer time   Equipment cost
Set-up time   Information cost

Cost and time reduction — change from business case to final outcome
Cost and time predictability — change from start to finish of contract
Number of defects at handover
Accident rate
Percentage of processes on target   Degree of confidence in process
                                         success
Error rate   Evidence of success
Resources needed: Degree of concern for process failure
    people   Evidence of failure
    equipment
Client satisfaction: Customer complaints
    measured on scale 0–10
Productivity
Profitability
No. of changes by client which affect business case
Staff morale
Degree of adaptability
etc.

Physical performance

Load/Strain   Displacement
Pressure   Settlement

Box 9.12   CALIBRE   Example

Hard evidence about on-site performance is very difficult to establish. CAL-IBRE has been developed by BRE Ltd to do just this. It is intended to provide a simple and consistent way of identifying how much time is being wasted on non-value adding activities. CALIBRE is intended to help us improve on-site performance on a day-to-day basis. It is designed to provide real time feedback about how certain KPIs are developing as the project is constructed on site.

It was realised early in the development of CALIBRE that time sheets which gave man hours per trade lacked detail and were often inaccurate. Conventional work study techniques concentrated primarily on measuring achieved output at one particular workplace and often on a single task.

CALIBRE consists at present of three tools, namely time utilisation, productivity, SEAS (Site Environmental Assessment System), with a further tool nearing implementation on Health and Safety.

CALIBRE provides a defined set of tasks and activities. At regular intervals (perhaps 16–20 times per day and, on a small site, down perhaps even to every 10 minutes) a trained observer tours the site with a hand held com-

continued

Box 9.12 continued

puter and records the tasks against standard codes. The captured data are then quickly analysed to identify how much time is being spent on activities that add value directly to the construction and how much time is being spent on non-value adding work. The output is in the form of charts and graphs which make it easy to see patterns of activity and to identify bottlenecks. CALIBRE enables monitoring in real time and, because standard codes are being used, information can be compared day by day and site by site, supplier by supplier for any combination of work, area, task, activity or operative.

A typical record is

- when the tour is carried out
- who the operatives are
- where they are working
- what package of work they are doing
- how they are doing it.

Standard activities may be positioning steel stanchions, positioning steel beams, fixing cladding, etc. They are classified as being either Added Value Time, Support Time, Non-Added Value Time, or Statutory Time. The latter, for example, includes breaks, being rained off or carrying out safety checks. Figure 9.20 shows a typical CALIBRE process measurement map for steel frame erection with typical coding patterns.

The SEAS tool enables the measurement of consumption of energy, water, electricity, diesel, etc. Material wastage is tracked by volume, type and product. Recently, the road mileage of all participants on a project has been measured with surprising results. This latter measure is a good example of an activity which is not normally considered directly as a part of a system (in the meta-system, see Chapter 2). Yet it is obviously in the system since all of the miles covered by all members of the supply chain have to be paid for. Such measures lead to new ways of thinking about how to reduce waste by considering the geographical location of contractors and sub-contractors or by requiring partnerships based partly on location. This is a good example of how measuring can change your perspective.

CALIBRE, however, cannot work unless the culture of the participants is appropriate. Such a system requires **trust.** This is a fragile commodity that depends upon total openness about all data that is made available to everyone concerned — including the site operatives themselves. Training is essential. The value added for all has to be agreed and shared. The focus is on non-financial added value for everyone, with cost savings for the client. Financial rewards to team members then flow later as a consequence of trust. The construction players all focus on doing it right first time which results in increased 'pride in the job' and in increased ownership of success. Managers will ask operatives for advice about specific operations. The status of everyone is enhanced. The measurement process drives the culture change. Higher level summary statistics have to be easily broken down into the parts. The interpretation of the data for the site has to be done by the site teams themselves and not by a third party — unless the site team specifically asks for help. Thus CALIBRE does not tell anyone to do anything — it simply provides data though which people can make more informed decisions.

If the site team, or even suspicious senior managers at HQ, choose to ignore the data then there will be no benefit. But the evidence is hard for any one individual, no matter how senior, to resist. Current experience is that very large savings are being made — Fig. 9.21 shows a typical footprint for a CAL-

continued

> *Box 9.12 continued*
>
> IBRE measured project that shows typical potential for waste reduction. One contractor found on one site that a maximum of 40% of the total time was spent actually adding value. By modularising, standardising, eliminating double handling and using process maps, he was able to increase the figure to an average of 65% with some periods at 80%, with consequent savings. There is an intention to develop CALIBRE as a benchmarking tool. Companies will be able to compare themselves with best practice through an anonymised set of data mounted on a web site. There are also plans to extend the measures used to other parts of the construction process including design. Several major companies are actively involved in the scheme, namely Sainsbury, McDonalds, BAA and Mace.
>
> Details from Vassos Chrysostomou, Director, CALIBRE, BRE Ltd, Garston, Watford, UK

Feed back to the future

As we saw in CALIBRE, the culture needed to make the difference is one of clarity of purpose, clarity of role (through clear responsibilities and accountabilities), openness and co-operation. It is a culture where performance is measured in a blame-free environment because people know it is through that knowledge that success will be attained for all. It is a culture where all, including senior management, genuinely care about the personal development of all of the players.

Such a culture should encourage a spiral of knowledge generation that feeds back an accelerating rate of improvement. The measurements enable us to record the process so we can track our path. The blame-free approach is crucial. It requires management to be 'hard on the problem but soft on the people'. It requires managers who are leaders to bring the best out of people. If we can tap into their desires for success then we can deliver the Egan challenge many times over.

Of course, what we describe is an ideal. The route to achieving it has to include a practical consideration of such critical factors as affordability, cash flow, etc. However, we believe that there is much that can be done once we realise the vision and establish the mission so that everything that we do acquires a **sense of purpose**.

9.9 Revisiting lean construction, value engineering and partnering

As we discussed in Chapter 1, the construction industry can learn from the experiences of other industries. However, we must resist an inappropriate imposition of ideas — they need to be tailored to the special circumstances of the construction industry.

One of the major recent drivers has been the idea of *Lean Production* (Box 9.13). Other well-known initiatives are *Value Engineering and Value Management* and *Partnering* (Boxes 9.16 and 9.17). Other, perhaps less well-known, ideas are *CALIBRE* (Box 9.12), the *Observational approach* (Box 9.9) and the *Dynamic Systems Development Method* (*DSDM* — Box 9.8) that we introduced earlier. It is clear that all of these ideas have great value. It is also clear that they have much in common. However, what is lacking is a set of ideas to integrate them. We believe that systems thinking through process holons that promote the creation of beneficial relationships and provide paths for dependable communications is that set of ideas.

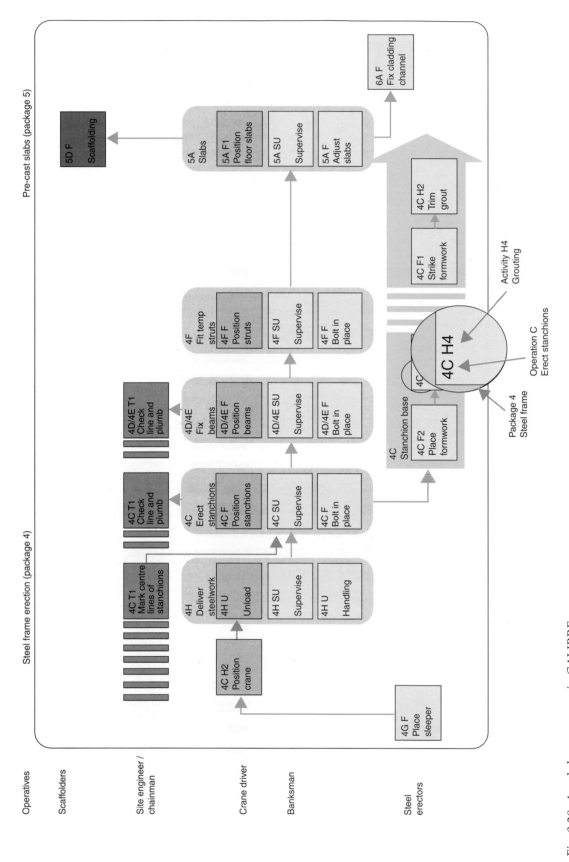

Fig. 9.20. A coded process map in CALIBRE

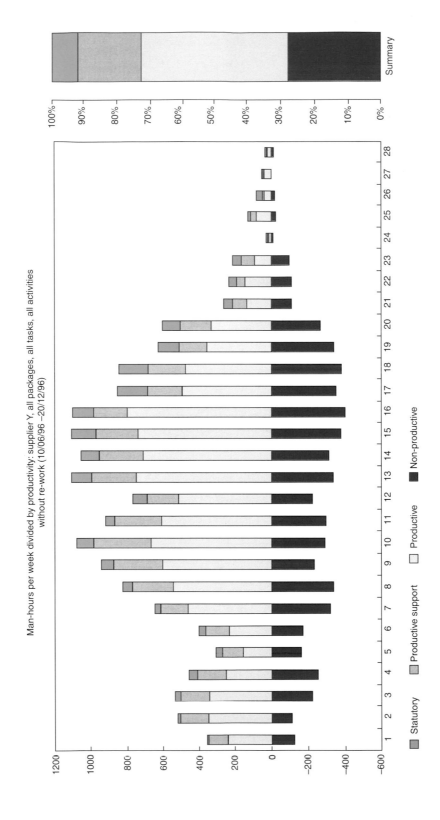

Fig. 9.21. A typical footprint of results from CALIBRE

Lean construction

In the *Machine that changed the world*, Womack, Jones and Roos described the dramatic reasons for the Japanese success in the manufacturing of cars worldwide. They presented the challenge to the rest of the world in terms of a new key idea *Lean Production*.

Box 9.13   Lean production of cars   Example

The truly lean plant has two key organisational features. Firstly, the maximum number of tasks and responsibilities are transferred to those workers actually adding value to the car on the line. Secondly, there is a system for detecting defects that quickly traces every problem, once discovered, to its ultimate cause.

(Womack *et al.*, 1990)

Thus the key requirement for lean construction is to understand where value is added and where it is not. The trick then is to reinforce that part of the system that adds value and reduce that which does not add value and is, by definition, wasteful.

Of course, it is important that value is not just identified with cost (which is undeniably important) but with a total set of values across the whole project and across all of the organisations involved. Without that set of rich values, lean construction, focusing only on cost, is likely to do more harm than good. For example, if we focus on cost alone we will sacrifice activities that improve our relationship with the community, the planning processes will become more and more obstructive, environmental protesters will get more and more support. If we ignore the soft benefits of customer experience we can leave ourselves vulnerable to competitors who have understood its importance. If we obstruct the generation of trust in our relationships then most communication is a waste of effort.

In projects which involve a number of organisations there are many processes which cross organisational boundaries. It is at these interfaces that much of the waste occurs.

Now in order to introduce lean production into the construction industry we need to examine the prerequisites for its introduction. Clearly, if we do not know what values are we will continue to attempt to squeeze out cost. This will not work, however, without major new thinking because the industry has been squeezing costs for a long time. If the leaders of the industry try to introduce these ideas without a clear idea about the values used then those at the 'coal face' lose confidence in the leaders. Their behaviour is then not consistent with the message. Here comes another 'initiative', they cry! They think 'My best strategy is to look helpful and duck'!

Box 9.14   The lean principles   **Principle**

Understand value
Measure value
Identify the processes that deliver value
Identify those processes that don't add value (waste)
Eliminate waste
Pursue continuous improvement

Box 9.15 sets out the crucial success factors for Lean Construction — they are all by now quite familiar to you as a systems thinker.

Box 9.15   Critical success factors for lean construction   Example

Understanding of process
Responsibility and authority clear
Real time feedback
Training and multi-skilling
Lack of reliance on formal contracts (relationships before contracts)
Benchmarking against each other
Close relations with suppliers
Transparency of costs

Value management

Value management and engineering are ideas that have also been used successfully — see Box 9.16. In a sense they are a subset of lean construction since they are also about identifying and adding value. However, at a recent seminar a group of value management experts were asked to describe how they would help a client to identify value from construction. Most speakers, just like the project managers we referred to in Section 1.4, restricted their answers to how they would add value by reducing costs. They seemed to have little or no concept of business case. In this case, value management will not stop the downward spiral we introduced in the Preface. We have to widen the concept of what value is and how to add value to our clients and to ourselves.

Box 9.16   Value engineering and management   **Explanation**

Value management is a structured approach to defining what value means to the client and to delivering that value in the design and construction. Value engineering is a subset of value management to deliver the required functions at lowest cost without detriment to quality.

The focus is on *value for money*. Clearly, value engineering as defined is limited and should only be part of the whole. The core stages are: define the problem; identify the options; evaluate them; select the best option in terms of value for money. This is a simple problem solving loop as defined in Fig. 2.16. Emphasis is placed on creative ways of meeting needs and, therefore, a series of workshops is commonly held to define, develop, challenge and evaluate the project.

Value management is therefore a part of process management. Values are the criteria used to define the success of a process and to identify performance indicators. A value hierarchy is a hierarchy of success for a project, e.g. Fig. 9.22. It can be extracted from the process model as required.

Value is often defined in value management as *function/cost*. It is possible to misinterpret this as function is only one aspect of quality. Really the numerator should be *delivering quality* and meeting the specification.

(Connaughton and Green, 1996)

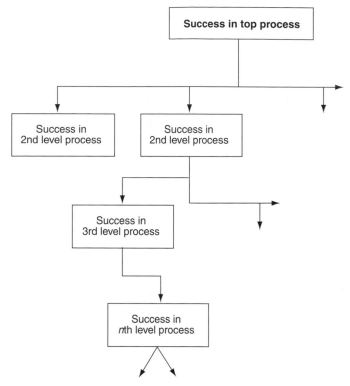

Fig. 9.22 Value hierarchy for a project

Partnering

Another initiative is in the use of partnering (Box 9.17). Again, this can be seen as a subset of lean production. The aim is to reduce waste and confrontation by agreeing to work in a co-operative relationship with the other player organisations in a process.

Of course, there are situations where such a relationship is not necessary. Where a commercial deal is simple and straightforward, partnering may not be appropriate — a simple transaction is the best way forward. This is the case, for example, when you are buying a reasonably straightforward product with little uncertainty in what you are getting for your money and you are doing it infrequently. An example is the buying of a car. However, the fleet purchase of many cars every year by a large company might indeed lend itself to a partnering arrangement.

The important factor is that the relationship between all of the players in a process is thought through first. Then that relationship is nurtured and built upon through a process of delivering success. The relationship has to be the most appropriate for the circumstances. If this is done well then the contractual arrangements become only a back stop because the relationship is so strong and the path to mutual success so clear. Of course, many will say that a change of culture of such magnitude is not possible. However, if there is a collective will, with committed leadership, with a quality agenda and professionals willing to use a wider set of skills, then it can happen as demonstrated by alliancing projects offshore.

Systems thinking about process enables a synthesis

It is obvious that the ideas behind lean production, value engineering and man-

---

Box 9.17   Partnering   **Explanation**

Partnering is a structured management approach to facilitate teamworking across contractual boundaries. The early ideas were simply about agreeing mutual objectives, making open decisions and aiming at continuous improvement. Later the *Seven Pillars of Partnering* (Bennett and Jayes, 1998) were proposed as:

- Strategy: develop client's objectives
- Membership: identify team, ensure skills are available
- Equity: ensure all are rewarded fairly
- Integration: improve the way people work together to build trust
- Benchmark: set measured targets for continuous improvement
- Process: establish standards and procedures
- Feedback: capture the lessons.

Some propose that the next stage is to develop a 'virtual organisation'. The idea is to enable construction professionals to work together to provide clients with products that they want and can invest in.

However, partnering is not suitable for all situations. Where transactions between parties are straightforward, involving little uncertainty, then it is unnecessary and probably uneconomic. However, where contracts are complex and there is much uncertainty to be managed, then the potential benefit of co-operation is high. However, we should recognise that *relationships* and mutual *values, needs and objectives* should be established *before* the *contracts* are written. Contracts should be designed to enable successful relationships — not to demotivate them as is too often the outcome.

---

agement, partnering all have much in common with systems and process thinking. Indeed, the whole initiative relies on integrating people and processes as stated in *Rethinking Construction*. The process holon provides a way of mapping what we do so as to achieve that integration, thereby realising the potential in rethinking construction and enabling these other methods to be more effectively applied. We emphasise that we can use the idea of process as a peg on which to hang all other initiatives. In Fig. 9.23, we can see how each initiative is a view, an aspect, of the same essential thing — the process — that which we do.

It seems to many practising construction players that each initiative is promoted by a group (some with commercial short-term objectives) who create an insider group with their own expertise and jargon which they attempt to propagate. Unfortunately, as a consequence, they tend to exclude the very people who need to be influenced, the very people from whom they need to learn. We suspect that the industry is tired of that and is suffering from initiative fatigue. Thus expectations have to be raised to an unrealistic level to get any buy in at all. The expectation of success in time is too short and the outcome is that successive good ideas fall by the wayside. There is a sort of strain hardening against innovation — a resistance to innovation and new language and to knowledge, which is very unfortunate. One participant in a seminar given by one of us, said *this is too bloody clever by half*. He was voicing a widely held anti-intellectual reaction to new ideas which has spawned and grown in an unfortunate professional climate. This has been created by an insufficient understanding by construction players of the genuine intellectual status and rigour of engineering practice, i.e. reflective practice. We have been intimidated by our intellectual heritage of the scientific search for truth. It has made the problems we face much more wicked than they need be — it has created a fog in our communications. Historically, this is not a new phenomenon (Box 9.18).

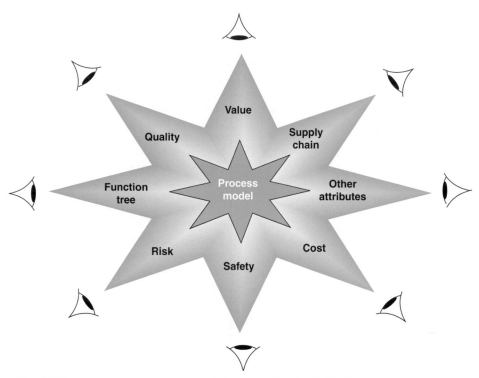

Fig. 9.23. A systems view of process integrates all other initiatives

In one very real sense in this book **we, the authors, are no better** – we have introduced new terms and jargon. We believe that while systems thinking does bring new terms and ideas, they are ideas with a difference — **because they are** *generic* — systems thinking has been used successfully in many contexts.

The industry has to stop attempting to introduce bolt-on techniques (especially those from other industries) — **the construction industry must learn from all sources but construct its own success.**

We should remember the following words from the Egan Report: 'The UK Construction industry is at its best excellent and **matches any other in the world'.**

The ideas developed in this book are intended to continue to expand that excellence and will be exportable to other industries worldwide.

Box 9.18   The dome of St Peter's, Rome   Example

In 1742, three experts were asked by Pope Benedict XIV to examine the dome of St Peter's and to find the cause of the cracking. They assessed the size of the tie force required to stabilise the dome at its base, by postulating a collapse mechanism and using an equation of virtual work with a safety factor of 2. The report they produced was severely criticised at the time. 'If it is possible to design and build St Peter's dome without mathematics and especially the new fangled mechanic of our time, it will also be possible to restore it without the aid of mathematicians...Michaelangelo knew no mathematics and yet was able to build the dome.' 'Heaven forbid that the calculation is correct,' said another critic, 'for in that case not a minute would have passed before the entire structure had collapsed.'
We would add that many other structures built with similar ignorance did!

(Straub, 1949)

9.10   Checking for success

The success targets for this chapter set out at the beginning were that, after reading it, you will be able to:

Success target	Review
• describe the importance of the whole life cycle to the client;	through their use of the product, our **clients** or their products add far greater value than is represented by the first construction cost. Consider the value of the product that passes through a factory or depot compared with its infrastructure cost. The life cycle value is dominated by its **purpose**;
• state how a process model may be developed with practical rigour;	processes at one level should, as far as is practicable, be **necessary and sufficient** for processes at the higher level with, as far as is possible, dependable measures of success;
• decide on appropriate attributes for each process;	the important ones are process owner role, purpose, success, building the team, managing the risks. A full list is given in Box 2.12;
• show how a process model contains all supply and value chains and how specific chains can be picked out;	all processes receive and send resources (including information) to others in a supply network. Specific supply chains can be picked out for specific purposes;
• describe the importance of planning to learn;	a dialogue about the needs for success of the company and of the person can develop motivation and encouragement that changes the whole perspective. We will fail to change if all we do is to deliver another procedural bolt-on with shrink-wrapped training packages, supported by pep-talks from management. For it to work we have to show we **value the learning process**;
• discuss the generalisation of the Observational Method in Geotechnics into the Observational approach;	if we have to manage a process to success and if there is a great deal of uncertainty about the future, then the close involvement of all players and stakeholders is required. This has to be through a well-understood and agreed process to review events as they evolve and to consider strategies and actions every step of the way;
• describe how lean construction, value management and partnering relate to the systems approach.	the ideas behind these initiatives have much in common — but what seems to be lacking is a set of ideas to integrate them — systems thinking provides those ideas.

We hope that we have reached our success targets for this chapter — please use the feedback form at the end of the book.

10. Looking to the future

10.1 Reviewing progress

The key ideas that we have promoted in the chapters of this book are that through systems thinking we:

- see process in a completely new way; we use it as the central structure on which all else, including quality, value, risk, uncertainty and supply chain management, is 'hung'; process becomes the common form through which all other 'views' can be expressed as attributes;
- identify process through what we do or have to do — we name a process — we see that it is tangible and productive and because we use active language (doing a process) we communicate a sense of purpose which provides a basis to integrate people and the hard systems with which we interact;
- realise that *process holons* are the simple way to deal with complexity and wicked problems — they provide an underlying framework to communicate all aspects of successful construction;
- understand that hard systems are embedded in soft ones — but all are process holons;
- see process holons are about people and success — they integrate processes and teams;
- realise that appropriate communication between process holons is vital;
- understand that wicked problems often stem from poor or non-existent communication between processes defined at appropriate levels;
- have a richer and wider view of quality, value, risk and uncertainty;
- understand that a success target is to add value;
- have a clearer understanding of measurement and of subjective, objective and dependable evidence;
- can classify all process holons into BCIOD+R;
- can connect mind maps of impelling propositions to process models;
- can build the relationships between all of the current initiatives such as lean construction, value management, partnering and supply chain management;
- understand the importance of the drivers identified in *Rethinking Construction*;
- can develop a new set of skills to 'do it differently'.

Now we need to look forward to how we can get the maximum benefit in the future for the construction industry.

10.2   Targeting success for this chapter

The success targets for this chapter are that, after reading it, you will be able to:

- state how process holons can be the central idea within a computer support tool for any construction project;
- describe how a simple intranet could be set up using that tool;
- appreciate how a process enactment intranet tool could be set up;
- state the added value that these tools could bring;
- describe how process holons help to create a sustainable business;
- state how the success targets set out for the whole book in Chapter 1 have been met;
- describe how systems thinking can contribute to *Rethinking Construction*.

The loopy logical processes within this chapter are set out in Fig. 10.1.

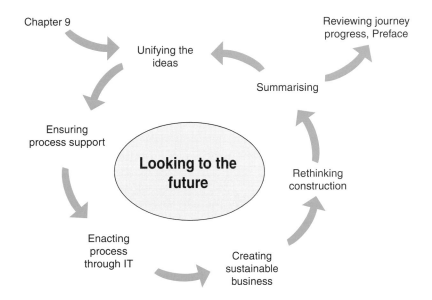

Fig. 10.1. Looking to the future

10.3   Unifying the ideas

In Chapter 4, we distinguished clearly between hard and soft systems. Hard systems consist of an action and a reaction whereas a soft system has the extra ingredient of intentionality. The differences are summarised in Box 10.1 — note that where there are no differences (e.g. in the attributes where and when) the attributes are not included.

We have said that all hard systems are embedded in soft ones. We can see from Box 10.1 that systems thinking about process holons shows us that hard systems are a restricted subset of soft systems.

It is perhaps curious at first to think of them in this way because, in many ways, hard systems are more advanced than soft ones. Certainly, scientific progress in the classical physics of hard systems has been very much greater than in soft ones. These hard systems, which are at the root of much of engineering science, are relatively easily measured and hence modelled. They are, on the whole, useful for tame problems as distinct from wicked ones. However, that is changing since many of the modern hard systems problems have now developed to a point where they have become wicked. Problems such as quantum physics,

Box 10.1	**Differences between hard and soft systems**	**Explanation**
Attribute	**Hard**	**Soft**
Who	Role as function	Role as responsibility
	No process owner	Crucial to have process owner
	No client/stakeholders, etc.	All roles including clients, stakeholders, etc., explicitly addressed
Why	Purpose attributed from players	Crucial to identify purpose
What	Closed system	Open system
	Relatively low interconnectivity	Highly interconnected
	Expressed mathematically	Descriptions in natural language
	Dependable measurement	Difficult to measure dependably
	Context clear	Context often unclear
How	Many predictive models	Few predictive models
	Success defined by players	Processes defined by working back from future success defined by clients and stakeholders
	Little uncertainty	Highly uncertain
	Limited number of future scenarios	Infinite number of future scenarios
	Risk predictable in bounds	Risk must be managed
	Dependable evidence	Uncertain evidence
	Few unintended consequences	Many unintended consequences of decisions.

cosmology, non-linear dynamics and chaos theory provide issues that are essentially unpredictable precisely. The truth, the absolute truth about the Universe remains elusive as it has from the time of Plato. Absolute truth (as distinct from the everyday dependable information which in commonsense we refer to as true) is still really a matter of faith. There is a tendency to assert truth when all that is available is a degree of evidence.

However, much of our thinking about science has been developed through classical physics and hard systems which are predictable and hence controllable.

Soft systems are soft because of people and their intentionality — they are therefore more general than hard systems. Of course, our physical bodies are just as subject to the laws of mechanics as any hard system. Perhaps, in the future, through developments in biology, we may come to understand intentionality through hard systems analysis — this would need a scientific breakthrough in the modelling of life itself. For our purpose here, however, we can model all systems (hard and soft) using a process holon and the attributes we have described. The approach we believe, therefore, is quite general and consequently potentially powerful in ways we have yet to discover.

10.4 Ensuring process support

A key idea of process holons and process modelling is to develop the capacity to deliver **the right information to the right people at the right time and in the right place**. We see information being delivered through information technology.

There is already computer software that will allow you to draw process models and to share them with all of the relevant players in a process. The ones we have used are Flowmap (Howard, 1992) and Visio Professional, but there are many others on the market. Even Microsoft Office enables us to share process information. Using Flowmap it is possible to build a process model in a matter of minutes and to associate the attributes with each process and to connect processes with other pieces of software. Thus, for example, it is possible to connect to a word processor to access QA documents in which specific roles are defined. Likewise, it is possible to connect to a spreadsheet in which is recorded the results of the monitoring of some variables such as the settlement of a footing or the deflection of a retaining wall.

Ideas promoted in earlier chapters, which are presently being implemented using groupware tools, are risk registers and more sophisticated risk management tools such as MARIUN as described in Chapter 6.

The benefits of this approach are straightforward. People are able to see clearly how what they do affects the total performance of their team and the whole project of which they are a part. The provision of appropriate information to people when they need it is a crucial lever to team success since it helps them do their job effectively and it helps to create a more coherent **sense of purpose.**

10.5 Enacting process through IT

The focus of current IT software for the construction industry is on product

Computer models of products are already taking the place of traditional documents. Paper drawings are rapidly becoming things of the past. Product models are already enabling much richer descriptions of the products. Visualisations can help understand concepts. For example, clients can now be provided with a computer simulated walk through the various rooms of their new building or even see the visual impact of it on the immediate environment. Holograms will soon be available for use in practice. Through these tools clients can develop a much better feel for what they are buying which lessens the risk of late changes when they realise something is not as they thought.

Current group ware software, such as ProjectWise (www.bentley.com) is designed to enable construction players to work together in real time around the world to develop designs of products. Since players are all working on the same data in a 'single model environment', whether architects, structural or service engineers or others, the data are constantly changing. The computer models are therefore moving from being passive to being active data. This is already bringing issues of ownership and authority to the fore. It will be a natural next step, therefore, to consider these product models as processes, as we have suggested in this book.

Current group ware software is really focused currently on data sharing and document exchanges. Thus different players working together on the same project view the same data. They can edit those parts for which they have authority and their colleagues see these changes instantly. They can make comments on other parts of the product and send them to their colleagues. They can exchange information readily. Progress information can be created for specific purposes (e.g. progress report to the client, a project schedule for a player), site information such as photographs can be exchanged, suggestions for edits to engineering drawings made from a remote site, and correspondence managed). Soon operatives will have hand-held computers on site in order to receive the information they need.

The computer will have a process role — multi-agent systems

All of these exchanges are controlled by the players involved. In the near future many of these processes will be computer controlled. Products will become intelligent so that windows will respond to light intensity, lighting will be controlled to suit the needs of the occupants.

Clearly, all that was described in the previous section can be put into a project intranet using existing software. By clicking on key words, team members can navigate the systems to find information that they need and are authorised to see.

However, an extra ingredient is already emerging through multi-agent systems (Ferber, 1999) and distributed artificial intelligence. It is already possible to program a computer to take an active role in a process — the computer itself becomes a player. Clearly, the computer has to be able to recognise the input messages and be programmed to transform them into outputs. A system where this is implemented is known as a *process enactment model*.

Consider, for instance, a very simple example of a process such as *writing a document* which is already supported by existing software as controlled by the players. Assume that this process has two simple sub-processes *drafting the document* and *checking the document*. However, we now add a third process and allocate it to a computer and that is *controlling the progress of the document*. We program the computer to send a request to the owner of *drafting the document* for the owner of that process to write the document in a word processor file. As soon as he has finished writing and has clicked on a 'finished' button, the computer automatically sends the file to the owner of *checking the document*. If the checker is not satisfied and adds comments to the file when he clicks on the appropriate button the computer sends the file back to the writer again automatically. If the checker is satisfied then the computer sends the document to whoever requested it in the higher level process to which our process is accountable. The computer in a process enactment model has a role that helps the players to enact their roles — the computer facilitates the smooth transition of information. The computer is able to send the right information to the right people at the right time — as long as it is programmed to do so!

Clearly, this simple example indicates only the potential of such a system. A computer could be programmed to take a process owning role for some of the process holons if appropriate. In this way some of the unintended consequences may be managed and consistent safeguards provided by suitable monitoring algorithms. These ideas are now being actively researched and explored for safety critical computer control systems. These techniques will enable extra added value and more competitive advantage than would otherwise be the case.

The world of computing moves so fast that it is difficult to predict what may be possible in the next decade. For example, Ferber (1999) has described a new discipline that he calls kenetics. This consists of being able to plan, design and create organisations of artificial agents (electronic or computing agents). These agents are capable of acting, collaborating in common tasks, communicating, adapting, reproducing, perceiving the environment in which they move. They can plan their actions to fulfil objectives defined externally (e.g. by human programmer) or intrinsically on the basis of a general objective of, at best, competitive success and, at least, survival. Any business that relies on the movement of information for its survival would do well to keep these developments in its sights.

10.6 Creating sustainable business

In Chapter 5, Fig. 5.2 we referred to the various stages in our collective and developing view of the basic nature of engineering. There is still a widely held academic view that engineering is simply applied science. It continues with the again widely held view that design is a creative and important activity — but one that is rather lacking in rigour. It progresses to the recognition that the management of projects is important but so difficult to do successfully that it is all rather ad hoc and hardly the subject of proper rigorous study.

In this text we have promoted the idea that really construction players, including engineers, are concerned with **managing a system** to a successful outcome. This is a much wider view than many people currently hold. It was the fourth stage in the list of Fig. 5.2. We maintain that all of these views need not be ad hoc and lacking in rigour if a systems thinking approach based on process holons is used. Indeed, we believe that the rigour of good construction players is largely unrecognised because of the undeveloped nature of our thinking about these matters.

We would now like to consider the final stage in Fig. 5.2, i.e. that construction is really, in essence, about sustainable business.

We interpret a sustainable business as one which has the basis for long-term success in harmony with the environment and which integrates people and things. It is one with a set of clearly thought through values.

Systems thinking, we maintain therefore, provides essential building blocks for sustainability. The essential root of sustainable business is a clear sense of responsibility to the whole environment (the physical world, the animal world and ourselves) and a mature recognition of the interdependence of all of these parts of the world we live in.

A necessary but not sufficient condition for sustainable business is that we have a wide and mature view of our values and a way of connecting those values to processes. We then have the capacity to manage those processes to successful conclusions, coping on the way with unintended and unwanted consequences of what we do and managing the risks. Of course, in the end these tools are not sufficient and we depend upon an understanding of our human nature in the final analysis. Trust, wisdom and good judgement will always be essential requirements. A clear sense of ethics must be nurtured and valued as the cornerstone on which trust is founded.

We believe that systems thinking is a powerful vehicle for living in harmony and balance with the world. It is a way of reducing waste, of preserving our natural resources for as long as we can, of reducing pollution, of reducing risk and stress, of increasing safety, self-worth and fulfillment and providing better health and reduced illness.

In short, if we think systems we have the potential to increase our collective quality of life.

10.7 Rethinking Construction

After those wide-ranging claims let us focus back down on construction and revisit each one of the five key drivers of change identified in *Rethinking Construction* (Box 1.1). Let us examine them again from a systems thinking point of view.

Committed leadership

Systems thinking emphasises the ideas of leaders as team coaches or as conductors of the orchestra. Their role is to bring out the best in their players by encouraging and developing them. Every process owner is a leader at his level in a project or organisation. All of us, therefore, have leadership roles to play in what we do — it is not just about top management. We all have many roles to play in many processes sometimes as leader (if only of what we ourselves do) and often as players in the team. It is just as important to support the team leader by appropriate behaviour as it is to lead. Success is about team behaviour as a whole. As Senge (Box 3.12) has written, shared vision and team learning are crucial ideas in thinking through these ways of behaving. Too often, senior managers are so involved in the day-to-day hurly burly of life that these essential leadership qualities are missed.

Focus on customer

Systems thinking helps us to be clear about the *why* questions — the purpose. So often we get totally absorbed by the *how* questions — the techniques. By answering the *why* questions we can target success — and we can do it to add value. Systems thinking helps us to understand values and not just to focus on cost. We think about the whole life cycle of process and this helps to look for opportunities to deliver value to customers. Value originates from our clients and ourselves. The motivation derives from both. One without the other is not sustainable. Systems thinking helps us to make the connection and in the process to do less of what is not needed and more of what adds real value.

Integrated processes and teams

Systems thinking about process holons naturally integrates processes and teams — that is what it is all about. It is a new way of thinking about process that does this integration — the old idea that process, product, entities, procedures, etc. are all different is swept away. We have just one idea which integrates all of these things and that idea concerns what we actually **do** — process. We make sure every process is identified by naming them all and by nominating a process owner for each one. We do this because we recognise that many of the difficulties in wicked problems are there because there are processes happening that go unrecognised. This happens because companies are so often organised around functions. We believe that functions are better conceived as roles and as attributes of process — companies could then organise themselves around processes, i.e. around what people actually do. We then create teams to deliver success for every process we have identified.

We take shared vision seriously and attempt to get ownership — we do not allow vision statements dreamt up by senior managers to be foisted on an unwilling work force — that is a waste of everyone's time. Vision is what vision does!

Quality driven agenda

Systems thinking gives a much wider understanding of what quality is — including safety, risk reduction (particularly unintended consequences), waste reduction, opportunities taken (particularly those not realised at start).

The same is true for values. Value is not just about cost or the ratio of functionality to cost — it has a much wider meaning with an underpinning in ethics. This richness helps us to know how to make the difference. It is not just the costs of rectifying defects that matter it is also loss in the confidence of the client, the customers and the stakeholders.

Commitment to people

Systems thinking puts an emphasis on people both inwards in their personal development and outwards as taking roles (responsibilities) i.e. being players in processes and as process owners at different levels. Systems thinking gives real empowerment to people. It can unlock their natural creativity and present exciting opportunities for improvement and self-fulfillment at all levels. Above all, it helps people to know what success looks like for themselves and to recognise what to do to improve. There are few things more motivating to all of us than a genuine recognition, from deep within ourselves or from those people around us, that we are being successful.

Create — the six principles

In Box 2.13, we set out our six principles of process equivalent to the drivers of *Rethinking Construction*. It is clear that there is much in common. They represent the priority attributes and are:

- focus on the **C**ustomer to define **purpose**;
- be clear about **R**oles to deliver the purpose;
- be clear about what is in the system and what is not — **E**nvironment or meta system — there are often differences of understanding that lead to problems later on;
- make sure the system is **A**ppropriate for the purpose;
- the best evidence is **T**estable — this is what makes it dependable and measurable, if evidence is not dependable then try to make it so and keep checking it whilst it matters;
- values are based in **E**thics — be sure you are clear about your own values.

What do I do now?

The ideas set out in this book are just as applicable to your personal role as a construction player as they are to the projects in which you work. They work at all levels: individual, project, organisation and national. If each construction player starts to think about and apply these ideas immediately then as well as improving his own performance it would influence others to take up the ideas. In this way, we can together make a difference and help the industry as a whole to **Do It Differently.**

10.8 Summarising and checking for overall success

In the Preface and Chapter 1, we set out the overall success target for the book. We said that after reading the book you will be able to:

- deliver some new customer focused strategies;
- work back from success;

- realise values by integrating people and process;
- generate simplicity out of complexity by process mind mapping;
- inject practical rigour;
- create tools for managing uncertainty.

In summary the major points for each of these targets are:

- develop an impelling proposition for your client and produce a process product mind map;
- use it to get a consensus on what is success for every appropriate process at every level and at the right time;
- associate attributes with each process such that people and tasks are totally integrated;
- see the essential simplicity of process mind maps and appreciate the way in which so many disparate ideas are pulled together and applied at any level;
- see that this process of building process models injects an objective practical rigour for all to see;
- use the Italian Flag to estimate evidence both for and against eventual success — use the flags to generate discussion and to identify and resolve differences of understanding.

The diagram of the book contained in Chapter 1 had a simple message. It is that in the past we have focused almost exclusively on cost. Whether the culture of confrontation causes this, or is a result of it, does not matter — the diagram shows how there is a reinforcing loop of influence that leads to dissatisfaction both of clients and construction players alike. We have tried to set out a wider view, a systems view of quality and value in a process to delight the client and customer, to promote a climate of co-operation, and feelings of worth and self-worth and status.

The added values of systems thinking include:

- a reduction in confrontation, hence saving time and money on non-value adding activity;
- new leverage on wicked problems from simplicity in complexity;
- less fragmentation — seeing how wholes and parts fit together;
- increased levels of consensus and agreement;
- a reduction in misunderstandings and communications;
- increased safety levels by careful monitoring of relevant KPIs;
- increased product quality by providing the right information to the right people at the right time;
- reduced risks;
- the creation of new opportunities;
- greater accountability — clearer audit streams and justifiability;
- a clearer ethical basis for difficult decisions;
- a tool for getting to grips with wicked, messy issues;
- a way of reducing waste — non-added value;
- better added value delivered to the client and helping him to add value to his customers;
- increased feelings of self-worth by construction players;
- a better understanding of the relationship of applied science to practice;
- more confidence in the rigour of practice.

We promised to tell you of the unanticipated benefits that flowed to us, as authors, during the writing of this book. In fact, they are many but the key ones are that we discovered:

- a realisation that this is a way in which the intelligence and knowledge of people who work at the front line of our industry can be synthesised to create a more rewarding future for us all;

- a connection between process holons and balanced scorecards and we realised the potential power of the process holon idea at company board level for strategic management;
- a connection between mind maps of impelling marketing propositions and process models to enhance the creative act of potentially adding value to the client;
- the potential for managing organisational change through process holons — particularly where change can have a serious implication for safety as, for example, in the nuclear industry;
- an increased confidence through prototype testing with some potential customers in the simplicity and the power of the process holon idea to cut through complexity in a way much more than first anticipated;
- the motivating force that is unleashed when we focus on our customers, our people and our success together — it makes a real difference. The help and encouragement we have received in writing this book from people at all levels in the industry is testimony to it.

10.9   Checking for success

Our success targets for this chapter set out at the beginning were that, after reading it, you will be able to:

Success target	Review
• state how process holons can be the central idea within a computer support tool for any construction project;	existing standard software can be used to represent process holons and hence for all players in a process to share;
• describe how a simple intranet tool could be set up using that tool;	this software can be part of a project intranet also using existing software;
• appreciate how a process enactment intranet tool could be set up;	the computer can be programmed to take specific roles in a process and hence can facilitate active process enactment between players;
• state the added value that these tools could bring;	providing the right information to the right people at the right time, coherent sense of purpose, helping people to know the impact of what they do and a clear sense of their contribution to success;
• describe how process holons help to create a sustainable business;	sustainable business is one which is in harmony with the environment and which integrates people and things. It is one with a set of clearly thought through values. Systems thinking, therefore, provides the essential building blocks for sustainability;
• state how the success targets set out for the whole book in Chapter 1 have been met;	the way in which the targets for the book have been reached are set out in Section 10.8;

• describe how systems thinking can contribute to *Rethinking Construction*.	systems thinking provides the three essential concepts necessary to understand and build on the key drivers indicated in the report. To rethink construction and to do it differently we need the three essential features of systems thinking, i.e. holons, connectivity and process.

We hope that we have reached our success targets with you for the book.

You will recall that in the Preface we said that the book was a stage in a process of joint success for all of those who want to be involved. The next stage is feedback to allow experiences to be developed for best practice.

If you wish to pursue the next stages of the process, please return the feedback form at the end of the book and monitor our web site at the address given on the form.

References

Argawal J., Woodman N. J., Blockley D. I. (1998) Safety of non-linear dynamic systems, *J. Structural Engng.*, **25**, No. 1, April, 37–42.

Barnard M. (ed.) (1998), *Health and safety for engineers*, Thomas Telford, London.

Belbin R. M. (1993), *Team roles at work*, Butterworth–Heinemann, Oxford.

Belbin R. M. (1981), *Management teams*, Butterworth–Heinemann, Oxford.

Benjamin J. R. and Cornell C. A. (1970), *Probability, statistics and decision for civil engineers*, McGraw-Hill, London.

Bennett J. and Jayes S. (1998) *The seven pillars of partnering*, Thomas Telford, London.

Blanchard K., Carew D. and Parisi-Carew E. (1994), *The one minute manager builds high performing teams*, HarperCollins, London.

Blockley D. I., Pilsworth B. W. and Baldwin J. F. (1983), Measures of uncertainty, *Civil Engng. Syst.*, **1**, No. 1, 3–9.

Blockley D. I. (1980), *The nature of structural design and safety*, Ellis Horwood, Chichester.

Blockley D. I. (ed.) (1992), *Engineering safety*, McGraw-Hill, London.

Blockley D. I. (1995), Computers in engineering risk and hazard management, *Archives of Computational Meths in Engng.*, **2**, 2, 67–94.

Blockley D. I. (1999), Risk based structural safety methods in context, *J. Struct. Safety*, **21**, 4, 335–348.

Buzan T. (1988), *Make the most of your mind*, Pan Books, London.

Carter R. (1998), *Mapping the mind*, Weidenfeld & Nicolson, London.

Checkland P. (1981), *Systems thinking, systems practice*, John Wiley, Chichester.

CIRIA (1992), *Site safety*, SP 90, London.

CIRIA (1997), *CDM regulations — work sector guidance for designers*, Report 166, London.

CIRIA (1997), *The observational method in ground engineering*, Funders Report/CP/49, London.

Conklin E. J. and Weil W. (1999), *Wicked problems: naming the pain in organisations*, http://www.gdss.com./wicked.htm

Connaughton J. N. and Green S. D. (1996), *Value management in construction: a client's guide*, CIRIA SP 129, London.

Connolly T. (1980), *Scientists, engineers and organisations*, Brooks/Cole Engineering Division, California.

Covey S. R. (1992), *The seven habits of highly effective people*, Simon & Schuster, London.

Cui W. C. and Blockley D. I. (1990), Interval probability theory for evidential support, *Int. J. Intelligent Systems* **5**, Part 2, June 183–192.

de Bono E. (1976), *Teaching thinking*, Penguin Books, London.

de Bono E. (1971), *Practical thinking*, Penguin Books, London.

Department of the Environment, Transport and the Regions (1998), *Rethinking construction*, London.

Engineering Council (1993), *Guidelines on risk issues*, London.

Elms D. G. (1989), Wisdom engineering: the methodology of versatility, *Int. J. of Applied Eng. Education*, **5** (6), 711–717.

Ferber J. (1999), *Multi-agent systems*, Addison-Wesley, UK.

Finch B. (1997), *30 minutes to write a business plan*, Kogan Page, London.

Fisher J. G. (1996), *How to improve performance through benchmarking*, Kogan Page, London.

Fisher R. and Ury W. (1997), *Getting to yes*, 2nd edn, Arrow Business Books, London.

Flanigan E. M. and Scott J. (1996), *Process improvement*, Kogan Page, London.

Glass P. R. and Powderham A. J. (1994), Application of the Observational Method at the Limehouse Link, *Géotechnique*, **44**(4), 665–679.

Godfrey P. S. (1993), The holistic approach, Institution of Mechanical Engineers Seminar, Railway Division, *Coping with complexity in procurement*, London, Jan.

Godfrey P. S. (1995), Ambition control, *HSE Conf. on Risk Management in Civil, Mechanical and Structural Engineering*, Thomas Telford, London, Feb.

Godfrey P. S. (1995), *Control of risk*, CIRIA SP125, London.

Haines S. G. (1998), *Successful strategy planning*, Kogan Page, London.

Hall J. W., Davis J. P. and Blockley D. I., (1998), Uncertain inference using interval probability theory, *Int. J. Approx. Reasoning*, **19**, No 3–4, 247–264.

Hampel Committee (1998), *Committee on corporate governance, final report*, Jan, Gee Publishing Ltd, London.

Handy C. B. (1985), *Understanding organisations*, Penguin Business, London.

Haynes M. E. (1988), *Make every minute count*, Kogan Page, London.

Hammer M. and Champy J. (1993), *Re-engineering the corporation*, Nicholas Brealey, London.

Hammer M. (1996), *Beyond re-engineering*, HarperCollins, London.

Health & Safety Executive (1993), *The costs of accidents at work*, HMSO, London.

Howard D. (1992), An approach to improving management performance, *Engineering Management Journal*, April, London.

ISO 8402 (1994), *Quality management and quality assurance. Vocabulary* (Part of ISO 9000 family of standards), BSI, London.

Johnson G. and Scholes K. (1999), *Exploring corporate strategy* (5th edn), Prentice Hall Europe.

Kaplan R. S. and Norton D. P. (1996), *The balanced scorecard*, Harvard Business School Press, Boston.

Koestler A. (1967), *The ghost in the machine*, Picador, London.

Latham M. (1994), *Constructing the team*, The Stationery Office, London.

Le Masurier J., Muir Wood D. and Blockley D. I. (1999a), Value management and efficient geotechnical design, *3rd Int. Conf. Hong Kong Inst. Value Management*, 5–7 May 1999.

Le Masurier J., Muir Wood D. and Blockley D. I. (1999b), Process modelling the observational method *The Value of Geotechnics in Construction*, 147–153, Emap Construct, London.

Lovelock J. (1992), *Gaia: a new look at life on earth*, Oxford.

Lownds S. (1998), *Fast track to change on the Heathrow Express*, Institute of Personnel and Development, London.

Lu Z., Yu Y., Woodman N. J. and Blockley D. I. (1999) A theory of structural vulnerability, *Struct. Eng.* **77**, 18, 17–24.

Magee B. (1973), *Popper*, Fontana Modern Masters, London.

Norton B. R. and McElligott W. C. (1995), *Value management in construction*, Macmillan.

Peck R. B. (1969) Advantages and limitations of the observational method in applied soil mechanics, *9th Rankine Lecture, Géotechnique*, **19**, No. 2, 171–187.

Penrose R. (1989), *The emperor's new mind*, Vintage, London.

Pidgeon N. F., Blockley D. I. and Turner B. A. (1988), Site investigations: lessons from a late discovery of hazardous waste, *Struct. Engr.*, **66**, 19/4, London.

Pidgeon N. F., Blockley D. I. and Turner B. A. (1986), Design practice and snow loading—lessons from a roof collapse, *The Structural Engineer*, 64A, 3, London.

Pirsig R. M. (1976), *Zen and the art of motor cycle maintenance*, Corgi Books, London.

Porter M. E. (1985), *Competitive advantage*, The Free Press, New York.

Roberts J. (1999), Demolition of Marks & Spencer, Manchester (a six-storey commercial building supported by post-tensioned beams), *Struct. Engr.*, **77**, 2, 19 Jan, London.

Rorty R. (1982), *Consequences of pragmatism*, Harvester Wheatsheaf, Herts, UK.

Royal Society (1992), *Risk*, London.

Saaty T. L. and Alexander J. M. (1981), *Thinking with models*, Pergamon Press, London.

Schon D. (1983), *The reflective practitioner*, Basic Books, New York.

Senge P. (1990), *The fifth discipline*, Century Business, London.

Sibly P. G. and Walker A. C. (1977), Structural accidents and their causes, *Proc. Instn. Civ. Engrs.*, Part 2, **62**, May, 191–208.

Stapleton J. (1997), *Dynamic systems development method*, Addison-Wesley, London.

Straub H. (1949), A history of civil engineering, translated from *Die Geschickte der Bauingenieurkunst* by Rockwell E., Leonard Hill Ltd, London, 1952.

Turner B. A. and Pidgeon N. F. (1998), *Man-made disasters (2nd ed.)*, Butterworth–Heinemann, Oxford.

Warnock M. (1998), *An intelligent person's guide to ethics*, Duckworth, London.

Womack J. P., Jones D. T. and Roos D. (1990), *The machine that changed the world*, Maxwell Macmillan, Oxford.

Index

Feedback

Purpose of feedback

Learning is an iterative process in which our ability to apply new thinking will improve with each cycle of experience. That process is accelerated if we deliberately seek to understand what we feel is good and bad about the experience.

Similarly, your learning experience from reading this book is a rich source of knowledge that will help us as authors and other readers to improve faster.

So we see feedback as having two parallel objectives:

- to provide a systematic framework for you to check back on your learning process and find ways of improving it;

and if you wish

- to guide us with feedback which we can share with other readers on a web site.

We have provided a form for you to copy for your feedback, whether on a particular chapter or on the whole book. There is also a feedback form on the web site.

Relationship with people feeding back

It is important that the feedback process is open and transparent. We ask you, therefore, for your name and e-mail address and, if you wish, a few biographical details to help us understand the context of your views.

Blame-free reporting

We will be reporting your feedback without identifying who has said what, so as to encourage blame-free dialogue. We will be pleased to include your name as a contributor to the site if you want us to.

The web site address is
http://www.fen.bris.ac.uk/civil/staff/dib/doingitdifferently.htm
from where you can fill out and return the feedback form

Feedback form: Doing it differently

Your Name . . . .   E-mail address . . . .

Which chapter(s) do you wish to comment on

1 ❑   2 ❑   3 ❑   4 ❑   5 ❑   6 ❑   7 ❑   8 ❑   9 ❑   10 ❑   Whole book ❑

Consider the success targets for these chapters and complete the following:

a) How useful did you find this chapter? (please tick one)

  Not at all ❑   Partly ❑   Useful ❑   Very useful ❑

b) Please judge the amount of evidence that you feel you have that this chapter fulfilled its purpose for you.   ❑ %

  Please provide bullet points to indicate topics or parts of the chapter that were particularly successful for you, indicating why.

   • . . . .
   • . . . .
   • . . . .

c) Please judge the amount of evidence that you feel you have that this chapter did not fulfil its purpose for you.   ❑ %

  Please provide bullet points to indicate topics or parts of the chapter that were particularly disappointing for you, indicating why.

   • . . . .
   • . . . .
   • . . . .

d) 100 minus the sum of percentages a) and b) is the evidence that you are uncertain about the success of this chapter for you.   ❑ %

  Please provide bullet points to indicate what action could be taken to reduce this uncertainty to an acceptable level for you.

   • . . . .
   • . . . .
   • . . . .

e) Please provide comment, suggestions or ideas that would be of interest to others concerned with understanding why they need to do it differently.

   • . . . .
   • . . . .
   • . . . .

f) Please tick as many of the following you think apply to this chapter.

  useful   ❑   stimulating ❑   too long   ❑   focused   ❑

  waste of time ❑   dull   ❑   too short ❑   woolly   ❑

Please send your response to David Blockley, Department of Civil Engineering, University of Bristol, Bristol BS8 1TR, UK